# TUDOR AND STUART
# NORWICH

Cowgate in 1867.

# TUDOR AND STUART
# NORWICH

## John Pound

Phillimore

1988

Published by
PHILLIMORE & CO. LTD.
Shopwyke Hall, Chichester, Sussex

ISBN 0 85033 657 0

Printed in Great Britain by
UNWIN BROTHERS LIMITED
at The Gresham Press, Old Woking, Surrey

*For Catherine and Richard*

# Contents

## List of Illustrations

*Frontispiece:* Cowgate in 1867

*Acknowledgements*

Illustration 9 is reproduced from M. W. Atkin, H. Sutermeister *et al.*, 'Excavations in Norwich, 1977/8: The Norwich Survey – Seventh Interim Report', *Norf. Arch.*, xxxvii, 1978, Fig. 6, and numbers 17, 18 and 46 from M. Atkin and S. Margeson, *Life on a Medieval Street*, Norwich 1985, by kind permission of Mr. Alan Carter, Director of the Norwich Survey, University of East Anglia. Illustrations 3, 5, 7, 8, 10, 11, 16, 19-24, 26, 28, 29, 32-6, 38, 41-3, 45, 47, 50 and the frontispiece are reproduced by kind permission of Norfolk Museums Service (Norwich Castle Museum).

## List of Tables

Chapter One

# Wealth and Occupation in Tudor and Stuart Norfolk

Throughout the 16th and 17th centuries Norwich was the major city of one of the largest and wealthiest counties in England, a county which comprised some 1,300,000 acres and around 700 parishes if Norwich itself is excluded. It was split into three unequal parts: the Fenlands, which covered the extreme west as well as a narrow coastal strip stretching from King's Lynn to Cromer; an extensive area of unenclosed light and medium soils in the north and west of the county which, while renowned for barley and other grain crops, was given over to sheep and corn husbandry and contained the homes of some of the greatest sheep owners in the country; and, finally, an area to the south of the county, long enclosed, which was composed essentially of heavy boulder-clay and supported dairy farming and the rearing of cattle.[1]

The major towns in Norfolk, Norwich apart, were King's Lynn and Great Yarmouth, and they were supplemented by a further 28 market towns.[2] King's Lynn controlled the commerce passing along the Great Ouse, Nene and Welland and their tributaries, and through them had access to eight or more counties. Indeed it has been suggested that towns as far inland as Northampton, Leicester and Oakham saw Lynn as their natural port.[3] The town's fortunes were largely based on its increasing participation in the coal trade and, to an even greater extent, on its activities in the corn trade; it was not unusual for Lynn to ship more corn in a month than most ports shipped in a year. In the process it had contact with nearly every port between Berwick and Bristol, concentrating especially on the Tyne, Yorkshire, London and Berwick itself. Yarmouth was also involved in the corn trade but on a much smaller scale, most of its exports going to London with lesser quantities being shipped to Kent, Sussex and the West Country. It also imported grain and sent some abroad.[4] It was the steady rise of Norwich to the position of second city in the kingdom, however, which guaranteed Yarmouth's fortunes; goods passed along the River Yare in both directions. Norwich's merchants used Yarmouth essentially for their cloth exports. In return they received a miscellany of produce. Coal intended for Norwich alone amounted to some 2,000 chaldrons a year. This apart, they imported goods as diverse as 'fish, corn, sugar and prunes, hops and wine; woad, madder, fullers' earth, soap, alum, wools from Spain and from Lincolnshire, yarn and woolcards; paper, salt, bricks, tiles, timber, glass, iron, pewter and tin'.[5]

Activity of the kind outlined above suggests that Norfolk was a major maritime county and surveys of shipping taken in 1565 and 1582 confirm this impression. The tonnage of the vessels belonging to Norfolk harbours was greater than that of any other county, its 7,787 tons being exceeded only by the port of London itself. In terms of skilled masters it was supreme, the 232 listed for Norfolk contrasting markedly with the 143 from London, the 81 from the Yorkshire ports, 48 from Bristol and Somerset, 46 from Southampton and no more than 29 from Newcastle.[6] In all, 1,570 Norfolk men earned their living from the sea, 75 of them being recorded as shipwrights in 1580, an essential skill in a county which relied so heavily on the activities of its seamen.[7]

The market towns of Norfolk were equally dependent on the activities of the major ports, whether they received and dispatched produce by way of its navigable rivers, such as the Bure, Yare or Ouse, or overland. Whatever the method the larger market towns, at least, appear to have been relatively prosperous and to have steadily widened their activities throughout the early-modern period. Our knowledge of this is heavily dependent on Dr. John Patten's analysis of wills for the 16th and 17th centuries, essential sources but ones which are almost invariably socially selective, do not always supply the requisite information and whose survival tends to be spasmodic.[8] Poorer people, almost by definition, are virtually excluded from such analysis which means that the apparent omission of trades such as tailor and blacksmith from some areas, as well as many of the building trades, may reflect the poverty of the practitioners rather than the real situation. Nevertheless, such analysis is valuable as a broad indicator of trends and does show those trades which are virtually ubiquitous and those others which gradually make an appearance on the urban scene.

With this proviso in mind, the evidence suggests that each of the larger market towns had at least one representative of the major trade groupings – building, clothing, food and drink, leather and metal – within it throughout the 16th and 17th centuries, with occupations like carpenter and tailor, cordwainer, blacksmith and weaver being commonplace. Others, such as draper, grocer, baker and tanner, were present in half or more of the towns and by the second half of the 17th century, if not before, brewers, innkeepers, linen weavers and, above all, members of the professions, were to be found virtually everywhere. People living in towns such as Wymondham, Harleston, Holt and Attleborough had access to twice as many trades at the end of the 17th century as their predecessors had had at the beginning of the 16th; in smaller towns like Fakenham, Loddon, Watton and Wells, the range of activities had trebled.

All of the larger market towns had their own specialisations, important corn markets being found at Diss, North Walsham, Swaffham and Thetford as well as at King's Lynn and Great Yarmouth, cattle markets at Attleborough, Lynn and possibly Norwich, and good markets for sheep at Attleborough and for swine at Norwich. Diss and East Dereham joined the county town as the major entrepôts for wool and yarn, with Norwich alone concentrating on cloth and leather.[9]

The market towns apart, industry steadily penetrated the rural areas of Norfolk as the Tudor and Stuart periods progressed. Table 1.4 lists the number of occupations recorded in individual parishes in the years concerned, the information again being taken from the surviving wills. Their limitations have been mentioned already, as has the number of parishes in the county as a whole. With these provisos in mind the figures largely tell their own tale.[10]

The general distributive trades, including grocers, merchants and victuallers among their ranks, the food and drink, leather and professional trades all made considerable inroads into the rural parishes during this period, but the greatest increase, by far, was in the worsted and linen trades. The revival of the worsted industry largely reflects the growth of the new draperies and their tremendous importance in 17th-century Norwich. By 1600 worsted weavers could be found in over ninety of the towns and villages in Norfolk, quite apart from Norwich and the village of Worstead itself, almost all of them situated in the central and north-eastern parts of the county. The linen trades, whose growth was stimulated at least in part by governmental activity which encouraged the development of canvas and linen weaving in the county, were based primarily in south Norfolk in areas where worsted weaving was largely absent.[11] As Acts of Parliament which stipulated that a quarter of an acre of hemp and flax should be grown on farms of 60 or more arable acres were passed as early as 1533 and 1563 respectively, the boom in linen weaving in 17th-century Norfolk may partly reflect increasing specialisation in an occupation which had previously been subsumed under the general title of weaver.

**Table 1.1 Occupations in Norfolk market towns as recorded in wills and inventories, 1500-1599**

| | Diss | East Dereham | Wymondham | Aylsham | Downham Market | Thetford | Cromer | Harleston | Swaffham | North Walsham | Burnham Market | Holt | Little Walsingham | Attleborough | Fakenham | Loddon | Watton | Wells | Foulsham |
|---|---|---|---|---|---|---|---|---|---|---|---|---|---|---|---|---|---|---|---|
| Bricklayer/maker | - | - | x | - | - | - | - | - | x | - | - | - | - | - | x | - | - | - | - |
| Carpenter | x | x | x | - | x | x | - | x | x | - | - | - | - | - | - | - | - | - | - |
| Glazier | - | - | - | - | - | - | - | - | - | - | - | - | - | - | - | - | - | - | - |
| Joiner/Turner | - | - | x | x | - | - | - | - | x | - | - | - | - | - | - | - | - | - | - |
| Limeburner | - | - | - | - | - | - | - | - | - | - | - | - | - | - | - | - | - | - | - |
| Mason | - | - | - | - | - | - | - | - | - | - | - | - | - | - | - | - | - | - | - |
| Painter | - | - | - | - | - | - | - | - | - | - | - | - | - | - | - | - | - | - | - |
| Capper/Hatter | - | x | - | - | - | x | - | - | - | - | - | - | - | - | - | - | - | - | - |
| Feltmaker | - | - | - | - | - | - | - | - | - | - | - | - | - | - | - | - | - | - | - |
| Furrier | - | - | - | - | - | - | - | - | - | - | - | - | - | - | - | - | - | - | - |
| Hosier | - | x | - | - | - | - | - | - | - | - | - | - | - | - | - | - | - | - | - |
| Tailor | x | x | x | x | x | x | x | x | - | x | x | x | x | - | - | - | - | - | - |
| Chandler | - | - | - | - | - | - | - | - | - | - | - | - | - | - | - | - | - | - | - |
| Draper | x | - | x | x | - | x | - | - | x | - | - | - | x | - | x | - | - | - | - |
| Grocer | x | x | x | - | - | x | - | - | - | x | - | - | - | x | - | - | - | x | - |
| Haberdasher | - | - | - | - | - | - | - | - | - | - | - | - | x | - | - | - | - | - | - |
| Mercer | x | x | - | - | - | x | - | - | x | - | x | - | - | x | - | - | - | - | - |
| Merchant | - | - | x | - | - | - | - | - | x | - | - | - | - | - | - | x | - | - | - |
| Baker | x | x | x | x | x | - | - | - | x | - | - | - | x | x | - | - | - | x | - |
| Brewer | x | - | - | - | - | - | - | - | - | - | - | - | - | - | - | - | - | - | - |
| Butcher | x | - | x | - | - | x | - | - | - | - | - | - | x | x | - | - | - | - | - |
| Cook | - | - | x | - | - | - | - | - | - | - | - | - | - | - | - | - | - | - | - |
| Fisherman | - | - | - | - | - | - | - | - | - | - | - | - | - | - | - | - | - | - | - |
| Fishmonger | - | - | - | x | - | x | - | - | x | - | - | - | - | - | - | - | - | - | - |
| Innholder | x | x | - | - | - | - | - | - | x | - | - | x | x | - | - | - | - | - | - |
| Innkeeper | - | - | - | - | - | - | - | - | - | - | - | - | - | - | - | - | - | - | - |
| Vintner | - | x | - | - | - | - | - | - | x | - | - | - | - | - | - | - | - | - | - |
| Cordwainer | x | x | x | x | x | x | - | x | x | - | x | - | - | x | - | - | - | - | - |
| Glover | x | x | x | x | - | x | - | - | - | - | - | - | - | x | - | - | - | - | - |
| Tanner | x | x | x | x | x | - | - | - | x | - | - | - | - | x | - | - | - | - | - |
| Blacksmith | - | x | x | x | x | x | - | x | - | - | - | x | - | - | - | - | x | - | - |
| Brazier | - | - | - | - | - | - | - | - | - | - | - | - | - | - | - | - | - | - | - |
| Cutler | - | - | - | - | - | - | x | - | - | - | - | - | - | - | - | - | - | - | - |
| Goldsmith | x | - | - | - | - | - | - | - | x | - | - | - | - | - | - | - | - | - | - |
| Ironmonger | - | - | - | - | - | - | - | - | - | - | - | - | - | - | - | - | - | x | - |
| Locksmith | - | - | - | x | - | - | - | - | - | - | - | - | - | - | - | - | - | - | - |
| Pewterer | - | - | - | - | - | - | - | - | x | - | - | - | - | - | - | - | - | - | - |
| Plumber | - | - | - | - | - | - | - | - | - | - | - | - | - | - | - | - | - | - | - |
| Gardener | - | - | - | - | - | x | - | - | - | x | - | - | - | - | - | - | - | - | - |
| Roper | - | x | - | - | - | x | - | - | - | - | - | - | - | - | x | - | - | - | - |
| Upholsterer | - | - | - | - | - | - | - | - | - | - | - | - | - | - | - | - | - | - | - |
| Apothecary | - | - | - | - | - | - | - | - | x | - | - | - | - | - | - | - | - | - | - |
| Barber | - | - | - | x | - | - | - | - | x | - | - | - | - | - | - | - | - | - | - |
| Doctor/Surgeon | x | - | x | - | - | - | - | - | x | - | - | - | - | - | - | - | - | - | - |
| Minstrel/Musician | - | - | - | - | - | - | - | - | - | - | - | - | - | - | - | - | - | - | - |
| Notary | - | - | - | - | - | - | - | - | - | - | - | - | - | - | - | - | - | - | - |
| Schoolmaster | - | - | - | - | - | - | - | - | - | - | - | - | - | - | - | - | - | - | - |
| Scrivener | - | x | - | - | - | - | - | - | - | - | - | - | - | - | - | - | - | - | - |
| Carrier | - | - | - | - | - | - | - | - | - | - | - | - | - | - | - | - | - | - | - |
| Sailor/Boatman | - | - | - | - | - | - | x | x | - | - | - | - | - | - | - | - | - | - | - |
| Shipbuilder | - | - | - | - | - | - | - | - | - | - | - | - | - | - | - | - | - | - | - |
| Clothier | - | - | - | - | - | - | - | - | - | - | - | - | - | - | - | x | - | - | - |
| Linen Weaver | - | - | - | - | - | - | - | - | - | - | - | - | x | - | - | - | - | - | - |
| Textile Trades | x | x | x | x | x | - | - | - | - | - | - | - | x | - | - | - | - | - | - |
| Weavers | x | x | x | x | x | x | x | x | x | x | - | x | x | x | x | - | - | - | - |
| Worsted Trades | - | x | - | - | - | x | - | - | x | - | - | - | - | - | - | - | - | - | - |
| Coopers | x | x | - | x | - | - | - | - | - | x | - | - | - | - | - | - | - | x | - |

## Table 1.2 Occupations in Norfolk market towns as recorded in wills and inventories, 1600-1649

| | Diss | East Dereham | Wymondham | Aylsham | Downham Market | Thetford | Cromer | Harleston | Swaffham | North Walsham | Burnham Market | Holt | Little Walsingham | Attleborough | Fakenham | Loddon | Watton | Wells | Foulsham |
|---|---|---|---|---|---|---|---|---|---|---|---|---|---|---|---|---|---|---|---|
| Bricklayer/maker | - | - | x | x | - | x | - | - | - | - | - | - | - | - | - | - | - | - | - |
| Carpenter | x | x | x | - | x | x | - | - | x | x | - | x | x | - | - | x | - | x | - |
| Glazier | - | - | - | - | - | - | - | - | x | x | - | - | - | - | - | - | - | - | - |
| Joiner/Turner | - | - | x | x | - | x | - | - | - | - | - | - | - | - | - | - | - | - | - |
| Limeburner | - | - | - | - | - | x | - | - | - | - | - | - | - | - | - | - | - | - | - |
| Mason | - | x | - | - | - | x | - | - | x | - | - | x | - | - | - | - | - | - | - |
| Painter | - | x | x | - | - | - | - | - | - | - | - | - | - | - | - | - | - | - | - |
| Capper/Hatter | - | - | - | - | - | - | - | - | - | - | - | - | - | - | - | - | - | - | - |
| Feltmaker | - | - | - | - | - | - | - | - | - | - | - | - | - | - | - | - | - | - | - |
| Furrier | - | - | - | - | - | - | - | - | - | - | - | - | - | - | - | - | - | - | - |
| Hosier | - | - | - | - | - | - | - | - | - | - | - | - | - | - | - | - | - | - | - |
| Tailor | x | x | x | x | x | x | x | x | - | x | - | x | x | x | - | - | - | x | x |
| Chandler | - | - | - | - | - | - | - | - | - | - | - | - | - | - | - | - | - | - | - |
| Draper | x | - | x | - | x | - | - | - | - | - | - | - | x | - | - | x | - | - | x |
| Grocer | x | x | x | x | - | x | x | - | - | - | - | - | x | - | - | - | - | - | - |
| Haberdasher | - | - | x | - | - | - | - | - | - | - | - | - | - | - | - | - | - | - | - |
| Mercer | - | - | - | - | - | x | - | - | - | - | - | x | - | - | - | - | - | - | - |
| Merchant | - | - | - | - | - | - | x | - | - | - | - | - | - | - | - | - | - | - | - |
| Baker | x | x | x | x | - | x | - | - | x | x | - | x | - | - | - | - | - | x | x |
| Brewer | - | - | x | x | x | x | - | - | - | x | - | x | x | - | - | - | - | x | - |
| Butcher | x | x | x | x | - | x | - | - | x | - | - | - | - | - | - | - | - | x | - |
| Cook | - | x | - | - | - | x | - | - | - | - | - | - | - | - | - | - | - | - | - |
| Fisherman | - | - | - | - | - | - | - | - | - | x | - | x | - | - | - | - | - | - | - |
| Fishmonger | - | - | - | - | - | - | - | - | - | - | - | - | - | - | - | - | - | - | - |
| Innholder | x | x | x | x | x | x | - | - | - | - | - | - | - | - | - | x | - | x | - |
| Innkeeper | - | - | - | - | - | - | - | - | - | - | - | - | - | - | - | - | - | - | - |
| Vintner | - | - | - | - | - | - | - | - | - | - | - | - | x | - | - | - | - | - | - |
| Cordwainer | x | x | x | x | x | x | x | x | x | x | - | - | x | - | x | - | - | x | - |
| Glover | x | x | x | x | - | x | - | - | x | x | - | x | - | - | - | - | - | x | - |
| Tanner | x | x | x | x | x | x | - | - | x | - | - | - | - | x | - | - | - | - | - |
| Blacksmith | x | x | x | x | x | x | - | - | - | x | - | x | x | - | - | - | - | x | x |
| Brazier | - | - | - | - | - | - | - | - | - | - | - | - | - | - | - | - | - | - | - |
| Cutler | x | - | - | - | - | - | - | - | - | - | - | - | - | - | - | - | - | - | - |
| Goldsmith | - | - | - | - | - | - | x | - | - | - | - | - | - | - | - | - | - | - | - |
| Ironmonger | - | - | - | - | - | - | - | - | - | - | - | - | - | - | - | - | - | - | - |
| Locksmith | - | x | - | - | - | - | - | - | - | - | - | - | x | - | - | - | - | - | - |
| Pewterer | - | - | - | - | - | - | - | - | - | - | - | - | x | - | - | - | - | - | - |
| Plumber | - | - | - | - | - | - | - | - | - | - | - | - | - | - | - | - | - | - | - |
| Gardener | - | - | - | - | - | - | - | - | - | - | - | - | - | - | - | - | - | - | - |
| Roper | - | - | - | - | - | - | - | - | - | - | - | - | - | - | - | - | - | - | - |
| Upholsterer | - | - | - | - | - | - | - | - | - | - | - | - | - | - | - | - | - | - | - |
| Apothecary | - | - | - | - | - | - | - | - | - | - | - | - | x | - | - | - | - | - | - |
| Barber | - | x | - | - | - | - | - | - | - | - | - | - | - | x | - | - | - | - | - |
| Doctor/Surgeon | - | x | - | - | - | - | - | - | - | - | - | - | - | - | - | - | - | - | x |
| Minstrel/Musician | - | x | - | - | x | - | - | - | - | - | - | - | x | - | - | - | - | - | - |
| Notary | - | - | - | - | - | - | - | - | - | - | - | - | - | - | - | - | - | - | - |
| Schoolmaster | - | - | - | - | - | - | - | - | - | x | - | - | - | - | - | - | - | - | - |
| Scrivener | - | - | - | - | - | - | - | - | - | - | - | - | - | - | - | - | - | - | - |
| Carrier | - | - | - | - | - | - | - | - | - | - | - | - | - | - | - | - | - | - | - |
| Sailor/Boatman | - | - | - | - | - | x | x | - | - | - | - | - | - | - | - | - | - | - | - |
| Shipbuilder | - | - | x | - | - | - | - | - | - | - | - | - | x | - | - | - | - | x | - |
| Clothier | - | - | - | - | - | - | - | - | - | - | - | - | - | - | - | x | - | - | - |
| Linen Weaver | - | - | - | - | - | - | - | - | - | - | - | - | - | - | - | - | - | - | - |
| Textile Trades | - | x | x | x | - | x | - | - | - | x | - | x | - | x | - | - | - | - | - |
| Weavers | x | x | x | x | x | x | - | - | - | - | - | - | - | x | - | - | - | - | x |
| Worsted Trades | - | x | x | x | - | - | - | ~ | - | x | - | - | - | - | - | - | - | - | - |
| Coopers | - | x | - | x | - | - | - | - | - | - | - | - | x | - | - | - | - | - | x |

# Table 1.3 Occupations in Norfolk market towns as recorded in wills and inventories, 1650-1699

| | Diss | East Dereham | Wymondham | Aylsham | Downham Market | Thetford | Cromer | Harleston | Swaffham | North Walsham | Burnham Market | Holt | Little Walsingham | Attleborough | Fakenham | Loddon | Watton | Wells | Foulsham |
|---|---|---|---|---|---|---|---|---|---|---|---|---|---|---|---|---|---|---|---|
| Bricklayer/maker | x | - | x | - | x | x | - | - | - | - | - | - | x | x | - | x | - | - | - |
| Carpenter | - | x | x | x | x | x | - | - | - | - | - | x | x | x | x | x | x | x | - |
| Glazier | - | x | x | x | x | x | - | x | - | - | - | - | x | - | x | - | - | - | - |
| Joiner/Turner | x | - | x | x | - | - | - | - | - | x | x | x | x | x | - | x | - | - | - |
| Limeburner | - | - | - | - | - | - | - | - | - | - | - | - | - | - | - | - | - | - | - |
| Mason | - | - | - | - | - | - | - | - | - | - | - | - | - | - | - | - | - | - | - |
| Painter | - | - | - | - | - | - | - | - | - | - | - | - | - | - | - | - | - | - | - |
| Capper/Hatter | - | - | - | - | - | - | - | - | - | - | - | - | - | - | - | - | - | - | - |
| Feltmaker | - | - | - | - | x | x | - | - | - | x | - | - | x | - | x | - | - | - | - |
| Furrier | - | - | - | - | - | - | - | - | x | - | - | - | - | - | - | - | - | - | - |
| Hosier | x | - | x | - | - | - | - | x | - | - | - | - | - | - | - | - | - | - | - |
| Tailor | - | x | x | - | x | x | - | x | x | x | x | x | x | - | x | x | x | x | x |
| Chandler | - | - | - | - | x | - | - | - | - | - | - | - | x | - | - | - | - | - | - |
| Draper | x | - | - | - | - | - | - | x | - | - | - | x | x | x | - | - | x | - | - |
| Grocer | x | x | x | - | x | - | - | x | x | x | x | - | x | x | - | - | x | - | - |
| Haberdasher | - | x | - | - | - | - | - | - | - | - | - | - | x | - | - | - | - | x | - |
| Mercer | x | - | - | - | - | - | - | - | - | x | - | - | x | - | - | - | - | x | - |
| Merchant | - | - | - | - | - | - | - | - | - | x | - | - | - | - | - | - | - | x | - |
| Baker | x | x | x | x | x | x | - | - | x | - | - | - | x | x | - | - | - | - | - |
| Brewer | - | x | - | x | - | x | x | x | x | x | - | - | x | - | x | - | - | - | - |
| Butcher | x | - | x | x | x | x | - | x | x | - | x | x | - | - | - | x | - | x | - |
| Cook | - | - | - | - | - | - | - | - | - | - | - | - | x | - | - | - | - | - | - |
| Fisherman | - | - | - | - | - | x | - | - | - | - | - | - | - | - | - | - | - | x | - |
| Fishmonger | - | - | x | x | - | - | - | - | - | - | - | - | - | - | - | - | - | - | - |
| Innholder | - | - | - | - | - | - | - | - | - | - | - | - | - | - | - | - | - | - | - |
| Innkeeper | x | x | x | x | - | x | - | x | x | x | - | x | x | x | x | x | - | x | - |
| Vintner | - | - | - | - | - | - | x | - | - | - | - | - | x | - | - | - | - | - | - |
| Cordwainer | x | x | x | x | x | x | - | x | x | x | x | x | x | x | x | x | x | x | x |
| Glover | x | x | x | - | x | - | x | - | - | x | - | - | x | - | - | - | - | - | - |
| Tanner | x | x | - | x | x | x | - | - | x | - | - | - | - | - | - | - | - | - | x |
| Blacksmith | - | x | x | - | x | x | x | x | x | x | - | x | x | x | x | - | - | x | - |
| Brazier | x | - | x | - | x | - | - | - | - | - | - | - | - | - | - | - | x | - | - |
| Cutler | - | - | - | - | - | x | - | - | - | - | - | - | x | - | - | - | - | x | - |
| Goldsmith | - | - | - | - | - | - | - | - | - | - | - | - | - | - | - | - | - | - | - |
| Ironmonger | - | - | - | - | - | - | - | - | x | - | - | - | - | - | - | - | - | - | - |
| Locksmith | - | - | x | - | - | x | - | - | - | - | - | - | - | x | - | - | - | - | - |
| Pewterer | - | - | - | - | - | - | - | - | - | - | - | - | - | - | - | - | - | - | - |
| Plumber | - | x | - | - | - | x | - | - | - | - | - | - | - | - | x | - | - | - | - |
| Gardener | - | - | - | - | - | x | - | - | x | - | - | - | - | - | x | - | - | - | - |
| Roper | - | - | - | - | - | - | - | - | x | - | - | - | - | - | - | - | - | x | - |
| Upholsterer | - | - | - | - | - | x | - | - | - | - | - | - | - | - | - | - | - | - | - |
| Apothecary | x | x | x | - | x | - | - | - | - | x | - | x | - | x | - | - | - | x | - |
| Barber | x | - | - | x | x | x | - | x | - | x | - | - | x | - | - | x | - | - | - |
| Doctor/Surgeon | x | x | x | - | - | x | - | - | - | x | - | x | x | x | - | - | - | - | x |
| Minstrel/Musician | - | - | - | - | - | x | - | - | - | - | - | - | - | - | - | - | - | - | - |
| Notary | x | - | - | - | - | - | - | - | - | - | - | - | - | - | - | - | - | - | - |
| Schoolmaster | - | - | - | - | - | x | - | - | - | - | - | - | - | - | - | - | x | - | - |
| Scrivener | - | - | - | - | - | - | - | - | - | - | - | - | - | - | - | - | - | - | - |
| Carrier | - | x | - | - | x | - | - | - | - | - | - | - | - | - | - | - | - | - | - |
| Sailor/Boatman | - | - | - | - | - | - | x | - | - | - | - | - | x | - | - | - | - | x | - |
| Shipbuilder | - | - | - | - | - | - | - | - | - | - | - | - | - | - | - | - | - | - | - |
| Clothier | - | x | - | - | x | - | - | x | - | - | - | - | - | - | - | - | x | - | - |
| Linen Weaver | x | x | x | - | x | x | - | x | - | - | - | - | x | x | x | x | - | - | - |
| Textile Trades | x | x | x | x | - | x | - | - | - | x | - | - | - | x | - | - | - | - | - |
| Weavers | - | - | - | - | x | x | - | - | x | - | - | x | x | - | x | x | x | - | - |
| Worsted Trades | - | x | x | x | x | - | x | - | - | - | - | - | - | x | - | - | - | - | x |
| Coopers | - | x | - | x | x | - | - | - | x | x | - | - | - | x | x | x | - | - | x |

**Table 1.4 Occupations and occupational groupings in Norfolk rural parishes in the 16th and 17th centuries**

| Occupation or occupational grouping | Number of parishes in which occupation is recorded | | |
| --- | --- | --- | --- |
| | 1500-1599 | 1600-1649 | 1650-1699 |
| Brickmaker/layer ⎱ | 6 | 5 | 9 |
| Brickmaster/tiler ⎰ | | | |
| Carpenters | 100 | 119 | 172 |
| Masons | 6 | 10 | 8 |
| Tailors | 112 | 142 | 170 |
| Cloth distributive | 20 | 20 | 25 |
| General distributive | 10 | 15 | 54 |
| Bakers | 13 | 15 | 40 |
| Brewers | 2 | 13 | 15 |
| Butchers | 37 | 37 | 91 |
| Shoemakers | 8 | 22 | 26 |
| Other leather trades | 44 | 59 | 156 |
| Blacksmiths/smiths | 23 | 32 | 55 |
| Professions and services | 5 | 11 | 23 |
| Linen trades | 9 | 69 | 170 |
| Woollen trades | 87 | 99 | 120 |
| Worsted trades | 34 | 44 | 115 |
| Wood trades | 35 | 43 | 37 |

Activities of the kind outlined above, whether in urban or rural areas, brought wealth for many, as the material surviving for the beginning and end of the period makes abundantly clear. Unfortunately, much of the evidence for Norfolk as a whole has yet to be analysed. Consequently the picture presented below is incomplete. For the early 16th century it is based on a thorough analysis of the surviving portions of the military survey taken in 1522 which, in this instance, takes in Great Yarmouth and 11 hundreds stretching from Blofield and Walsham in the east to Gallow and Brothercross in the north of the county;[12] the payments made by the various hundreds to the subsidy of 1524;[13] and, finally, on the returns to the Anticipation, comprising all those people worth £40 and above who were required to pay their contributions to the subsidy in advance.[14] For the late 17th century we have a county wide assessment for the provision of arms in 1663, supplemented by an analysis of the Hearth Tax returns for the following year as they relate to those wealthy enough to be assessed on 10 hearths or more.[15]

The ostensible purpose of the survey was to provide an indication of the country's capacity to supply arms and armour in time of war, the provision of which was linked to a person's stated wealth. Everyone listed, whether clerical or lay, was required to state on oath the value of his goods and, where appropriate, the annual value of his freehold lands, benefice or stipend. As it was not known at the time that the survey was the prelude to an all-embracing and virtually unprecedented method of taxation, people tended to provide relatively accurate details of their wealth, possibly even exaggerating it in a minority of cases. Where such material survives, it provides a fuller and more accurate impression of the distribution of wealth than the subsidies which followed it, important and useful though those sources are.

The inequality of wealth in Tudor England is by now a virtual historical commonplace and in broad terms the Norfolk figures do no more than confirm an already established pattern. In some respects, however, they do more than this. In the first place they emphasise that wealth was more evenly distributed in both town and country districts in 1522 than an examination of the subsequent subsidy payments would suggest, and they also emphasise that any examination of clerical wealth must take into account the goods and lands owned by clerics as well as any benefice or stipend they may have had. Where Great Yarmouth, West Flegg, South Erpingham, Happing and Tunstead hundreds are concerned, the numbers of poor are given which allows a comparison to be made between urban and rural poverty. Finally, and perhaps most important of all, the survey provides us with details of the amounts of land in the possession of the freeholders, landholdings which were an important and, where the poorer classes were concerned, vital addition to their moveable goods. It should be noted that the percentages in brackets in the supporting table relate to the total numbers recorded, while the others are percentages of those actually owning goods, a distinction which allows for easier comparison of the groups concerned.

In Great Yarmouth what might be called the traditional picture can be discerned, an upper class of some seven per cent owning 52 per cent of the moveable goods, with no more than six per cent of the property being in the possession of those worth between £1 and £2. More than a third of those recorded had no goods at all to their names, although 17 of these 174 did own small parcels of land. Only Gallow hundred compares with Yarmouth in its distribution of wealth, for reasons which will be referred to below. Elsewhere, the bulk of the property tended to be in the hands of a middling group situated somewhere in the £5 to £39 range. This is especially noticeable in Blofield where the Anticipation class owned little more than 14 per cent of the hundred's wealth, in Tunstead where they owned less than one-fifth, and in Walsham where the proportion was just over one-quarter. Everywhere a majority of those with goods to their names owned a minority of the wealth but, in contrast to the larger towns assessed in 1524 and beyond where the wage-earners or those with £1 worth of goods usually comprised some forty per cent of all the taxpayers, such people in rural Norfolk seldom constituted one-third of the population and usually considerably less than that. Absolute poverty ranged from one in five in West Flegg to just over one-third in South Erpingham. Interestingly enough, some people, notably in Tunstead hundred, had goods recorded which were worth less than £1, a clear attempt to differentiate between the really destitute and those just above that level.

On the evidence of the survey the Norfolk clergy, with very few exceptions, ranged from the comfortably off to the wealthy.[16] Few of the stipendiary clergy received less than the standard rate of £5 6s. 8d., with almost half of them allotted stipends above this level. In addition to their stipends, however, a full 80 per cent owned property worth £2 or more, with a quarter of them in possession of moveables valued at £10 and above. Seven of the 116 stipendiary clergy were also landowners in their own right, with one individual owning in excess of 200 acres. Those with benefices were even wealthier, several of them being the richest men in their particular villages. Twenty-six of the beneficed clergy in Norfolk were non-resident, but of the remaining 119 one-quarter owned goods worth £20 or more, with a full 86 per cent having property worth £3 and above. The wealthier among them included pluralists like William Boleyn, vicar of Aylsham and member of a famous family who, in addition to a benefice of £20 and moveable goods worth £30 in his own town, had a still more rewarding benefice of £40 in St Peter's, Cheapside, in London. His near neighbour, who held the parsonage of Marsham in Holt hundred, owned £200 worth of goods and a personal landholding of some 15 acres, in addition to his benefice of £20. Over 50 of the resident clergy had benefices valued at £10 or more, in addition to their other property, with the residue virtually all exceeding £6 in value.

Information on monastic communities is limited to a valuation of the properties of the priors of Hickling, Cockford and Hampton. All three were wealthy. The prior of Hickling in Happing hundred had £140 worth of goods to his name as well as lands worth £100. The prior of Cockford, in Gallow hundred, was richer still, with a manor assessed at £120 and

## Table 1.5 Distribution of wealth in Great Yarmouth

| Goods, etc. | Land only | Nil | Under £1 | £1 | £2 | £3-£4 | £5-£9 |
|---|---|---|---|---|---|---|---|
| | **17** | **157** | **6** | **70** | **71** | **54** | **46** |
| Great | *(3.37)* | *(31.09)* | *1.81* | *21.15* | *21.45* | *16.31* | *13.90* |
| Yarmouth | | | 2 6 8 | 70 10 0 | 143 19 8 | 129 6 8 | 292 0 0 |
| | | | *0.07* | *2.08* | *4.25* | *3.81* | *8.61* |
| | - | - | - | **45** | **53** | **41** | **67** |
| Blofield | - | - | - | *15.79* | *18.60* | *14.39* | *23.51* |
| | | | - - - | 47 10 0 | 106 13 4 | 144 13 4 | 426 0 0 |
| | | | - | *2.15* | *4.84* | *6.56* | *19.31* |
| | **26** | - | - | **53** | **36** | **16** | **21** |
| Brothercross | *(13.98)* | - | - | *33.12* | *22.50* | *10.00* | *13.12* |
| | | | - - - | 59 3 4 | 75 0 0 | 54 6 8 | 125 0 8 |
| | | | - | *4.96* | *6.28* | *4.55* | *10.48* |
| | **13** | **480** | **2** | **302** | **192** | **156** | **124** |
| South | *(0.91)* | *(33.57)* | *0.21* | *32.23* | *20.49* | *16.65* | *13.23* |
| Erpingham | | | - 6 4 | 324 0 0 | 399 0 0 | 538 13 4 | 795 13 4 |
| | | | - | *5.23* | *6.44* | *8.70* | *12.85* |
| | **1** | - | - | **27** | **35** | **35** | **33** |
| East | *(0.43)* | - | - | *11.59* | *15.02* | *15.02* | *14.16* |
| Flegg | | | - - - | 27 0 0 | 70 10 0 | 124 0 0 | 201 13 4 |
| | | | - | *1.65* | *4.32* | *7.59* | *12.35* |
| | **1** | **71** | - | **64** | **54** | **52** | **43** |
| West | *(0.31)* | *(21.85)* | - | *25.30* | *21.34* | *20.55* | *17.00* |
| Flegg | | | - - - | 64 4 0 | 108 0 0 | 176 0 0 | 261 13 4 |
| | | | - | *4.39* | *7.38* | *12.03* | *17.89* |
| | **32** | - | **2** | **139** | **110** | **64** | **59** |
| Gallow | *(6.62)* | - | *0.44* | *30.82* | *24.39* | *14.19* | *13.08* |
| | | | - 17 4 | 153 6 8 | 223 0 0 | 217 13 4 | 374 0 0 |
| | | | *0.02* | *3.63* | *5.28* | *5.15* | *8.86* |
| | **19** | - | - | **137** | **132** | **82** | **67** |
| North | *(3.47)* | - | - | *25.90* | *24.95* | *15.50* | *12.66* |
| Greenhoe | | | - - - | 148 8 4 | 274 13 4 | 283 13 4 | 440 13 4 |
| | | | - | *3.41* | *6.30* | *6.51* | *10.12* |
| | **8** | **191** | **2** | **141** | **124** | **121** | **85** |
| Happing | *(1.08)* | *(25.74)* | *0.37* | *25.97* | *22.84* | *22.28* | *15.65* |
| | | | 1 0 0 | 141 16 8 | 248 13 4 | 412 0 0 | 534 13 4 |
| | | | *0.03* | *5.43* | *9.52* | *15.77* | *20.46* |
| | **28** | - | - | **186** | **137** | **121** | **105** |
| Holt | *(4.04)* | - | - | *27.97* | *20.60* | *18.19* | *15.79* |
| | | | - - - | 206 2 8 | 282 13 4 | 428 6 8 | 691 16 8 |
| | | | - | *4.36* | *5.99* | *9.07* | *14.65* |
| | **3** | **281** | **19** | **230** | **152** | **175** | **153** |
| Tunstead | *(0.26)* | *(24.43)* | *2.19* | *26.56* | *17.55* | *20.21* | *17.67* |
| | | | 10 13 4 | 236 6 8 | 308 13 4 | 589 0 0 | 943 13 4 |
| | | | *0.22* | *4.91* | *6.41* | *12.23* | *19.60* |
| | **4** | - | - | **46** | **60** | **58** | **75** |
| Walsham | *(1.36)* | - | - | *15.81* | *20.62* | *19.93* | *25.77* |
| | | | - - - | 48 3 4 | 120 0 0 | 191 0 0 | 494 13 4 |
| | | | - | *2.34* | *5.82* | *9.26* | *23.99* |

The number assessed in each category is given in bold and the total value of their assessment is given below i

| £0-£19 | £20-£39 | £40-£99 | £100-£299 | Over £300 | Totals |
|---|---|---|---|---|---|
| 36 | 26 | 18 | 4 | - | 505 |
| *0.88* | *7.85* | *5.44* | *1.21* | - | |
| 2 6 8 | 639 6 8 | 986 13 4 | 783 6 8 | - - - | 3,389 16 4 |
| *0.10* | *18.86* | *29.11* | *23.11* | - | |
| 51 | 22 | 5 | 1 | - | 285 |
| *7.89* | *7.72* | *1.75* | *0.35* | - | |
| 8 0 0 | 529 6 8 | 180 0 0 | 133 6 8 | - - - | 2,205 10 0 |
| *8.93* | *24.00* | *8.16* | *6.04* | - | |
| 18 | 8 | 7 | 1 | - | 186 |
| *1.25* | *5.00* | *4.37* | *0.62* | - | |
| 6 13 4 | 206 13 4 | 346 13 4 | 120 0 0 | - - - | 1,193 10 8 |
| *7.31* | *17.31* | *29.04* | *10.05* | - | |
| 83 | 50 | 22 | 6 | - | 1,430 |
| *8.86* | *5.34* | *2.35* | *0.64* | - | |
| 3 13 4 | 1,104 6 8 | 1,213 11 0 | 793 6 8 | - - - | 6,192 10 8 |
| *6.53* | *17.83* | *19.60* | *12.81* | - | |
| 23 | 13 | 7 | 2 | - | 234 |
| *9.87* | *5.58* | *3.00* | *0.86* | - | |
| 0 13 4 | 314 0 0 | 295 0 0 | 300 10 0 | - - - | 1,632 16 8 |
| *8.41* | *19.23* | *18.07* | *18.40* | - | |
| 18 | 15 | 7 | - | - | 325 |
| *7.11* | *5.93* | *2.77* | - | - | |
| 5 0 0 | 338 0 0 | 300 0 0 | - - - | - - - | 1,462 17 4 |
| *4.70* | *23.10* | *20.51* | - | - | |
| 42 | 21 | 10 | 3 | 1 | 483 |
| *9.31* | *4.66* | *2.22* | *0.66* | *0.22* | |
| 13 4 | 485 6 8 | 491 0 0 | 460 0 0 | 1,333 6 8 | 4,222 4 0 |
| *1.45* | *11.49* | *11.63* | *10.89* | *31.58* | |
| 56 | 30 | 17 | 8 | - | 548 |
| *0.59* | *5.67* | *3.21* | *1.51* | - | |
| 3 13 4 | 716 13 4 | 841 13 4 | 1,006 13 4 | - - - | 4,356 1 8 |
| *4.78* | *16.45* | *19.32* | *23.11* | - | |
| 51 | 13 | 5 | 1 | - | 742 |
| *9.39* | *2.39* | *0.92* | *0.18* | - | |
| 8 6 8 | 300 0 0 | 256 13 4 | 140 0 0 | - - - | 2,613 3 4 |
| *2.13* | *11.48* | *9.82* | *5.36* | - | |
| 60 | 32 | 19 | 5 | - | 693 |
| *9.02* | *4.81* | *2.86* | *0.75* | - | |
| 0 0 0 | 756 6 8 | 966 13 4 | 700 0 0 | - - - | 4,721 19 4 |
| *4.61* | *16.02* | *20.47* | *14.82* | - | |
| 91 | 32 | 10 | 4 | - | 1,150 |
| *0.51* | *3.69* | *1.15* | *0.46* | - | |
| 2 13 4 | 748 0 0 | 469 0 0 | 466 13 4 | - - - | 4,814 13 4 |
| *1.66* | *15.54* | *9.74* | *9.69* | - | |
| 40 | 5 | 5 | 2 | - | 295 |
| *3.75* | *1.72* | *1.72* | *0.69* | - | |
| 5 13 4 | 125 0 0 | 230 0 0 | 317 4 0 | - - - | 2,061 14 0 |
| *5.98* | *6.06* | *11.16* | *15.38* | - | |

£ s. d.; the percentage each represents of the whole is shown in italics.

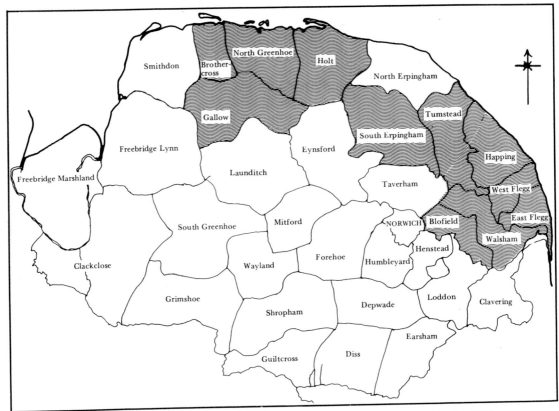

1.  The hundreds of Norfolk. The shaded areas indicate the hundreds recorded in the 1522 survey.

goods worth £333 6s. 8d., while the prior of Hampton in the same hundred was estimated to be worth £20 and £46 13s. 4d. respectively.

The richest clergy had few rivals in this part of Norfolk, the wealth of the parson of Marsham, for example, being matched by the Bishop family in Great Yarmouth and, apart from a man with goods valued at £240 in North Greenhoe hundred, exceeded by only four other individuals. They included the outstandingly wealthy Henry Fermor, lord of the manor of East Barsham, who declared himself worth £1,333 6s. 8d. in moveable goods, with a landholding valued at £166 13s. 4d., or possibly 5,000 acres. Fermor, one of the great sheep farmers of this part of Norfolk, owned well over 90 per cent of all the property in his own village and one-third of the goods in the entire hundred of Gallow.[17] His only serious rival in the county, was Robert Jannys of Norwich who was assessed on goods worth £1,100 in 1524 but whose landed wealth was most unlikely to have matched Fermor's.[18]

Landed wealth, however, whether great or small, is a feature of the Norfolk material. Tawney referred long ago to the large number of freeholders in the county, the manors he examined suggesting that about one in three of all landholders fell into this category.[19] Where we have figures for the poor as well as those with property to their names the 1522 survey largely confirms this figure, the proportions ranging from 22 per cent in Tunstead and West Flegg to as high as 46 per cent in Great Yarmouth.

If, on the other hand, we consider the freeholders solely in relation to those actually owning goods the proportions are decidedly higher. Such people were most numerous in

## Table 1.6 Numbers and percentages of people with freehold land in Great Yarmouth and 11 Norfolk hundreds in 1522

| Value of goods | Great Yarmouth | Blofield | Brothercross | South Erpingham | East Flegg | West Flegg | Gallow | North Greenhoe | Happing | Holt | Tunstead | Walsham | Totals |
|---|---|---|---|---|---|---|---|---|---|---|---|---|---|
| To 3s.4d. | 1 *0.43* | 3 *2.46* | 17 *14.41* | 46 *10.13* | 6 *5.71* | - - | 49 *14.85* | 61 *18.83* | 43 *16.67* | 60 *16.04* | 3 *1.18* | - - | 289 *10.51* |
| 4s.-6s.8d. | 28 *12.17* | 14 *11.47* | 38 *32.20* | 103 *22.69* | 27 *25.71* | 17 *23.29* | 113 *34.24* | 81 *25.00* | 62 *24.03* | 113 *30.21* | 33 *13.04* | 19 *17.43* | 648 *23.56* |
| 7s.-10s. | 70 *30.43* | 23 *18.85* | 19 *16.10* | 59 *12.99* | 15 *14.28* | 14 *19.18* | 59 *17.88* | 50 *15.43* | 46 *17.83* | 64 *17.11* | 33 *13.04* | 25 *22.93* | 477 *17.34* |
| 11s.-13s.4d. | 39 *16.96* | 16 *13.11* | 13 *11.02* | 49 *10.79* | 11 *10.48* | 12 *16.44* | 37 *11.21* | 28 *8.64* | 36 *13.95* | 41 *10.96* | 41 *16.20* | 7 *6.42* | 330 *12.00* |
| 13s. 4d. + | 5 *2.17* | 3 *2.46* | 1 *0.85* | 11 *2.42* | - - | - - | 4 *1.21* | 6 *1.85* | 1 *0.39* | 10 *2.67* | 2 *0.79* | 4 *3.67* | 47 *1.71* |
| £1 | 22 *9.56* | 27 *22.13* | 8 *6.78* | 55 *12.11* | 19 *18.09* | 14 *19.18* | 28 *8.48* | 25 *7.72* | 42 *16.28* | 30 *8.02* | 67 *26.48* | 24 *22.02* | 361 *13.13* |
| £1 + | 19 *8.26* | 10 *8.20* | 7 *5.93* | 53 *11.67* | 11 *10.48* | 5 *6.85* | 11 *3.33* | 24 *7.41* | 5 *1.94* | 22 *5.88* | 26 *10.28* | 10 *9.17* | 203 *7.38* |
| £2 | 21 *9.13* | 14 *11.47* | 5 *4.24* | 36 *7.93* | 12 *11.43* | 5 *6.85* | 9 *2.73* | 31 *9.57* | 10 *3.88* | 14 *3.74* | 27 *10.67* | 13 *11.93* | 197 *7.16* |
| £3-£4 | 17 *7.39* | 8 *6.56* | 4 *3.39* | 14 *3.08* | 1 *0.95* | 2 *2.74* | 9 *2.73* | 7 *2.16* | 7 *2.71* | 7 *1.87* | 9 *3.56* | 4 *3.67* | 89 *3.24* |
| £5-£9 | 3 *1.30* | 2 *1.64* | 3 *2.54* | 13 *2.86* | 2 *1.90* | 2 *2.74* | 6 *1.82* | 4 *1.23* | 2 *0.77* | 10 *2.67* | 7 *2.77* | 1 *0.92* | 55 *2.00* |
| £10-£25 | 5 *2.17* | 1 *0.82* | 3 *2.54* | 13 *2.86* | 1 *0.95* | 1 *1.37* | 3 *0.91* | 3 *0.92* | 3 *1.16* | 2 *0.53* | 4 *1.58* | 1 *0.92* | 40 *1.45* |
| £26-£50 | - - | - - | - - | 1 *0.22* | - - | 1 *1.37* | 1 *0.30* | 4 *1.23* | - - | - - | 1 *0.39* | 1 *0.92* | 9 *0.33* |
| Above £50 | - - | 1 *0.82* | - - | 1 *0.22* | - - | - - | 1 *0.30* | - - | 1 *0.39* | 1 *0.27* | - - | - - | 5 *0.18* |
| Totals | 230 | 122 | 118 | 454 | 105 | 73 | 330 | 324 | 258 | 374 | 253 | 109 | 2,750 |
| Percentage of freeholders owning goods | *64.35* | *42.81* | *63.44* | *47.79* | *44.87* | *28.74* | *68.32* | *59.12* | *46.82* | *53.97* | *29.11* | *36.95* | *48.28* |

## Table 1.7 Landholdings in Great Yarmouth and 11 Norfolk hundreds in 1522 related to value of goods

| Goods. etc. | Land only | % | £1 | % | £2 | % | £3-4 | % | £5-9 | % | £10-19 | % | £20-39 | % | £40-99 | % | £100-299 | % | Over £300 | % | Totals |
|---|---|---|---|---|---|---|---|---|---|---|---|---|---|---|---|---|---|---|---|---|---|
| To 3s. 4d. | 52 | *34.4* | 72 | *23.3* | 70 | *17.1* | 67 | *13.5* | 20 | *3.5* | 6 | *1.3* | 2 | *0.9* | - | - | - | - | - | - | 289 |
| 4s.-6s. 8d. | 53 | *35.1* | 145 | *46.9* | 155 | *37.8* | 148 | *29.8* | 109 | *19.3* | 31 | *6.9* | 5 | *2.3* | 2 | *1.7* | - | - | - | - | 648 |
| 7s.-10s. | 11 | *7.3* | 54 | *17.5* | 100 | *24.4* | 112 | *22.5* | 115 | *20.3* | 62 | *13.9* | 18 | *8.2* | 3 | *2.6* | 1 | *3.0* | - | - | 476 |
| 11s.-13s. 4d. | 10 | *6.6* | 21 | *6.8* | 39 | *9.5* | 74 | *14.9* | 110 | *19.5* | 54 | *12.1* | 17 | *7.7* | 5 | *4.3* | - | - | - | - | 330 |
| 13s. 4d.+ | - | - | 2 | *0.6* | 3 | *0.7* | 13 | *2.6* | 15 | *2.6* | 9 | *2.0* | 4 | *1.8* | 1 | *0.9* | - | - | - | - | 47 |
| £1 | 10 | *6.6* | 9 | *2.9* | 25 | *6.1* | 56 | *11.3* | 101 | *17.9* | 112 | *25.1* | 41 | *18.6* | 5 | *4.3* | 1 | *3.0* | - | - | 360 |
| £1+ | 4 | *2.6* | 3 | *1.0* | 11 | *2.7* | 16 | *3.2* | 55 | *9.7* | 67 | *15.0* | 36 | *16.4* | 11 | *9.5* | - | - | - | - | 203 |
| £2 | 7 | *4.6* | 3 | *1.0* | 4 | *1.0* | 10 | *2.0* | 31 | *5.5* | 62 | *13.9* | 45 | *20.4* | 29 | *25.0* | 6 | *18.2* | - | - | 197 |
| £3-£4 | 4 | *2.6* | - | - | - | - | - | - | 6 | *1.1* | 17 | *3.8* | 33 | *0.2* | 26 | *22.4* | 3 | *9.1* | - | - | 89 |
| £5-£9 | - | - | - | - | 2 | *0.5* | - | - | 2 | *0.3* | 15 | *3.4* | 14 | *6.4* | 16 | *13.8* | 6 | *18.2* | - | - | 55 |
| £10-£25 | - | - | - | - | 1 | *0.3* | 1 | *0.2* | 1 | *0.2* | 10 | *2.2* | 3 | *1.4* | 16 | *13.8* | 8 | *24.2* | - | - | 40 |
| £26-£50 | - | - | - | - | - | - | - | - | - | - | 1 | *0.2* | 2 | *0.9* | 2 | *1.7* | 4 | *12.1* | - | - | 9 |
| Above £50 | - | - | - | - | - | - | - | - | - | - | - | - | - | - | - | - | 4 | *12.1* | 1 | *100* | 5 |
| Totals | 151 | *5.5* | 309 | *11.2* | 410 | *14.9* | 497 | *18.1* | 565 | *20.6* | 446 | *16.2* | 220 | *8.0* | 116 | *4.2* | 33 | *1.2* | 1 | *0.03* | 2,748 |

Gallow, where they made up 68 per cent of the property-owning classes, closely followed by Great Yarmouth and Brothercross, each with around 64 per cent. More than half of those enumerated in the hundreds of North Greenhoe and Holt were similarly endowed, with the figure only falling below 30 per cent in West Flegg and Tunstead.

As a rough-and-ready guide, £1 worth of land may be equated with 30 acres, although obviously the value would vary according to the situation and quality of the land concerned. Some two-thirds of the landholdings were valued at less than this, smaller holdings being particularly numerous in the hundreds to the north of the county, such as Gallow, Brothercross and North Greenhoe, where between three-fifths and two-thirds of all freeholdings were valued at ten shillings or below. This was a proportion very similar to that prevailing in Babergh hundred in Suffolk, where two-thirds was again the norm and, as in Babergh, the smaller holdings were in the possession of people of all classes, ranging from the wage-earner on the one hand to the man with over £100 to his name on the other. Obviously the less wealthy a man was the smaller his landholding was likely to be, and over 90 per cent of the 309 men with goods worth £1 or less had landholdings valued at under £1, compared with eight per cent of those assessed at £40 and above. Nevertheless, the proportions of middling men owning small amounts of freehold land were quite high, with one-third of those with goods worth between £10 and £19 and one-fifth of those in the next category having similar holdings, quite apart from any lands they may have held as tenants.

Just over one-fifth of all the landholdings were valued at £1 or at sums such as £1 6s. 8d. or £1 13s. 4d. They were specially prominent in the hundreds of Blofield, Tunstead and Walsham where their numbers were decidedly above average, exceeding 30 per cent in every case. It may be of some significance that these were the hundreds where the Anticipation classes were less prominent than elsewhere, and suggests that people here preferred to invest their money in land rather than moveables, a suggestion which is partially reinforced by the equally above average number of holdings at the £2 level in the same hundreds.

The information on landholdings is especially interesting where the poorer classes are concerned. It is usual, when considering the extent of poverty in early-Tudor England, to link the wage-earners or those assessed on £1-worth of goods with those of no substance, to emphasise their large numbers, and make judgements accordingly. This is perfectly legitimate for many of such people lived on a knife's edge and could find themselves among the ranks of the very poor at any time. However, as has been mentioned above, a good number of these people owned lands as well as goods. They were to be found everywhere but were especially significant in North Greenhoe, Brothercross and Gallow hundreds, where the proportions of £1 men with lands to their names ranged from 34 and 35 per cent in the first two to as high as 43 per cent in the third. Less significant, but highly interesting for an urban area, are the 28 per cent of such people listed as holding lands or tenements in Great Yarmouth itself. Bearing in mind that some of them may also have had land other than freehold, the evidence suggests that in the country districts at least, poverty may have been a less serious threat than is sometimes suggested, and that one must be constantly aware of the gradations of poverty even in the larger towns.

Nothing comparable to the 1522 material survives for the county as a whole, but we do have details of the payments made by the various hundreds to the subsidy of 1524 which provide a broad impression of the distribution of wealth of early sixteenth-century Norfolk.

Norwich was supreme in the county, being almost three times as wealthy as King's Lynn and six times as wealthy as Great Yarmouth. Despite its own wealth, however, the city was surrounded by some of the poorer hundreds in Norfolk, the richer areas being to the north and west, with Freebridge Marshland outstanding. The hundreds of Loddon and Mitford contained a number of substantial parishes, as did those of Tunstead, South Erpingham and Forehoe, with their market towns of North Walsham, Aylsham and Wymondham. Diss and Guiltcross, in contrast, both in areas of inferior soils to the south, were distinctly poorer, while Thetford's wealth scarcely matched that of some of the larger market towns.

Detailed analyses of the subsidies have yet to be undertaken. Information is available for the Anticipation class, however, and an analysis of this material supplements the details outlined above and allows for some comparison with those areas detailed in the 1522 survey.

**Table 1.8 Norfolk contributions to the subsidy of 1524**

| Hundred | Number of parishes | Total Assessments | | | Average wealth per parish | | |
|---|---|---|---|---|---|---|---|
| | | £ | s. | d. | £ | s. | d. |
| Freebridge Marshland | 12 | 161 | 4 | 0 | 13 | 8 | 8 |
| Tunstead | 26 | 145 | 14 | 3 | 5 | 12 | 1 |
| North Erpingham | 32 | 143 | 18 | 4 | 4 | 9 | 11 |
| South Erpingham | 37 | 143 | 1 | 6 | 3 | 17 | 4 |
| Gallow | 32 | 136 | 12 | 0 | 4 | 5 | 4 |
| North Greenhoe | 17 | 135 | 11 | 2 | 7 | 19 | 6 |
| Holt | 27 | 128 | 17 | 6 | 8 | 1 | 1 |
| Freebridge Lynn | 34 | 117 | 14 | 4 | 3 | 9 | 3 |
| Forehoe | 32 | 107 | 11 | 4 | 3 | 7 | 3 |
| South Grenhoe | 23 | 107 | 5 | 8 | 4 | 18 | 0 |
| Launditch | 32 | 104 | 4 | 9 | 3 | 5 | 2 |
| Loddon | 20 | 100 | 11 | 4 | 5 | 6 | 10 |
| Mitford | 17 | 88 | 0 | 4 | 5 | 3 | 9 |
| Eynesford | 30 | 87 | 2 | 10 | 2 | 18 | 1 |
| Shropham | 20 | 75 | 17 | 2 | 3 | 16 | 10 |
| Smithdon | 18 | 68 | 7 | 0 | 3 | 15 | 11 |
| Earsham | 15 | 68 | 2 | 4 | 4 | 10 | 10 |
| Grimshoe | 16 | 65 | 8 | 6 | 4 | 1 | 9 |
| Depwade | 21 | 62 | 13 | 8 | 2 | 19 | 8 |
| Blofield | 17 | 62 | 7 | 8 | 3 | 13 | 5 |
| Walsham | 14 | 60 | 0 | 4 | 4 | 5 | 9 |
| Happing | 17 | 57 | 19 | 10 | 3 | 8 | 3 |
| Humbleyard | 19 | 47 | 17 | 6 | 2 | 10 | 5 |
| Wayland | 15 | 47 | 14 | 10 | 3 | 3 | 8 |
| Brothercross | 9 | 40 | 8 | 4 | 4 | 9 | 10 |
| Diss | 16 | 38 | 17 | 6 | 2 | 8 | 7 |
| Henstead | 19 | 36 | 7 | 6 | 1 | 18 | 3 |
| Taverham | 18 | 36 | 7 | 6 | 2 | 0 | 5 |
| Guiltcross | 13 | 36 | 3 | 10 | 2 | 15 | 8 |
| Clavering | 20 | 34 | 6 | 6 | 1 | 14 | 4 |
| West Flegg | 13 | 34 | 2 | 0 | 2 | 12 | 6 |
| East Flegg | 9 | 27 | 13 | 7 | 3 | 1 | 6 |

Source: N.R.O., Bradfer-Lawrence Papers, XIb. Details of all the payments referred to above are to be found among these papers in typescript, although there is no information for the hundred of Clackclose, which would probably have been high in the list. Full details of the individual assessments, as well as the payments, are provided for several of the hundreds, but not all of them, so a detailed analysis is not possible from this source. It may be noted, *int. al.*, that Little Walsingham in the hundred of North Greenhoe paid £57 7s. 6d., East Dereham in Mitford £27 17s. 10d. and Wymondham in Forehoe £41 3s. 8d. Norwich in the same year contributed £749 4s. 0d., King's Lynn £262 7s. 0d., Great Yarmouth £115 17s. 6d. and Thetford no more than £29 8s. 8d.

## Table 1.9 Anticipation payments – 1524

| Town or Hundred | Categories of Goods – £ | | | | | Value £ s. d. | | | Percentage of tax paid[*] |
|---|---|---|---|---|---|---|---|---|---|
| | 40-99 | 100-299 | 300-500 | over 500 | Totals | | | | |
| Norwich | 57 | 25 | 2 | 3 | 87 | 10,284 | 13 | 4 | 69 |
| King's Lynn | 23 | 9 | - | 1 | 33 | 3,006 | 0 | 0 | 57 |
| Gallow & Brothercross | 9 | 3 | - | 2 | 14 | 2,073 | 0 | 0 | 59 |
| North Greenhoe | 14 | 5 | - | - | 19 | 1,262 | 13 | 4 | 46 |
| Holt | 11 | 2 | 1 | - | 14 | 1,246 | 13 | 4 | 48 |
| Great Yarmouth | 13 | 3 | - | - | 16 | 1,206 | 13 | 4 | 53 |
| South Erpingham | 15 | 1 | - | - | 16 | 916 | 13 | 4 | 32 |
| Forehoe | 9 | 2 | - | - | 11 | 830 | 0 | 0 | 38 |
| Freebridge Marshland | 9 | 2 | - | - | 11 | 813 | 6 | 8 | 25 |
| Blofield & Walsham | 3 | 4 | - | - | 7 | 803 | 6 | 8 | 33 |
| North Erpingham | 16 | - | - | - | 16 | 706 | 13 | 4 | 25 |
| South Greenhoe | 6 | 3 | - | - | 9 | 673 | 6 | 8 | 31 |
| Tunstead | 8 | - | 1 | - | 9 | 620 | 0 | 0 | 21 |
| Shropham | 7 | 1 | - | - | 8 | 492 | 0 | 0 | 33 |
| Freebridge Lynn | 5 | 2 | - | - | 7 | 455 | 0 | 0 | 19 |
| East Flegg | 5 | - | - | - | 5 | 450 | 0 | 0 | 83 |
| Launditch | 6 | 1 | - | - | 7 | 386 | 13 | 4 | 19 |
| Clackclose | 6 | - | - | - | 6 | 350 | 0 | 0 | ? |
| Eynesford | 7 | - | - | - | 7 | 306 | 13 | 4 | 18 |
| Smithdon | 4 | 1 | - | - | 5 | 300 | 0 | 0 | 22 |
| Grimshoe | 2 | 1 | - | - | 3 | 280 | 13 | 4 | 22 |
| Mitford | 6 | - | - | - | 6 | 256 | 0 | 0 | 15 |
| Humbleyard | 5 | - | - | - | 5 | 230 | 0 | 0 | 24 |
| Loddon | 1 | 1 | - | - | 2 | 220 | 0 | 0 | 11 |
| Depwade | - | 1 | - | - | 1 | 200 | 0 | 0 | 16 |
| Thetford | 4 | - | - | - | 4 | 200 | 0 | 0 | 34 |
| Wayland | 3 | - | - | - | 3 | 167 | 0 | 0 | 17 |
| Taverham | 1 | 1 | - | - | 2 | 160 | 0 | 0 | 22 |
| Earsham | 3 | - | - | - | 3 | 120 | 0 | 0 | 9 |
| West Flegg | 1 | - | - | - | 1 | 60 | 0 | 0 | 9 |
| Diss | 1 | - | - | - | 1 | 40 | 0 | 0 | 5 |
| Guiltcross | 1 | - | - | - | 1 | 40 | 0 | 0 | 5 |
| Happing | 1 | - | - | - | 1 | 40 | 0 | 0 | 3 |
| Henstead | 1 | - | - | - | 1 | 40 | 0 | 0 | 6 |

[*] All those assessed at £20 and above, or on land, paid at the rate of one shilling in the pound, those with less than £20 in goods paid 6d. in the pound, and wage-earners paid a poll tax of 4d. This column is thus based on the total value of goods, etc., given here, divided by 20, and related, as a percentage, to the payments given in the previous table.

Source: *Norfolk Antiquarian Miscellany*, ii, 1883, pp.399-410, for all except Norwich, which is taken from my analysis of P.R.O., E179/150/208.

The 87 men assessed at £40 and above in Norwich paid 69 per cent of the city's contribution in 1524, those at King's Lynn and Great Yarmouth 57 and 53 per cent respectively. The wealthier inhabitants of Gallow, largely because of the substantial contributions of Henry Fermor and Sir Roger Townshend, matched Lynn and Yarmouth if not Norwich itself in this respect, with those of North Greenhoe and Holt providing almost half of their hundreds' payments to the subsidy. Elsewhere the share of the rich was considerably smaller, usually supplying between one-fifth and one-third of the tax, with half a dozen of the poorer hundreds providing under one-tenth.

Whether their share was large or small, a comparison of the assessments for 1522 with those actually used for taxation purposes two years later makes it abundantly clear that the rich were already resisting the new method of obtaining revenue. In virtually every case their alleged wealth in 1524 was considerably less than their earlier sworn statements had declared it to be. Collectively the numbers worth £40 and above in Great Yarmouth and the other hundreds for which we have the requisite information had fallen from 170 to 102, and their overall wealth from £13,131 to £8,039 – and this despite assessments of £600 for Sir Roger Townshend in East Raynham, £400 for Sir John Heydon in Stodey and £300 for Sir William Paston which were not recorded in the earlier return.[20] Virtually to a man, the wealthier members of the community had had their assessments reduced, the apparent decline of Henry Fermor's £1,333 6s. 8d. to a mere £666 13s. 4d. being only the most notable among many.[21] This was not unusual. Similar reductions can be found in Babergh hundred in Suffolk, for example, and in Norwich itself, and reflect the determination of the wealthy to extricate themselves from a financial trap which they had not originally anticipated.[22]

We have nothing comparable to the military survey and the Tudor subsidies until the levying of the Hearth Tax in the early days of Charles II's reign, and this has yet to be analysed in full where Norfolk is concerned. In parallel with this, however, the 1662 Militia Act allowed the king to raise a 'month's tax' to provide not more than £70,000 a year to supply the militia 'in case of apparent danger to the present government'.[23] The county of Norfolk, excluding Norwich, had to produce £3,622 3s. 4d. as its share, and a return for 1663 has survived in its entirety. It gives no real impression of individual wealth but does provide some indication of the relative importance of the individual hundreds and allows for at least broad comparison with the early-Tudor material.

Great Yarmouth was required to contribute £74 14s. 10d. a month, King's Lynn £55 12s. 6d. and Thetford no more than £10, a clear indication of its continuing decline. These apart, some two-thirds of all the parishes were rated on sums of up to £5, or just over, and a further quarter on amounts of between £6 and £10. As in the early 16th century, Freebridge Lynn and Freebridge Marshland hundreds were among the wealthiest areas of the county, and it was here that the largest assessments were to be found, five of their twelve parishes being rated at between £16 and £32, with Tilney and Walpole among the richest parishes outside the major towns.[24] The bigger of the market towns, such as Aylsham, North Walsham and Diss, were rated at between £17 and £19, the smaller ones, such as Holt, at little more than £5. At the other extreme, the parishes in the hundreds of Gallow, North Erpingham and Holt to the north and Blofield and East Flegg to the east all averaged under £4, the Fleggs, on this evidence, continuing to be among the poorest areas in the county. Holt's decline is the most noticeable among the various hundreds with Clavering's the most significant rise. Elsewhere, the hundreds stood in much the same relationship to each other as they had done in 1524.

**Table 1.10 Norfolk monthly assessments for furnishing ammunition, 1663**

| Hundred | Number of parishes | Total assessments £ s. d. | Average wealth per parish £ s. d. |
|---|---|---|---|
| Freebridge Marshland | 12 | 186 17  2 | 15 11  5 |
| Clackclose | 30 | 181 10  1 | 6  1  1 |
| South Erpingham | 37 | 167 19  2 | 4 10 10 |
| Freebridge Lynn | 34 | 156 18  6 | 4 12  2 |
| Launditch | 32 | 153 19  0 | 4 10  0 |
| Forehoe | 32 | 142  7  4 | 4  9  0 |
| Eynesford | 30 | 141  7  0 | 7  1  5 |
| Depwade | 21 | 135  0  0 | 6  8  7 |
| North Erpingham | 32 | 125  3  8 | 3 18  3 |
| Tunstead | 26 | 122 10 10 | 4 14  3 |
| South Greenhoe | 23 | 119 13 10 | 5  4  1 |
| Mitford | 17 | 117  2 10 | 6 17 10 |
| Shropham | 20 | 115 16  8 | 5 15 10 |
| Earsham | 15 | 114  6  6 | 7 12  5 |
| Loddon | 20 | 109 12  0 | 5  9  7 |
| Clavering | 20 | 108 16  8 | 5  8 10 |
| Gallow | 32 | 101 12 10 | 3  3  6 |
| Diss | 16 | 101 11  2 | 6  6 11 |
| Smithdon | 18 | 99  3 10 | 5 10  3 |
| North Greenhoe | 17 | 98 18  4 | 5 16  4 |
| Holt | 27 | 97 15  2 | 3 12  5 |
| Grimshoe | 16 | 83  8  6 | 5  4  4 |
| Wayland | 15 | 80  3  2 | 5  6 10 |
| Humbleyard | 19 | 77 10  4 | 4  1  7 |
| Walsham | 14 | 73 10 10 | 5  5  1 |
| Happing | 17 | 71  7  4 | 4  4  0 |
| Taverham | 18 | 69 11  2 | 3 17  3 |
| Guiltcross | 13 | 68 16 10 | 5  5 11 |
| Henstead | 19 | 67 12  6 | 3 11  2 |
| Blofield | 17 | 53  6  8 | 3  2  9 |
| Brothercross | 9 | 49 16  2 | 5 10  8 |
| West Flegg | 13 | 48 14  2 | 3 14 11 |
| East Flegg | 9 | 44  4  8 | 4  9  5 |

Source: R. M. Dunn, ed., *Norfolk Lieutenancy Journal, 1660-1676*, Norfolk Record Society, xlv, 1977, pp. 38-69. The material has been collated and re-arranged in rank order.

The Hearth Tax return for 1664, which has been analysed for the wealthy, can be used as a complement to the material contained in the military assessments.[25] The details in broad terms can swiftly be stated. In those areas for which the information is available, 188 men lived in houses with between 10 and 15 hearths, 50 in houses containing 16 to 20 hearths, and 29 in mansions which had between 21 and 58, the largest of them being Blickling Hall, occupied by Sir John Hobart. The information for Norwich is given elsewhere, but it may be noted here that its 88 or more houses with upwards of 10 hearths were five times as numerous as those of its nearest rivals in the county. As the evidence for the military assessments would suggest, a number of such buildings were to be found in west Norfolk but substantial houses existed throughout the county. Hobart's apart, Sir Robert Paston's Oxnead had 45 hearths, the house of Sir Ralph Hare at Stow Bardolph had 44 and Sir John Holland's at Quidenham, forty. Only marginally smaller were Sir Nicholas Le Strange's property at Hunstanton which contained 37 hearths, Thomas Bedingfield's Oxborough Hall with 34 and the house of Sir Thomas Pettus at Rackheath which had thirty.

**Table 1.11 Hearth Tax Assessments of the wealthy in Norfolk, 1664**

| Town or Parish | Households with | | | Total households | Total hearths | Av. no. hearths per household |
|---|---|---|---|---|---|---|
| | 10-15 | 16-20 | 21+ | | | |
| | | hearths | | | | |
| King's Lynn | 13 | 3 | 1 | 17 | 214 | 12.59 |
| Eynesford | 11 | 5 | - | 16 | 216 | 13.50 |
| Henstead | 9 | 3 | 2 | 14 | 216 | 15.43 |
| Humbleyard | 10 | 3 | 1 | 14 | 203 | 14.50 |
| South Greenhoe | 12 | 1 | 1 | 14 | 186 | 13.29 |
| Holt | 9 | 2 | 2 | 13 | 183 | 14.08 |
| Forehoe | 7 | 4 | 1 | 12 | 182 | 15.17 |
| Taverham | 7 | 3 | 2 | 12 | 186 | 15.50 |
| Clackclose | 8 | - | 3 | 11 | 188 | 17.09 |
| Freebridge Marshland | 8 | 1 | 2 | 11 | 164 | 14.91 |
| Clavering | 6 | 4 | - | 10 | 150 | 15.00 |
| Earsham | 10 | - | - | 10 | 114 | 11.40 |
| Loddon | 6 | 3 | 1 | 10 | 146 | 14.60 |
| North Erpingham | 7 | 2 | 1 | 10 | 136 | 13.60 |
| South Erpingham | 5 | 1 | 4 | 10 | 225 | 22.50 |
| Tunstead | 7 | 1 | 2 | 10 | 150 | 15.00 |
| Diss | 7 | 1 | - | 8 | 96 | 12.00 |
| Launditch | 7 | 1 | - | 8 | 102 | 12.75 |
| Thetford | 4 | 4 | - | 8 | 120 | 15.00 |
| Shropham | 6 | - | 1 | 7 | 90 | 12.86 |
| Freebridge Lynn | 5 | 1 | - | 6 | 78 | 13.00 |
| Grimshoe | 5 | 1 | - | 6 | 81 | 13.50 |
| Depwade | 3 | 2 | - | 5 | 64 | 12.80 |
| Guiltcross | 3 | - | 2 | 5 | 101 | 20.20 |
| Smithdon | 2 | 2 | 1 | 5 | 93 | 18.60 |
| Gallow | 2 | 1 | 1 | 4 | 68 | 17.00 |
| North Greenhoe | 4 | - | - | 4 | 45 | 11.25 |
| Happing | 3 | - | - | 3 | 37 | 12.33 |
| Mitford | 1 | - | 1 | 2 | 51 | 25.50 |
| Wayland | 1 | 1 | - | 2 | 26 | 13.00 |
| Totals | 188 | 50 | 29 | 267 | 3,911 | 14.65 |

Source: M. S. Frankel and P. J. Seaman, eds., *Norfolk Hearth Tax Assessments, Michaelmas 1664*, Norfolk Genealogy, xv, 1983, *passim*. The assessments for Blofield, Brothercross, and East and West Flegg are missing from this return, as are parts of Great Yarmouth, Earsham, Forhoe, Gallow, North Erpingham and Shropham. The Great Yarmouth material which survives lists two houses at this level, one with ten hearths and one with eleven.

The Hobarts, Pastons, Bedingfields and Le Stranges were all county families of long standing who, with others of their kind, had served as J.P.s or in other spheres since at least the reign of the first Elizabeth and, in some cases, long before.[26] In Charles II's reign the names of Hobart and Le Strange appear among the deputy and lords lieutenant of the

2. Oxnead Hall in 1809, the seat of Sir Robert Paston in 1664.

county, along with Astley, Holland, Hare and others not referred to above. Sir Jacob Astley and Sir John Hobart were among the most assiduous attenders at such meetings and Astley, who lived to be 90, continued to serve the county until well into the next century.[27]

The foregoing material depicts a rich and prosperous county whose major town remained the largest and wealthiest provincial city in England throughout the 16th and 17th centuries. By the late 16th century many of its ruling class were being drawn from the lesser gentry of Norfolk and supplying cadet branches of such families in return. At a lesser level the city continued to attract large numbers of country youths as apprentices to the various crafts, some of whom extended their expertise to their native villages when they returned after finishing their training. The interrelationships between town and county, as well as those topics peculiar to Norwich alone, are discussed in detail below.

## Chapter Two

# *The Physical Appearance of the City*

Norwich had been in existence for almost a thousand years when the first of the Tudors came to the throne. Anglo-Saxon settlers, inspired partly by the natural advantages of the Yare and Wensum valleys, partly perhaps by the proximity of the former Roman town of *Venta Icenorum*, had settled on the site of the future Norwich by the sixth century, to be followed in their turn by Danish and Norman invaders. It was the latter who built the great stone castle which for so long dominated the town, and it was a Norman bishop, Herbert de Losinga, who was responsible for the construction of the cathedral when he transferred the see from Thetford to Norwich in 1096.[1] The Cathedral was the most resplendent building in a town which already boasted more than fifty churches, and it was around the outermost of these that the city began to build its walls in 1297. When they were completed in 1334 the walls embraced an area some six miles in circumference. Within them, or immediately adjacent to them, were the cathedral, 58 churches, 22 religious houses and hospitals, the castle, and the larger houses of the gentry and merchant classes, as well as those of their less prosperous neighbours. Even so, large areas of the city were not occupied by buildings of any kind, and farming took place on a limited scale within the walls as well as in the immediately adjacent suburbs.[2]

Admittance to the city could be gained by any one of 12 gates, separated at regular intervals by a number of towers. Bishops' Gate, situated astride the city's only stone bridge, formed the entrance to the eastern part of the city, an area given over almost entirely to the cathedral and its surrounds, the adjacent houses of the Grey and Austin Friars, and the Great Hospital, the major city institution for the aged and indigent. In close proximity, although separated by the river which wound its way through the town, was the priory of the White Friars, the remaining monastic house, that of the Black Friars, being situated in the neighbouring ward of Middle Wymer. Four gates admitted travellers to the Ward across the Water, the most northerly of the city's administrative areas, and a further five were to be found to the west of the town. Finally, two gates provided access to Conesford Ward to the south.

It was the more obvious features – the walls, the castle, the cathedral and the churches – which caught the eye of the traveller, almost invariably to the exclusion of anything else. The more perceptive visitor referred to the city's market place and the produce sold there, the 15th-century guildhall, the market cross, erected as recently as 1518, and, in later years, to the Duke of Norfolk's palace, but rarely to anything else. References to the churches are hardly surprising in a city which contained the greatest number of ecclesiastical buildings in England, but here, as elsewhere, a transformation took place in the middle years of the 16th century. Before the accession of Elizabeth, all of the city's monastic property had been swept away, with the single exception of the Blackfriars, which was bought by the citizens for secular purposes. A number of churches were secularised at the same time and by the end of the century no more than 36 were still in use.

Sixteenth century descriptions of Norwich are particularly unrewarding. Leland devoted one sentence to the walls. Camden referred to the 'neatness of buildings' and beautiful churches, and made brief reference to the city's textile industry, but neither he, nor anyone else, made any attempt to distinguish between the different trading areas of Norwich, and even a partial description of the market's activities had to await the arrival of Thomas

3. The Market Cross, erected in 1518.

Baskerville in 1682.[3] This is surprising for Norwich had one of the largest markets in England with butchers', fishmongers' and poulterers' stalls proliferating, as well as those for bread, cheese and the sale of wool. The butchers were particularly numerous, and they were not restricted to city tradesmen alone. As early as 1565 country butchers hired as many as 37 stalls for the sale of their wares, and the number had doubled a century later.

Fortunately, two maps produced in the middle years of the 16th century help to make good these deficiencies. The so-called Sanctuary Map of 1541 is particularly helpful in demonstrating the progress made in the city's 'housing revolution', the buildings depicted in the centre of the town being almost entirely two-storied and quite possibly of fairly recent construction or renovation. The second of the maps, produced by Cunningham in 1558, is a much fuller representation. The cartographer concerned made a realistic attempt to depict

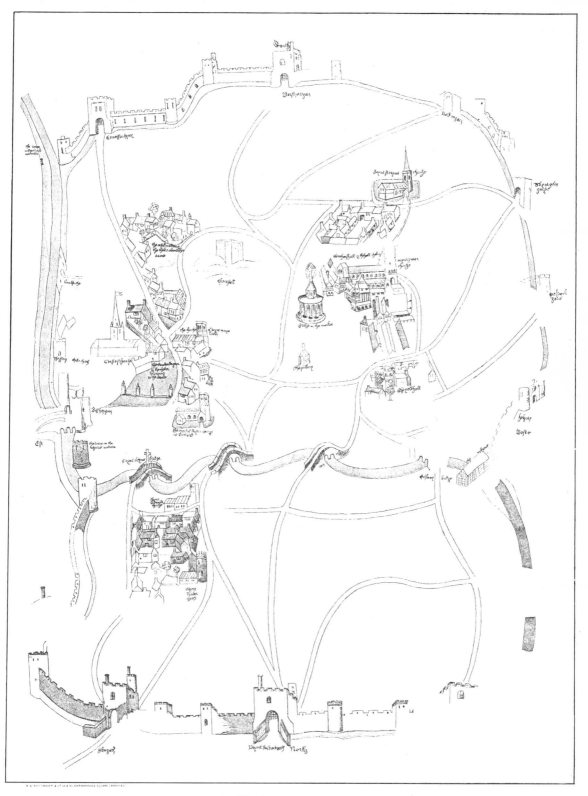

4. The Sanctuary Map, 1541.

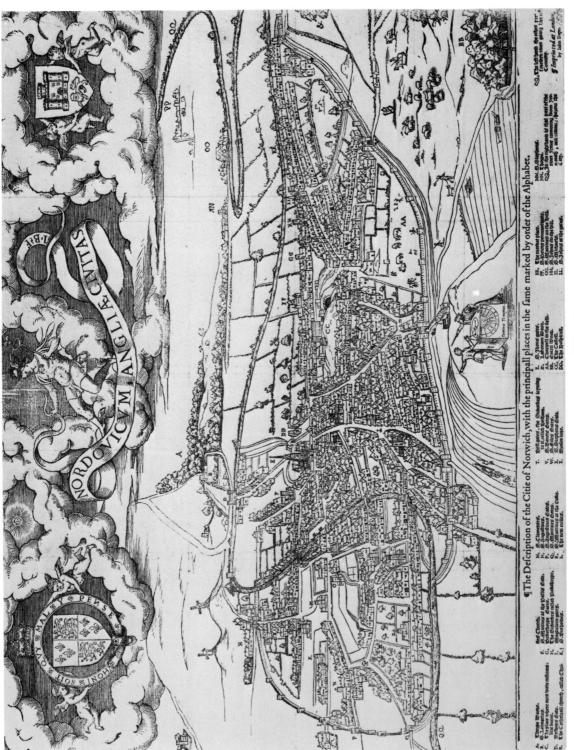

NORDOVICVM ANGLIÆ CIVITAS

**¶The Description of the Citie of Norwich, with the principall places in the same marked by order of the Alphabet.**

A. Kinge Wate.
B. S. Leonarte.
C. The place where our Ladie cumae:
D. Bishops Gate.
E. The Cathedrall churt, called the Chift.

F. Seid Church.
G. S. Martinus at the Pallia Gate.
H. S. Gylberlame.
I. S. Augustlane Gate.
K. S. Marlane or called Pockthorpe.
L. S. Botolphes.

M. S. Clementae.
N. S. Austlane.
O. S. Edmundae.
P. S. Sawlet Gate.
Q. S. Martinus at the Cate.

T. Bottgater, the Colledbat buylng.
    to cation brethare.
V. S. Sevete Gate.
W. S. Bent Woode.
X. S. Bent Gate.
Y. S. Stephanes at Gate.
Z. Bulen lane.

AA. Conneill in the fish.
BB. From Wode.
CC. S. Johnat Sepulchre.
DD. The Hospitall.
EE. The markeat place.
FF. S. Peters corner mighte.
GG. S. Martinur on the Hill.
HH. S. Andrewet on the Hill.
II. S. Gylforde.
JJ. S. Johur of the yeate.

MM. S. Stephend.
NN. Timper.
OO. In the typ forme of this part of the
    Conntie.

QQ. The Lestbrue the other part of
    London thou goat] lucd in the
    Countie.

¶Imprinted at London,
    by Iohn Daye.  1558.

5.  Cunningham's Map of Norwich, 1558.

the city as he actually saw it. He carefully distinguished between the different types of houses, as well as indicating the major buildings and uninhabited areas of the town. Norwich is shown as a city contained almost entirely within its walls. Suburbs, such as Pockthorpe and Heigham, were small and contained very few of the inhabitants. The bulk of the population is shown as living in the centre of the city in an area embracing the wards of Mancroft, Wymer and the most southerly part of Ultra Aquam, or the Ward across the Water. Conesford contained a number of houses spreading upwards from the river but, like its neighbour St Stephen's, had tracts of open land towards the walls. The eastern part of the city was almost entirely bereft of buildings due, in part, to the extent of the cathedral lands already referred to, and large areas to the north of the city were also unoccupied. All of the major buildings are shown, ranging from the castle, cathedral and churches on the one hand to the market place with its cross and the five bridges on the other.[4] Both maps tell another tale, however. They depict a city which had already experienced its 'housing revolution' some fifty years before the generally accredited dates.[5] By far the majority of the houses shown are two-storied or larger and contain chimneys; this evidence of a transformation from the older medieval pattern is fully supported by recent archaeological work which suggests that the introduction of the built fireplace was almost universal by the early 16th century.[6]

There was a housing boom in Norwich in the last quarter of the 15th century and the first quarter of the 16th, a period when especially large numbers of building workers were admitted to the freedom of the city. Although there was a major setback in 1507, when fire destroyed some seven hundred houses, the evidence suggests that the city recovered far more quickly from this disaster than has been previously thought. The oft-quoted Act of 1534 which stipulated the re-building of certain areas apparently neglected after the fire may be an indirect tribute to the city's energy in this respect. Of the seven hundred or so houses destroyed almost thirty years earlier, little more than two dozen remained unbuilt, a figure which, if interpreted literally, implies that much of the devastated areas had already been re-edified. Almost all of the houses in Elm Hill, for example, can be dated to between 1508 and 1525. Isolated plots in Pottergate and Cowgate remained unoccupied until the late 17th and 18th centuries, but in general terms the evidence suggests both energy and pros-

6.  *The Britons Arms*, the only building in Elm Hill to survive the fire of 1507.

perity in early 16th-century Norwich rather than the reverse. The fire of 1507 provided the impetus for the development of new ideas and new building techniques in the city as a whole. There was a rapid acceleration in the development of building design, and there is clear archaeological evidence for an increase in the size of houses and, possibly, for increasing specialisation within them.

7.  Elm Hill, 1818. Many of the houses in Elm Hill were built soon after the fire of 1507.

8.  Crown Court, Elm Hill, 1829.

A number of houses appear to have been built between 1530 and 1550, most of the larger ones being situated in the broad belt of parishes, known collectively as Wymer, which stretched from St Benedict's in the west to St Helen's in the east. The ward of Mid-Wymer was especially prominent in this respect, but a number of aldermanic houses, in particular, were also to be found in the parish of St Peter Mancroft and in the Ward across the Water.

There is little evidence of the complete rebuilding of larger houses in Elizabethan Norwich but, in contrast, there is increasing evidence of a housing boom where the less wealthy are concerned. Until the arrival of the Dutch and Walloon refugees in the late 1560s and early 1570s the housing conditions of the poor appear to have been more than adequate. Many of these people lived in areas away from the centre of the city where there was freer availability of land, and recent archaeological excavation has suggested that when tenements were established there the houses were often disproportionately large for their class. This is borne out, to some extent, by the Norwich census of the poor which suggests that as late as 1570 overcrowding was the exception rather than the rule, even at the lowest level. Thereafter the situation changed radically. The English population, which had been rising steadily, would have created pressures of its own before long, but the steady influx of the Dutch and Walloons made conditions intolerable. Within a few years they numbered some six thousand of a total population of sixteen thousand or so, far more than could be absorbed within the existing housing stock, and radical changes had to be made to accommodate them.[7]

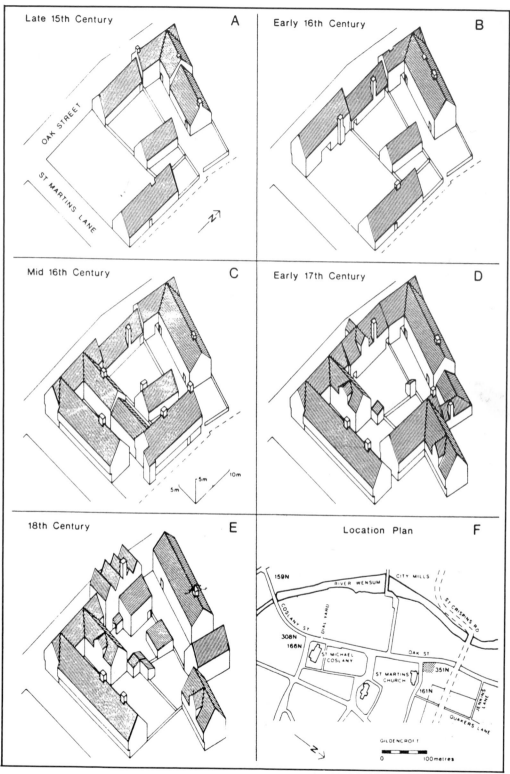

| Late 15th Century | A | Early 16th Century | B |
| Mid 16th Century | C | Early 17th Century | D |
| 18th Century | E | Location Plan | F |

9. Reconstructions of buildings excavated by the Norwich Survey in Oak Street, Coslany.

Somewhat surprisingly, the city authorities made little or no attempt to contain the alien population within the open spaces in the city, most of which continued to be unoccupied until the end of the 17th century. The problem was partially solved by the steady development of 'cottage' housing in the yards behind the existing street frontages, and in some cases by the multiple occupation of existing houses. Large numbers of small, single-hearthed buildings were erected on once-open yards, and the discovery of considerable amounts of imported pottery in recent excavations suggests that many of these houses were occupied by Dutch and Walloon refugees.[8]

Buildings of this type must have proliferated in the 17th century when the population virtually doubled, but by their very nature they are seldom, if ever, commented upon by the traveller and we must rely on the combined evidence of the Hearth Tax returns of the 1670s and archaeological excavation to indicate their whereabouts. Documentary evidence, for example, shows the parish of St Peter's, Southgate, as being composed almost entirely of households containing a single hearth, and large numbers of similar households were to be found in the industrial areas of Wymer and Ultra Aquam.[9] While many of these may have been individual houses there is little doubt, too, that some buildings previously occupied by wealthier people were taken over by the poor and were in multiple occupation.

As in the 16th century, the complete re-building of larger houses was comparatively rare under the early Stuarts, the most notable exception being the Duke of Norfolk's town house in the parish of St John Maddermarket, which was first demolished and re-built in 1602 and reconstructed yet against some seventy years later. In 1671 it was the largest house in Norwich, being assessed on 60 hearths, although it was closely rivalled by Sir John Hobart's mansion on the site of the present Assembly House which itself contained 50 hearths.[10] Adaptation appears to have been the order of the day and Celia Fiennes, who visited the city in 1698, commented on this conservatism. She observed that all the houses were 'of the old form, mostly in deep points and much tiling . . . their building timber and their plaster of laths . . . but none of bricks except some few beyond the river which are built of some of the rich factors like London buildings'.[11] The extensive tiling was itself of fairly recent origin. When Fuller saw Norwich some thirty years earlier he commented especially on the large numbers of thatched houses which were then in evidence.[12]

Nevertheless, although there were few new buildings to delight the eye, most visitors to Norwich were impressed by what they saw. Fuller, who visited the city some time before his death in 1662, was fulsome in his praises. To him, Norwich was '. . . pleasant and populous . . . either a city in an orchard or an orchard in a city, so equally are houses and trees blended in it, so that the pleasures of the country and the populousness of the city meet here together'. John Evelyn, who came to Norwich in 1671, was equally impressed. He described the town as 'one of the noblest of England, for its venerable cathedral, number of stately churches, cleanness of the streets and buildings of flint so exquisitely headed and squared . . .', but he was less impressed than Fuller with the Duke of Norfolk's palace which he described as 'an old wretched building', and he noted in passing that the city's churchyards were so full that they seemed to have been built in pits.[13]

Celia Fiennes commented especially on the condition of the walls which, to her, were 'the best in repair of any walled city I know' and on the streets, many of which were very broad and 'all well pitched with small stones and very clean'. She also noted the presence of a piped water supply for at least some of the houses.[14]

Comments on the city's industrial activities were few, although Thomas Baskerville, writing in 1682, was sufficiently impressed with the hustle and bustle of the Norwich market place to leave his impressions in full.

A little way from this [Norwich] castle on the opposite side of a hill is the chief market place of this city, and this being the only place where all things are brought to be sold for the food of this great city, they not as in London allowing markets in several places, make it vastly full of provisions, especially on Saturdays, where I saw the greatest shambles for butchers' meat I had ever yet seen, and the like also for poultry and dairy meats, which dairy people also bring many quarters of veal with their butter and cheese, and I believe also in their seasons pork and hog-meats. These people fill a square of ground on the side of a hill twice as big [as] Abingdon market place. They setting their goods in ranges as near as may be one above another, only allowing room for single persons to pass between; and above these the butchers have their shambles and such kind of people as sell fish, of which there was plenty of such kinds as the seas hereabouts afford, viz., crabs, flounders, mackerel, very cheap, but lobster for sea fish and pike or jack for river fish were dear enough. They asked me for one pike under 2 foot, 2s. 6d., and for a pot of pickled oysters they would have a shilling. Here I saw excellent oatmeal which being curiously hulled looked like French barley, with great store of gingerbread and other edible things. And for grain in the corn market, which is on the other side of the market house, as large for space of ground as that on which the dairy people stand, I saw wheat, rye, oats, malt ground and not ground, French wheat, and but little barley, because the season for malting was over.

The activity which Baskerville witnessed was not confined to the city traders alone. By the time of his visit the Norwich authorities were leasing stalls to more than seventy country butchers, a larger number than was available to the townsmen themselves.[15]

Baskerville apart, the only other comments of note were again those supplied by Celia Fiennes. She, too, made reference to the fish and meat markets, but she also made passing reference to other activities. In, or immediately adjacent to, the main market she noted markets for hay and corn, as well as fruit being sold at the market cross. A large space beside the castle was used for the sale of cattle and other animals, while in the sealing hall, near the guildhall, the city's stuffs were measured and checked for quality before being made available for sale. In general, like other visitors she was impressed by what she saw, concluding that 'the whole city looks like what it is, a rich, thriving, industrious place.[16]

It remains to sum up. The majority of the buildings erected by the middle years of Henry VIII's reign were still standing at the accession of Charles II. Many had been altered structurally, principally by the addition of sleeping chambers and extra windows, and in that sense, at least, the skyline of Restoration Norwich would have been different from that of 150 years earlier. Yards which had been relatively empty under the Tudors were largely built upon by the end of the 17th century, but the complete rebuilding of larger dwellings was rare, such new building as there was being instigated by members of the aldermanic class. The Henrician merchant would thus have found little difficulty in finding his way about the Restoration city. He would have been surprised at the overcrowding in the industrial areas of the city and the growth of 'cottage' housing in the yards, possibly saddened at the disappearance of the monastic houses and some of the older churches, and gladdened at the resurgence of the Norwich textile industry, but he would have found little that would have left him a puzzled man.

*Chapter Three*

# Population

Any estimate of the population of a pre-industrial city must be based, in part, on speculation even when a variety of sources survive which can be used as a basis for research. Subsidy returns are frequently used for this purpose, but an estimate has to be made of the numbers excluded from a particular return and the resulting figure must then be subjected to a multiplier which, in itself, is little more than an informed guess. As taxation lists are rarely full enough in themselves to be used for demographic purposes, recourse must invariably be made to such supplementary materials as muster returns, parochial estimates of births and deaths, lists of ratepayers and, more rarely, censuses taken for a particular purpose. The central and local archives contain examples of all of the materials referred to above and, between them, they provide a broadly accurate picture of the demographic history of Norwich between 1525 and 1675.

In 1525 1,414 citizens of Norwich contributed to the second instalment of the subsidy granted by parliament to assist in the financing of Henry VIII's French wars.[1] Assuming that at least one-quarter of the city's population would have been exempted on the grounds of poverty, the total male population would have been in the region of 1,885. If this figure is multiplied by 4.5 we obtain a total of 8,482 or, in round numbers, a minimum population of some 8,500 people. If we make the same assumptions and use the same multiplier for other towns, Bristol in the same period would have had a population in the region of 6,500, Exeter 4,600, York 5,250 – if the Ainsty is included, 7,350 – and Salisbury 3,500.[2]

The population of the country as a whole rose steadily from 2.774 millions in 1541 to 4.110 by the turn of the century and to as high as 5.281 millions in 1656. Having virtually doubled, a period of decline then set in with the numbers falling to some 4.865 millions by the mid-1680s.[3] The proportion living in towns rose much faster than this, however, the larger towns more than doubling their populations in the same period.[4]

**Table 3.1 An estimate of the population of Norwich between 1591 and 1640**

| Period | Number of baptisms | Yearly average | Estimated population |
|---|---|---|---|
| 1591-1600 | 3,696 | 369.6 | 11,088 |
| 1601-1610 | 4,786 | 478.6 | 14,358 |
| 1611-1620 | 7,489 | 748.9 | 22,467 |
| 1621-1630 | 8,362 | 836.2 | 25,086 |
| 1631-1640 | 7,106 | 710.6 | 21,318 |

Where Norwich is concerned, we are next in position to estimate the population in 1569-70, a very full muster return being taken in the former year and the comprehensive census of the poor the year after that.[5] Both sources suggest a native population of around eight thousand, supplemented already by some 3,000 Dutch and Walloon immigrants. The population of the latter group doubled during the next decade, and by the plague year of 1579 the combined totals of English and aliens must have comprised between 14,000 and 15,000 people.

At least six thousand of these people perished in the outbreaks of plague between 1579 and 1580, and although natural increase and further immigration built up the population again the frequent recurrence of plague prevented any rapid progress. One result of the initial outbreak was the appointment of what amounted to a registrar of births and deaths. The city fathers were so concerned at the heavy toll that they appointed one Thomas Usher to record the deaths and, subsequently, to list both baptisms and burials. The records maintained by Usher and his successors provide us with population statistics for the next 65 years or so, the last entries being made in 1646. The figures were presented once a week at the meeting of the mayor's court and were evidently derived from the parish registers. As not all of these registers have survived for the period concerned, we are heavily dependent on the transcriptions made, particularly in the absence of any reliable alternative source.[6]

The baptismal records begin in July 1582 and can be used from then until they finally peter out to provide an impression of the city's population at the end of each 10-year period. It has been suggested that if the average number of births over a 10-year period is multiplied by 30 it will provide a

10. St Peter's Steps.

figure which is correct to within 10 per cent either way. Using this method, the details shown in Table 3.1, opposite, emerge over a 50-year period.[7]

The fall in population from the 14-15,000 suggested earlier is quite compatible with the mortality figures we have for the same period. Plague deaths alone totalled some 3,500 in the late 1580s and early 1590s, and a similar number perished in the onslaught of 1603. The rapid rise in the early decades of the 17th century is accounted for both by natural increase and by immigration; the retraction in the subsequent decades by further outbreaks of plague in 1625-6, 1631 and 1637-8 and by some emigration from the city for religious reasons in the 1630s.[8]

No further estmates can be made until the 1670s when we are again dependent on taxation returns, supplemented in this case by the Compton return of 1676. During the first decades of Charles II's reign Norwich, in common with other cities, was called upon to contribute to the Hearth Tax, a new fiscal measure designed to extract the maximum return from the highest number of people. The fullest returns include lists of those exempted on the grounds of poverty, as well as those actually taxed and thus, in theory at least, the total number of households should be recorded. Inevitably, there was some evasion and not all returns have survived, but sufficient remain for Norwich, in both the local and central archives, to enable the number of households to be reconstructed with reasonable accuracy. In 1671 there were approximately 5,000 households in the city as a whole. If we apply the currently accepted multiplier of 4.25 to this figure we obtain a total of 21,250. The Compton census of 1676 listed 12,562 communicants in the city and its hamlets. Assuming that these referred to the 60 per cent generally considered to be above 16 years of age, it would suggest a total population of 20,937, sufficiently near to that derived from the Hearth Tax material to confirm a figure of around 21,000 as a satisfactory approximation.[9]

This figure differs little from that apparently reached in the middle years of the century and in this respect Norwich mirrors the picture to be found in the country at large. Various factors contributed to this local stagnation, all of which may have discouraged immigration: the decline of the Spanish trade in the 1650s; the heavy plague mortality in 1665-6 when 2,231 deaths were attributed to the disease out of a total of 3,012; and, to a lesser extent, outbreaks of smallpox. While none of them provides the complete answer, the fact remains that the final disappearance of plague in 1666 saw rapid growth thereafter. By 1693 the city contained 28,881 persons and by the end of the century the total may have reached 30,000.[10]

While the populations of the other towns referred to earlier in the chapter rose at a less rapid rate than that of Norwich, their demographic history broadly paralleled that of the East Anglian town. The population of Bristol had apparently reached 10,549 by 1607, some 15,200 by the 1670s and as much as 19,400 by the mid-1690s. Exeter's population just exceeded 10,000 in the 1670s, according to its Hearth Tax assessment, with that of York standing at around 9,100. Salisbury progressed more slowly, but by 1695 its population stood at 6,976, having almost doubled in the 170 year period.[11]

The experiences of Salisbury and York closely parallel the national picture, with neither town quite doubling its population between the middle years of Henry VIII's reign and that of Charles II. Norwich and Bristol, and possibly Exeter, in contrast all contained twice as many inhabitants in the 1670s as in the 1520s, and in the case of the former towns subsequent increase was rapid.

*Chapter Four*

# The Pattern of Wealth

The basic sources for a study of the pattern of wealth in Tudor and Stuart Norwich are threefold; the subsidy returns of the 1520s, particularly that of 1525 which survives in its entirety; the 1671 Hearth Tax return, which again is virtually complete; and some nine hundred and fifty probate inventories, beginning in 1584, which provide a link between the two. They can be supplemented at intervals by less complete subsidy returns, in the sense that they were less all-embracing, and by parochial rates which were levied for specific purposes during the 17th century.[1]

The Tudor subsidies were intended to provide a realistic assessment of an individual's wealth, and despite the fact that the rich were quick to get their assessments reduced they can be used to provide a reasonably accurate picture of the distribution of wealth among some three-quarters of the city's population.

Inequality of wealth was prevalent everywhere in Tudor England and Norwich was no exception to the rule. The wealthiest citizens in 1525 were the 29 men who owned moveable goods worth between £100 and £1,000. Although comprising little more than two per cent of the taxable population they owned, between them, more than 40 per cent of the taxable wealth. Immediately below them, and forming what can conveniently be described as an upper middle class, were a further 52 men, or four per cent of the whole, who were assessed on amounts varying between £40 and £99. These men, and those above them, were recognised as the most influential citizens in the community. As such they, and their peers elsewhere, were called upon to pay their contributions in advance when the tax was first levied in 1523 and they were taxed at a high rate for the ensuing three years. The 204 people (14 per cent) assessed on goods worth between £10 and £39 may also be considered middle-class while the 141, including a few of the city's common councillors, who were worth between £5 and £9 may reasonably be described as comfortably-off. Below this we are approaching the less wealthy sections of the community. The 30 per cent of the citizens taxed on goods worth between £2 and £4 formed an effective buffer between their more affluent fellows and those who, by any standards, must be considered relatively poor. A full 40 per cent of the taxpayers were assessed on wages of £1, or little more, a year, and broad as this base was at least a quarter of the inhabitants – possibly more – would have been too poverty-stricken to contribute at all.[2]

The situation was not unusual. Wage-earners and exempted everywhere made up some two-thirds of the urban population, and while few historians would now accept Professor Hoskins' pioneering suggestion that all of these people lived on or just above the poverty line, life for a majority of them was precarious in the extreme.[3] At the drop of a hat they could become unemployed, with no guarantee of support for themselves or their families whatsoever. This is fully borne out by the Norwich census of the poor which included 71 men who had taken up their freedom and a further 41 who had served an apprenticeship, the two groups comprising some 20 per cent of all those recorded. Even so, we must be careful not to exaggerate the situation. Mr. Phythian-Adams has pointed to the widespread distribution of servants in early 16th-century Coventry, many of whom were to be found in the households of those with nil assessments in 1522, while others at this level lived in houses with higher annual rents than those of the poorest cottagers.[4] Equally, in East Anglia at least, a proportion of those assessed on £1 worth of goods were landowners in their own right, the proportions ranging, at their highest, from 29 per cent in Great Yarmouth to as high as 46 per cent in the hundred of Gallow in west Norfolk.[5] Poverty is necessarily a relative term, with those at the bottom end of the scale especially vulnerable to changing economic conditions. While we may accept that 'grinding poverty' was only present intermittently, this precarious situation needs to be borne constantly in mind.

In virtually every town in England a minority of people owned much of the taxable wealth. In Norwich about six per cent of those taxed owned approximately 60 per cent of the property; at Exeter an upper class of seven per cent were in possession of two-thirds of the town's goods. Men of the same social standing in Bristol, Salisbury and Canterbury, never numbering more than seven per cent of the population, all owned more than half of the property in the town concerned. In the relatively small, but extremely wealthy, cloth town of Lavenham an unusually large upper class of 12 per cent had more than four-fifths of the town's property in their hands. At the other end of the scale, the 570 Norwich wage-earners owned less than four per cent of their city's wealth. At Lavenham, where men of that class made up more than half of the population, the wage-earners' share of the taxable wealth was less than three per cent. The proportions were similar elsewhere, ranging from two and three per cent at Stamford and Thetford respectively to seven per cent at Bury St Edmunds. The only exception to this was at Lincoln where a wage-earning class of 57 per cent owned about one-eighth of the moveable goods.[6]

Much of a town's wealth was usually in the hands of a few exceptionally rich men. Richard Marler, a Coventry grocer, and Thomas Guybon of King's Lynn, for example, each paid about one-ninth of their town's contributions to the subsidy, while William Wigston of Leicester paid just over one-quarter. The widow and daughter of Thomas Spring of Lavenham, assessed on £1,000 and £333 6s. 8d. respectively, contributed just over 30 per cent while Thomas Smyth of Long Melford, taxed on £600, contributed more than 46 per cent.[7]

Norwich had several wealthy men, all of whom were called on to pay their contributions in advance. Robert Jannys, grocer and alderman of the city, was assessed on £1,100 in 1523, a sum which almost equalled that contributed by the town of Rochester as a whole. Thomas Aldrych, a draper, was considered to be worth £700, John Terry, a grocer, £550, and Edward Rede and Thomas Pykerell, mercers, £500 and £300 respectively. In all, 32 Norwich men were assessed on personal estate to the value of £100 or more in that year, although all of them had their assessments significantly reduced by 1525, and reduced yet again two years later.[8]

Most of those people lived in the wards of St Peter Mancroft and Middle Wymer, although the wards of West Wymer, Coslany and Colegate also contained a number of rich

11.   Robert Jannys, mayor of Norwich in 1517 and 1524.

## Table 4.1 The pattern of wealth in 12 English towns, 1524-5

| Town | Numbers owning moveable goods valued at: Under £2 | £2-4 | £5-9 | £10-19 | £20-39 | £40-99 | £100-299 | £300-500 | Over £500 | Totals |
|---|---|---|---|---|---|---|---|---|---|---|
| **Norwich** | **570** | **416** | **141** | **124** | **80** | **52** | **25** | **1** | **3** | **1,414** |
| *Percentages* | *40.37* | *29.46* | *9.98* | *8.78* | *5.66* | *3.68* | *1.77* | *0.07* | *0.21* | |
| Value of goods | 570 6 8 | 1,037 0 0 | 869 13 4 | 1,484 13 4 | 2,016 0 0 | 2,850 6 8 | 3,585 0 0 | 400 0 0 | 2,066 13 4 | 14,879 13 4 |
| *Percentages* | *3.83* | *6.96* | *5.84* | *9.97* | *13.54* | *19.15* | *24.90* | *2.68* | *13.88* | |
| **Bristol** | **398** | **404** | **88** | **73** | **47** | **67** | **18** | **-** | **-** | **1,095** |
| *Percentages* | *36.35* | *36.89* | *8.04* | *6.67* | *4.29* | *6.12* | *1.64* | - | - | |
| Value of goods | 410 12 4 | 934 6 0 | 571 0 0 | 932 6 8 | 1,152 0 0 | 3,660 0 0 | 2,990 0 0 | - - - | - - - | 10,650 5 0 |
| *Percentages* | *3.85* | *8.77* | *5.36* | *8.76* | *10.82* | *34.37* | *28.07* | - | - | |
| **Exeter** | **307** | **234** | **70** | **60** | **41** | **27** | **27** | **1** | **-** | **767** |
| *Percentages* | *40.03* | *30.50* | *9.13* | *7.82* | *5.34* | *3.52* | *3.52* | *0.13* | - | |
| Value of goods | 343 15 8 | 566 17 4 | 426 6 8 | 710 0 0 | 909 6 8 | 1,146 13 4 | 3,903 15 4 | 300 0 0 | - - - | 8,306 15 0 |
| *Percentages* | *4.14* | *6.83* | *5.13* | *8.55* | *10.95* | *13.80* | *46.99* | *3.61* | - | |
| **Salisbury** | **218** | **174** | **60** | **60** | **33** | **27** | **16** | **1** | **-** | **589** |
| *Percentages* | *37.01* | *29.54* | *10.19* | *10.19* | *5.60* | *4.58* | *2.72* | *0.17* | - | |
| Value of goods | 253 0 0 | 437 13 4 | 393 0 0 | 812 3 4 | 853 10 0 | 1,460 0 0 | 2,132 0 0 | 400 0 0 | - - - | 6,741 6 8 |
| *Percentages* | *3.75* | *6.49* | *5.83* | *12.05* | *12.66* | *21.66* | *31.63* | *5.93* | - | |
| **York and Ainsty*** | **387** | **499** | **147** | **114** | **59** | **13** | **4** | **-** | **-** | **1,223** |
| *Percentages* | *31.64* | *40.80* | *12.02* | *9.32* | *4.83* | *1.06* | *0.33* | - | - | |
| Value of goods | 406 13 2 | 1,256 0 0 | 856 6 8 | 1,440 13 4 | 1,339 6 8 | 582 0 0 | 640 0 0 | - - - | - - - | 6,520 19 10 |
| *Percentages* | *6.24* | *19.26* | *13.13* | *22.09* | *20.54* | *8.93* | *9.81* | - | - | |
| **Canterbury** | **395** | **167** | **59** | **62** | **39** | **31** | **13** | **-** | **-** | **766** |
| *Percentages* | *51.57* | *21.80* | *7.70* | *8.09* | *5.09* | *4.05* | *1.70* | - | - | |
| Value of goods | 396 4 0 | 435 6 8 | 363 6 8 | 612 0 0 | 941 6 8 | 1,612 0 0 | 1,516 13 4 | - - - | - - - | 5,876 17 4 |
| *Percentages* | *6.74* | *7.41* | *6.18* | *10.41* | *16.02* | *27.43* | *25.81* | - | - | |
| **Bury St Edmunds** | **301** | **207** | **48** | **49** | **27** | **16** | **8** | **-** | **-** | **656** |
| *Percentages* | *45.88* | *31.55* | *7.32* | *7.47* | *4.12* | *2.44* | *1.22* | - | - | |
| Value of goods | 301 0 0 | 554 0 0 | 302 13 4 | 559 6 8 | 715 0 0 | 680 13 4 | 1,150 0 0 | - - - | - - - | 4,262 13 4 |
| *Percentages* | *7.06* | *13.00* | *7.10* | *13.12* | *16.77* | *15.97* | *26.98* | - | - | |
| **Lavenham** | **100** | **37** | **12** | **8** | **12** | **13** | **9** | **-** | **1** | **192** |
| *Percentages* | *52.08* | *19.27* | *6.25* | *4.17* | *6.25* | *6.77* | *4.69* | - | *0.52* | |
| Value of goods | 100 0 0 | 83 13 4 | 78 0 0 | 97 6 8 | 330 13 4 | 668 0 0 | 1,343 6 8 | - - - | 1,000 0 0 | 3,701 0 0 |
| *Percentages* | *2.70* | *2.26* | *2.11* | *2.63* | *8.93* | *18.05* | *36.30* | - | *27.02* | |
| **Lincoln** | **435** | **152** | **77** | **61** | **23** | **16** | **1** | **-** | **-** | **765** |
| *Percentages* | *56.86* | *19.87* | *10.07* | *7.97* | *3.01* | *2.09* | *0.13* | - | - | |
| Value of goods | 461 6 8 | 390 0 0 | 500 13 4 | 808 13 4 | 565 13 4 | 804 0 0 | 100 0 0 | - - - | - - - | 3,630 6 8 |
| *Percentages* | *12.71* | *10.74* | *13.79* | *22.27* | *15.88* | *22.15* | *2.76* | - | - | |
| **Great Yarmouth** | **111** | **273** | **34** | **43** | **18** | **14** | **3** | **-** | **-** | **496** |
| *Percentages* | *22.38* | *53.04* | *6.86* | *8.67* | *3.63* | *2.82* | *0.60* | - | - | |
| Value of goods | 111 6 8 | 636 0 0 | 214 0 0 | 535 0 0 | 441 0 0 | 753 6 8 | 500 0 0 | - - - | - - - | 3,190 13 4 |
| *Percentages* | *3.49* | *19.93* | *6.71* | *16.77* | *13.82* | *23.61* | *15.67* | - | - | |
| **Southampton** | **179** | **89** | **36** | **28** | **14** | **7** | **4** | **-** | **-** | **357** |
| *Percentages* | *50.14* | *24.93* | *10.09* | *7.84* | *3.92* | *1.96* | *1.12* | - | - | |
| Value of goods | 179 0 0 | 218 0 0 | 217 6 8 | 363 6 8 | 293 6 8 | 400 0 0 | 483 6 8 | - - - | - - - | 2,154 6 8 |
| *Percentages* | *8.31* | *10.12* | *10.09* | *16.87* | *13.62* | *18.55* | *22.44* | - | - | |
| **Stamford** | **51** | **107** | **40** | **12** | **16** | **13** | **2** | **-** | **-** | **241** |
| *Percentages* | *21.16* | *44.40* | *16.60* | *4.98* | *6.64* | *5.39* | *0.83* | - | - | |
| Value of goods | 51 0 0 | 255 0 0 | 231 0 0 | 137 0 0 | 397 0 0 | 806 0 0 | 220 0 0 | - - - | - - - | 2,097 0 0 |
| *Percentages* | *2.43* | *12.16* | *11.02* | *6.53* | *18.93* | *38.44* | *10.49* | - | - | |

* I have retained my analysis of York *and* the Ainsty as Professor Palliser's analysis of York alone does not exactly conform to the categories used above. Both of us have used P.R.O., E179/217/92, my work on the sources being carried out some years before the appearance of his book on Tudor York. According to Professor Palliser, 874 people were taxed in York itself and were worth £4,480. Three hundred and thirty-one, or 37.9 per cent of these, were assessed on the minimum of £1, although no figure is given for their share of the wealth. In contrast, the 62 men taxed on goods worth £20 or more (7 per cent of the whole) owned just over half of the town's moveables. D. Palliser, *Tudor York*, 1979, p. 136.

Sources: Norwich, P.R.O., E179/150/218; Bristol, P.R.O., E179/113/192; Exeter, M. M. Rowe, ed., *Tudor Exeter*, Devon and Cornwall Records Society, xxii, 1977, pp. 35-44; Salisbury, P.R.O., E179/197/154; Canterbury, P.R.O., E179/124/188; Bury St Edmunds, S. H. A. Hervey, ed., *Suffolk in 1524*, Suffolk Green Books, x, 1910, pp. 348-58; Lavenham, ibid., pp. 24-9; Lincoln, P.R.O., E179/136/323; Great Yarmouth, P.R.O., E179/150/210; Southampton, P.R.O., E179/173/175; Stamford, P.R.O., E179/136/315.

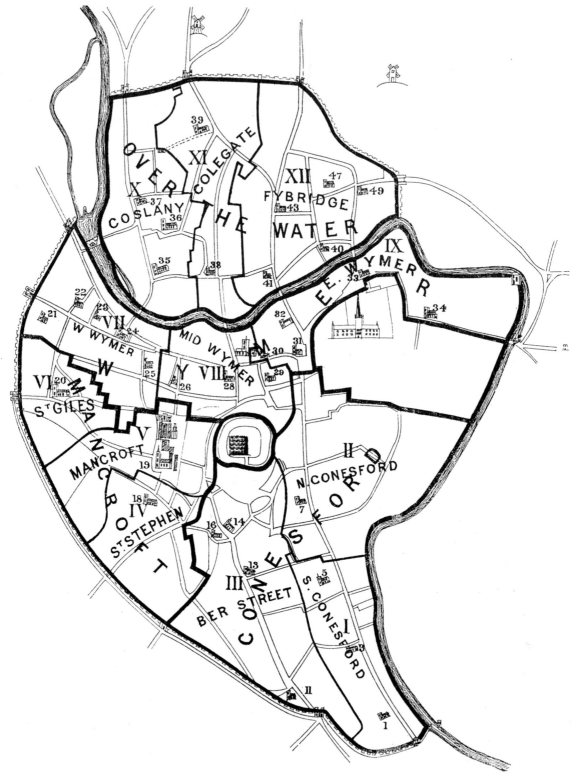

12.   The Great and Small Wards of Norwich, reproduced from W. Hudson and J. C. Tingey, eds., *The Records of the City of Norwich*, 1910.

men. Almost a quarter of the city's wealth was to be found in the single ward of Middle Wymer, and a similar proportion was shared by those living in Coslany and Colegate, albeit with a combined population three times as great as that of the former ward. Conesford contained the houses of a few wealthy men and women but, with the exception of the small ward of St Giles, tended to be the poorest section of the city.

**Table 4.2 Distribution of the taxable population and wealth throughout Norwich in 1525***

| Area of the city | Numbers taxed | % | Total wealth of group £ s. d. | | | % | Average wealth per head to the nearest shilling |
|---|---|---|---|---|---|---|---|
| South Conesford | 82 | 5.80 | 486 | 6 | 8 | 3.27 | 124 |
| North Conesford | 72 | 5.09 | 508 | 0 | 0 | 3.41 | 141 |
| Ber Street | 128 | 9.05 | 622 | 13 | 4 | 4.18 | 97 |
| **CONESFORD** | **282** | **19.94** | **1,617** | **0** | **0** | **10.86** | **115** |
| St Stephen's | 63 | 4.45 | 1,106 | 0 | 0 | 7.43 | 351 |
| St Peter's | 122 | 8.63 | 1,342 | 6 | 8 | 9.02 | 220 |
| St Giles' | 33 | 2.33 | 144 | 13 | 4 | 0.97 | 88 |
| **MANCROFT** | **218** | **15.41** | **2,593** | **0** | **0** | **17.42** | **238** |
| West Wymer | 166 | 11.74 | 1,612 | 13 | 4 | 10.84 | 194 |
| Middle Wymer | 112 | 7.92 | 3,383 | 13 | 4 | 22.74 | 604 |
| East Wymer | 147 | 10.40 | 1,091 | 6 | 8 | 7.33 | 149 |
| **WYMER** | **425** | **30.06** | **6,087** | **13** | **4** | **40.91** | **287** |
| Coslany | 161 | 11.39 | 1,581 | 6 | 8 | 10.63 | 196 |
| Colegate | 174 | 12.30 | 1,758 | 0 | 0 | 11.82 | 202 |
| Fyebridge | 154 | 10.89 | 1,242 | 6 | 8 | 8.35 | 161 |
| **ULTRA AQUAM** | **489** | **34.58** | **4,581** | **13** | **4** | **30.80** | **187** |
| Totals | 1,414 | | 14,879 | 6 | 8 | | 210 |

* Based on an analysis of P.R.O., E179/150/218.

In Norwich, at least, it seems that more people were called upon to contribute to the subsidy in 1525 than in the previous year, but several of the taxpayers had their assessments radically reduced. In the absence of a complete 1524 return, it is impossible to give many details of lesser men, but the members of the city's upper classes were treated ever more generously in each successive year. Of the 96 people worth £40 and above who were taxed in both 1524 and 1525, 56 had their assessments reduced, four were increased and 36 remained the same. Twenty-four of these had their assessments reduced yet again in 1527. Some of these reductions were considerable. Robert Jannys paid on £1,100 in 1523, £960 in 1525 and on only £600 in 1527. Aldrych's assessment of £700 in 1523 was reduced to £566 13s. 4d. in the following year. Edward Rede's wealth allegedly fell from £500 in 1523 to £266 13s. 4d. three years later, Pykerell's from £300 to £160 in the same period, virtually halved in both cases. In contrast, although on a more modest scale, Thomas Grewe, a butcher, who had paid on £30 in 1523, was assessed on £66 13s. 4d. four years later.

# Table 4.3 The value of the moveable goods owned by the freemen of Norwich in 1525

| Occupational grouping | Under £2 | £2-4 | £5-9 | £10-19 | £20-39 | £40-99 | £100-299 | £300-500 | Over £500 | Totals |
|---|---|---|---|---|---|---|---|---|---|---|
| **Distributive** | **5** | **18** | **14** | **20** | **16** | **17** | **12** | **1** | **3** | **106** |
| *Percentages* | *4.72* | *16.98* | *13.21* | *18.87* | *15.09* | *16.04* | *11.32* | *0.94* | *2.83* | |
| Value of goods | 5 0 0 | 46 13 4 | 89 0 0 | 251 13 4 | 404 13 4 | 922 6 8 | 2,006 13 4 | 400 0 0 | 2,066 13 4 | 6,192 13 4 |
| *Percentages* | *0.08* | *0.75* | *1.44* | *4.06* | *6.53* | *14.89* | *32.40* | *6.46* | *33.37* | |
| **Textiles** | **54** | **80** | **27** | **18** | **17** | **9** | **3** | **-** | **-** | **208** |
| *Percentages* | *25.96* | *38.46* | *12.98* | *8.65* | *8.17* | *4.33* | *1.44* | *-* | *-* | |
| Value of goods | 54 0 0 | 212 13 4 | 164 3 4 | 213 13 4 | 441 6 8 | 524 13 4 | 546 13 4 | - - - | - - - | 2,157 3 4 |
| *Percentages* | *2.50* | *9.86* | *7.63* | *9.90* | *20.46* | *24.31* | *25.34* | *-* | *-* | |
| **Food and Drink** | **23** | **30** | **9** | **16** | **6** | **7** | **2** | **-** | **-** | **93** |
| *Percentages* | *24.73* | *32.26* | *9.68* | *17.20* | *6.45* | *7.53* | *2.15* | *-* | *-* | |
| Value of goods | 23 0 0 | 75 13 4 | 58 0 0 | 198 13 4 | 165 0 0 | 430 0 0 | 293 6 8 | - - - | - - - | 1,243 13 4 |
| *Percentages* | *1.85* | *6.09* | *4.66* | *15.97* | *13.26* | *34.58* | *23.59* | *-* | *-* | |
| **Leatherwork** | **25** | **26** | **10** | **8** | **7** | **2** | **-** | **-** | **-** | **78** |
| *Percentages* | *32.05* | *33.33* | *12.82* | *10.26* | *8.97* | *2.56* | *-* | *-* | *-* | |
| Value of goods | 25 0 0 | 62 13 4 | 62 13 4 | 96 13 4 | 170 6 8 | 95 0 0 | - - - | - - - | - - - | 512 6 8 |
| *Percentages* | *4.88* | *12.23* | *12.23* | *18.87* | *33.25* | *18.54* | *-* | *-* | *-* | |
| **Building** | **9** | **34** | **11** | **10** | **2** | **-** | **1** | **-** | **-** | **67** |
| *Percentages* | *13.43* | *50.75* | *16.42* | *14.92* | *2.99* | *-* | *1.49* | *-* | *-* | |
| Value of goods | 9 0 0 | 85 6 8 | 71 6 8 | 126 6 8 | 46 13 4 | - - - | 106 13 4 | - - - | - - - | 445 6 8 |
| *Percentages* | *2.02* | *19.16* | *16.02* | *28.37* | *10.48* | *-* | *23.95* | *-* | *-* | |
| **Metalwork** | **8** | **6** | **5** | **9** | **6** | **1** | **-** | **-** | **-** | **35** |
| *Percentages* | *22.86* | *17.14* | *14.29* | *25.71* | *17.14* | *2.86* | *-* | *-* | *-* | |
| Value of goods | 8 0 0 | 16 6 8 | 31 6 8 | 107 6 8 | 161 13 4 | 40 0 0 | - - - | - - - | - - - | 364 13 4 |
| *Percentages* | *2.19* | *4.48* | *8.59* | *29.43* | *44.33* | *10.97* | *-* | *-* | *-* | |
| **Clothing** | **11** | **21** | **8** | **9** | **3** | **2** | **-** | **-** | **-** | **54** |
| *Percentages* | *20.37* | *38.89* | *14.81* | *16.67* | *5.36* | *3.70* | *-* | *-* | *-* | |
| Value of goods | 11 0 0 | 51 6 8 | 48 13 4 | 96 6 8 | 60 0 0 | 60 0 0 | - - - | - - - | - - - | 360 13 4 |
| *Percentages* | *3.05* | *14.23* | *13.50* | *26.71* | *16.63* | *16.63* | *-* | *-* | *-* | |
| **Professional** | **3** | **7** | **6** | **2** | **2** | **-** | **1** | **-** | **-** | **21** |
| *Percentages* | *14.29* | *33.33* | *28.57* | *9.52* | *9.52* | *-* | *4.76* | *-* | *-* | |
| Value of goods | 3 0 0 | 16 6 8 | 35 13 4 | 20 0 0 | 62 0 0 | - - - | 120 0 0 | - - - | - - - | 257 0 0 |
| *Percentages* | *1.17* | *6.36* | *13.88* | *7.78* | *24.12* | *-* | *46.69* | *-* | *-* | |
| **Woodwork** | **5** | **5** | **4** | **3** | **1** | **-** | **-** | **-** | **-** | **18** |
| *Percentages* | *27.78* | *27.78* | *22.22* | *16.67* | *5.56* | *-* | *-* | *-* | *-* | |
| Value of goods | 5 6 8 | 13 0 0 | 27 13 4 | 30 0 0 | 20 0 0 | - - - | - - - | - - - | - - - | 96 0 0 |
| *Percentages* | *5.56* | *13.54* | *28.82* | *31.25* | *20.83* | *-* | *-* | *-* | *-* | |
| **Transport** | **6** | **3** | **3** | **1** | **-** | **-** | **-** | **-** | **-** | **13** |
| *Percentages* | *46.15* | *23.08* | *23.08* | *7.69* | *-* | *-* | *-* | *-* | *-* | |
| Value of goods | 6 0 0 | 8 0 0 | 19 0 0 | 13 6 8 | - - - | - - - | - - - | - - - | - - - | 46 6 8 |
| *Percentages* | *12.95* | *17.27* | *41.01* | *28.77* | *-* | *-* | *-* | *-* | *-* | |
| **Total of Freemen** | | | | | | | | | | **693** |
| Value of goods | | | | | | | | | | 11,675 16 8 |

13. A 16th-century house in Ber Street. The adjoining house is of similar date but was refronted in the 18th century.

Significantly, he had been elected an alderman in 1526 and the higher assessment occurred in the year that he was elected sheriff.[9]

All of these men, with the exception of Grewe, were members of the Norwich merchant classes, and it was among such people that the bulk of the city's wealth was to be found. As a class they comprised no more than 15 per cent of the 693 men recognisable as freemen in 1525, but they owned more than half of the taxable property. They were comfortably off almost to a man, little more than one in five owning goods worth less than £5. The textile workers, numerically almost twice as large, owned almost one-fifth of the property, while just under 11 per cent was in the hands of those concerned with food and drink. The city's metalworkers were reasonably well off, as were the few men employed in a professional capacity, but the bulk of the remainder were either poor or, at best, of moderate wealth.

Two-thirds of the building workers and those employed in the leather trades owned moveable goods worth less than £5 a year. Almost 70 per cent of the small number of freemen concerned with transport were in the same category. A lone freemason assessed on £100 was the only really wealthy man among the builders, while the leather-workers had two men who could claim to be more than comfortably off. The transport workers and the woodworkers alone among the city's freemen had nobody in this category.

Although there was reasonable opportunity for social mobility in Tudor Norwich, the distribution of wealth among the various classes altered little between the reigns of Henry VIII and Elizabeth. The bulk of the city's wealth remained in the hands of a few men, a select group which included all of the aldermen and the richest third of the common councillors. Exactly how wealthy they were is difficult to ascertain. Thomas Wilson, writing at the end of the 16th century, said that he knew 24 Norwich aldermen worth at least £20,000 apiece, some much more, and several lesser men worth half as much.[10] Wilson was obviously generalising about the aldermanic body as a whole, and the so-called 'lesser citizens' may well have been the common councillors. In almost every case, the greater part of this wealth was held in lands and, to a lesser extent, plate and jewellery. Even so, fairly large sums of money were disbursed on occasion. Clement Hyrne and Thomas Whall, both of whom served as mayor in the Elizabethan period, bequeathed £950 and £1,382 respectively. Thomas Sotherton, mayor in 1605, left instructions for the disposal of more than £8,000 at his death in 1608. This was unusual. In the late 16th century typical aldermanic wills disposed of between £300 and £500 in cash.[11] A rare survival of an aldermanic inventory from this period, that of Robert Suckling who died in 1589, contained possessions worth little more than £196, but he was able to dispose of £147 in cash and his will also referred to lands in Topcroft, Woodton and Newton near Norwich.[12]

**Table 4.4 The median value of Norwich inventories, 1584-1675***

| Occupational grouping | 1584-1600 £ s. d. | | 1601-25 £ s. d. | | 1626-50 £ s. d | | 1651-75 £ s. d. | |
|---|---|---|---|---|---|---|---|---|
| Building | 7 13 4 | *13* | 19 13 5 | *21* | 60 9 10 | *5* | 61 10 0 | *5* |
| Clergy | 9 7 6 | *8* | 59 19 4 | *11* | 88 16 8 | *6* | 89 16 5 | *3* |
| Clothing | 12 18 11 | *17* | 34 14 6 | *29* | 28 2 2 | *17* | 80 10 2 | *10* |
| Distributive | 38 17 10 | *18* | 92 6 6 | *19* | 111 3 11 | *16* | 116 19 1 | *8* |
| Farming | 27 17 6 | *5* | 66 8 8 | *13* | 41 7 2 | *6* | 176 2 5 | *2* |
| Food & Drink | 88 15 11 | *13* | 75 11 1 | *24* | 92 9 5 | *28* | 136 6 6 | *16* |
| Gentry | 353 14 0 | *6* | 339 3 0 | *11* | 336 3 8 | *15* | 167 16 0 | *6* |
| Leatherwork | 15 19 3 | *10* | 36 16 0 | *24* | 19 8 11 | *5* | 66 6 8 | *4* |
| Metalwork | 14 12 10 | *8* | 46 11 5 | *7* | 41 5 3 | *6* | 105 16 1 | *6* |
| Miscellaneous | 22 6 1 | *18* | 20 3 6 | *13* | 28 2 4 | *6* | 63 9 0 | *4* |
| Professional | - - - | - | 212 15 11 | *5* | 141 5 7 | *4* | 90 3 1 | *1* |
| Textiles | 8 8 3 | *21* | 64 5 0 | *29* | 73 11 1 | *39* | 92 7 8 | *40* |
| Transport | 85 7 10 | *2* | 113 16 0 | *2* | 11 1 4 | *4* | - - - | - |
| Woodwork | 17 12 3 | *5* | 18 5 0 | *7* | 40 10 6 | *2* | - - - | - |
| Women | 15 2 11 | *36* | 15 6 6 | *46* | 38 16 0 | *60* | 55 10 0 | *29* |
| Unstated | 6 14 11 | *42* | 10 19 10 | *70* | 15 10 8 | *29* | 24 10 0 | *18* |
| Median of all inventories for the period | 15 15 11 | *222* | 31 13 0 | *327* | 57 8 0 | *253* | 74 7 3 | *148* |

*The figures in italics indicate the number of inventories from which the median is taken.

While inventories for the upper classes are relatively rare, a reasonable number survive for people of lower status. The earliest date from 1584 and there is a total of 222 for the 16th century, with a further 728 for the period ending in 1675, or 950 in all. Between them, they provide a reasonable coverage of Norwich society in these periods, although the bulk of them are concerned essentially with people of the middle classes. As such, they are less satisfactory as a source for the distribution of wealth than either the early Tudor subsidies or the Hearth Tax returns of the Restoration period, but they provide a broadly accurate picture of the situation in Norwich at different periods and thus allow for some consideration of the changing fortunes of the various sections of the community.

It is perfectly obvious that one can only speak with confidence about the changing fortunes of a particular trade grouping when a reasonable number of inventories survive; and working from this premise we must immediately discount the figures for the clergy and other professional men, the farming community, the gentry and the transport and woodworkers. Similarly, while the overall wealth of the metalworkers undoubtedly increased, it is unlikely that they experienced a threefold rise between the second and third quarters of the 17th century. In every case, the figures represent the chance survival of particular inventories.

Having said this, however, it is unlikely that an analysis of the sum total of inventories for a period, varying in number between 148 and 327, would give an unduly false impression, and the steady rise in the median value of the inventories as a whole is striking. This is particularly so when the rise is considered against the overall rise in the cost of living, as evinced by the oft-used Phelps-Brown and Hopkins index. On their evidence the cost of living rose by 38 per cent between 1584 and the turn of the century, increased by another 16 per cent during the reign of James I and, after a period of stability in the middle years of the century, rose by a further 30 per cent between 1655 and 1675. There were considerable variations during the years concerned, but in 1675 the cost of living was 108 per cent higher than in 1584.[13] During the same period the median value of the Norwich inventories increased almost fivefold, having doubled by the end of James I's reign and almost doubled again during the next 25 years.

The rising standards of living of at least a section of the populace is particularly well documented in the case of the city's textile workers. At the end of the 16th century the median value of their goods was £8 8s. 3d., or little more than half the average. The next quarter of a century saw a substantial improvement in their fortunes, due principally to the development of the New Draperies, and by the end of this period the value of their goods had increased eightfold, subsequently rising to a level 12 times what it had been a century earlier.

If only because of their initial poverty, the rise in the fortunes of the textile workers was almost meteoric. None of the other trade groupings could compete with them in this respect, but most of them experienced some improvement in their living standards. Bearing in mind that the cost of living doubled in the period concerned, the median value of the merchant classes inventories trebled between 1600 and 1625; the leather-workers experienced a similar increase; while the fortunes of the building workers more than doubled. There seems no reason to doubt that this improvement continued, but the relatively small number of inventories which survive for the later period make the extent of this improvement uncertain. There is no such uncertainty where the women of the city are concerned, and their fortunes rose steadily as the 17th century progressed.

Although the major 'housing revolution' in Norwich occurred during the first quarter of the 16th century, if not earlier, people continued to adapt their existing houses. This is evinced both by increased building activity and by the rising standard of living experienced by at least some of the building workers. The 17th century witnessed a considerable increase in alterations to existing property and – at least after 1670 – the building of new ones. The

14.  Seventeenth-century houses with dormer windows, King Street.

15.  The Music House, King Street.

proportion of inventories recording cellars doubled; those referring to 'false roofs' increased fourfold; while specialised chambers, including larders, washing houses and pantries, increased in number and variety. At the same time some of the older terms became less fashionable. The hall, which was mentioned in almost half of the inventories at the end of the 16th century, was referred to in only one inventory in four 75 years later, being replaced in many cases by the kitchen. The parlour and buttery suffered a similar decline in popularity.[14]

On the evidence of their surviving inventories, at least a section of the building trades prospered as a result of the activity outlined above. At his death in 1616, for example, Robert Aldred, one of the city's tilers, had assets exceeding £450. Bills and debts totalled £143 13s. 4d. of this, and leases made up another £147, but he had nearly £26 worth of plate and money in his house and almost £17 worth of brass and pewter as well as other domestic goods which were valued at some £80.[15] Palfryman Sheffield, a carpenter and common councillor who died 45 years later, was even wealthier; his inventory included stock of £98 and debts of £815 out of a grand total of £1,049.[16]

Despite investing money in altering the physical appearance of their houses, not everyone was prepared to provide a similar investment in improving their overall standards of comfort. In a number of cases the value of domestic goods simply kept pace with the rise in the cost of living and, in some cases, actually failed to maintain such a pace. Between 1600 and 1675, for example, the median value of the domestic goods of the women and those in unstated occupations merely doubled in a period when the cost of living rose by some 108 per cent, while that of the people engaged in the distributive and food and drink trades actually declined. In contrast, the value of such goods recorded in the inventories of clothing and textile workers quadrupled. The overall picture, however, is one of a city in which the value of domestic property rose as the cost of living rose, and rarely went beyond it.[17]

During the same period, for whatever reason, the proportion of debts recorded in inventories rose steadily. Whereas in the last years of Elizabeth's reign little more than a quarter of the inventories recorded details of such transactions, the figure for the years 1651-75 was 61 per cent. Virtually all sections of the community had sums of money owed to them, whether great or small, and they often made up a large proportion of the sum total of the inventories concerned. The proportion of debts of 21 Norwich people with inventories deposited in the Prerogative Court of Canterbury, for example, averaged 70 per cent of the total value of their moveable goods, with five of them having debts in excess of 90 per cent.[18] While the majority of these were probably the results of normal trading transactions, it seems fairly certain that others stemmed from money-lending for a profit.[19]

Scriveners were particularly engaged in such activities. William Edgeley, for example, was owed almost £492 out of an inventory total of just under £747. The gentry, too, often had large sums due to them in debts. Thus Matthew Sotherton was owed £1,162 out of a total sum of £2,257 at his death in 1611; Augustine Woode, who died in the same year, had £1,800 due to him, the residue of his property being worth little more than £72; while William Pearce, who died some thirty years later, had an inventory total of £5,529 8s. 1d., of which £5,393 was made up of 'good debts, as bonds, bills and mortgages and ready money'.[20]

Men concerned with the distributive trades and worsted weavers exporting their products abroad as well as elsewhere in this country were as likely to have goods outside the city as in it. John Kettill, a merchant who died in 1661, for example, had goods recorded in Cambridge, St Neots, Bedford and Newport Pagnell as well as stock in his shop worth £1,136, or some forty per cent of the total value of his inventory. Symeon Jerman, a worsted weaver worth no more than £222, had debts owing to him in Lincolnshire, Huntingdonshire and Cambridgeshire, as well as in his native county and city. Other worsted weavers died with stock still in their warehouses in London and, occasionally, abroad. Kettill was unusual in having so much of his property in stock in trade, although even he was outshone in this respect by a linen draper with stock of £2,462 out of an inventory total of £4,592. For most of the wealthier men stock comprised little more than a quarter of their recorded possessions, and often less than this.[21]

Investment in things agricultural was often a necessary concomitant of a person's trade. At his death in 1664 Robert Beecroft, a carter, had three acres of roots, 53 acres containing winter corn and a further 20 acres with beans, peas and vetches in them. As he also owned four bullocks and 28 horses with the five waggons that they pulled, some of this, at least, must have gone on feed for his animals. Beecroft also owned two barns with barley in them and his agricultural investments comprised some three-quarters of the total value of an inventory of some £512.[22]

This was unusual, but many people of more moderate means had what amounted to subsidiary occupations that boosted the value of their inventories. Richard Clarke, described as a clothier, had 35 dozen bowstaves in his house, as well as 1,500 patching tiles, when his inventory was taken, quite apart from looms for broadcloth and blankets. Katherine Warwick, a widow, included 160 knit stockings, worth £37 19s. 0d., among her possessions, or almost half the total value of her property. Martyn Stevens, described as a fishmonger, owned seven acres of rye worth £8 and eight loads of hay as well as the more obvious tools of his trade. An innkeeper of St Paul's had even more of the same commodity, his seven score combs of barley and five combs of oats being assumed to be worth £49. This may have been intended in part for his customers, but it made up almost half the total value of his inventory. A reeder who died in 1592 worth the comfortable sum of £192 16s. 5d. also gave evidence of farming activities, his property including four milking cows worth £10, horses worth £8 and pigs priced at £4 as well as eight combs of wheat totalling £2 13s. 4d. in value. The minister of St Edmund's parish was similarly occupied, keeping cows and horses priced at £13 10s. as well as owning three hens and barley, wheat and hay worth £4 13s. 4d. Farming was not the only alternative occupation. A reeder of St Peter's Southgate took advantage of the fact that his parish was near the river and evidently plied a boat for hire. At his death in 1601 this was one of his most valued possessions, being priced at £1 13s. 4d. second only to his bedding which was worth £3 and being of rather greater value than the cow and calf which he also kept and which were deemed to be worth 30s.[23]

A number of people appear to have been full-time farmers, despite living within the city precincts, and on the evidence of their inventories found the occupation generally profitable.

**Table 4.5 The distribution of wealth in Norwich and five other provincial towns in the 1670s**

|  | Number and percentage of households containing: | | | | | | | | | Totals |
|---|---|---|---|---|---|---|---|---|---|---|
|  | 1 hearth | | 2 hearths | | 3-5 hearths | | 6-9 hearths | | 10 & above | | |
| Norwich | 2,290 | *51.62* | 1,087 | *24.50* | 710 | *16.00* | 261 | *5.88* | 88 | *1.98* | 4,436 |
| Bristol | 714 | *19.94* | 1,150 | *32.67* | 1,312 | *36.64* | 338 | *9.42* | 67 | *1.87* | 3,581 |
| Exeter | 1,073 | *45.31* | 579 | *24.50* | 451 | *19.00* | 203 | *8.50* | 62 | *2.50* | 2,368 |
| York | 715 | *33.25* | 481 | *22.37* | 619 | *28.79* | 250 | *11.63* | 85 | *3.97* | 2,150 |
| Ipswich | 171 | *10.55* | 685 | *42.26* | 477 | *29.43* | 224 | *13.82* | 64 | *3.95* | 1,621 |
| Leicester | 537 | *52.44* | 175 | *17.09* | 236 | *23.04* | 58 | *5.66* | 18 | *1.76* | 1,024 |

The Norwich figures include the parishes of St Peter Hungate, St Edmund's, St Paul's and Pockthorpe for which there is no information other than the numbers exempted. Percentages are in italic.

| A = Households taxed | E = Total households |
|---|---|
| B = Households exempted | F = Total number of hearths |
| C = Hearths taxed | G = Average no. of hearths per household |
| D = Hearths exempted | H = Percentage of households exempted |

|  | A | B | C | D | E | F | G | H |
|---|---|---|---|---|---|---|---|---|
| Norwich | 1,818 | 2,618 | 7,289 | 2,900 | 4,436 | 10,189 | 2.30 | *59.02* |
| Bristol | 2,842 | 739 | 9,855 | 1,156 | 3,581 | 11,011 | 3.07 | *20.64* |
| Exeter | 1,433 | 935 | 5,037 | 1,084 | 2,368 | 6,121 | 2.59 | *39.48* |
| York | 1,722 | 428 | 6,014 | 449 | 2,150 | 6,463 | 3.00 | *19.91* |
| Ipswich | 1,031 | 590 | 4,594 | 1,057 | 1,621 | 5,651 | 3.49 | *36.40* |
| Leicester | 743 | 281 | 2,145 | 281 | 1,024 | 2,426 | 2.40 | *27.44* |

Sources:
Norwich: N.R.O., Norwich City Assessment Books, 1671; P.R.O., E179/254/701 and E179/336.
Bristol: P.R.O., E179/116/541.
Exeter: W. G. Hoskins, *Industry, trade and people of Exeter, 1688-1800*, 1935, pp. 112, 115 and 117.
York: P.R.O., E179/218/180.
Ipswich: *Suffolk in 1674*, Suffolk Green Books, xi, pp. 160-77.
Leicester: W. A. Jenkins and C. T. Smith, 'Social and Administrative History, 1660-1835', *V.C.H. Leicestershire*, iv. 1958, pp. 156-9.

They included both English and Dutchmen, and their holdings ranged from the 10 acres held by Francis van Dijcke to the 110 acres or so farmed by Thomas Potter of Trowse.[24]

Like their counterparts in other occupations, they were not averse to entering the money market. Davy Coshing, described as a yeoman of St Julian's, had debts due from people as far afield as Trowse, Earlham, Felthorpe, Hevingham and Aylsham at his death in 1619. He had evidently loaned animals as well as cash, for his debtors included people in possession of some of his cows as well as those responsible for monetary repayments.[25]

On the evidence quoted above, one would expect to find the Norwich of the 1670s a much more prosperous place than it was a century and a half earlier. In fact, the Hearth Tax returns suggest the reverse, for some 60 per cent of the city's households were exempted, a distinctly higher proportion than any other provincial town of comparable size, and probably higher than most smaller ones.

The proportion exempted was three times greater than that at Bristol and York, more than twice as high as that at Leicester, and half as great again as the proportions exempted at Exeter and Ipswich. Three-quarters of the people of Norwich were housed in dwellings with either one or two hearths, again a distinctly higher proportion than any of the other towns with which the city is compared. The only explanation for the apparent conflict between the evidence of the inventories and that of the Hearth Tax returns is that the gulf between the rich and poor had widened in the 17th century, that the relative dearth of inventories for the lower classes reflects the fact that they had little property worth recording. It is, perhaps, no coincidence that full records of the maintenance of the poor survive for this particular decade whereas they are absent, except at a parochial level, for much of the preceding century.[26]

It is clear from an analysis of the returns themselves that the distribution of wealth in Norwich had altered relatively little between the reigns of Henry VIII and Charles II, with the poor continuing to predominate. Some areas of the city were composed almost entirely of people in this category, rather more than 90 per cent of the parishioners of St Peter's, Southgate, for example, living in households containing a single hearth. Almost as bad were the parishes of St Michael at Thorn and St Paul's, with over 80 per cent of the inhabitants exempted from the Hearth Tax, and those of St Julian's, St Peter per Mountergate, All Saints', St John Sepulchre and St Augustine's which had three-quarters or more of their occupants designated poor. Significantly, six of these eight parishes were to be found in the single ward of Conesford.

In contrast, almost three-quarters of the householders of St Andrew's, St Peter Mancroft and St Michael at Plea paid the tax, and as many as 60 per cent in St John Maddermarket. These were the areas in which some of the largest houses in the city were to be found, ranging in size from the huge mansions of the Duke of Norfolk and Sir John Hobart, with 60 and 50 hearths respectively, to the more modest, but still large, houses of the city's gentry and aldermen which had between 10 and 25 hearths each. There were just under

16. Sir Benjamin Wrench's Court, in the 19th century.

ninety houses in Norwich with 10 hearths or more. Twenty-two of these were to be found in the single large parish of St Peter Mancroft, while St Andrew's and St Stephen's each had seven and St Gregory's six. The rest were distributed more or less evenly throughout the city.

Rather more than one-fifth of the houses in Norwich had between three and nine hearths, the type inhabited by all the common councillors of the city and by some of the less affluent aldermen. A similar proportion lived in houses with two hearths. Some of these were exempted from paying the tax on the grounds of poverty, but most were probably above subsistence level.

### Table 4.6 The distribution of wealth among the Norwich wards in 1671

A = Total number of households
B = Total number of hearths
C = Average number of hearths per household

| | 1 | % | 2 | % | 3-5 | % | 6-9 | % | 10+ | % | A | B | C |
|---|---|---|---|---|---|---|---|---|---|---|---|---|---|
| South Conesford | 264 | 74 | 50 | 14 | 30 | 8 | 9 | 3 | 2 | 1 | 355 | 548 | 1.54 |
| North Conesford | 224 | 61 | 106 | 29 | 29 | 8 | 8 | 2 | 3 | 1 | 370 | 630 | 1.70 |
| Ber Street | 373 | 60 | 152 | 25 | 68 | 11 | 18 | 3 | 6 | 1 | 617 | 1,140 | 1.85 |
| **CONESFORD** | **861** | **64** | **308** | **23** | **127** | **9** | **35** | **3** | **11** | **1** | **1,342** | **2,318** | **1.73** |
| St Stephen's | 147 | 51 | 65 | 23 | 52 | 18 | 15 | 5 | 7 | 2 | 286 | 681 | 2.16 |
| St Peter's | 105 | 30 | 85 | 24 | 99 | 25 | 40 | 11 | 22 | 6 | 351 | 1,281 | 3.18 |
| St Giles' | 78 | 53 | 30 | 20 | 25 | 17 | 11 | 7 | 3 | 2 | 147 | 341 | 2.32 |
| **MANCROFT** | **330** | **42** | **180** | **23** | **176** | **22** | **66** | **8** | **32** | **4** | **784** | **2,303** | **2.94** |
| West Wymer | 337 | 54 | 158 | 25 | 90 | 14 | 27 | 4 | 15 | 2 | 627 | 1,342 | 2.14 |
| Middle Wymer | 82 | 25 | 80 | 24 | 102 | 31 | 56 | 17 | 11 | 3 | 331 | 1,226 | 3.70 |
| East Wymer | 155 | 42 | 101 | 27 | 74 | 20 | 35 | 9 | 6 | 2 | 371 | 997 | 2.69 |
| **WYMER** | **574** | **43** | **339** | **26** | **266** | **20** | **118** | **9** | **32** | **2** | **1,329** | **3,565** | **2.68** |
| Coslany | 337 | 59 | 137 | 24 | 61 | 13 | 13 | 3 | 3 | 1 | 551 | 959 | 1.74 |
| Colegate | 151 | 50 | 73 | 24 | 56 | 19 | 16 | 5 | 6 | 2 | 302 | 673 | 2.23 |
| Fyebridge | 37 | 29 | 50 | 39 | 24 | 19 | 13 | 10 | 4 | 3 | 128 | 371 | 2.90 |
| **ULTRA AQUAM** | **525** | **54** | **260** | **26** | **141** | **14** | **42** | **4** | **13** | **1** | **981** | **2,003** | **2.04** |
| Grand Totals* | 2,290 | 52 | 1,087 | 25 | 710 | 16 | 261 | 6 | 88 | 2 | 4,436 | 10,189 | 2.30 |

*The lists of payers in the parishes of St George Tombland, and St Simon and St Jude in East Wymer were defective and most of the Ward of Fyebridge is missing. Their deficiencies are not likely to have altered the overall picture. A more detailed table, listing the parish totals, is provided in J. F. Pound, 'Government and Society in Tudor and Stuart Norwich, 1525-1675', Univ. of Leicester Ph.D. thesis, 1974, pp. 49-50.

We know the occupations of about one-third of those recorded in the Hearth Tax returns, as well as their social status. Significantly, 80 per cent of the building workers lived in dwellings with either one or two hearths and were thus poor or, at best, in modest circumstances, a picture which contrasts sharply with that produced by the inventories of their wealthier colleagues. Over 60 per cent of the wood, leather, clothing, metal and textile workers were in similar circumstances, and more than half of those occupied with food and drink. Only the city's merchants and professional men had small numbers in those categories, with 19 and 13 per cent respectively. The bulk of the men following such occupations as draper, grocer, haberdasher and general merchant lived in houses containing three hearths or more, as did the Norwich apothecaries, clerks, doctors and scriveners.

**Table 4.7 The social status of the freemen of Norwich, 1671**

|  | Distribution of hearths: | | | | | | | | | | |
|  | 1 | % | 2 | % | 3-5 | % | 6-9 | % | 10+ | % | Totals |
|---|---|---|---|---|---|---|---|---|---|---|---|
| Building | 61 | 51 | 35 | 29 | 22 | 18 | - | - | 1 | 1 | 119 |
| Clothing | 52 | 32 | 56 | 34 | 39 | 24 | 12 | 7 | 6 | 4 | 165 |
| Distributive | 6 | 5 | 18 | 14 | 51 | 41 | 40 | 32 | 10 | 8 | 125 |
| Food & Drink | 26 | 22 | 32 | 27 | 39 | 33 | 15 | 13 | 5 | 4 | 117 |
| Leatherwork | 53 | 37 | 46 | 32 | 39 | 27 | 4 | 3 | 2 | 1 | 144 |
| Metalwork | 29 | 34 | 28 | 33 | 20 | 23 | 8 | 9 | 1 | 1 | 86 |
| Miscellaneous | 5 | 20 | 11 | 44 | 7 | 28 | 2 | 8 | - | - | 25 |
| Professional | 3 | 6 | 3 | 6 | 18 | 38 | 15 | 32 | 8 | 17 | 47 |
| Textiles | 203 | 34 | 162 | 27 | 166 | 28 | 49 | 8 | 16 | 3 | 596 |
| Transport | 2 | 50 | 1 | 25 | 1 | 25 | - | - | - | - | 4 |
| Woodwork | 6 | 40 | 5 | 33 | 3 | 20 | 1 | 7 | - | - | 15 |
| Totals | 446 | 31 | 397 | 28 | 405 | 28 | 146 | 10 | 49 | 3 | 1,443 |

Trade groupings can, of course, conceal the differences between individual trades. Thus, one-third of the city's carpenters and tailors and a majority of the hosiers were men of some substance. Most of the bakers and brewers were comfortably off, and both cordwainers and tailors contained a number of men of the middle classes in their ranks. The same story is true of the metalworkers, where goldsmiths, ironmongers, pewterers and pinners were predominantly men of the middle rank, and the textile workers, where individual worsted weavers were among the wealthiest men in the city.

If the information derived from the inventories has been interpreted correctly, men of the middle and upper classes had raised their standard of living almost to a man. The lot of the poor, in contrast, appears to have either altered little or grown progressively worse. In part, this reflects the changes in the city's economy, in part the general effects of economic change and pestilence. The city suffered severely from plague throughout the last quarter of the 16th century, notably in 1579 when it lost one-third of its population, and it was hit almost as hard during the 1620s and 1630s when, in common with other parts of the country, it had to combat economic recession as well. The poor, as always, were the hardest hit, whereas their wealthier neighbours prospered, however indirectly, from the successful introduction of the New Draperies. By the second decade of Charles II's reign, following yet another severe outbreak of pestilence, the gulf between the richer and poorer sections of the community was wider than it had ever been, and the problem of the poor remained one that was to haunt the city fathers for decades to come.

*Chapter Five*

# The Trade Structure of Tudor and Stuart Norwich

Norwich is rich in materials relating to the trade structure of the city. The lists of freemen range in unbroken sequence from the reign of Edward II to that of Victoria; apprenticeship indentures are available for the period 1548-1719, albeit with many omissions; while, even more significantly, returns are available which give occupational details of the poor in 1570 and of the vast majority of the city's householders in 1589, returns which can themselves be supplemented by the occupational details appearing in censuses of the Dutch and Walloons, taken in 1568 and 1622 respectively.[1]

Admission to the freedom of Norwich, a necessary prerequisite to normal trading activities, was obtainable in three ways: on completion of a period of apprenticeship, usually of seven years duration but extending on occasion to 10, 12 and, exceptionally, 14 years; by patrimony; and, progressively less frequently, by purchase. All apprenticeship indentures should have been enrolled in the book provided for the purpose, but there was much slackness in this respect, particularly in the middle years of the 17th century. Between 1551 and 1675 details of 4,992 apprentices are recorded, of whom little more than one-quarter (1,253) ultimately proceeded to their freedom. In the same period the freemen's lists record 3,351 people obtaining their freedom by apprenticeship and a further 1,741, the majority of whom had also served a period as an apprentice, who claimed their freedom by patrimony, figures which suggest that between sixty and seventy-five per cent of the apprenticeship indentures were not officially recorded.

The apprenticeship indentures are nonetheless, indispensable for the incidental details which they supply. They invariably list fathers' occupations and places of origin, as well as details of the trades entered. It is also possible to determine, in some cases, the length of time elapsing between a person completing his apprenticeship and taking up his freedom, and the proportion of apprentices ultimately proceeding to their freedom in a given trade.

On the evidence available, most of the people apprenticed in Norwich had their origins in the city itself or in the surrounding countryside. Some three-quarters of the city's apprentices in the second half of the 16th century were born in Norfolk and the proportion rose to more than 90 per cent as the 17th century progressed. During the period as a whole apprentices were drawn from between 150 and 160 of the Norfolk towns and villages, and it seems probable that local migration of this sort was general. In Kent, for example, over 70 per cent of the apprentices coming to Maidstone between 1567 and 1599 were drawn from a radius of up to 11 miles; 61 per cent of those entering Faversham between 1592 and 1642 came from similar distances.[2]

Those taking up apprenticeships in Norwich from outside the county came predominantly from Suffolk and Yorkshire with regular, but smaller, contingents from Cambridgeshire, Lancashire, Leicestershire and Lincolnshire. Individuals arrived in the city, at intervals, from most parts of the British Isles, but the bulk of the apprentices came from the same areas throughout the 16th and 17th centuries.

The apprentices were drawn from all ranks of society, with the exception of the peerage, their fathers, collectively, following almost as many occupations as were to be found in Norwich itself. Initially, it was primarily the craftsmen and husbandmen who sent their sons to be apprenticed in the city, but with the resurgence of the textile industry in the 17th century apprentices were increasingly recruited from the ranks of the yeomen, the clergy and the gentry.

**Table 5.1 Places of origin of people taking up apprenticeships in Norwich between 1551 and 1650**

|  | 1551-75 | 1576-1600 | 1601-25 | 1626-50 |
|---|---|---|---|---|
| Norfolk | 269 70.4 | 311 60.5 | 283 67.2 | 312 90.6 |
| Suffolk | 42 11.0 | 34 6.6 | 39 9.2 | 32 8.2 |
| Yorkshire | 32 8.3 | 68 13.2 | 29 6.9 | 13 3.4 |
| Lincolnshire | 6 1.6 | 10 1.9 | 21 5.0 | 10 2.6 |
| Lancashire | 5 1.3 | 16 3.0 | 4 0.9 | 3 0.8 |
| Leicestershire | - - | 17 3.2 | 8 1.9 | 1 0.3 |
| Cambridgeshire | 3 0.8 | 8 1.5 | 6 1.4 | 3 0.8 |
| Other areas | 25 6.5 | 50 9.7 | 31 7.4 | 13 3.4 |
| Totals | 382 | 514 | 421 | 387 |

The figures in italic are percentages.

**Table 5.2 The social origins of Norwich apprentices**

|  | 1551-75 | 1576-1600 | 1601-25 | 1626-50 |
|---|---|---|---|---|
| Building | 8 6.5 | 12 4.1 | 13 4.5 | 7 2.2 |
| Clergy | 1 0.8 | 16 5.5 | 31 10.8 | 37 11.5 |
| Clothing | 6 4.9 | 30 10.3 | 23 8.0 | 15 4.7 |
| Distributive | 8 6.5 | 7 2.4 | 12 4.2 | 9 2.8 |
| Food & Drink | 11 8.9 | 19 6.5 | 12 4.2 | 14 4.4 |
| Gentlemen | 4 3.2 | 13 4.5 | 33 11.5 | 63 19.6 |
| Husbandmen | 33 26.8 | 90 31.0 | 56 19.5 | 41 12.8 |
| Leatherwork | 11 8.9 | 25 8.6 | 12 4.2 | 9 2.8 |
| Metalwork | 3 2.4 | 2 0.7 | 9 3.1 | 3 0.9 |
| Miscellaneous | 5 4.1 | 8 2.8 | 10 3.5 | 3 0.9 |
| Professional | - - | 2 0.7 | - - | 2 0.6 |
| Textiles | 16 13.0 | 9 3.1 | 6 2.1 | 17 5.3 |
| Transport | - - | 2 0.7 | 2 0.7 | 3 0.9 |
| Yeomen | 17 13.8 | 55 19.0 | 68 23.7 | 98 30.5 |
| Totals | 123 | 290 | 287 | 321 |

The figures in italic are percentages.

The Norwich textile industry, particularly that section relating to worsted weaving, was in decline for much of the 16th century, and fathers were increasingly reluctant to commit their sons to a trade in which unemployment could well become widespread. Gentry, clergy and yeomen all tended to avoid the industry and the more conservative husbandmen, although always supplying more recruits than the others, slowly followed their example.[3] The clothing industry, in contrast, remained relatively popular throughout, and tailoring especially always attracted a number of recruits even when the textile industry was at its height again. The husbandmen were particularly attracted to this trade and consistently supplied the same proportion of apprentices throughout the 16th and 17th centuries. They remained equally faithful to the leather and building industries which suffered a dearth of recruits from other sources as the textile industry revived.

Initially attracted to the clothing trades and to those concerned with mercantile activity, the gentry apprenticed an increasing proportion of their sons to worsted weaving as the 17th century progressed. Even so, such occupations as grocer, mercer, draper and merchant remained a popular choice with people of this class, both from the point of view of status and prospective wealth. In contrast, a small number of gentry either chose, or felt constrained, to apprentice their sons to the building, leather or metal trades, a decision which may reflect diminishing fortunes or unduly large families.

The clergy favoured the textile and clothing industries, and the same is broadly true of the yeomen, although they tended to distribute their favours rather more widely than the other non-craftsmen groups. Yeomen tended to interpret the economic picture rather more shrewdly than their fellows. In the last quarter of the 16th century fewer than 15 per cent of them sent their sons into the textile trades, while a healthy 29 and 35 per cent respectively were apprenticed to the prospering distributive and clothing trades. They changed course abruptly in the 17th century when half of the yeomen sent their sons to receive training in the, by now, booming textile industry. A minority retained an interest in the clothing, leather and food and drink trades, but far fewer sons of yeomen were apprenticed in the distributive trades than heretofore.

When we turn to the sons of craftsmen, whether native-born or immigrants, one fact immediately stands out: more than half of them were apprenticed to trades which were vastly different to those of their fathers.[4] This is partly explained by what has been called 'betterment migration' – the desire to rise in the social hierarchy – but there is also the reverse side of the picture when a youth is apprenticed to a trade which is obviously inferior to that of his father. This has already been noticed in the case of a few of the gentry. In the industrial sphere, to instance some of the more obvious cases, sons of grocers and merchants became building and leather workers, the trade of cordwainer appealing particularly to them, while the sons of professional men were apprenticed, in some instances, to the metal trades. The situation varied from trade grouping to trade grouping. Textile workers were more conservative than most, even when the industry was at its nadir. The proportion of those following their fathers was never lower than 46 per cent, and rose eventually to as high as two-thirds. The same applies to the clothing trades where the tailors were particularly prone to follow their fathers, the proportion varying between one-half and 62 per cent. Sons of leather workers, in contrast, frequently moved to a different trade. In the middle years of the 16th century fewer than one-third chose to follow their fathers, and although the proportion rose steadily, about half of those apprenticed always sought another occupation. This clearly reflects the ambitions of those concerned, and the same argument applies to the metal, building and transport workers. It is more surprising to find the sons of merchants and professional men seeking an alternative occupation, particularly in the 16th century when there was an increasing demand for their products or services.[5]

Broadly speaking, the number of apprentices entering the various trade groupings remained surprisingly constant throughout the period 1551-1650. The one notable exception was the textile industry, which increased its share of apprentices from 25 per cent in the second half of the 16th century to 42 per cent in the first half of the seventeenth. In the process it naturally reduced the proportions entering the other trades, but all of them were affected equally, no one trade grouping showing a radical decline in the number of potential entrants.

'Potential' is the operative word in this context. The vast majority of the apprenticeship indentures relate to people who were never to proceed to their freedom, the non-free element never falling below two-thirds of those recorded in a given period and rising to as high as 94 per cent in the last quarter of the 16th century – a period of high plague mortality.[6]

Apprenticeship indentures, as such, do not tell the full story, however; as admissions to the freedom make abundantly clear, the numbers being admitted by apprenticeship and patrimony were far in excess of those whose indentures were actually recorded.[7] It is impossible to correlate the two sources absolutely, for while the apprenticeship indentures indicate that a person began his training at a particular time, the freemen's lists record the date of his admission as a freeman and the trade concerned but nothing else. Nevertheless, a rough-and-ready check can be made by comparing the numbers apprenticed in one period of 25 years with those actually taking up their freedom in the next. The men who attained their freedom, either as the result of an apprenticeship or by patrimony, added to those who never became freemen correspond, very broadly, to the total number of apprentices in any one period. Clearly, few apprentices took as long as 25 years to attain their freedom from the time they were originally bound to a master, but as several served apprenticeships in excess of seven years and, as discussed below, took up to ten years subsequently to attain the freedom, the linking of the successive periods does not greatly distort the facts.[8]

**Table 5.3 An estimate of the proportion of apprentices proceeding to their freedom**

|  | 1576-1600 | 1601-25 | 1626-50 | 1651-75 |
|---|---|---|---|---|
| Numbers attaining their freedom by apprentice-ship or patrimony | 666 | 975 | 1,253 | 1,621 |
| Number of apprentices from preceding period never attaining their freedom | 526 | 641 | 1,360 | 797 |
| Totals | 1,192 | 1,616 | 2,613 | 2,418 |
| Percentage attaining freedom on this basis | 56 | 60 | 48 | 66 |

One can only suggest reasons for this relatively high loss of potential freemen. A number of those completing an apprenticeship undoubtedly returned to their home towns or villages; others would have stayed in Norwich as journeymen; some, possibly many, may have fallen victim to the recurrent attacks of plague.

Theoretically, all apprentices should have taken up their freedom on completion of their apprenticeships. In practice, if only because of the costs involved, this was seldom done promptly. An apprentice was mature at the end of his term, usually 24 years of age, sometimes older, but unless he came from a reasonably affluent family he needed time to build up his capital and establish himself as a householder.[9] When he had done this to his satisfaction he would seek enrolment as a freeman. If he was the son of a freeman himself it would cost him nothing.[10] Other apprentices had to pay a standard fee of 13s. 4d.[11] These fees were not unduly onerous and although admission to the freedom meant accepting the duties of a master craftsman, together with a number of civic responsibilities, a certain number of apprentices were always ready to be enrolled, usually after a short period as a journeyman. On the limited evidence available, more than 80 per cent of those that took this step did so within 10 years of completing their apprenticeships. Of these, 11 per cent sought almost immediate enrolment and a further 51 per cent did so within five years. Others took decidedly longer. One in eight of the apprentices waited between 11 and 20 years before seeking admission to the freedom; five per cent of them allowed more than twenty years to elapse before taking this step. One worsted weaver, almost incredibly, waited 40 years between the completion of his apprenticeship and taking up his freedom, and 17 of his fellows in the same trade allowed more than twenty-five years to pass before taking the same course. Half a dozen others – two cordwainers, a barber, a brewer, a feltmaker and a hosier – took up their freedom more than thirty years after their term of apprenticeship had expired. One must assume that a combination of poverty and disinclination to serve the community is the main explanation for such delay. No non-freeman could trade on his own account for very long. He was allowed to maintain a shop for two years and a day, but was forbidden to take any apprentices. After the period had expired he had the choice of taking up his freedom or closing the shop.

**Table 5.4 Number of years elapsing between completion of apprenticeship and enrolment as a freeman, 1551-1675***

| Occupational grouping | Nil | 1-5 | 6-10 | 11-15 | 16-20 | 21-25 | Over 25 | Totals |
|---|---|---|---|---|---|---|---|---|
| Building | 11 | 40 | 13 | 5 | 3 | 1 | - | 73 |
| Clothing | 26 | 130 | 32 | 10 | 8 | - | 3 | 209 |
| Distributive | 21 | 66 | 17 | 1 | 4 | 2 | 1 | 112 |
| Food & Drink | 13 | 23 | 13 | 1 | 4 | - | 1 | 55 |
| Leatherwork | 8 | 66 | 22 | 9 | 4 | 2 | 4 | 115 |
| Metalwork | 4 | 31 | 7 | 6 | 2 | 1 | - | 51 |
| Professional | 5 | 6 | 1 | 2 | 1 | - | - | 15 |
| Textiles | 39 | 211 | 114 | 49 | 32 | 19 | 21 | 485 |
| Transport | - | 2 | - | - | - | - | - | 2 |
| Others | - | 4 | 1 | 1 | 1 | 1 | - | 8 |
| Totals | 127 | 579 | 220 | 84 | 59 | 26 | 30 | 1,125 |
| *Percentages* | *11* | *51* | *20* | *7* | *5* | *2* | *3* | |

* The details in this table are based on those examples in P. Millican, *The Freemen of Norwich, 1548-1713*, 1934, where the dates of apprenticeship and of taking up the freedom are both given, and the Norfolk Record Office supplement to Millican which is mainly concerned with the years 1601-25.

Despite the fact that so many apprentices did not take up their freedom, and others were reticent about doing so, the numbers admitted as freemen increased steadily throughout the 16th and 17th centuries. In contrast to the apprenticeship indentures, there was little, if any, under-recording of the freemen and the lists provide a reasonably accurate picture of the trade structure of Tudor and Stuart Norwich.[13] Very broadly speaking, the story is one of the decline and resurgence of the local textile industry and of the development of the city as a regional capital. In the process Norwich grew to rely progressively less on the skilled tradesman coming in from outside its confines, and more on its own freemen's sons and on those people who were apprenticed in the town. Initially, certain trades, notably those concerned with clothing, food and drink and transport, relied heavily on outsiders. Eighteen of the carriers, keelmen, watermen and wheelwrights purchased their freedom in the period 1551-75, for example, the only exceptions being a keelman who was the son of an existing freeman and a wheelwright who served an apprenticeship. All of the brewers, cooks, innholders and innkeepers were admitted non-apprentice in the same period, as were more than one hundred of the 142 tailors. The influx of such newcomers caused some resentment, however, as that of the Dutch and Walloons was to do in another context, and legislation attempted to restrict their admission to the freedom. In theory, admissions by redemption were limited to four per year after 1622.[14] In practice, this rule proved difficult to implement but by the third quarter of the 17th century the proportion of men admitted to the freedom other than by apprenticeship had fallen to 11 per cent compared to the 44 per cent admitted between 1551 and 1575. In the same period the proportion of apprenticeship admissions increased by 50 per cent while those by patrimony almost doubled.[15]

In the first half of the 16th century potential freemen had between eighty and ninety trades to choose from, a number which had risen to more than one hundred by the early years of Elizabeth's reign. In the first quarter of the century textiles still employed the greatest number of freemen, the 209 textile workers admitted during that period accounting for rather more than 28 per cent of the whole. The distributive trades, employing just under one in five of such people, were formidable rivals, while the building, clothing and leather trades, each accounting for some ten per cent of the freeman body, were the most important minority groupings. Thereafter the decline of the textile trades was rapid. By the end of the century they attracted little more than 14 per cent of the city's freemen, the void being largely filled by such occupations as draper, grocer and mercer at the higher levels and by the booming clothing and leather trades at the lower.

**Table 5.5 Admissions to the freedom in the 16th century**

| Occupational grouping | 1501-25 | | 1526-50 | | 1551-75 | | 1576-1600 | |
|---|---|---|---|---|---|---|---|---|
| Building | 72 | 9.8 | 53 | 6.5 | 109 | 10.1 | 122 | 11.0 |
| Clothing | 69 | 9.4 | 97 | 12.0 | 173 | 16.1 | 207 | 18.6 |
| Distributive | 142 | 19.3 | 151 | 18.6 | 212 | 19.7 | 175 | 15.8 |
| Food & Drink | 63 | 8.6 | 87 | 10.7 | 131 | 12.2 | 133 | 12.0 |
| Leatherwork | 75 | 10.2 | 100 | 12.3 | 135 | 12.6 | 166 | 14.9 |
| Metalwork | 40 | 5.5 | 59 | 7.3 | 67 | 6.2 | 64 | 5.8 |
| Miscellaneous | 2 | 0.3 | 3 | 0.4 | 10 | 0.9 | 4 | 0.4 |
| Professional | 36 | 4.9 | 34 | 4.2 | 27 | 2.5 | 44 | 4.0 |
| Textiles | 209 | 28.5 | 189 | 23.3 | 171 | 15.9 | 164 | 14.8 |
| Transport | 6 | 0.8 | 15 | 1.8 | 20 | 1.9 | 11 | 1.0 |
| Woodwork | 20 | 2.7 | 23 | 2.8 | 20 | 1.9 | 20 | 1.8 |
| Totals | 734 | | 811 | | 1,075 | | 1,110 | |

The figures in italic are percentages.

The broad trends throughout the century are indicated above. They are made clearer by a comparison of the city's trade structure in specific years. In 1525 and 1569 the names of the freemen can be extrapolated from the subsidy and muster returns respectively, and in 1589 a full occupational census of a majority of the city's householders was provided, possibly as the prelude to a muster.

Just under half of the 1,414 people who were taxed in 1525 are identifiable as freemen, occupying between them 78 different trades. When the individual occupations are linked together in their respective trade groupings, the picture which emerges is broadly similar to that provided by the freemen's admissions for the first quarter of the 16th century, the distributive and professional trades being marginally fewer and those concerned with transport rather more than the admissions themselves would suggest.

Important as the textile industry undoubtedly was (and one has constantly to bear in mind the involvement of the merchant classes in this sphere, as well as the unknown number of women and children and those employed in country districts) seven out of 10 of the freemen were primarily involved in other activities. Of these, the distributive trades were both the second largest and wealthiest group by far. The food and drink trades employed more than 12 per cent of the Norwich freemen, the most numerous being the butchers, bakers and fishmongers. These trades also included a number of wealthy men, the three leading groupings supplying more than 85 per cent of those citizens who were called upon to pay their tax in advance of the others in 1523.[16]

The majority of the remaining freemen were engaged in the leather, building, clothing and metal trades. The first two of these, employing between them one-fifth of the city's freemen, were among the poorer occupational groupings, two-thirds of the builders and over two-thirds of the leather workers being worth less than £5 in personal estate.[17] The bulk of the masons, glaziers and reeders in the building trades and the curriers, saddlers and shoemakers in the leather trades fell into the same category.

**Table 5.6 Trade groupings in 1525**

| Occupational grouping | Number of freemen | % |
|---|---|---|
| Textiles | 208 | 29.9 |
| Distributive | 106 | 15.2 |
| Food & Drink | 93 | 13.4 |
| Leatherwork | 78 | 11.2 |
| Building | 67 | 9.6 |
| Clothing | 54 | 7.8 |
| Metalwork | 36 | 5.2 |
| Professional | 21 | 3.0 |
| Woodwork | 18 | 2.6 |
| Transport | 13 | 1.9 |
| Miscellaneous | 1 | 0.1 |
| Total | 695 | |

Of the 78 occupations being practised in the city, just over a dozen stand out as being especially significant. The worsted weavers alone provided employment for almost one-fifth of the entire freeman body, a similar proportion being occupied by tailors, cordwainers and mercers who, between them, accounted for a further fifth. Carpenters and masons, butchers and bakers, grocers and raffmen represented the non-textile trades among the residue, with dyers, shearmen and coverlet-weavers providing further evidence of the importance of the textile industry in Henrician Norwich.

**Table 5.7 Occupations with the largest number of freemen in 1525**

| Trade | No. | % |
|---|---|---|
| Worsted weavers | 127 | 18.3 |
| Tailors | 48 | 6.9 |
| Mercers | 47 | 6.8 |
| Cordwainers & Shoemakers | 44 | 6.3 |
| Butchers | 33 | 4.7 |
| Grocers | 24 | 3.5 |
| Shearmen | 23 | 3.3 |
| Bakers | 22 | 3.2 |
| Carpenters | 22 | 3.2 |
| Masons | 18 | 2.6 |
| Raffmen | 17 | 2.4 |
| Coverlet weavers | 16 | 2.3 |
| Dyers | 16 | 2.3 |
| Others | 238 | 34.2 |
| Total | 695 | |

A full listing of all the trades being practised in Norwich in 1525 is provided in Appendix I.

None of the crafts was spread equally throughout the city. Thus almost three-quarters of the textile workers were to be found in the wards of Wymer and Ultra Aquam, with Wymer alone housing some sixty per cent of the metalworkers, forty per cent of those concerned with the leather trades and half of the woodworkers. Similarly, almost all of the 13 transport workers who had taken up their freedom plied their trade on the water in the Conesford area, while the majority of the builders and those concerned with food and drink lived in the two wards of Conesford and Wymer.

**Table 5.8 Distribution of occupational groupings throughout the city, 1525**

| Occupational grouping | | Great Ward | | |
|---|---|---|---|---|
| | Conesford | Mancroft | Wymer | Ultra Aquam |
| Building | 39 | 16 | 28 | 16 |
| Clothing | 20 | 30 | 35 | 15 |
| Distributive | 13 | 25 | 35 | 27 |
| Food & Drink | 38 | 21 | 28 | 13 |
| Leatherwork | 18 | 24 | 42 | 15 |
| Metalwork | 17 | 17 | 58 | 8 |
| Professional | 24 | 19 | 33 | 24 |
| Textiles | 16 | 10 | 25 | 48 |
| Transport | 77 | 8 | 8 | 8 |
| Woodwork | 11 | 28 | 50 | 11 |
| Freemen in each Great ward | 23 | 19 | 32 | 26 |

These figures are given as percentages of the whole. The numbers from which they are derived are given on page 52.

**Table 5.9 Occupational groupings most common to the petty wards of the city, 1525**

| Occupational grouping | | | | | | Ward | | | | | | |
|---|---|---|---|---|---|---|---|---|---|---|---|---|
| | SC | NC | BS | StS | StP | StG | WW | MW | EW | Cos | Cg | Fib |
| Building | 13 | 22 | 16 | - | - | - | 11 | - | - | - | 11 | 6 |
| Clothing | - | 12 | - | - | 15 | - | - | - | 15 | 7 | - | - |
| Distributive | - | - | - | 23 | 22 | - | 13 | 28 | - | 16 | 11 | 21 |
| Food & Drink | 23 | 16 | 24 | 16 | 15 | 14 | - | 14 | 15 | 10 | 5 | - |
| Leatherwork | - | - | 12 | 16 | - | 14 | 13 | - | 20 | - | - | 9 |
| Metalwork | - | - | - | - | - | - | - | 15 | - | - | - | - |
| Textiles | 28 | 16 | 21 | 14 | 15 | 29 | 37 | 14 | 15 | 55 | 63 | 48 |
| Transport | 18 | - | - | - | - | - | - | - | - | - | - | - |
| Percentage employed in major groupings | 82 | 66 | 73 | 69 | 67 | 57 | 74 | 71 | 65 | 88 | 90 | 84 |
| Number of freemen in each of the petty wards | 40 | 31 | 86 | 43 | 73 | 14 | 91 | 72 | 61 | 58 | 58 | 67 |

Fewer than half of the 78 trades were to be found in any one of the petty wards, and in most cases considerably less than this.[18] Thus St Giles contained no more than 10 of those available, South Conesford 18 and Coslany 19, rising to the 30 in Ber Street and East Wymer and the 34 in the West Wymer district of the city. Individual trades were particularly prone to concentrate in certain areas, with butchers predominating in Ber Street, mercers in Middle Wymer, coverlet-weavers in West Wymer, shearmen in the Charing, or Shearing,

Cross area of Middle Wymer and worsted weavers throughout Ultra Aquam. One in four of the city's cordwainers was to be found in St Peter's, with a similar proportion of the less-skilled shoemakers in East Wymer.[19]

With the exception of the tiny ward of St Giles, each of the 12 petty wards housed craftsmen employed in four main trade groupings which, between them, accounted for between sixty-six and ninety per cent of the workforce of the area concerned. The figures are again given as a percentage of the whole.

The textile trades rank as one of the most important occupational groupings in each of the 12 wards and of major significance, in terms of numbers employed, in Ultra Aquam as a whole, in West Wymer, St Giles and South Conesford. The food and drink trades were a major employer in 10 of the wards and, although pre-eminent in Ber Street alone, ranked second in six of them. The building, distributive and leather trades were among the most pre-eminent groupings in half of the city's wards, with building and leather being of primary importance in North Conesford and East Wymer respectively, and the distributive trades reigning supreme in the wealthy wards of St Stephen's, St Peter's and East Wymer. The remaining occupational groupings were less equally distributed. The clothing trades appear as one of the leading employers in four of the petty wards but, with metal and transport, were of primary importance in none; the two latter groupings were of significance in Middle Wymer and South Conesford alone.

Important as the textile trades were in 1525, the seeds of decay were already present. The change in the fortunes of the industry was brought about by the lessening demands for its products. As early as 1536 complaints were made that worsted could not be sold, one weaver, at least, attributing his failure to pay subsidy to that cause, and the tax collectors were obliged to collect reduced amounts in the city. Competition abroad, where a better class of worsted was produced, caused considerable distress in Norwich and the government showed itself aware of the problem by making specific provision for the city's merchants to buy and sell worsted elsewhere. The decline continued, however. Up to 1535 between one thousand and three thousand Norwich worsteds were exported annually from Great Yarmouth. Thereafter the numbers fell steadily until by the third year of Elizabeth's reign no more than 38 left for foreign markets.[20]

In an attempt to restore the city's fortunes new industries were fostered, the hatters becoming a separate company in 1543, the russel weavers in 1554. Neither trade was particularly successful. The hatters, although briefly appearing among the city's leading trades between 1551 and 1575, suffered from the apparent total inability of the city fathers to control their activities, with the result that inferior products were put onto the market. Initially, there was no effective training, no specific period of apprenticeship, and a number of people from depressed occupations (worsted weavers, shearmen etc.) tried their hands at the new trade. It also attracted some people from the surrounding country districts, few of whom ever proceeded to their freedom. The difficulties were not finally resolved until the 1560s, several hatters in the meantime having left the city to escape possible craft restrictions. The russel weavers, when they began, introduced foreign craftsmen and repeatedly made better products than their continental rivals but their output was small, numbering only a few hundred cloths a year.[21]

The depression did not affect those engaged in the textile trades alone. In May 1549 the common council complained that masons, carpenters, reeders and tilers had left to find work in the country, the void created being filled by 'foreigners' and beggars.[22]

To add to the depression in the textile industry, the city suffered severely from the influenza epidemic which swept the country in 1556.[23] No precise figures are available, but Blomefield records the deaths of 10 aldermen and a number of common councillors, classes that usually survived similar outbreaks in the Elizabethan period, and the poor almost certainly suffered severely.[24]

Nevertheless, while much has been written about the decline of Norwich as a textile town and its subsequent revival with the coming of the New Draperies, to paint a picture of complete economic stagnation before the arrival of the Dutch and Walloons would be misleading in the extreme. Far from being a depressed town there is every evidence, textiles apart, that the economy of Norwich was in a very healthy state in the first decades of Elizabeth's reign due, at least in part, to the increasing demands of the surrounding gentry. This is made abundantly clear by an examination of the occupations of 1,250 freemen included in a muster taken in 1569. The number of tailors alone suggests a considerable demand for clothing from beyond the city. If we add to this the large numbers of the occupied population engaged in the provision of food and drink, household goods and building facilities it becomes apparent that the tradesmen of Norwich served many customers outside its immediate precincts. At least 80 per cent of the freemen were engaged, directly or indirectly, in providing goods for the consumer, and it is hardly possible to envisage four people producing goods for the other one. In a period of less than fifty years, the numbers employed in the clothing trades and in the professions had more than trebled, those concerned with the distributive trades had doubled, and the numbers of building, leather and metalworkers had almost doubled. The increased number of freemen – an average of 49 a year compared to the 28 earlier in the century – and, in particular, the spheres in which they had increased, reflect a major change in the economy of the city, and one which more than filled the void created by the decline of the textile industry.

#### Table 5.10 Trade groupings in 1569

| Occupational grouping | Number of freemen | % |
|---|---|---|
| Textiles | 264 | *21.1* |
| Distributive | 251 | *20.1* |
| Clothing | 186 | *14.9* |
| Leatherwork | 153 | *12.2* |
| Food & Drink | 121 | *9.7* |
| Building | 116 | *9.3* |
| Metalwork | 65 | *5.2* |
| Professional | 38 | *3.0* |
| Woodwork | 32 | *2.6* |
| Transport | 21 | *1.7* |
| Miscellaneous | 3 | *0.2* |
| Total | 1,250 | |

It seems perfectly clear that by the middle years of the 16th century Norwich had become increasingly attractive as the capital city of its region – in effect, a lesser London. On a reduced scale the city had much the same advantages as the metropolis. The Duke of Norfolk held court there in a very real sense; the quarter sessions attracted the country gentry, and others, at frequent intervals and many gentry were in residence for at last part of the year; the city's grammar school made provision for a number of people outside the town's boundaries; it was a minor port, albeit an inland one; and the great fairs, held at regular intervals throughout the year, brought in a vast concourse of people.

In this respect Norwich resembled many of the other large towns that played the part of capital cities to their regions. Professor Hoskins has pointed out that many towns of this type – Exeter, Salisbury, Newcastle and Bristol, as well as York and Norwich – were in the process of becoming social capitals 'in which a growing proportion of the larger gentry had a town house to which they migrated for the winter months', while Professor Dickens has noted the steady increase in the number of those engaged in the luxury trades at York, a town which, like Norwich, increased its population during the 16th century.[25]

### Table 5.11 Occupations with the largest number of freemen in 1569

| Occupation | No. | % |
|---|---|---|
| Worsted weavers | 166 | *13.3* |
| Grocers | 150 | *12.0* |
| Tailors | 146 | *11.7* |
| Cordwainers | 59 | *4.7* |
| Mercers | 48 | *3.8* |
| Dornix weavers | 35 | *2.8* |
| Hatters | 35 | *2.8* |
| Tanners | 34 | *2.7* |
| Bakers | 32 | *2.6* |
| Carpenters | 31 | *2.5* |
| Butchers | 29 | *2.3* |
| Masons | 26 | *2.1* |
| Others | 459 | *36.7* |
| Totals | 1,250 | |

### Table 5.12 Number of freemen admitted to the 12 leading occupations in 16th century Norwich[*]

|  | 1501-25 | | 1526-50 | | 1551-75 | | 1576-1600 | |
|---|---|---|---|---|---|---|---|---|
| *1* | Worsted Ws | 134 | Worsted Ws | 114 | Tailors | 142 | Tailors | 170 |
| *2* | Mercers | 70 | Tailors | 72 | Grocers | 121 | Grocers | 96 |
| *3* | Tailors | 67 | Mercers | 69 | Worsted Ws | 103 | Cordwainers | 78 |
| *4* | Cordwainers | 34 | Grocers | 53 | Cordwainers | 55 | Worsted Ws | 74 |
| *5* | Grocers | 31 | Cordwainers | 43 | Mercers | 49 | Dornix Ws | 38 |
| *6* | Carpenters | 27 | Smiths | 32 | Butchers | 29 | Carpenters | 32 |
| *7* | Shearman | 26 | Shearmen | 29 | Hatters | 29 | Glovers | 32 |
| *8* | Masons | 21 | Butchers | 26 | Dornix Ws | 27 | Masons | 32 |
| *9* | Raffmen | 21 | Tanners | 25 | Masons | 24 | Butchers | 30 |
| *10* | Butchers | 20 | Bakers | 19 | Carpenters | 23 | Masons | 29 |
| *11* | Barbers | 15 | Masons | 18 | Tanners | 22 | Drapers | 27 |
| *12* | Scriveners | 15 | Carpenters | 17 | Haberdashers | 20 | Brewers | 24 |

[*] For a comparative table see Palliser, *The Age of Elizabeth*, 1983, p. 244.

That much of the demand in Norwich was for luxury goods is evidenced both by the increasing quantity of groceries being imported and by the phenomenal rise of the grocers themselves. The quarter of a century ending in 1525 saw the admission of 31 grocers to the freedom. That figure was almost doubled in the succeeding period of 25 years and it more than doubled again between 1551 and 1575 when 121 men were admitted to the freedom in the trade. In consequence 150 grocers are identifiable in 1569 compared to the 24 who were present when the subsidies were levied some fifty years earlier. A contemporary noted the change as early as 1550, remarking in a tavern that 'there were more merchants now by the hundred thousand in carrying and conveying victual and such like things'.[26] If the number of merchants was exaggerated it is difficult to exaggerate the variety of goods being brought into the city at this time, whether food, textiles, building materials or household goods.[27]

By the 1570s the East Anglian ports were importing ever-increasing quantities of sugar, molasses and syrup, figs and prunes, raisins and currants. In 1581 a cargo of 20,000 oranges and 1,000 lemons reached Norwich in time for the St Bartholomew's Fair. The grocers were mainly responsible for this activity, but they were not the only ones to take advantage of the opportunities offered. The Norwich mercers, possibly extending their activities, imported large quantities of French and sweet wines at about the same time. Even the Bishop of Norwich imported beer for his household, rather surprisingly, for the number of local beer brewers increased considerably.

The innkeepers were able to make large profits on occasion, particularly when the quarter sessions brought in the justices and other notables, and by 1575 one of them, Nicholas Baker, had achieved aldermanic status. The business of the tailors increased only less than that of the grocers, while the ever-increasing river traffic enabled John Stingate, keelman and common councillor, to quote but one example, to leave over £250 to his children at his death, as well as real estate within the city. The development of the leather trades increased the status of the cordwainers, ordinances passed in 1561 allowing them to become common councillors for the first time, while Richard Durrant, the Norwich bone-setter, prospered sufficiently to bequeath over £280 at his death in addition to large sums owed him, almost certainly, by wealthy patrons.[28]

The increasing wealth of at least a section of the community is reflected, too, in what appears to have been considerable building activity in Norwich between 1576 and 1590, activity only temporarily halted by the various outbreaks of plague. There is evidence of an increasing substitution of brick for timber and slate for thatch, large quantities of bricks and tiles being brought up-river, mostly from the Low Countries. By 1580 the volume of river traffic had grown to such an extent that the authorities found it necessary to construct a new common staithe.[29]

There was, of course, a reverse side to the picture, and the census of the poor, taken in 1570, makes it clear that there was considerable poverty in the town, with labourers and textile workers predominating among the men and spinners, with a miscellany of other occupations, among the women.[30] The reorganisation of the city's poor law policy is discussed elsewhere, but steps had been taken to alleviate the situation as long ago as 1564. An unusually wet autumn, followed by severe frost, in that year had aggravated the employment problem which was already made bad by the decline of the textile trades. Aware of the skills of the Dutch and Walloon refugees who had begun to arrive in the country in large numbers following the invasion of the Netherlands by the Duke of Alva, the mayor, Thomas Sotherton, approached the Duke of Norfolk and the Privy Council in turn. He pleaded the decline of the worsted trade, the large numbers of unemployed, and the fact that several artisans were leaving the city causing the decay of many houses which had to be let at small prices.[31] The appeal was successful and Letters Patent, dated 5 November 1565, authorised 30 families with their servants to settle in the city. Twenty-four of these were to be Dutch and six Walloon, the total number being limited to 300 people, i.e., 10 per family, including servants. They were expected to introduce bayes, arras, sayes, tapestry, mockadoes, carsays 'and other outlandish commodities' not previously manufactured in this country. The common council of the city, possibly fearing the competition of so many strangers, refused to put their seal to the orders, but the opposition was overcome by the mayor using his own seal of office.[32]

The numbers authorised were soon exceeded. In the year that the Letters Patent officially authorised their settlement in Norwich, at least forty-two families, comprising 174 people in all, had already arrived in the town, and by 1568 the men alone numbered over four hundred, more than half of whom were employed in the textile trades. Of these, 193 were woolcombers, an occupation which took some time to gain popularity in Norwich, and 62

17. *(left)* Slipware vessels imported from Germany and Holland found during excavations at Alms Lane, possibly owned by immigrants.

18. *(above)* A late 16th-century Dutch fire-cover, decorated with yellow and green slip, excavated at Alms Lane.

were weavers. Among the more interesting of the miscellaneous occupations were those of printer, one of whom set up in the city, and bookseller. Anthony de Solen was apparently the first printer to become established in Norwich, certainly the first to become a freeman in the trade, an activity he combined with importing Rhenish wine.[33]

Despite the fact that the aliens arrived at the express invitation of the Norwich authorities they were regarded with the utmost suspicion. They were placed under severe restrictions, being forbidden to buy or sell any goods except those of their own make, and even these could only be sold to members of their own nation, restrictions which were to cause incessant disputes between the 'strangers' and the city authorities. How unwise the city fathers were to antagonise the aliens was proved by the almost immediate revival in trade, the pieces produced by the Russel Company, for example, promptly increasing from 276 to 1,048 and reaching 2,845 by 1572.[34]

Despite this initial stimulus, there was no wholesale co-operation between the English and the aliens. The English weavers experienced keen competition from the strangers over the available wool supplies, and there is no record of the English being instructed in new methods until the 1570s and 1580s and then only in the making of bays. In 1581 the Dutch refused to pass on the secrets of fulling and scouring, while the English, in their turn, did nothing to prevent unskilled shearmen from having access to the new cloths nor was there any attempt made to compel native dyers to comply with the Strangers' Book of Orders.[35]

Nevertheless, the stimulus provided by the Dutch and Walloons gave a welcome boost to the textile industry and by the 1580s it had been restored to the position of pre-eminence it had occupied earlier in the century.

### Table 5.13 Trade groupings in 1589

| Occupational grouping | Number of tradesmen | % |
|---|---|---|
| Textiles | 259 | 18.9 |
| Labourers | 162 | 11.8 |
| Leatherwork | 155 | 11.3 |
| Clothing | 150 | 11.0 |
| Food & Drink | 149 | 10.9 |
| Distributive | 109 | 8.0 |
| Building | 104 | 7.6 |
| Professional | 57 | 4.2 |
| Metalwork | 56 | 4.1 |
| Farming | 36 | 2.8 |
| Woodwork | 32 | 2.3 |
| Transport | 31 | 2.3 |
| Others | 69 | 5.0 |
| Total | 1,369 | |

This is made abundantly clear by the chance survival of a relatively full occupational census of the city's householders, taken in 1589, which recorded all classes from the gentleman to the labourer.[36] Under normal circumstances, we are heavily dependent on freemen's lists for an impression of the occupational structure of the city. The significant and important distinction between that source – useful and reliable though it is – and the census is the number of non-free occupations recorded in the latter. The labourers are especially numerous, but the census also includes husbandmen, yeomen and gentry, as well as such professional men as schoolmasters, attorneys, doctors and surgeons for whom specific numbers are usually lacking. Aldermen are listed as such. Most of them were members of the distributive trades, as were some of those described as gentry and a few of those with no specific designation.

From the evidence of the census, the freemen of Norwich comprised some 50 per cent of the city's householders, with considerable variations among the different trade groupings. The distributive trades had the largest proportion of freemen, almost 82 per cent of them being master craftsmen in 1589. The clothing trades, with 64 per cent, and the leather-workers, with 52, also had significant numbers of freemen. At the other extreme, only two of the nine miscellaneous craftsmen and nine of those concerned with transport had achieved, or desired, this status when the census was taken.

It is the submerged 52 per cent of the textile workers which is of immediate significance here. Admissions to the freedom over successive periods of 25 years suggest a steady decline in the importance of the textile industry, which reached its nadir in the last quarter of the 16th century when no more than 14 per cent of the freemen admitted were concerned with such trades. It is clear from the census, however, that the industry was already reviving and employed half as many men again as the wider analysis would imply.[37]

**Table 5.14 Proportion of freemen to non-freemen in 1589**

| Occupational grouping | Number of freemen | Number of non-freemen | Totals | Percentage of freemen |
|---|---|---|---|---|
| Distributive | 104 | 23 | 127 | 81.9 |
| Clothing | 98 | 54 | 152 | 64.5 |
| Leatherwork | 81 | 76 | 157 | 51.6 |
| Metalwork | 28 | 30 | 58 | 48.3 |
| Textiles | 113 | 149 | 262 | 48.1 |
| Building | 47 | 57 | 104 | 45.2 |
| Professional | 26 | 32 | 58 | 44.8 |
| Food & Drink | 60 | 91 | 151 | 39.7 |
| Woodwork | 12 | 20 | 32 | 37.5 |
| Transport | 9 | 22 | 31 | 29.0 |
| Miscellaneous | 2 | 7 | 9 | 22.2 |
| Totals | 580 | 561 | 1,141 | 50.8 |

The table includes the trades of those aldermen, gentlemen etc. which are obtainable from the freemen's lists.

In part, at least, this reflects the advent of the Dutch and Walloons. By the turn of the century, the major difficulties between the English and their alien counterparts had been overcome. In 1598 the strangers were admitted to the freedom for the first time and allowed to buy and sell as readily as any English freemen.[38] The English, although never mastering the art of bay making which declined with the Dutch congregation, took more easily to the Walloon grograines, mockadoes, vellums, buffins and other caungeantry, and by the last years of Elizabeth's reign the manufacture of traditional worsteds was all but extinct.[39] The scene was set for the tremendous boom in the textile industry which was to occur in the 17th century.

The disinclination, or inability, of the English craftsmen to take to the Dutch methods meant that the sale and production of bays declined rapidly. French products, on the other hand, went from strength to strength. According to Professor Wilson, the particular strength of the Norwich industry was the light, bright, stuffs often made of a mixture of wool and silk 'which came to be the popular wear of the not too affluent squire's lady or tradesman's wife'.[40] The sheer diversity of these cloths is well brought out in a letter written by Thomas Anguish, the mayor of Norwich, in 1611 when he refers to some three dozen different varieties of cloth being produced at that time.[41]

Both the home and the foreign markets were captured by the men producing the New Draperies and their success encouraged more and more people to enter the worsted industry. If the 16th century can be seen, however broadly, as a story of the steady decline of the textile trades in Norwich, the 17th century must be seen as one of their phenomenal rise. On three separate occasions during the reign of James I more than one hundred youths were apprenticed as worsted weavers in a single year, and over eight hundred are known to have been apprenticed to the trade during the first 25 years of the century.[42] Admissions to the freedom never reached this level, but more than 260 men were admitted as worsted weavers in the first quarter of the century, half as many again in the succeeding period and a further 680 between 1651 and 1675.[43] In the process the textile industry's share of the freemen rose from 26 to 40 per cent, a much greater proportion than that achieved in the preceding century.

Most of the other occupations maintained themselves at the same level, in an absolute sense, the leather and metal workers admitted actually increasing in number between 1626 and 1650, but virtually all of them declined in relative importance as an ever-increasing number of apprentices entered the textile trades. Only the building and clothing trades reversed the general trend. The builders had reached their high point at the end of Elizabeth's reign. They lost ground over the next 50 years, recovering slightly between 1651 and 1675. The clothing trades continued to attract much the same proportion of freemen throughout the 17th century, and the number of admissions actually rose by some twenty-five per cent during the Commonwealth and Restoration periods.

**Table 5.15 Admissions to the freedom in Norwich, 1601-75**

| Occupational grouping | 1601-25 | | 1626-50 | | 1651-75 | |
|---|---|---|---|---|---|---|
| Building | 101 | 7.0 | 103 | 6.6 | 135 | 7.4 |
| Clothing | 224 | 15.4 | 216 | 13.8 | 266 | 14.5 |
| Distributive | 220 | 15.1 | 203 | 13.0 | 159 | 8.7 |
| Food & Drink | 157 | 10.8 | 149 | 9.6 | 124 | 6.8 |
| Leatherwork | 178 | 12.2 | 197 | 12.6 | 174 | 9.5 |
| Metalwork | 97 | 6.7 | 111 | 7.1 | 97 | 5.3 |
| Miscellaneous | 3 | 0.2 | 8 | 0.5 | 10 | 0.5 |
| Professional | 59 | 4.1 | 59 | 3.8 | 71 | 3.9 |
| Textiles | 387 | 26.7 | 492 | 31.5 | 748 | 40.9 |
| Transport | 9 | 0.6 | 3 | 0.2 | 6 | 0.3 |
| Woodwork | 17 | 1.2 | 18 | 1.2 | 41 | 2.2 |
| Totals | 1,452 | | 1,559 | | 1,831 | |

The figures in italics are percentages.

**Table 5.16 Number of freemen admitted to the 12 leading occupations in Norwich, 1601-75**

| | 1601-25 | | 1626-50 | | 1651-75 | |
|---|---|---|---|---|---|---|
| 1 | Worsted weavers | 261 | Worsted weavers | 392 | Worsted weavers | 680 |
| 2 | Tailors | 165 | Tailors | 160 | Tailors | 192 |
| 3 | Cordwainers | 81 | Cordwainers | 107 | Cordwainers | 115 |
| 4 | Grocers | 75 | Grocers | 88 | Grocers | 70 |
| 5 | Merchants | 57 | Bakers | 59 | Bakers | 58 |
| 6 | Dornix weavers | 45 | Masons | 35 | Carpenters | 46 |
| 7 | Hosiers | 42 | Hosiers | 33 | Hosiers | 38 |
| 8 | Bakers | 41 | Barbers | 30 | Masons | 36 |
| 9 | Mercers | 36 | Merchants | 30 | Barbers | 34 |
| 10 | Brewers | 34 | Carpenters | 29 | Butchers | 27 |
| 11 | Butchers | 29 | Butchers | 28 | Blacksmiths | 26 |
| 12 | Masons | 29 | Blacksmiths | 27 | Woolcombers | 24 |
| | | | Dornix weavers | 27 | | |
| | | | Mercers | 27 | | |

The fortunes of the individual trades naturally varied as much as those of the trade groupings. Worsted weavers, tailors, cordwainers and grocers held the first four places throughout while the hosiers, newly emerged as a separate occupation, maintained themselves in seventh place. The fortunes of the rest fluctuated. Bakers, butchers and masons were always among the leading trades. The drapers and brewers, in contrast, the former permanently, the latter temporarily, made an early exit to be replaced by carpenters, blacksmiths and, for a short while, mercers. The barbers increased in number during the reign of Charles I and held their position thereafter.

Any discussion of the distribution of occupations in 17th-century Norwich would be incomplete without some mention of the aliens. They continued to have a strong bias towards textiles, 62 per cent of them being placed in that category in an occupational census of Dutch and Walloons taken in 1622. By then some of them had turned to other fields, however. The presence of 27 hosiers suggests that aliens may have been responsible for the introduction of that trade in Norwich. A small group of eight gardeners and farmers indicates the Dutch interest in agriculture, and the presence of a small proportion of schoolmasters, physicians and surgeons reveals their professional interests.[44]

Professional men are consistently underestimated if we rely on freemen's lists alone. Clerics are omitted for obvious reasons, as are those concerned with teaching and the law. Significantly, the census of 1589 mentions nine schoolmasters, seven attorneys, a doctor and two surgeons, few of whom would have been detected from other sources. Barbers and barber-surgeons are listed, but they give no real idea of the extent of medical practice in Norwich during the 16th and 17th centuries which was, in fact, considerable. It has been estimated, on the basis of known names, that a total of at least seventy-three persons were practising some form of medicine in the city between 1570 and 1590, reflecting 'a consistently high demand for medical services in the early modern period, probably at every level of society'. In the middle years of the 17th century a minimum of 19 doctors were practising in Norwich, several of whom were university trained and some, at least, comfortably off.[45] In Norwich, as elsewhere, a number of men were engaged in subsidiary occupations, even if they adhered primarily to their nominal profession.[46] Tippling was commonplace, the 142 houses licensed for that purpose in 1651, for example, being owned by members of 38 different trades. It was a popular by-employment and 20 years later the number of tipplers had risen to two hundred and forty-three.[47] Forty new occupations appeared in the freemen's lists between 1601 and 1675, but some of these had been practised in the city by non-freemen for some time.[48] Roger Horton was described as a furrier as early as 1563 but no freeman was enrolled as such until 1694.[49] John Porter was engaged as a clockmaker before 1598, but none appears in the freemen's lists until 1613 when, surprisingly, the youth in question was apprenticed to a man who had begun his career as a grocer.[50] Lastmakers, coppersmiths and crossbow-makers appear among the occupations to which boys were apprenticed, but no freeman was officially practising as such. Barber-surgeons had long-standing connections with net-making and with music, the latter being commonplace throughout Europe. During the 1630s, for example, John Adkin, barber of Norwich, indentured three apprentices in the art and science of music and barbering while in 1618 it was actually stipulated that a barber of Great Yarmouth should instruct his apprentice in the use of musical instruments.[51] Basket-makers and locksmiths, as well as tailors, took hosier apprentices while the first of the city's ironmongers had their origins as grocers.[52]

Finally, some mention must be made of the servant class. They were clearly numerous but usually appear anonymously among the fifty per cent or so of the adult population to whom no trade can be ascribed. The only occasion on which their numbers can be ascertained with any certainty is in 1694. A return survives for that year which gives full details of 255 households in the large and wealthy parish of St Peter Mancroft. One hundred and fifty of the households, or 60 per cent of the whole, employed servants, the larger of them having between five and seven, the smaller between one and two, giving an average of just over two per household. There were approximately six female servants for every four males, and their total of 316 comprised just under 39 per cent of the entire adult population of the parish.[53] This can in no way be described as an average number but it does give some impression of the importance of this class in the city's occupational structure.

19.   Norwich market place in 1799.

20.   Norwich market place, *c.* 1812.

The tremendous boom in the textile trades might suggest relative prosperity for much of the 17th century. In part this is true. In 1576 the only worsted weavers in the city's government were the five men who sat as common councillors. A century later half of the aldermen and one-third of the common councillors were drawn from the trade, an eightfold increase which reflects their increasing wealth. On the other hand, 55 per cent of the people who lived in households containing a single hearth in 1671 were also worsted weavers.[54] The difference partly reflects the economic fluctuations of the century. A combination of trading depression and plague between 1625 and 1630 caused the poor rate to be trebled and large numbers were unemployed.[55] By 1650 relatively few cloths were being exported overseas and the clothiers relied heavily on the home market for the sale of their produce.[56] As in the 16th century, when there was a trading slump the members of the largest trade suffered the most, and it is not without some significance that in 1671 sixty per cent or so of the city's households were exempted from payment of the Hearth Tax on the grounds of poverty, a distinctly higher proportion than elsewhere.[57]

### Table 5.17 Trade groupings in 1671

| Occupational grouping | Number of freemen | % |
|---|---|---|
| Textiles | 596 | 41.3 |
| Clothing | 165 | 11.4 |
| Leatherwork | 144 | 10.0 |
| Distributive | 125 | 8.7 |
| Building | 119 | 8.2 |
| Food & Drink | 117 | 8.1 |
| Metalwork | 86 | 6.0 |
| Professional | 68 | 4.7 |
| Woodwork | 15 | 1.0 |
| Miscellaneous | 4 | 0.3 |
| Transport | 4 | 0.3 |
| Total | 1,443 | |

### Table 5.18 Occupations with the largest number of freemen in 1671

| Occupation | No. | % |
|---|---|---|
| Worsted weavers | 521 | 36.1 |
| Tailors | 125 | 8.7 |
| Cordwainers | 90 | 6.2 |
| Grocers | 54 | 3.7 |
| Butchers | 43 | 3.0 |
| Bakers | 41 | 2.8 |
| Carpenters | 30 | 2.1 |
| Roughmasons | 30 | 2.1 |
| Blacksmiths | 23 | 1.6 |
| Hosiers | 23 | 1.6 |
| Barbers | 21 | 1.5 |
| Tanners | 21 | 1.5 |
| Others | 421 | 29.2 |
| Total | 1,443 | |

Wealth apart, the Hearth Tax returns provide an opportunity to compare the distribution of occupations in Norwich in 1671 with their distribution some one hundred and fifty years earlier. Some 1,443 of those paying the tax are recognisable as freemen, the proportions in the various trade groupings broadly reflecting the admissions in the previous 25 years.

Between them the contributors to the Hearth Tax followed 106 distinct trades, almost half as many again as their counterparts in Henrician Norwich. As in the earlier period, however, a dozen occupations stand out as being especially significant, employing between them some 71 per cent of the freeman body. Worsted weavers were again supreme, providing employment for four times as many people as the tailors who, as in 1525, stand second in the table. By 1671 blacksmiths, hosiers, barbers and tanners had replaced mercers, shearmen, raffmen, coverlet weavers and dyers as leading employers in the city, with the residue of occupations being the same as in the earlier period.

As in 1525, occupational groupings in Restoration Norwich tended to be concentrated in specific areas of the city, albeit with some changes from the earlier period. Mancroft housed twice as many builders as in the Tudor period while the proportion of the same workers in Conesford had fallen by one third. Mancroft had also attracted a higher proportion of grocers, mercers, merchants and men of similar occupations, as well as a large influx of metalworkers at the expense of Wymer. These occupations apart, Conesford housed almost half of those concerned with the provision of food and drink, while two-thirds of the leather-workers were to be found in the wards of Mancroft and Wymer. The textile trades were distributed a little more equally throughout the city than they had been in Henrician Norwich, but fully two-thirds of those employed in this field were still to be found in the two wards of Wymer and Ultra Aquam.

**Table 5.19 Distribution of occupational groupings in Restoration Norwich**

| Occupational grouping | Great Ward | | | |
|---|---|---|---|---|
| | Conesford | Mancroft | Wymer | Ultra Aquam |
| Building | 27 | 34 | 22 | 18 |
| Clothing | 22 | 27 | 33 | 18 |
| Distributive | 18 | 45 | 23 | 14 |
| Food & Drink | 45 | 18 | 17 | 20 |
| Leatherwork | 19 | 31 | 35 | 15 |
| Metalwork | 20 | 49 | 16 | 15 |
| Professional | 15 | 44 | 34 | 7 |
| Textiles | 20 | 14 | 25 | 40 |
| Freemen in each great ward | 23 | 25 | 26 | 26 |

The figures, which should be compared with those in Table 5.8, are again given as a percentage of the whole. The four miscellaneous tradesmen and those concerned with transport and woodwork are excluded as being too few for meaningful percentages to be applied. The numbers from which they are derived are given on page 64.

As with Henrician Norwich, the industrial character of the city can be made clearer by an examination of the occupational groupings which are most characteristic of each ward. In contrast to the earlier period, the relevant information is available for the great wards only. To make comparison easier, the percentages are given below for both 1525 and 1671.

Table 5.20 tells its own story. The leather and textile industries were of importance in each area of the city in both Henrician and Restoration Norwich. Textiles, which were of secondary importance in both Conesford and Mancroft in 1525, reigned supreme in every part of the city by 1671, while the proportion of leatherworkers employed remained remarkably constant throughout. The fortunes of the other crafts varied. The clothing industry, which was of importance in Mancroft alone in 1525, had risen to a position of some significance in all parts of the city by the later date. The drapers, grocers, mercers and merchants, who were the most important members of the distributive trades, in contrast, were of less importance numerically than their Henrician counterparts. They still featured among the leading trades in the wealthy wards of Mancroft and Wymer, but were no longer among the top five employing groups in Conesford and Ultra Aquam. A similar story is true of the food and drink trades. They remained an important minority group in Ultra Aquam and continued to be of significance in Conesford, if only because of the presence of the butchers there, but were no longer a major employer in Mancroft and Wymer in 1671. The fortunes of the building trades were equally varied, their story being one of decline in Conesford, of maintaining the *status quo* in Ultra Aquam, and of rising to a position of minor importance in Wymer. The metal trades, which were represented among the top five groupings in Wymer in 1525, had changed their venue by 1671 and were of primary importance in the great ward of Mancroft.

**Table 5.20 Occupational groupings most common to the city in 1525 and 1671**

|  | Great Ward | | | | | | | |
| Occupational grouping | Conesford | | Mancroft | | Wymer | | Ultra Aquam | |
|  | 1525 | 1671 | 1525 | 1671 | 1525 | 1671 | 1525 | 1671 |
| Building | 16 | 10 | - | - | - | 7 | 6 | 6 |
| Clothing | - | 11 | 13 | 12 | - | 14 | - | 8 |
| Distributive | 9 | - | 20 | 15 | 17 | 8 | 16 | - |
| Food & Drink | 22 | 16 | 16 | - | 12 | - | 7 | 6 |
| Leatherwork | 9 | 8 | 15 | 12 | 15 | 14 | 6 | 6 |
| Metalwork | - | - | - | 11 | 9 | - | - | - |
| Textiles | 21 | 38 | 16 | 23 | 24 | 40 | 55 | 64 |
| Percentages employed in major groupings | *77* | *83* | *80* | *73* | *77* | *83* | *90* | *90* |
| Number of freemen in each of the great wards | 157 | 327 | 130 | 364 | 224 | 376 | 183 | 376 |
| Percentages of freemen in each great ward | *23* | *23* | *19* | *25* | *32* | *26* | *26* | *26* |

As one would expect, the Norwich of 1671 had a greater variety of trades to offer than in 1525, and the increase in number from 78 to 106 is reflected throughout the city. In Mancroft the number of individual metal trades trebled and the building and distributive trades there doubled. Conesford, which in 1525 had tailors alone among its freemen in the clothing sphere, was a major centre for feltmakers in 1671 as well as sheltering hosiers and an upperbodymaker, and it housed twice as many representatives of the distributive trades as in the earlier period. Wymer was also a centre for feltmakers in Restoration Norwich, as well as providing employment for many of the city's hosiers, while Ultra Aquam was able to offer the services of nine distinct types of metalworker compared with the two which were present 150 years earlier.

Individual trades continued to concentrate in specific parts of the city. No fewer than 35 of the 43 butchers were to be found in the single ward of Conesford, which also housed a majority of the city's masons and, combined with Mancroft, the bulk of blacksmiths. Mancroft proved attractive as a residential area to a number of the Norwich freemen. By 1671 it contained: three-quarters of the painters and glaziers; most of the drapers and mercers, and almost half of the grocers; and the greater part of the city's cutlers, goldsmiths, locksmiths and pinners as well as individual spurriers and watchmakers. Combined with Wymer it was the major place of residence for the cordwainers and glovers among the leatherworkers, and the doctors and scriveners among the professional men; and with Ultra Aquam it shared the bulk of the dyers and carpenters. Wymer continued to attract the city's tanners as well as providing homes for the three vintners and many of the worsted weavers, while Ultra Aquam was the most important single area of the city's textile trades. Other occupations were spread equally throughout the city as a whole.

**Table 5.21 The number of different trades in each ward in 1525 and 1671**

| Occupational grouping | Great Ward | | | | | | | |
|---|---|---|---|---|---|---|---|---|
| | Conesford | | Mancroft | | Wymer | | Ultra Aquam | |
| | 1525 | 1671 | 1525 | 1671 | 1525 | 1671 | 1525 | 1671 |
| Building | 8 | 9 | 7 | 8 | 8 | 10 | 8 | 10 |
| Clothing | 1 | 4 | 3 | 4 | 2 | 5 | 2 | 2 |
| Distributive | 4 | 8 | 6 | 10 | 5 | 7 | 5 | 6 |
| Food & Drink | 7 | 5 | 7 | 5 | 6 | 7 | 3 | 5 |
| Leatherwork | 4 | 8 | 7 | 9 | 7 | 8 | 5 | 5 |
| Metalwork | 4 | 5 | 4 | 13 | 9 | 9 | 2 | 9 |
| Miscellaneous | - | - | 1 | 1 | - | 1 | - | 2 |
| Professional | 2 | 6 | 3 | 7 | 1 | 7 | 3 | 3 |
| Textiles | 8 | 9 | 7 | 8 | 8 | 10 | 8 | 10 |
| Transport | 4 | 1 | 1 | 1 | - | 1 | 2 | - |
| Woodwork | 2 | 3 | 2 | 1 | 4 | 3 | 2 | 1 |
| Totals | 44 | 58 | 48 | 67 | 50 | 68 | 40 | 53 |

While the importance of textiles in 17th-century Norwich can hardly be denied, much of the wealth in the city continued to be in the hands of its distributive traders and those concerned with food and drink and the professions. Their wealth reflects the continuing demand for the city's products from people outside its own confines and emphasises that, in many respects, Norwich was even more of a regional capital in the reign of Charles II than it had been in the reign of Elizabeth I. The Restoration city has been succinctly described by Macaulay.

It was the residence of a Bishop and of a chapter. It was the chief seat of the chief manufacture of the realm. Some men distinguished by learning and science had recently dwelt there; and no place in the kingdom, except the capital and the Universities, had more attractions for the curious. The library, the museum, the aviary and the botanical garden of Sir Thomas Browne, were thought by Fellows of the Royal Society well worthy of a long pilgrimage. Norwich had also a court in miniature.[58]

To the visitor, the more obvious signs of poverty were concealed. The traveller saw the wealth and affluence of both the great and not so great, and he was usually impressed. Sir John Harrington sums up the views of many:

I should judge this City to be another Utopia. The people live so orderly, the streets kept so cleanly, the tradesmen, young and old, so industrious, the better sort so provident and withal so charitable, that it is as rare to meet a beggar there, as it is common to see them in Westminster.[59]

## Chapter Six

# The Government and Governing Classes of Norwich, 1525-1625

## I

The men who ruled Tudor and Stuart Norwich were the inheritors of a system of government which had its origins in the days of the Plantagenets. The city received its original charter during the reign of Henry II, but the first of any real significance was the one granted in 1194 which gave the municipality its independence. It authorised the citizens to take burgage rents, tolls and profits of the borough court for themselves in exchange for a fee-farm rent of £108, and at the same time gave them the right to elect a reeve, coroners and other subordinate officials and to hold a leet or local court. Forty years later, in the reign of Henry III, the reeve was replaced by four bailiffs, a move connected with the assumption of leet, or police, jurisdiction by the citizens. The city was divided into four leets, the bailiffs acting in the dual capacity of city heads and police officers.[1]

Succeeding charters confirmed these major privileges and occasionally added to them, and by the end of the 13th century a well-defined class of leading citizens had come into being on whom fell the burden of the city's administration. By 1378 this body, the most prominent of whom were the 24 who sat in the assembly, were seeking to accumulate power in their own hands rather than share it with the community as a whole. The refusal of Richard II to grant their request for a mayor caused them to espouse the cause of the future Henry IV, and in return for their support he promised them the desired charter.

The granting of the charter in January 1404 was an important landmark in the city's history. It transformed the citizens from a self-governing community in which each of them had at least a theoretical voice in the government and administration into that of a body under the virtually permanent control of a magistracy combined, for legislative purposes, with a limited number of elected representatives.

In the process Norwich was elevated to the dignity of a county in its own right, a status already achieved by Bristol in 1372, York in 1397 and Newcastle in 1400. The bailiffs were replaced by a mayor and two sheriffs, the governing body being henceforth described as 'The mayor, sheriffs, citizens and commonalty of the city of Norwich'. Later in the year the charter was supplemented by an act of assembly which created a body of 80 citizens, but disputes over the relative authority of aldermen and councillors in the early years of Henry V's reign led the ruling body to request the arbitration of its leading citizen, Sir Thomas Erpingham. His decisions, recorded in a document known as the Composition of 1415, represent the final stage in the development of the city's government.[2] The 24 were confirmed as the major legislative body, but it was agreed that they should enact nothing binding on the city without the consent of the commonalty, and that all ordinances passed by them and the mayor should be declared to the common council, or lower house, by the recorder or his deputy. The councillors, now reduced to 60, were to be allowed time for deliberation before giving assent.

The situation which had evolved in Norwich was succinctly described by a nameless writer about the close of the 17th century.

The Government of the City consists of 24 Aldermen, out of which is yearly chosen on the first of May and sworn the Tuesday before St John the Baptist (if it happens not to fall on a Wednesday) a Mayor who is a Justice of the Peace and quorum during the year of his Mayoralty and after a

Justice of the Peace during his life. It also hath two Sheriffs chosen the last day in August and sworn on Michaelmas Day. The Mayor and Aldermen keep Court twice in the week to hear complaints and order such things as concern the peace and well governing of the city on Wednesday and Saturday. The Sheriffs also keep Court on Wednesdays and Fridays to try actions of debt and trespass between man and man, they have also Assistant to them two learned Lawyers in Commission of the Peace and quorum whereof one is Recorder and the other Steward. The Recorder assisteth the Court of the Mayor and Aldermen and the Steward in the Sheriffs' Court is as Chief Judge, although the Sheriffs and Steward are called into the Mayor's Court as often as occasion serveth. The Corporation consisteth of the Mayor, Sheriffs and Aldermen with the Commonalty which are of the number of 60 chosen out of the Commons to be of the Assembly with the Mayor to consult and enact, pass and determine anything which concerns the state of the city. The stated days of the Assembly are four, St Matthew, St Matthias, May 3rd and the day before the swearing of the new Mayor, and they are summoned by the Mayor to meet at other times and upon any emergent occasion.[3]

The Norwich system of government was broadly similar to that which had developed in towns such as York, Exeter, Worcester and Oxford, varying only in the numbers appointed to the two bodies and the relative importance of the lower house.[4] As in Norwich, the senior citizen in York and Exeter was the mayor whereas bailiffs continued to be appointed in the smaller towns of Worcester and Oxford. In the East Anglian city the numbers of aldermen and common councillors remained constant. In York, in contrast, the numbers of councillors fluctuated and were sometimes fewer than the official twenty-four.[5]

The common councillors of Norwich, who were apportioned according to the size of their particular ward, were elected in the week following the fifth Sunday in Lent.[6] Like their compatriots in Oxford, a majority of them would have served as ward constable before election, fewer than one in five avoiding this office in the 16th century.[7] There was no guarantee of regular tenure of office nor, in most cases, was it desired. Some men were rejected after serving the community for a single year, others were regularly re-elected. Continuity of service normally implied that the person concerned was a potential alderman, but there are cases of individuals serving for several years and never achieving higher status, even when they were wealthy and had not sought to avoid the office.

Aldermanic service was normally for life and elections were thus intermittent. When they did occur, a man could be chosen from any part of the city to represent a particular ward, in contrast to the councillors, who were drawn exclusively from the areas in which they lived and who were expected to resign if they moved to a different part of the town.[8]

The election of the sheriffs was left to the Chamber, one being chosen by the mayor and aldermen, the other by the common councillors. For a majority, such election was the prelude to admittance to the upper house whenever a vacancy occurred. Whether potential aldermen or not, however, election to the shrievalty almost invariably followed a period of service as a common councillor and never coincided with such service, although occasionally a person was elected sheriff before serving as either common councillor or alderman.[9] Councillors apart, there were always some aldermen who had yet to attain the shrievalty and the sheriffs could thus be drawn exclusively from the aldermanic body, from previous common councillors, or from a combination of both. The sheriffs were primarily responsible for the judicial aspects of city administration and for the payment of the fee farm rent. They were aided by the under-sheriff, appointed from the city's scriveners, who acted as sheriffs' clerk, making entries, records and returns; by the sheriffs' sergeants, who executed plaints or received them to present to the court and who served distresses and warrants; and by attorneys who were bound to give true counsel to clients, to be obedient to the sheriffs and court, and to attend all courts of oyer and terminer, of gaol delivery and of quarter sessions. About 1520 these officials were supplemented by a steward who was appointed a legal adviser to the sheriffs in the same way as the recorder was to the mayor.[10] Apart from dealing with petty offences in their own court, the sheriffs' biggest responsibility was the payment of the fee farm rent. They were given £30 towards the cost of this and every sheriff claimed unspecified perquisites of office at his election, but most of them were out of pocket at the end of their year's service.[11] For the ambitious, the major reward was the prospect of ultimate election to the mayoralty, a position open only to a person who was both a serving alderman and a past sheriff.

The mayor, appointed from one of two aldermen nominated by the freemen, was supreme in all departments. As chief magistrate he was responsible for maintaining the city's laws and keeping the peace, a position in which he was advised by the recorder, and as clerk of the markets he was expected to deal with regulations concerning food. His immediate assistants were his brother aldermen. Further assistance came from the mayor's sergeants who were primarily concerned with market regulations, and the ward constables who were responsible for keeping the peace.

The expenses incurred by the mayor were normally so onerous that only a really wealthy man could afford to serve. No more than one in three of the aldermen appointed during Elizabeth's reign filled the office, and a further nine (13 per cent) became mayor during the early Stuart period. A similar number (32) were elected sheriff but never mayor while six aldermen attained neither position. Eight of the Elizabethan mayors served twice, six on three occasions, but after 1620 a man could legally serve once only.

Although there was no lack of candidates for high office, the cost was more than some could bear and throughout the 16th and 17th centuries both aldermen and common councillors sought to avoid the more exacting positions. The assembly was always paid for avoidance of duty. An alderman, once elected, was fined £40 if he declined to serve. Fines for asking to be relieved of the shrievalty for various periods ranged from £10 to £20 in the Elizabethan period and rose to as high as £50 during the succeeding 50 years. Attempts to avoid the mayoralty normally involved a penalty of twice as much.[12]

21. Peter Read, 1568, son of Edward Rede or Read. He was knighted by Charles V at the siege of Tunis, a knighthood which was not recognised in England.

Wealthy though those accepting office may have been, the mayors still found the cost of office burdensome and their salary was increased at intervals throughout Elizabeth's reign, after which it remained static. Beginning at £20 it was raised to £33 6s. 8d. in 1566, and by 1573 it had been increased again to £52 for the first two mayoralties and to £66 13s. 4d. for a third. Further increases were made in 1582 and 1594. In the former year the salary of a man serving for a second time was set at £66 13s. 4d., while in the latter it was ordained that a man serving for a third time should be paid £100. By 1594 there were thus distinct salaries for men serving for the first, second or third time, and by the turn of the century £100 had become the fixed fee for any period of mayoral service.[13]

Despite the expenses involved, the attainment of the mayoralty was the pinnacle of fame and in the ambitious Elizabethan age, in particular, it was a prize that was eagerly sought. A man was nominated for the position by virtue of his standing in the community, and there was no question of his being chosen by virtue of his seniority alone. Sufficiency of wealth was an absolute pre-requisite. Given this, the mayors tended to be chosen from either the senior alderman who had yet to pass the chair or from those who had already achieved this status. There is no doubt, however, that the freemen had their favourites and they sought, whenever possible, to get them into office. As tradition demanded that the senior of the two nominated should be chosen, except when a man had served previously, it was not difficult for the electorate to nominate someone of their choice and match him with a man who had entered the aldermanic body at a later date. This eventually led to younger men being appointed ahead of their elders, and the latter's protests sparked off the constitutional crisis discussed later in the chapter. Before considering this, it will be useful to look at both the common councillors and the aldermen in greater detail.

## II

Theoretically, any person who was the son of a freeman, who had served an apprenticeship with a freeman, or who had brought his freedom after entry into the city from outside, was eligible for election to the common council. In practice, this basic qualification had to be supplemented by adequate wealth and membership of an acceptable trade. Adequate wealth, by the standards of the 1525 subsidy, meant possession of an absolute minimum of £5 worth of moveable goods, and a place among the wealthiest quarter of the city's population. Membership of an acceptable trade restricted the choice of candidates to those following between forty and fifty of the trades practised in the city, and almost invariably to those engaged in fewer than half of those occupations. In practice this excluded most of the handicraftmen, for few of them were capable of meeting the basic financial requirements.

The 60 common councillors were divided into three almost equal groups according to their wealth, the so-called 'first, second and third sorts' who were referred to whenever a rate was levied. The twenty or so men who were the richest among them possessed wealth comparable to, and sometimes in excess of, that owned by many of the aldermanic body, and were the natural successors of their seniors in the upper house. The middle group included those who were willing and able to devote many years of their lives to civic responsibilities. Those in the third category mainly comprised the craftsmen among the councillors, men who could spare little time for civic duties and who returned to their own onerous tasks as soon as circumstances permitted. Some of the councillors, of course, were in a transitional stage and could expect to accumulate greater wealth and, if inclination and opportunity permitted, a correspondingly higher place in the social scale. Others had achieved all that they were likely to achieve and were content to maintain the *status quo*. There is some evidence that the threefold division among the councillors was deliberately maintained. In the 1520s those completing their period of service were almost always replaced by men of similar standing, and the same phenomenon can be detected, although with less certainty, in the 1670s.[14]

Where occupations are concerned, the ruling classes of Norwich, whether aldermen or councillors, were almost invariably drawn from the same dozen occupations. Worsted weavers, bakers, drapers, grocers, mercers and scriveners were nearly always represented, in varying numbers, among the common councillors. Scarcely less common were the brewers, butchers, goldsmiths, tanners, tailors and – after 1561 – cordwainers.[15] Even among this elite certain crafts predominated. The grocers and mercers were outstanding in the 16th century, and the grocers continued to be the dominant trading group until finally ousted by the worsted weavers in the second half of the 17th century. The fortunes of the latter trade waxed and waned according to the state of the economy. Even at its nadir people made sufficient from the trade to find a place on the city council, and at its zenith worsted weavers comprised almost one-third of the whole common council. In the middle years of the 17th century the Ward across the Water, or Ultra Aquam, was almost wholly represented by worsted weavers and several were to be found among the 20 representatives of the great ward of Wymer.

**Table 6.1 Occupational groupings of all common councillors not proceeding to aldermanic rank**

A = 1526-1550      D = 1601-1625
B = 1551-1575      E = 1626-1650
C = 1576-1600      F = 1651-1675

| Occupational grouping | A | B | C | D | E | F |
|---|---|---|---|---|---|---|
| Textiles | 46 | 19 | 13 | 17 | 33 | 50 |
| *percentage* | *28.39* | *13.67* | *12.74* | *19.77* | *28.70* | *37.88* |
| Distributive | 45 | 41 | 33 | 33 | 35 | 30 |
| *percentage* | *27.78* | *29.50* | *32.35* | *38.37* | *30.43* | *22.73* |
| Food & Drink | 19 | 21 | 19 | 11 | 18 | 15 |
| *percentage* | *11.73* | *15.11* | *18.63* | *12.79* | *15.65* | *11.36* |
| Building | 11 | 5 | 4 | 1 | 2 | 4 |
| *percentage* | *6.79* | *3.60* | *3.92* | *1.63* | *1.74* | *3.03* |
| Metalwork | 11 | 10 | 4 | 3 | 6 | 10 |
| *percentage* | *6.79* | *7.19* | *3.92* | *3.49* | *5.22* | *7.57* |
| Leatherwork | 10 | 15 | 10 | 7 | 10 | 7 |
| *percentage* | *6.17* | *10.79* | *9.80* | *8.14* | *8.70* | *5.30* |
| Clothing | 7 | 14 | 11 | 4 | 7 | 9 |
| *percentage* | *4.32* | *10.07* | *10.78* | *4.65* | *6.09* | *6.82* |
| Professional | 7 | 5 | 6 | 7 | 4 | 7 |
| *percentage* | *4.32* | *3.60* | *5.88* | *8.14* | *3.48* | *5.30* |
| Transport | 3 | 6 | 1 | 3 | - | - |
| *percentage* | *1.85* | *4.32* | *0.98* | *3.49* | - | - |
| Woodwork | 3 | 3 | 1 | - | - | - |
| *percentage* | *1.85* | *2.16* | *0.98* | - | - | - |
| Unspecified | 24 | 5 | 4 | 1 | 3 | 1 |
| Totals | 186 | 144 | 106 | 87 | 118 | 133 |
| No. of different trades | 42 | 39 | 36 | 29 | 28 | 41 |

Given the requirements noted above, any man was eligible for election by the freemen of the ward concerned. Quite often an opulent outsider was chosen, a qualified tradesmen who had opted to reside in the city and had purchased his freedom from the authorities. In the last quarter of the 16th century, the first period in which we have sufficient statistical material on which to base an opinion, more than one-third of the people elected to the council came from this background. The aldermanic body was never entirely happy with the position and, more in an effort to protect the local tradesman from outside competition than to change the composition of the council, passed an ordinance in 1622 which restricted the number of non-apprentices to four per year. As in so many cases, the ordinance was not strictly adhered to, but it was sufficient of a deterrent to reduce the numbers of such people.

In the first quarter of the 17th century the proportion of non-apprentice common councillors dropped to 18 per cent of the total, falling to 15 per cent during the Restoration period.

Many of the local-born representatives either came from families with a background of civic service or were apprenticed to men who had devoted part of their working life to a period as alderman or councillor. The proportion was as high as two-thirds during the period 1576-1600, but thereafter it fell gradually, dropping a century later to just under one-half. Not infrequently, son followed father as a common councillor. In some cases three and even four generations served the city. In the process they contributed to the creation of the dynasties which sprang up in the 16th century in particular, and which are discussed in more detail below.[16]

A minority of freemen came from sufficiently substantial backgrounds to embark on a civic career almost as soon as they had completed their apprenticeships.[17] They never numbered more than five per cent of those elected as common councillors during any 25-year period, and they were almost invariably drawn from the wealthier trades of grocer and mercer. Most men had to wait longer for their first experience of local government, an experience almost always preceded by service as a ward constable, but between 1526 and 1575 almost sixty per cent of those elected had begun their service within ten years of becoming a freeman. Subsequently this became exceptional, the proportion falling below 30 per cent in the second quarter of the 17th century. In contrast, the number of those who began their civic careers in middle, or even old, age rose steadily. In the period ending in 1550 14 per cent of the councillors were elected when they had been freemen for more than twenty years. The proportion fell to five per cent in the succeeding 25 years but thereafter rose steadily to reach almost one-third in the Civil War years and as high as 36 per cent during the Commonwealth and Restoration periods. In extreme cases, in both the first and last periods under discussion, men were elected to serve as common councillors who had been freemen for between forty and fifty years, and who were thus anything between sixty-five and seventy-five years of age.[18]

Under such circumstances service was unlikely to be lengthy. In the early 16th century, however, whether a man was young or old his period as a common councillor tended to be brief. Two-thirds of the men elected between 1526 and 1550 completed their service within a five-year span, and of these some twenty per cent served for a single year. Short service was a phenomenon peculiar to all classes of society, whether they were humble craftsmen or wealthy members of the merchant guilds, and is partly explained by the depressed state of the city's economy in those years. As the situation improved, first under the auspices of the grocers and other men catering for those wishing to be entertained in the provincial capital, and subsequently with the revival of the textile trades, service became progressively longer. Men could afford to devote more of their time to civic affairs and short service gradually became the exception rather than the rule. By the end of the 16th century the percentage of councillors serving for five years or less had fallen to 39 and in the succeeding 25 years it fell still further to just under one quarter. Thereafter there was a relapse and by the first decade of Charles II's reign the proportion of people serving for short periods of time had risen to 47 per cent, a situation largely brought about by the disruptions of the Civil War and Restoration.

As service increased in the century before the Civil War the number of men elected inevitably fell. By James I's reign the proportion of councillors willing and able to serve for between eleven and twenty years had trebled, and the proportion of those serving in excess of this had increased fivefold. The change is clearly reflected in the numbers elected. Between 1526 and 1550 186 men were chosen as common councillors; during the 25 years ending in 1625 the number had fallen to eighty-seven.[19]

Some councillors devoted most of their working lives to serving the community, the 42 years served by Thomas Cony, a grocer of Wymer ward, being only the most exceptional of many. Periods in excess of twenty-five and thirty years were by no means infrequent. Most people, whether by personal inclination or the whim of the electors, served on one occasion only. Between 1526 and 1550 some sixty per cent of the men elected did not return for a further term. The proportion fell to 52 per cent in the third quarter of the 16th century but thereafter rose steadily until by the Restoration era over 88 per cent of the common councillors met their commitment with a single period of service. It follows that, with the exception of the period 1651-75, between thirty and forty per cent of the councillors were returned for a further period of service in subsequent years. Sometimes a second term sufficed, sometimes a third, but until well into Elizabeth's reign men were occasionally elected to serve for a fourth, fifth or even sixth time.

Among the latter were John Pettus, a tailor of Wymer ward, who, although devoting no more than eight years to civic service, was elected five times between 1533 and 1557, and was followed by a son and two grandsons, all of whom became aldermen and mayors of the city; James Lynne, a tanner of the same ward, who was elected six times and served for a total of 24 years between 1531 and 1564; and Edward Pye, a worsted weaver, who represented his ward on five occasions between 1553 and 1580 and completed 20 years of service in the process. Pye, like Pettus, began a tradition of service to the community. John Pye, baker, was returned on four occasions between 1554 and 1588, serving for a total of 13 years, while Edward's sons, Henry and Thomas, both became aldermen of the city. Henry died young having spent 10 years of his life as a councillor and three as an alderman, but Thomas represented his ward for 51 years between 1574 and 1625, including 40 years as an alderman. He was mayor in 1597. Other families who served the city for an extended period included the two branches of the Cock family which produced four aldermen and five councillors between 1526 and 1682, the Skottowes, who had five members of the family serving at various times between 1585 and 1655, and, above all, the Sothertons who provided Norwich with four common councillors and seven aldermen between 1520 and 1664, none of whom served for less than twelve years.

It was from among men of this sort, and not from the rank and file of the common councillors, that the various city offices were filled. Little more than one quarter of those elected as councillors were ever called upon to serve in an official capacity and, significantly, those selected were almost invariably drawn from the wealthier wards of Mancroft and Wymer and were usually members of the merchant guilds.

The offices of chamberlain, foreign receiver and common speaker were filled exclusively by members of the lower house, the first two of these following a period of service as a common councillor. Five others, those of sheriff, clavor, auditor, coroner and counsellor to the chamber, were shared by councillors and aldermen alike. The mayoralty alone was confined to members of the upper house. Of those offices filled solely by common councillors, that of chamberlain was the most prestigious by far. The holder was responsible for husbanding the city's fortunes, and could rely on assistance from the clavors, or city treasurers, only in times of real emergency. The foreign receiver, as the name implies, was originally concerned with collecting the admission fees of those admitted to the freedom of the city from outside its confines, but his duties were widened to include all sums paid by those taking up their freedom. The common speaker was the 'link-man' between the upper and lower houses, and beyond exercising this task he was a person of no great significance. Most posts were held for a single year, although a person could be returned for a second term of office. Those of coroner, chamberlain and foreign receiver sometimes remained in the same hands for an extended period.[20]

22.  The interior of the hall of Strangers' Hall, home of the Sotherton family.

23.  The exterior of the hall of Strangers' Hall, 1842.

24. The courtyard of Strangers' Hall.

Of posts open to aldermen and councillors alike, that of sheriff was by far the most important. It was a pre-requisite for attainment of the mayoralty and, in practice, it had become the virtual gateway to promotion as alderman. As early as the last decades of Henry VIII's reign some 62 per cent of the aldermen had been appointed sheriff before elevation to the upper house. By the end of the 16th century the proportion had risen to 81 per cent and it reached its peak of 89 per cent in the succeeding 25 years. Before the end of that period the position had been officially recognised. In 1620 complaints had reached the ears of the king that far too many younger men were usurping the authority of their elders, and that some were elected mayor with scarcely any aldermanic service. The dispute was essentially an aldermanic one and, as such, is dealt with in greater detail below, but its aftermath led to changes which made the shrievalty of even greater importance. James I, in letters to the mayor and corporation, stipulated that from henceforth every person promoted to aldermanic rank should be a past or present sheriff.[21]

## III

Compared to the aldermanic body of London which, by the 17th century, demanded a £10,000 property qualification and fines of between £600 and £1,000 for refusal to serve, the Norwich body was relatively liberal.[22] The transition from councillor to alderman was by no means an easy one, however. All of the stipulations applying to prospective members of the common council applied to those aspiring to admittance to the upper house, but they were applied much more stringently. Those ultimately elected were normally wealthier, were drawn from fewer trades, usually had experience of local government sooner than the majority of their fellows and, in the earlier period at least, were much more likely to have come from families with a background of civic service.

If the 1525 subsidy can again be used as a guide, a prospective alderman would need to be in possession of at least £40 worth of moveable goods, the minimum amount on which any alderman was assessed in that year. Possession of such a sum would have placed him among the richest third of the common councillors at his election, but his fortune would have been small compared to that amassed by his elders. He would be sitting cheek by jowl with men taxed on goods worth anything from £100 to £1,000 and who, at their wealthiest, had few peers in East Anglia.

Membership of a suitable trade was absolutely essential at this level, and most aspiring aldermen would be members of the merchant classes, following such occupations as grocer, mercer and draper. Between 1526 and 1625 men drawn from such trades comprised between two-thirds and three-quarters of the entire aldermanic body. It was only in the second half of the 17th century that members of the textile trades, in effect worsted weavers, came into their own, and even then they captured no more than 38 per cent of the seats. The proportion of merchants on the aldermanic bench was more than halved, however, the residue being held mainly by representatives of the food and drink and metal trades.

**Table 6.2 Occupational groupings of all aldermen elected between 1526 and 1675**

| Occupational grouping | 1526-50 | 1551-75 | 1576-1600 | 1601-25 | 1626-50 | 1651-75 |
|---|---|---|---|---|---|---|
| Distributive | 28 | 34 | 28 | 18 | 33 | 8 |
| percentage | 70.00 | 77.27 | 75.68 | 64.29 | 60.00 | 27.59 |
| Textiles | 5 | 1 | 2 | 2 | 10 | 11 |
| percentage | 12.50 | 2.27 | 5.40 | 7.14 | 18.18 | 37.93 |
| Food & drink | 3 | 4 | 1 | 2 | 4 | 4 |
| percentage | 7.50 | 9.09 | 2.70 | 7.14 | 7.27 | 13.79 |
| Professional | 2 | 1 | 2 | 4 | 1 | 1 |
| percentage | 5.00 | 2.27 | 5.40 | 14.28 | 1.82 | 3.45 |
| Clothing | 1 | 4 | 2 | - | 6 | 2 |
| percentage | 2.50 | 9.09 | 5.40 | - | 10.91 | 6.90 |
| Metalwork | 1 | - | 2 | 1 | 1 | 3 |
| percentage | 2.50 | - | 5.40 | 3.57 | 1.82 | 10.34 |
| Leatherwork | - | - | - | 1 | - | - |
| percentage | - | - | - | 3.57 | - | - |
| Unspecified | - | 1 | - | - | - | - |
| Totals | 40 | 45 | 37 | 28 | 55 | 29 |
| Number of different trades | 13 | 14 | 11 | 11 | 14 | 13 |

As well as being wealthier and drawn from fewer trades, the aldermanic body contained far more men with a background of civic service. More than twice as many aldermen as councillors had parents who had served the city before them, and many of the rest had been apprenticed to men with such a background. There was always a proportion of outsiders among them, men who had come to the city from elsewhere and purchased their freedom, and on occasion they were sufficiently affluent and influential to be elected to the aldermanic body without having served previously as a common councillor. These apart, it was rare for a man to enter the upper house whose father or former master had not been there before him, the proportion being as low as three to four per cent between 1576 and 1625. The purges of the Civil War and Restoration periods brought an abrupt end to the traditional picture. One-third of those elected during the reigns of Charles I and II were sons of neither alderman nor councillor, and their masters had never been called upon to serve in any capacity whatsoever.[23]

Men destined to become aldermen began their civic careers much earlier, on the whole, than their less ambitious, or less wealthy, counterparts. In the last decades of Henry's VIII's reign almost 60 per cent of the future members of the upper house were elected common councillors within five years of becoming freemen, and four out of five of them had achieved this status within 10 years. In the succeeding 25 years the proportions rose to 69 and 87 per cent respectively, and to the end of James I's reign it was still possible for some seven out of every 10 prospective aldermen to achieve councillor status within 10 years of becoming a master craftsman. Thereafter the situation changed. Four out of every 10 aldermen in the second quarter of the 17th century had been councillors for more than fifteen years before achieving promotion, a proportion which increased to 60 per cent in the Commonwealth and Restoration periods.[24]

Except possibly during the Civil War years, prospective aldermen were normally recognised as such from the outset of their political careers. On election to the council they were usually placed at the head of the list of members. They were described as 'Mr.', or titular gentlemen, and were promoted as soon as an aldermanic vacancy occurred. Sometimes this was quite soon. In the reigns of both Henry VIII and Charles II some three-quarters of them achieved aldermanic status within ten years of becoming a common councillor, and for 40 per cent of them promotion occurred within five years. In the intervening years progress was less rapid, and under both Elizabeth and James I between one-third and one-half of the potential members of the upper house had to wait for periods in excess of ten years before they achieved their aim. Despite the purges of the 1640s, the Civil War did little to alter this pattern.[25]

Once a man had achieved aldermanic status he had tenure for life unless he transgressed in some way, and then his brother aldermen had the right to remove him. Removals before the Civil War were rare. In 1598 Cuthbert Brereton was dismissed for inadequate service, and also towards the end of Elizabeth's reign Nicholas Sotherton and Sir Robert Wood were disfranchised for insisting on living outside the city.[26] There were some anomalies, however. During the 1520s and 1530s Thomas Moore, a wealthy draper of Mancroft ward, regularly alternated between councillor and aldermanic service. Moore was elected to the common council in 1501, the year after he had attained his freedom and served as a constable, and between then and 1531 he served the city for 20 years as a councillor, alternating this with seven years of service as an alderman for both St Giles' and St Stephen's wards. He was essentially a 'link-man', appointed until someone else was willing and able to take his place. He finally avoided this somewhat anomalous situation in 1532 when he paid £20 to be dispensed from the offices of both alderman and mayor, but his services to the city were not yet over and he served for a further 11 years as common councillor between 1534 and 1545. Moore's career was almost unique. Its nearest parallel was that of Anthony

Style, mercer and notary, who twice served as councillor for Mancroft ward between 1559 and 1565, served as alderman for St Stephen's between 1565 and 1567, and returned as councillor for his ward for a further two periods between 1567 and 1568.

Aldermanic election was normally a peaceful affair and, the Civil War years apart, there were only two disputed elections during the whole of the 16th and 17th centuries. Both resulted from the normally passive freeman body showing its teeth, and both had to be resolved by central government intervention.

The first of these occurred in 1595 with the nomination of one William Peters, mercer, for the vacancy in St Stephen's ward. Peters had all the obvious attributes of an alderman. He had served as sheriff in 1590, was a member of a prestigious trade, and had twice represented his ward as a common councillor. Despite this, the aldermanic body rejected him, claiming that he had been elected by 'many of the inferyor sorte . . . who exceded the nombre of the most fytt and hablest men in the saide warde' and that 'for diverse consider-acions best knowne to themselves and not fytt here to be expressed' his election would not be ratified. The place was left void for a year, and when the upper house again rejected him at the end of this time Peters took out a writ in Chancery to compel them to concede the point. The aldermen took their stance on 'charter and ancient custom' which allowed the mayor the right to disallow an election, and they were supported in this by Sir Thomas Egerton, Lord Keeper of the Great Seal of England, who duly cancelled the writ. Despite having the legal situation explained to them by the city's steward, 'the meane sorte of the inhabitants . . . did of a hedy wilfulnes preache and cotynewe their former nomynacion', which was just as promptly rejected. Ultimately, at another meeting of the inhabitants, held on 19 October 1596, a man acceptable to the aldermanic body was elected, and his election was ratified four days later.

The man elected, one George Downing, had been admitted a freeman of the city only four days before his election to aldermanic rank. He was not apprenticed, and thus, almost certainly, not a native of Norwich. He served as sheriff two years later and attained the mayoralty in 1609. The speed with which he was elected, and the presence of more of the 'better sort', implies that some financial gain to the city was anticipated, but this is pure speculation. Peters had little alternative but to accept defeat and he continued to serve his ward as a common councillor for a further 12 years, finally disappearing from the lists in 1608.

The second clash between the aldermen and the electors of a particular ward occurred some thirty years later, and was a direct consequence of the constitutional changes of the 1620s. These are discussed more fully below, and it is sufficient to note here that in 1620 it was agreed that from henceforth the mayors of the city should be chosen exclusively from the senior aldermen, a principle well established in London, and that all future aldermen should be elected from the senior of the surviving sheriffs in a ward. In other words, once a man was elected sheriff he was bound to be ultimately elected mayor, assuming that he lived long enough. Such changes meant that the Peters incident could not be repeated. If a man was legally elected as sheriff nothing the aldermen could do would prevent his ultimate election to the upper house, and it was thus more imperative than ever that he should be of suitable standing.

As it happened, the constitutional changes occurred at a time when both the common councillors and the electorate in general were becoming increasingly aware of their potential power. It was the nomination of men relatively new to the aldermanry as prospective mayors which had led the king to insist on the changes referred to above. As their hands were tied in this respect after 1620, the electors determined to make their presence felt at the elections to the shrievalty. The crisis came in 1627 when the aldermanic choice of sheriff proved unacceptable to the electorate at large. In retaliation 'a great multitude of mechanical men and other citizens of meanest quality' nominated one John Kettle, basketmaker, as their man. Kettle, a former servant of Sir Charles Cornwallis, had been admitted to the freedom, non-apprentice (i.e. by redemption), in 1609. He was a born trouble-maker. At intervals, his name appears in the court books charged with obstructing the market place, refusing to contribute to the poor rate, abusing the aldermanry and accusing them of corruption. It is hardly surprising that they were totally opposed to the election of a man they described as 'so unworthy of a place of magistracy [and] so rude and uncivil as he is not fit for common society, a man so addicted to railing and drunkenness as he hath been often bound to his good behaviour and yet never reformed . . .'

In the event, Kettle was defeated by 10 votes in the ensuing poll, significantly by Thomas Atkins, a leading Puritan and future Lord Mayor of London. The threatened disruption which followed Kettle's defeat led the authorities to appeal to the Privy Council who declared the election valid and cast Kettle into the Fleet Prison for a period. After his release he was ordered to return to Norwich, to make humble submission to the mayor and corporation, and pay a fine of £40 for refusing to contribute to the mayor's feast. Kettle sought the aid of his former patron, Sir Charles Cornwallis, and both men, with some servants of Cornwallis, appeared before the court to dispute the validity of the judgment. Kettle was eventually obliged to submit, but not before he had again abused the corporation and Cornwallis' grandson and some of his servants had abused the mayor to his face.[27]

An event such as this could not be allowed to create a precedent and the magistrates made a further appeal to the Privy council, this time to have the commons' sheriff chosen by the councillors alone rather than by the whole body of the freemen, and for the aldermen to be chosen from the whole body of sheriffs rather than from the most ancient in rank. The Privy Council agreed to the request, although it seems that the freeman body continued to participate in elections.

The aldermanic body seldom had cause to examine the antecedents of its members. Not only were they socially acceptable but by the Elizabethan period they were virtually a closed caste. Eleven families predominated in the later 16th century, nearly all of whom had origins outside the city. Four families, the Anguishes, Barretts, Davies and Layers, were gentle in origin; five others, the Ferrors, Hyrnes, Mingays, Sothertons and Sucklings came from yeoman stock; the Aldriches were descended from bailiffs of Great Yarmouth and the Pettus clan from lesser Norwich tradesmen. Eight of these families were connected by marriage and the Pettus and Sotherton families, although not connected to the main group, were related to other aldermanic families, the Sothertons being linked to no fewer than 11 of them. Between them, the 11 major families produced 31 generations of

25.  Thomas Layer, mayor 1576 and M.P. 1586.

Norwich aldermen and 28 mayors. At one stage, if one includes connection by apprenticeship, 23 of the 24 aldermen were linked together in one way or another.[28]

Although many of them served as aldermen for a number of years, none of the men concerned showed any desire to forge permanent links with the city. In common with members of the merchant classes in other towns they sought connections with the land, and the length of their stay reflects their success or otherwise in doing so. Three broad phases can be detected in this transformation. In the first of these, which ended around 1550, the aldermen were recruited almost exclusively from the merchant class and had little or no social connections with the surrounding gentry. Civic affairs absorbed much of their time, and if they invested their money it was almost always in property within the city walls, few aldermen buying land outside the city boundaries.

In the Elizabethan period an increasing number of aldermen began to invest their money in landed estates outside the city, albeit within a distance of fifteen miles or so. The amount of land purchased grew steadily year by year. Manors, rectories, advowsons, tenements, meadows, pastures, mills and marshes came into aldermanic hands. When manors were bought, branches of the leading families frequently settled in the country and became respected members of the minor gentry. With the exception of Sir Robert Wood, none of these men were knighted, none became sheriffs of the county, and very few married members of the greater Norfolk families.

This tendency increased sharply during the 17th century, and in the process the ruling group gradually changed from an exclusively merchant class to one with more connections with the county aristocracy. Far more of the aldermen had gentle origins and they tended to marry into their own class, 14 such alliances taking place in this period compared to four in the previous half century. In consequence, several of them became heads of gentry families in their own right. Three of the city's aldermen – Sir Thomas Hyrne, Sir John Pettus and Sir Peter Gleane – became sheriffs of the county, having already served the city in this capacity.[29] The first of these is a perfect example of the rapid rise to pre-eminence of a family not of gentle stock. Sir Thomas Hyrne's grandfather was a yeoman of Drayton, a village just outside Norwich. The yeoman's son, Clement was apprenticed in Norwich as a grocer, and he subsequently prospered and rose to aldermanic rank. At his death he bequeathed £1,305 in cash, a number of houses, and a manor at Haveringland which Thomas inherited.[29] The latter's rise was meteoric. He took up his freedom as the city's first ironmonger on 16 October, 1596, succeeded to his father's place as alderman five days later, was sheriff within less than a year and served the first of his three terms as mayor seven years later.[30] Ultimately, he became the first man to serve as sheriff of both city and county, was knighted by James I and represented his native city in parliament.

Broadly speaking, those families which rose highest did so most rapidly, purchased the least amount of city property, and left Norwich for the county earlier than the other groups. This inevitably meant that they attained the shrievalty and mayoralty sooner than men many years their senior, both in age and civic service. Whereas in Elizabeth's reign a man had to have at least seven years' aldermanic experience, on average, before becoming mayor, at least one man in every subsequent decade attained this status in a shorter time. Richard Rosse, for example, became mayor in 1618 within one year of his election to the upper house. Others reached this position after three to five years aldermanic service. At the same time the average period of aldermanic service became shorter, but this can be explained almost entirely by the purges of the Civil War and Restoration periods. In the decade 1641-50 alone, 29 men, or twice the normal average, were elected to the aldermanry, and there was a similar turnover in the years immediately following 1660.

Partly, no doubt, because of their origins, the city assembly became increasingly title conscious during the 17th century. A man entering the council ranks as a gentleman was either placed at the top of the list or immediately below those of similar status, and was ready to step as quickly as possible into the shoes of an alderman. After 1620 those councillors appointed sheriff and thus, by definition, potential aldermen, were immediately designated gentlemen if they had not begun their civic service as such. From the 1640s all aldermen who had passed the chair were described as esquire, and those who could proclaimed their armigerous status.

Very few of the city's upper classes were descended from lesser tradesmen in the 17th century. It was much more common for men to enter Norwich sufficiently endowed to become wealthy merchants in the first generation. As in the 16th century, the civic careers of the major families spanned, at the most, some four generations. They usually began when a second son was sent to the city to begin his apprenticeship. Already having financial backing, he accumulated further wealth as he progressed to aldermanic status and eventually bought a manor and settled a branch of his family on it. That branch of the family would settle permanently on the land and have little or nothing to do with civic affairs. Other sons continued in city trade for a further two or three generations, providing more aldermen and mayors, but each generation sent some members out of Norwich. Eventually the last member of the family would retire to the country and that particular clan would cease to have direct contact with Norwich or with trade. Now much wealthier than before, the family owned many manors where previously they may have had one or none at all. They were accepted in local society and many married into the leading county families. Thus the Hyrnes formed associations with the Knyvetts, the Hobarts, the Bacons and the Pastons. The family of Mingay had ties with the Gawdys (twice), the Wentworths, the Jernegans, the Cokes and the Cornwallises. The Sucklings intermarried with the Drurys, the Woodhouses and the Knyvetts, the Sothertons with the Bacons, and the Pettus family with the Heveninghams, the Saltonstalls and the Knyvetts. In every case they had used their connection with Norwich trade to rise high in the county hierarchy.

The rise of the Hyrnes has already been charted. Of many other possible examples, another two can be cited to illustrate the general trend. The Mingays had their origins in the village of Shotesham, some seven miles to the south of Norwich. The first member of the family to move to Norwich was Robert, a cordwainer. He inherited some lands and tenements from his yeoman father but was able to add little to these, leaving no more than £26 in cash and two tenements in Norwich at his death in 1545. Of this meagre fortune, his son William was bequeathed the houses and £10, but he was a sound businessman. He had already climbed beyond his father's status by being apprenticed as a mercer, and he increased his patrimony by shrewd buying and selling of monastic lands. In due course he became an alderman and attained the mayoralty in 1561. At his death in 1564 he had enhanced the family fortunes to such a degree that he owned manors in both Norfolk and Suffolk, lands, tenements and a rectory at Shotesham and lands at Framingham. He was also able to bequeath more than £600 in cash. Significantly, with the exception of his Suffolk property, all of his land purchases were in the vicinity of the ancestral home at Shotesham. None of his three sons went into trade. Two became lawyers and a third became the squire of Arminghall. Another branch of the family was even more successful. John Mingay, nephew of William – whom he emulated as mayor in 1617 – and a Norwich apothecary, was able to purchase a manor at Swainsthorpe, just outside the city, lands and houses in Norwich, including the site of the Austin Friars on which he built three houses, and meadows and lands at Shotesham and Lakenham. At his death in 1625 he had three warehouses full of goods and a total of £3,777 in cash.[32]

The Pettus family, in contrast to the Mingays, had their origins in Norwich. Thomas, who died in 1491, was described as an 'opulent citizen'. His son John, referred to earlier in the chapter, was a member of the common council and married his daughter to Richard

26. *(left)* Sir John Pettus, 1612, aged 62. Mayor in 1608, Pettus was one of the few men to be sheriff of both city and county.

27. *(above)* A timber-framed house, all that remains of Pettus House, Elm Hill.

Corpusty, a Norwich alderman. His son, Thomas, joined his father as a common councillor, became an alderman in 1568, served the city as mayor in 1590, and before his death in 1598 had married into the Dethick family, gentry from South Elmham in Suffolk. Thomas prospered exceedingly during his civic career. At his death he owned the manor of Rackheath, purchased in 1591, two small manors near Worstead, houses and lands at Hethersett and Holt and in other parts of the county and, uniquely, houses and lands in London. He also bequeathed more than £2,000 in cash. Both of his sons followed him as aldermen and mayors of Norwich and one of them, John, was knighted in 1603. Sir John Pettus made a prosperous marriage with a Suffolk heiress and in due course both of his sons were knighted, one of whom, Sir Thomas Pettus, was appointed High Sheriff of Norfolk in 1632 and made a baronet nine years later.

While not every alderman aspired to a position among the leading families of the county, virtually all of them invested in land outside the city and either they, or their successors, took up residence there. With the notable exception of the Sothertons, few aldermanic families stayed in the city for more than three generations, a fact amply illustrated by the changing names of the members of the upper house. In this respect, they were emulating their peers elsewhere, and allowed for an influx of new blood and new attitudes. The new men came well to the fore in the Civil War years.

## Chapter Seven

# Civil War and Instability, 1620-1675

For much of the hundred years between 1526 and 1625 the government of Norwich was carried out in an atmosphere of almost studied calm. During the whole of that period the city had to contend with only one major uprising, but one of sufficient seriousness to bring it to the forefront of national politics between early July and late August 1549.

The tale of Kett's rebellion has been often told, notably and most recently in the accounts of Julian Cornwall and Barrett Beer, and the barest outline of events is necessary here.[1] A rebellion which had its beginnings in the pulling down of enclosures at Hethersett on 8 July soon swelled into a major uprising led by Robert Kett, a yeoman farmer and tanner of some substance. Backed by a large band of men, at the outset mostly comprising yeomen and tenant farmers, he descended on Norwich, ignoring the conciliatory overtures of the mayor, Thomas Codd. By 12 July they had established themselves on Mousehold Heath overlooking the city, and were soon joined by large contingents from most parts of the county, with the notable exception of the arid south-west. At the height of the rising the rebel forces numbered some sixteen thousand men, perhaps half as many again as the entire population of Norwich itself. The corporation negotiated with the rebels, but at first made little attempt to resist them and the insurgents contented themselves with manning the city's gates. Subsequently, after rejecting an offer of pardon from York Herald on 21 July, the city was twice occupied and partly sacked by the rebels who were sufficiently numerous and skilled in arms to defeat thoroughly a combined force of English soldiers and Italian mercenaries led by the Marquis of Northampton. It took a major campaign eventually to bring the rebels to heel; a force of some ten thousand men commanded by the Earl of Warwick, and supplemented by German mercenaries, finally destroyed them at Dussindale on the outskirts of the city. Both Robert Kett and his brother William were convicted and hanged, the former at Norwich Castle, the latter from the tower of Wymondham Abbey. Before this, Warwick had hanged 49 men the day he entered Norwich, some 3,000 had died at Dussindale and possibly 200 of those sent to relieve the city had perished in the fighting.

The events of July and August had emphasised the total inadequacy of the city's defences and its almost complete inability to defend itself, despite the presence of a dozen cannon and other ordnance. It is not without significance that repairs to the walls feature prominently in the Chamberlains' Accounts throughout the Elizabethan period and beyond.[2]

Kett's rebellion was an exception, almost an aberration, however, and would have been beyond the control of most, if not all, of the corporations at that time. In normal circumstances, the whole of the city assembly, aldermen and councillors alike, were concerned to maintain good order, and a form of continuity was ensured by the ever-longer periods of time served by those elected. When members of the same family were present in both the upper and lower houses, and when the family ties were made stronger by the presence of both former master and former apprentice among the ruling body, there was little cause for friction.[3]

The first decades of the 17th century saw the disappearance of some of the leading families from the stage, however. The men who replaced them had no tradition of service within the city. Many were imbued with strong religious ideals, in some cases to the point of fanaticism, and they were far less inclined than their predecessors to accept with good grace every ruling of the upper house. When the more wealthy among them were elected to aldermanic

28.  Augustine Steward's house, Tombland. Occupied by Kett's men and later used to entertain the Marquis of Northampton when he relieved the city.

rank they placed ever greater pressure on their more conservative colleagues, and ultimately succeeded in purging the old guard completely.

The first signs of conflict appeared in the second decade of the 17th century. It became increasingly noticeable that men were being nominated mayor over the heads of their older and more experienced colleagues. This was not necessarily a new departure. It had always been accepted that a man must be both willing and able to bear the city's highest office, and seniority alone did not ensure he did. Nevertheless, seniority was something to be jealously guarded. On all feast days the mayor took precedence, followed by his predecessors in the order that they had attained the chair, and finally by the other aldermen in order of election. The only exception to the strict observance of this rule was if a man was knighted, whereupon he automatically became second to the serving mayor. Bickerings over precedence even took place among the aldermen's wives. Under such circumstances, any men who aspired to the mayoralty and were superseded by their juniors would be bitterly resentful.[4]

In due course, James I felt constrained to intervene. He wrote to the authorities in April 1619 urging them to conform to the London system where seniority was rigidly adhered to.[5] The aldermanic body was, on the whole, willing to concur but any such alteration to the constitution had to have the assent of the majority of both houses. On 11 October the proposed amendment was introduced and the common council immediately requested time to consider the implications of such a change. A committee was set up to consider the matter but it dragged its feet and by December the Lord Chief Justice and the Justices of Assize began to agitate for a decision. When no decision had been reached three months later the justices presented their own scheme, and even then a further two months elapsed before it was presented to the assembly for consideration. Ultimately on 29 May 1620, more than a year after the king's original letter, the matter was put to the vote. The meeting was barely quorate, 15 aldermen and 33 common councillors being present, but after some consideration the motion was accepted by the narrow majority of 25 to 23. This led to an immediate protest by the councillors who pointed out that while 14 of the 15 aldermen supported the motion it had had the support of only one-third of the councillors present. The assembly accepted the protest, but it took until 4 August when the Chief Justice of Common Pleas and two justices of assize were present, as well as the mayor, sheriffs, 18 aldermen and 48 councillors, before the matter was finally settled. The seniority principle was agreed to, and at the same time it was accepted that in future all aldermen were to be elected from the senior surviving sheriffs among the common councillors.[6]

The weaknesses of the new system were fully brought out in the Kettle controversy already referred to, and required further amendment in 1627. What is immediately significant here is that the councillors had shown their teeth, an ominous portent for the future.

Throughout the constitutional controversies of the 1620s Norwich had looked to, and received support from, the central government. The accession of Charles I, however, marked the beginning of a steady deterioration in relations between the city and the crown. Norwich, as other places, protested against the severity of the financial exactions imposed upon it, not least because they coincided with a severe outbreak of plague in 1625-6 which led to 1,431 deaths and a doubling of the poor rate.[7] Writs for the payment of ship-money in the spring of 1626 were followed by demands for a forced loan in the following January. Despite aldermanic suggestions that the collection of ship-money might cause difficulties over the collection of the loan, the crown was prepared to accept no excuses and the corporation received a writ of *quo warranto*. By September one-third of the loan was still uncollected, but the city complied thereafter where ship-money was concerned and the tax was levied promptly throughout the following decade.[8]

The financial exactions of the crown were more than paralleled by the continuing attempts of the central government to curb the activities of the local Puritans. Norwich had a tradition of dissent which stretched back to pre-Reformation times. As early as 1574 Elizabeth I had privately instructed Archbishop Parker to commence any purge of Puritan ministers with those of Norwich.[9] Such attempts were resisted and the intermittent activities of the Jacobean and Caroline bishops to undermine the Puritan cause were matched by the equal determination of the local aldermen to support it.

29. Bishop Hall's Palace, Heigham.

In Caroline Norwich the Puritans were essentially concerned with a zealous attitude towards daily life and worship and they were given assistance by the mayor's court which functioned, *inter alia*, as a 'moral policeman'. Individual aldermen exercised considerable patronage where advowsons and lectureships were concerned while the assembly itself had obtained control over two lectureships at St Andrew's before 1620 where they almost invariably sponsored Puritans.[10] The ecclesiastical authorities reacted with a mixture of authoritarianism and apparent indifference. In 1615 the bishop of Norwich blocked an appointment to a lectureship because the man concerned 'refused to subscribe to the Articles of Religion and form of Church Government' and his still more zealous successors, Harsnet and White, launched a fierce attack on nonconformist preachers which culminated in a total ban on Sunday morning sermons and an insistence that the ordinary parishioners attend the Cathedral instead. Despite pressures from White, the Norwich authorities purchased the advowson of St Peter Hungate in 1630 and invited William Bridge, one of the more notorious Puritan preachers, to the city to officiate there. Characteristically, Bridge took the opportunity to establish combination lectureships at the church of St George Tombland which involved at least a dozen Puritan preachers. The laxer attitude of White's successor, Bishop Corbet, a man not averse to heavy drinking on occasion, did nothing to undermine the Puritan cause. It was clear that a strong man was needed and Matthew Wren was duly translated from Hereford to Norwich in November 1635.[11]

Wren 'was one of Laud's most loyal supporters, and in complete agreement with his views – a lover of ceremony and order, a rigid disciplinarian, resolute and energetic in all that he undertook. He was also a man of deep piety and learning, and of an unfaltering courage'.[12] He arrived in a city where the Puritans were united in their concern for the establishment of, and support for, godly ministries, their defiance of certain Anglican forms of worship, their determination to maintain the purity of the Sabbath, and their hopes for the creation of communities who would share these objectives.

While Wren was concerned, with reason, at the attitudes of some of the lecturers in his diocese it was never his aim to abolish lectureships in their entirety but rather to suspend those clergymen who refused to conform. He expected them to read the divine service in surplice and hood, to behave themselves modestly and to preach faith, obedience and good works. They were not to 'meddle with matters of state, news or questions late in difference, nor favour or abet any schismatics or separatists, either by special prayer for them, or otherwise approving of them'.[13] Wren objected strongly to those lecturers who observed no order in their services nor in their presentation, and claimed that people knew beforehand who was going to preach. Lecturers who were factious or controversial could guarantee full houses. For others, the church was often half empty.

Wren launched an immediate attack, ordering that Sunday mornings were to be used for sermons and homilies, the afternoons for catechising, and that all magistrates were to attend the cathedral service and sermon every Sunday morning. He also suspended eight of the more recalcitrant lecturers, including the notorious William Bridge, who took up temporary residence in Holland.[14] Despite this apparent intransigence, Wren subsequently claimed that, far from being concerned with total abolition, he had actually created some lectureships as well as confirming and restoring others. In Norwich alone he increased the number of sermons from three or four to at least one in every church on Sunday.

While the Puritans were not hostile to Whitehall or Canterbury, as such, they were deeply opposed 'to the aggressive episcopal effort to extirpate an already entrenched Puritanism'. It was this determination which, allegedly, led to the emigration of some 500 people from Norwich alone, quite apart from large numbers from the rest of the county.[15] Significantly, most sought refuge in Holland. While a Puritan community was undoubtedly established at Rotterdam, Wren claimed that the exodus owed more to the prevalence of low wages in the county and the fact that the Dutch were prepared to pay them half as much again to be taught the new methods of textile manufacture.[16] If he was right it was an interesting reversal of the trend prevalent in the 1560s when the Dutch and Walloon refugees were brought to this country for precisely the same purpose. An additional factor was undoubtedly the presence of plague in both London and Norwich which brought normal commerce to a halt. As a contemporary noted, with some exaggeration, 'the city trade doth consist all most wholly in commerce with Londoners'.

While Wren undoubtedly had a case, his policies caused considerable resentment among a majority of the citizens. The aldermanic body responded initially with the time-honoured method of petitioning Wren and even sending a delegation to him to outline their objections to his proposals. The failure of these approaches led to what was to become a permanent split in the aldermanic body. A minority among them sought to petition the king himself, a policy which required the support of a majority within the assembly. When the more conservative aldermen opposed such a petition the mayor obtained the assent of a sufficient number of common councillors to outvote them. The petition was received, and almost inevitably rejected, but was countered with another from Wren's supporters among the aldermen who dissociated themselves from it.[17] Wren's support was not confined to the laity. Fourteen of the Norwich clergy, including representatives from St Andrew's, signed a declaration referring to him as one 'by whose pious care and great pains herein, the public worship and service of God is much advanced amongst us already, and will doubtless, every day, more increase, as all moderate and truly religious men will fully testify'.[18]

Protests against Wren's policies were to no avail. By 1639 his successor, Bishop Montague, was able to inform Charles I that the diocese of Norwich was 'as quiet, uniform, and conformable as any in the kingdom, if not more'.[19] His very success, however, had convinced the local Puritans that they must look to parliament for support, rather than the king, an attitude which was to be significant during the Civil War years.

The split in the aldermanic ranks made it perfectly clear to the Puritans among them that the only way forward was the gradual replacement of the conservatives by others more amenable to their cause. In terms of political sympathies, the common councillors in the industrial wards of Wymer and Over the Water tended to lean towards what was to be the parliamentary side while their colleagues in Mancroft and Conesford were more inclined to royalist sympathies. The freemen electorate, however, while occasionally ambivalent, were largely antagonistic towards the policies of Wren and, by definition, those of the Crown, and could be relied upon to elect pro-Puritan sheriffs, and future aldermen, whenever the opportunity arose. In the event, what looked like a long drawn out policy of attrition was expedited by the events of the Civil War years.

Until 1640 at least half of the aldermanic body remained conservative in their political outlook. By the eve of the Civil War in 1642, however, future supporters of parliament just outnumbered their royalist counterparts and within a year a purge, albeit a legitimate one, gave the parliamentarians a firm majority.

The purge followed a gradual hardening of attitudes as warfare appeared increasingly inevitable. Although Norwich tended to respond to events in the capital, the city was not slow to react to apparent injustice. Thus the ruling body indicated its support for parliament over the attempted arrest of the Five Members in January 1642. By July the supporters of parliament had formed a volunteer company and had broken their silence on national affairs, alleging that many thousands of the inhabitants of Norwich were opposed to 'the dayly growing evils and almost desperate diseases which have overspread the whole body of this kingdom, both in Church and State'. Not surprisingly, bearing in mind their recent experiences with Wren, the city's petition to the House of Lords referred specifically to 'the multitude of frivolous, ridiculous, and unwarranted [religious] ceremonies, pressed with the vehemence of suspension, excommunication, and deprivation' of many Puritan ministers. The petition went on to cite monopolies, illegal taxations and imprisonment, 'as if government had been set free from restraint of laws'. They saw those responsible as mainly evil councillors, courtiers, Jesuits and bishops, but parliament also came in for some criticism. The city sought the return of the king and the removal of Catholic peers from the Upper House, but was also concerned that the country should be armed and ready for war.[20]

Readiness for warfare did not extend to providing soldiers for the king, however, and when Captain Moses Treswell entered the city on 28 July 1642, bearing a commission signed by the Earl of Lindsey to gather 100 volunteers, he received very short shrift. When he ignored an order to desist he was promptly arrested and turned over to the House of Commons. The House expressed its gratitude to the city, but the aldermanic body was sufficiently cautious to send details of their actions, with an explanation, to the king. The die was cast, however, and when a proclamation from the king seeking the aid of his subjects to suppress the rebels arrived in Norwich in late August it was totally ignored.[21]

Earlier in the month, deputy-lieutenants had been appointed for the city, with responsibility for the trained bands and other military affairs. The formation of the Eastern

Association in December was linked to a parliamentary demand for local officials to raise the necessary money for fortifications and munitions, any people who refused to pay being liable to have both weapons and horses confiscated. A month later, in January 1643, the order was put into effect, the sheriffs being instructed to enter the homes of any who resisted and to seize all horses, arms and ammunition. The attempt of the mayor, William Gostlyn, to obstruct the order simply led to his own imprisonment and provided the opportunity for the supporters of parliament to move against the remaining royalists on the aldermanic bench. Some of the city's magistrates were allegedly involved in a royalist plot to take over the city of 5 March. Whether this was true or not, three of them – Lane, Daniel and Osborne – had been absent from key aldermanic meetings. Letters were sent asking them to explain their absence or be removed from office. When no such explanations were forthcoming, a hastily convened meeting of the mayor's court ejected them from their position. With the mayor in gaol, another royalist alderman desperately ill and yet another, Alexander Anguish, due to be removed for alleged misconduct the following year, the parliamentary-puritans had established a position of absolute supremacy.[22]

The return of aldermen amenable to puritanical ideas allowed the more radical among them to turn their attention to the Church. The House of Commons had already passed an order as early as September 1641 which forbade the practice of bowing at the name of Jesus, and ordered the removal of rails from the communion table and the abolition of images. It was fortified by an ordinance of August 1643 which sought the destruction of all so-called monuments of superstition and idolatry. The city's Puritans needed no second bidding. Aldermen Greenwood and Lindsey, assisted by one of the sheriffs, Thomas Toft, led a mob to the Cathedral. Their subsequent depredations are best described in the words of Bishop Hall himself:

> It is no other than tragical to relate the carriage of that furious sacrilege, whereof our eyes and ears were the sad witnesses, under the authority and presence of Lindsey, Toft the Sheriff, and Greenwood. Lord, what work was here. What clattering of glasses! What beating down of walls! What tearing up of monuments! What pulling down of seats! What wresting out of irons and brass from the windows and graves! What defacing of arms! What demolishing of curious stonework, that had not any representation in the world, but only of the cost of the founder, and skill of the mason! What tooting and piping upon the destroyed organ pipes, and what a hideous triumph on the market day before all the country, when in a kind of sacrilegeous and profane procession, all the organ pipes, vestments, both copes and surplices, together with the leaden cross which had been newly sawn down from over the Green Yard pulpit, and the service-books and singing-books that could be had, were carried to the fire in the public market-place, a lewd wretch walking before the train, in his cope trailing in the dirt, with a service-book in his hand, imitating in an impious scorn the tune, and usurping the words of the Litany used formerly in the Church. Near the public cross, all these monuments of idolatry must be sacrificed to the fire, not without much zealous joy in discharging ordnance, to the cost of some who professed how much they had longed to see that day.[23]

This activity received the hearty approbation of the aldermanic body. Within a fortnight they had named a committee to search the parish churches with the specific intention of destroying scandalous pictures, crucifixes and images. In March the following year some religious paintings which had survived the initial onslaught were discovered in St Swithin's and St Peter Mancroft. They were duly burnt in the open market place.[24]

To all intents and purposes, Norwich was essentially a Puritan city by the mid-1640s. The parliamentary triumph at Marston Moor in 1644 was decreed a day of thanksgiving, proclaimed by the roar of cannon and the ringing of bells. By 1645 the old church services were discontinued and the celebration of Christmas was forbidden.

This apparent unity was something of a delusion, however. In 1643, when Parliament looked to its supporters for financial assistance, the 229 Norwich contributors to the relief of Newcastle were outnumbered by the 274 who were named as refusing to donate, a figure which would undoubtedly have been larger if all the non-contributors of Mancroft had been included. The aldermanic body contained seven refusers while the common council was almost equally divided between the 27 who were prepared to pay and the 33 who refused to do so. Significantly, over two-thirds of the members of Wymer and Over the Water (22 out of 32) contributed whereas the Wards of Conesford and Mancroft were able to muster no more than five contributors between them. In the same context, the nine out of 10 sheriffs elected between 1641 and 1645 who were named as donors were almost all residents of the northern wards. While parsimony undoubtedly accounted for some of the refusals to donate, the majority of the non-contributors were probably anti-Puritan if not overtly royalist.[25]

The Puritans themselves were far from a united body.[26] They were unanimous in their opposition to Laudian ceremony and what they considered to be episcopal tyranny, but completely at variance when it came to deciding on a new form of worship. The whole question had been delegated to a body of churchmen, known as the Westminster Assembly of Divines, as early as June 1643, a body who favoured a Presbyterian form of worship and church government and who were strongly influenced by Scottish participation in their discussions. After apparently interminable delays, parliament approved the abolition of the Book of Common Prayer in January 1645, replacing it with a Directory of Worship. Eight months later, following the predictable recommendation of the Assembly to adopt a form of Presbyterianism based on the Scottish model, an ordinance was passed which regulated the election of Church elders and divided London into 12 classical presbyteries. At this juncture, Lenthall, the Speaker of the House of Commons, judged it appropriate to write to the mayor and aldermen of Norwich suggesting that similar methods be adopted 'with all expedition'. His letter was totally ignored.

The following May the London Puritans devised the Humble Remonstrance and Petition which sought, *inter alia*, to prevent anyone opposed to the new Church from holding office, as well as a speedy settlement with the king and a close understanding with the Scots. Despite opposition from the Independents and others, the House of Commons agreed to implement the Presbyterian religious system and the Directory of Worship, with the proviso that appeals from the hierarchy of church courts should be filed with a committee of parliament.

As was so often the case, Norwich responded to events in the capital. A body of Presbyterians, led by a minister named Thornbeck, not only sought support for the London Remonstrance but attempted to bring pressure on the mayor and aldermen to approve their own remonstrance. Like its London counterpart, it stipulated that any who opposed them should be ejected from office in church, commonwealth

30.  A 17th-century house, Princes Street.

and army, and claimed that because of the uncertainty of the religious situation three-quarters of the parishes were without ministers, that there were no church officers to look after the poor and children were frequently not baptised. The contents of the Presbyterian petition were leaked to the Norwich Independents who were totally opposed to both its local and national goals. In contrast to the Presbyterians, they favoured the independence of the individual congregation, advocated religious toleration, and had already set up their own church in the city.

Furious pamphlet warfare followed. The Presbyterians described the supporters of the Independents as either drunkards or the worst malignants in Norfolk. The Independents responded with a pamphlet entitled 'Vox Populi, or the Voice of the People', alleging that the Presbyterians were little more than the old priest writ large.

Is this all the quarrel and cause of our wasting wars? What, to pull down the prelate and set up the Presbyter? To change only the name and not the nature of a tyrannizing state? To take away the miter from the head of the prelate and fasten it upon the head of the Presbyter?

Vox Populi was officially condemned by the Norwich ruling body in September 1646, with both aldermen and common councillors denying all knowledge of its authorship. In December a committee was appointed to determine who should nominate elders of the church and who should organise classes. In the event nothing was done, an outcome which probably reflects the divisions within the city assembly, despite its rejection of Vox Populi.

The Presbyterian and Independent uncertainties were matched by the discontent of the lesser tradesmen over the whole question of the payment of excise duties. The duties, which had been first imposed in 1643, covered a variety of goods, including meat and ale, and tended to fall especially heavily on the poorer classes. Demonstrations against the tax were followed by serious riots in December 1646 and the following month, with the aldermen claiming to be in danger of their lives. Attempts to arrest some of the insurgents were prevented by the armed intervention of the rioters, with the butchers to the forefront, and the houses of some of the aldermen were badly damaged. With the tax rebellion spreading into Norfolk and riots also prevalent elsewhere in the country, parliament had little alternatve but to modify the tariff. This had the effect of cooling tempers, but the situation continued volatile in Norwich until the summer months and remained threatening thereafter.

The royalists in the city were equally discontented. An act passed in September 1647 prevented the election to municipal office of any man who had been in the royalist armies, had assisted them or been sequestered from office. A month later such men were disfranchised as well as being ineligible for election. In March 1648 the House of Commons prepared an ordinance specifically for Norwich, stipulating that all persons who had been imprisoned, sequestered, refused to obey the ordinances of parliament, or who had assisted the crown at any time were ineligible to be elected to the position of mayor, recorder, steward, alderman, sheriff or common councillor for a period of one year. Such people were also disfranchised. The ordinance also decreed that no existing office-holders faithful to parliament should be displaced under any circumstances.

By the spring of 1648 the discontentment of Presbyterians, Royalists and lesser tradesmen had coalesced into outright opposition to the army and central government. In defiance of the parliamentary ordinance, the freemen of Mancroft Ward elected Roger Mingay to the position of alderman in March 1648, a man who had never been sheriff and who was an avowed royalist. Mingay was ineligible for office both under the terms of the 1620 ordinance and that passed by parliament earlier in the month. Despite this, the mayor, John Utting, refused to declare the election void and permitted bonfires and feasting on the anniversary of the accession of Charles I six days later.

The anti-Royalists were sufficiently alarmed for an alderman, one of the sheriffs and several other citizens to ride to London to present personally a petition to the House of

Commons. The Commons responded by ordering the March ordinance to be put into effect and passed the petition to the Committee of Complaints who sent a messenger to escort Utting to London to answer to the charges.

The messenger arrived in Norwich on 21 April. Utting responded by calling a special meeting of the Court of Aldermen for the following day to draw up a petition testifying to his good behaviour and providing reasons why he should stay in Norwich. Only six aldermen, one of whom was Mingay, attended the meeting, but the petition was passed around the city over the weekend, allegedly attracting the signatures of hundreds of supporters. By the Sunday a large group was determined to prevent Utting's departure, going so far as to lock the city's gates. By Monday their numbers had grown to around one thousand and individuals among them were heard to shout for God, King Charles and the mayor and of their intention of purging the assembly of any supporters of the Puritan cause.

An emergency meeting of the aldermanic body was called, but suggestions to raise the city forces or to send for troops in the county were blocked by Utting's supporters. The messenger of the House of Commons was forced to flee, pursued by the mob who broke into Sheriff Ashwell's house and secured arms. By 2 p.m. they were roaming the city, sacking the houses of known supporters of parliament. In the confusion, some citizens succeeded in escaping and made their way to a contingent of soldiers, commanded by Colonel Fleetwood, who were mustering some twelve miles outside the city. These troops arrived in Norwich by 4 p.m., immediately fired on the insurgents, and finally cornered them in the Committee House where 100 barrels of gunpowder were stored. The explosive was ignited, by accident or design, with inevitable loss of life, but it had the effect of quelling the riot and leaving Fleetwood's men in control.

The situation was sufficiently serious for it to be thoroughly investigated by a Committee of the House of Commons which took until September 1649 to complete its findings. Apart from his general support for the royalists, Utting was accused of favouring their religious inclinations, allowing a revival of Anglicanism to the exclusion of many Presbyterian ministers. He and Alderman John Tooly, who had been his principal supporter, were declared 'Grand Delinquents'. They were debarred from holding office, fined £500 and £1,000 respectively, and committed to the Fleet Prison, Utting being imprisoned for six months and Tooly for three. Their fines were subsequently reduced to £200 and £400. The leaders of the riot were less lucky. They remained in prison throughout the summer and autumn, finally being brought to trial on Christmas Day, 1648. Twenty-four were fined £30 and sentenced to remain in prison until the fines were paid. Nine were acquitted and eight were sentenced to death, the latter being hanged in the Castle Ditches on 2 January 1649.

Two days after the riot, when Utting had left voluntarily for London, the assembly met to confirm a grant of £200 to Fleetwood's soldiers as a gesture of gratitude for putting down the rebellion, together with £50 for expenses. At the same time, by 40 votes to 12, they declared Mingay's election to be illegal. Fleetwood's men had one further duty to perform. On the orders of the House of Commons, troops were placed around the city to ensure that the mayoral election of 1 May was allowed to proceed peacefully. They were not allowed to interfere with free elections and in the event the matter was conducted in an atmosphere of 'quietness and peaceableness as was wonderful'.

It was perfectly clear to the aldermanic body that others, apart from Utting and Tooly, in the upper house had been concerned with the riots of 1648. On 26 January 1649 the assembly decreed the parliamentary ordinance of the preceding March should remain in force for the forthcoming elections. This was reinforced by an additional stipulation declaring that all men who had spread the petition defending Utting or who had taken part in the riot were ineligible to vote or be elected to office, and that any who had been guilty of complicity were to be displaced. Although their actual roles were undeclared, this led to the removal of Aldermen Croshold, Sotherton, Gostlyn and Thacker, in addition to Utting and Tooly. The deaths of five other aldermen during 1649 led inevitably to further changes in the composition of the upper house.

The changes in the lower house were, on the surface, even more radical than those among the aldermanic body. Twenty common councillors were replaced in 1649 and a further 25 the following year. Some of those displaced in 1649 may have been concerned with the riot of the previous year, while some of those leaving in 1650 may have been reluctant to take the Engagement which required an oath of loyalty to the Commonwealth. These men would have been in a minority, however. Thirteen of the 45 men leaving the common council in the years 1649-50 were promoted to aldermen and a further 15 returned to do subsequent service, although in the case of two of them this was deferred until the Restoration. Two of the remaining 17 were replaced on their deaths, while others would have left in the normal course of events. In consequence, it seems unwise to talk of a purge of the common council at this time.

Dr. Evans has stressed correctly that the ages and occupations of the new men were broadly similar to those that they had replaced. There were significant differences in two important areas, however. With the possible exception of Mancroft, those elected to the common council during the Commonwealth period were decidedly poorer, in a relative sense, than their immediate predecessors. Of even greater significance was their almost total lack of experience or background of civic service. In 1648 14 of the common councillors had fathers who had served before them, with fully half of them having either this background or one of apprenticeship to an existing or past alderman or councilman. As a group they had a median period of service of five years, with one in five of them having served 10 years or more. The contrast with their successors could hardly be more marked. Twenty men were elected for the first time, many beginning their civic service in middle or old age, with the median years of service falling to one, while no more than seventeen of them (28 per cent) had any connection with past or present members of the assembly. As was pointed out at the Restoration, many of these councilmen would not have been elected in the first place had it not been for the parliamentary election ordinance passed 'in those times of defection'. Half of these men were able to provide the city with less than five years service, eight of them serving for no more than a year. Eleven of them, in contrast, were still there at the Restoration.

The decade leading up to the return of Charles II was significant mainly for the slow, but clearly perceptible attempt of the freeman body to undermine the Puritan supremacy. As early as 1651 they gave notice of their intentions by nominatng for the mayoralty the only two eligible aldermen who had not voted for the replacement of Mingay in 1648. Two years later, in September 1653, Mingay himself was one of two moderates nominated as sheriff despite the fact that he was still technically ineligible by virtue of the parliamentary ordinances for municipal elections; and both he and his fellow sheriff, Christopher Jay, were promoted to the aldermanry within a month of their election as sheriffs.

Jay and Mingay used their period as sheriffs to oppose openly the parliamentary ordinances yet again. At the elections for the first parliament of the Protectorate, two strong supporters of Cromwell, Colonel Charles George Cock and Thomas Baret were opposed by two moderates, John Hobart and Bernard Church. Both Cock and Baret had served on parliamentary commissions, both had military backgounds, Baret having been promoted to lieutnant-colonel as recently as 1650, and both had served as deputy lieutenants for the city. They were in a seemingly strong position, for the Instrument of Government which had brought the Protectorate into being included among its provisions a stipulation that any men who had acted against parliament at any time since 1641 should be excluded from either voting or standing in parliamentary elections. In the event, although Cock was initially returned unopposed Baret was beaten in a straight fight for the second seat by Bernard Church. There the matter should have ended, but instead of accepting the decision Jay and Mingay declared that a second election should be held at a different location with all the freemen being allowed to vote, despite the parliamentary ordinance to the contrary. On this occasion Cock was opposed and defeated by John Hobart and Hobart and Church were duly returned as the city's representatives to parliament.

A subsequent petition, signed by 101 people who supported Cock and Baret, led to nothing. Two months after the election, Joseph Paine, a known Royalist who had already been imprisoned for his beliefs, was elected commons' sheriff in place of Mingay, completing a year in which the freeman body had consistently elected moderates to the shrievalty, the aldermanry and the House of Commons. They continued in the same vein by nominating Robert Holmes, another acknowledged royalist, to a vacant aldermanic position.

Despite the clearly expressed preference of the freemen, and despite the elections of Paine and Holmes, the aldermanic body continued to support parliament. They made their sympathies abundantly clear in 1658 when they sent an entirely unsolicited letter of support to Cromwell. Significantly, the petition was taken to Cromwell by Puritan aldermen Puckle and Parmenter rather than by the mayor, the moderate Christopher Jay, who had been appointed to his position in 1657, only three years after becoming alderman. The assembly as a whole declared its loyalty to Richard Cromwell on Oliver's death in 1658 and affirmed their support by electing William Davy, a strong Independent and supporter of parliament, to the mayoralty in 1659.

The assembly was out of tune with many, if not most, of the citizens by 1659, however. Like their counterparts in London who were agitating for a free parliament and who took every opportunity to elect moderates and conservatives to the Common Council and even to the aldermanry, the Norwich freemen were waiting for an opportunity to express their discontent. General Monck's march to London provided the opportunity. When he was within 30 miles of the capital in January 1660 he was presented with a Declaration signed by 794 of the gentry of Norfolk and citizens of Norwich, including 14 of the aldermen and 25 of the common councillors. It referred specifically to 'the miseries of an unnatural war, the too frequent interruptions of government, the impositions of several heavy taxes, and the loud outcries of undone and almost famished people, occasioned by the general decay in trade', the latter referring genuinely to an economic slump in the city. It proposed, as a remedy, that the excluded members of Parliament should be returned without the obligation of taking the Engagement or any other oath, and that until this was done 'the people of England cannot be obliged to pay any taxes'. As the Declaration was essentially a criticism of the Rump rather than a statement of support for Monck himself it received an understandably cool response. Nevertheless, the document implied a strong preference for a restoration of the Stuarts, but as Monck did not declare for this until 19 March it refrained from openly saying so. However, when the Convention Parliament finally declared on 1 May that 'the government was and ought to be by King, Lords and Commons', the city was not slow to respond and by 11 May had begun several days of celebration.

In an immediate attempt to ingratiate themselves with the crown, the assembly voted for the restoration of the fee farm rent which it had purchased in 1650, and followed this with the provision of a free gift of £1,000. In August the aldermen and common councillors voluntarily took the oath of allegiance and supremacy.

As Evans rightly stresses, the total volte-face of the ruling body, which was very similar to that adopted by other towns, almost certainly reflects the frantic desire of the aldermen to remain in office. 'They were willing to make declarations, pass legislation, take oaths, and open their pocket-books precisely because they had no guarantees against Crown intervention.'[27] Only one alderman, Nicholas Pointer, willingly resigned his seat. The rest waited on events, attempting to placate the central government by accepting the election of two previously ejected aldermen to positions which became vacant.

In the event, their hands were forced. In January 1661 a letter from Whitehall instructed the corporation to implement the Act of Indemnity which had come into being the previous August. This stipulated that any person who had given sentence of death in the High Courts of Justice since 1648 or who had signed a warrant of execution for any person condemned in the courts should be debarred from office or serving as a Member of Parliament. The assembly was ordered not only to restore any surviving royalists to office but also to remove any existing aldermen who had been unduly elected. Three days later, on 29 January, a body of 17 aldermen and 38 common councillors voted for the removal of Robert Allen, John Andrewes, Thomas Ashwell, William Davy and William Rye, all of whom had replaced men ejected in the purges of 1649-50. On 2 February Thomas Baret and Edmund Burman were ordered to appear before the assembly to defend themselves against charges that they were ineligible to hold office under the provisions of the Act of Indemnity. Burman succeeded in defending himself but Baret refused to appear and was removed from office. Just over a year later, in July 1662, a further four aldermen were evicted under the terms of the Corporations Act, an Act which gave the crown's commissioners *carte blanche* to remove any person from office that they thought fit. ·

The freeman body had already undertaken a similar purge of the common councillors. Eight of the men replaced were elected aldermen, either immediately or within a few years. For most of them, however, it meant the end of a civic career which might never have begun but for the instability of the Civil War years. Thirteen of the new men elected in 1660 and 28 of those beginning their service in 1661-2 had never previously held political office. Thus by 1662 a full two-thirds of the common council was composed of men who had never served during the Civil War or Interregnum. Notable among the survivors was Samuel Allen. He had been elected a member for Conesford in 1637 and continued in office throughout the turmoil of the 1640s and 50s, being finally replaced in 1664. He and Thomas Norris of the Ward across the Water, whose service was intermittent, were the only survivors of the common council which had been in existence before the purges of the 1640s.

31. Augustine Briggs, mayor 1670 and M.P. 1677.

The constitutional changes of the early 1660s created a thoroughly royalist assembly which, for all its loyalty, had to fight to preserve its liberties when the crown began to issue new charters to the various corporations. In May 1661, during the opening session of the Cavalier Parliament, attempts were made to insert four specific clauses into all new charters. These would have allowed the crown to reserve to itself the first nomination of all aldermen, the final choice of common councillors from nominations presented by the corporation and the first and future appointment of recorders and town clerks; most significant of all where Norwich was concerned, was a stipulation that the election of borough M.P.s should be confined to the common councillors alone, a move which would have given the crown an indirect control over the election of a majority of the members of parliament.[28]

The assembly fought the crown on every issue, pointing to precedent and the dangers of overturning a tried and tested system, and their efforts were largely successful. In the final analysis the changes were minimal. The dates for the elections of the sheriffs were altered. All aldermen elected in future were to be Justices of the Peace for the wards which elected them, and they were to be chosen from the 'most worthy and sufficient citizens' and not solely from the sheriffs as in the immediate past; in the same context the seniority ordinance for mayoral elections, which had been repealed in 1644, was not restored. The position of the common councillors was strengthened by a provision that any by-laws passed by the upper house would need the consent of a majority of the common councillors, but the franchise remained, as before, in the hands of the whole freeman body.

The purges of the 1660s marked the end of an uncertain period in Norwich history, at least for the foreseeable future. The following decade was an essentially tranquil one, marred only by the appalling death rate resulting from the plague of 1666 which led to the deaths of over two thousand people and caused considerable unemployment and hardship. The seeds for future conflict were there, however. The Act of Uniformity, which passed through parliament in 1662, placed both Presbyterians and Independents outside the Church of England. Those concerned responded by setting up conventicles which attracted hundreds of people, and despite the necessity of taking an oath of allegiance Nonconformists were elected to the common council as occasional conformists. Many of the aldermen either sided with, or were sympathetic to, the Nonconformist cause. Nevertheless, as Evans has emphasised, in the 1660s and early 1670s 'Norwich achieved a degree of political stability unknown since the 1630s', with the occasional conflict between Anglicans and Dissenters causing no problems to the established authority.

The subsequent difficulties of the Dissenters and the political turmoil of James II's reign lie outside the scope of this book, and at this juncture we can turn our attention to matters which were the permanent concern of the ruling body. A healthy financial situation was essential for the good governing of the city, as was the maintenance of law and order. Both aspects were affected by the presence of the poorer classes. The cost of maintaining the indigent led to a steady increase in the rates paid by the more affluent citizens, while a steady influx of vagrants placed a heavy burden on the shoulders of the constables and their helpers. These topics are considered in detail below.

*Chapter Eight*

# Financial Affairs

The accounts of the city of Norwich during the Tudor and Stuart periods were many and varied. Apart from those maintained by the major financial officials, known as the clavors and chamberlains respectively, a number of separate accounts were kept by other officials: for the care of the river and streets; for sums received on admission to the freedom of the city; for the provision of a corn stock; for the hospital for the aged and destitute; for profits received from the aliens' customs and for dyeing and sealing their manufactures; for aulnage profits; for sums received from court and other miscellaneous fines; and, for at least the decade 1570-80, for money received and distributed to the poor. Most of these accounts were self-supporting. If absolutely necessary, sums were occasionally borrowed from one or the other to support a particular city venture but repayment was always prompt. Normally, apart from paying the officials concerned with the account and workmen responsible for any relevant tasks, the scribe had little to do apart from rendering his account and adding the profits to the next year's receipts. The chamberlain and foreign receiver (the person responsible for money received on admission to the freedom of the city) were the only officials expected to contribute their surplus to the city treasury and the clavors' accounts record the intermittent receipt of such sums. This chapter will be concerned with the activities of the clavors, or city treasurers, and, in much greater detail, with the normal city business recorded in the chamberlains' accounts.

The clavors' primary task seems to have been to maintain a reserve stock of money which could be drawn on in time of need. In part, their funds were derived from the profits accumulated by the chamberlains and foreign receivers, but this was, at best, an insecure source of revenue. It was rare for the chamberlains to record a profit in the 16th century, and although the position improved in the succeeding period it was much more common for the chamberlains to receive help from the city treasurers than it was for them to provide it. The foreign receivers, in contrast, always received more than they had to pay out and yet they were frequently in debt.[1] The chamberlains regularly recorded the receipt of sums derived from admission to the freedom but these seldom bore any relationship to the profits actually made. It would seem that the foreign receivers were allowed the use of the sums they controlled, repaying the city as and when they could. One would have expected the city to receive interest on such 'loans', but it is impossible to establish this from the accounts. The remainder of the treasurers' income was normally derived from loans made to the various city officials, again presumably with interest, and from fines for being relieved of the office of alderman or sheriff. Occasionally it was bolstered from other sources. The profits from aulnage, granted to the city for six years from 1580, brought in over £600.[2] Fines for re-admission to the freedom of the city, following disfranchisement for various offences, brought in a small, but relatively regular, income. Almost without exception the clavors made a profit due to the careful handling of their resources. They rarely undertook tasks which were beyond their financial capabilities. When it was absolutely necessary to do so they borrowed from other city accounts, drawing on the funds of the corn stock and the Great Hospital, for example, in 1578 when the city purchased the manor of Little Ellingham, but repayment was always quick.[3]

The payments which the clavors were called upon to make were usually more diverse than their receipts. Regularly throughout the 16th century and intermittently thereafter the treasurers had to bolster the chamberlains' finances. Almost without exception this commitment was the result of heavy expenditure on repairs to civic buildings, a point which will be discussed in more detail below. Other payments were made on an *ad hoc* basis and reflect the temporary importance of particular issues. Thus money was spent from time to time on city business in London. In times of scarcity corn had to be bought and sold cheaply to the poor. The conveyance of water from the New Mills to the Market Cross cost nearly £700 between 1583 and 1585. A new prison cost almost £220 in 1600. During the 17th century payments are recorded, among others: of £163 in 1630 for the defence of the Palatinate; of £10 for the entertainment of local dignitaries in 1635 when the ship money issue was discussed; of £25 for the purchase of 100 swords in 1645; of £22 5s. 8d. in 1650 for the provision of clothing for poor boys sent to New England; and, as late as 1665, of a sum of £116 for the repair of the city walls.[4] These payments, and others like them, were mainly in addition to the usual city business and the normal day-to-day expenditure came within the province of the chamberlains.

**Table 8.1 Receipts and expenditure of the Norwich clavors at five yearly intervals**

| Date | Receipts £ s. d. | | | Expenditure £ s. d. | | |
|---|---|---|---|---|---|---|
| 1561 | 81 | 5 | 2 | 72 | 19 | 4 |
| 1565 | 194 | 7 | 2 | 82 | 18 | 11 |
| 1570 | 154 | 11 | 5 | 40 | 3 | 4 |
| 1575 | 286 | 6 | 7 | 80 | 4 | 4 |
| 1580 | 962 | 11 | 10 | 1,056 | 2 | 3 |
| 1585 | 258 | 4 | 1 | 431 | 3 | 0 |
| 1590 | 416 | 10 | 11 | 126 | 3 | 1 |
| 1595 | 583 | 6 | 8 | 63 | 17 | 10 |
| 1600 | 670 | 11 | 11 | 448 | 1 | 9 |
| 1605 | 210 | 17 | 9 | 85 | 3 | 4 |
| 1610 | 301 | 6 | 5 | 158 | 13 | 4 |
| 1615 | 372 | 10 | 6 | 320 | 15 | 3 |
| 1620 | 308 | 16 | 11 | 179 | 8 | 10 |
| 1625 | 160 | 1 | 6 | 153 | 11 | 2 |
| 1630 | 426 | 3 | 11 | 422 | 17 | 5 |
| 1635 | 420 | 3 | 5 | 203 | 0 | 4 |
| 1640 | 235 | 18 | 3 | 101 | 18 | 8 |
| 1645 | 436 | 17 | 6 | 182 | 12 | 4 |
| 1650 | 326 | 5 | 2 | 328 | 17 | 10 |
| 1655 | 152 | 6 | 2 | 132 | 6 | 5 |
| 1660 | 178 | 8 | 5 | 168 | 0 | 0 |
| 1665 | 553 | 11 | 1 | 550 | 9 | 9 |
| 1670 | 191 | 6 | 4 | 140 | 3 | 4 |
| 1675 | 745 | 9 | 0 | 741 | 0 | 3 |

The city's income, as recorded in the chamberlains' accounts, was derived from much the same sources throughout the Tudor and Stuart periods. The greatest single source of revenue was the so-called New Mills, bought from the Abbot of St Benet's as long ago as 1430.[5] Substantial sums were obtained from the lease of city property, both landed and otherwise, and from the rents derived from the stalls and shops in the market place, and smaller amounts were received from the profits of tolls and customs. At the end of each account were listed the foreign receipts, primarily the sums paid by the clavors for repairs although short-term renting of city property was included among them and, especially in the 17th century, large sums which were in arrears.

The New Mills were a particularly profitable investment. One hundred years after their original purchase they were providing the city with no more than £10 a year. Thereafter, partly in response to the price rise, they rose steadily in value. The rent had quadrupled by 1535, increased by almost a further 50 per cent five years later, and reached £53 13s. 4d. by the early years of Elizabeth's reign, by which time the local bakers were obliged by act of assembly to grind their corn there. For 25 years the rent remained stable. It then jumped to £95 in 1588, £100 by the turn of the century and had reached £120 before the beginning of James I's reign, a fourfold increase in a period of some seventy years. Subsequent increases took the rent for the Mills to £160 a year in 1615 and to an all-time high of £212 10s. in 1625. Thereafter there was a gradual decrease in revenue, the rent finally becoming stabilised at £170 a year in 1655.[6] Needless to say, the Mills were not entirely a source of profit. At an assembly meeting held on 16 November 1562, for example, it was noted that the New Mills and Blackfriars Bridge were 'in decay and required moche costes'.[7] The following year £116 8s. 1d. was spent on the Mills alone. Twenty-five years later, when the rent was almost doubled, a further £168 14s. was spent on them, and smaller sums were expended at regular intervals.[8] Nevertheless, even allowing for this expenditure, the profits from the New Mills greatly exceeded the sums spent on them. The available accounts for Elizabeth's reign show that in a period of 35 years the city obtained £2,411 18s. 8d. in rents from this source and spent rather more than £348 on repairs.[9] It was undoubtedly the greatest single source of city revenue.

If the irregular sums for foreign receipts and arrears are excluded, rents for lands and tenements made up some forty per cent of the city's revenue. The tenements can be classified into three broad categories, namely: those held by the city for centuries and whose rents, apparently, could not be legally raised; others also owned for a long period of time but whose rents did show some increase; and those which had previously belonged to monastic establishments and were obtained after the dissolution of the monasteries, primarily through the good offices of the Duke of Norfolk. Between 1525 and 1565 rents from the tenements and from lands owned by the city approximately doubled every 20 years; they had doubled again by 1615 at which point they were bringing in almost £200 a year; while 50 years later receipts exceeded £300.[10] In part, this increase was the result of enhanced rents, in part the result of increased investment in property of this kind. Thus the rent of the lime kilns was increased from £2 6s. 8d. to £10 a year on the expiration of a 60-year lease in 1625.[11] Tenements and grounds which were rented yearly were subject to rapid increase, others had their rents increased on the expiration of their leases. Against this, all city property was subject to periodic repair and the city fathers had to combat increased labour costs as well as a rise in the price of materials. As with the New Mills, however, repair bills were never sufficiently high to offset the gains made from incoming rents.

The same story is true of the stalls and shops rented or leased to the various city traders. These comprised the rows of stalls rented to both city and country butchers, fish stalls and wool shops. The return from the butchers' stalls was particularly lucrative, both from increased rents and from the greater number of stalls actually rented. Rents from this source increased fivefold between 1531 and 1535, remained relatively stable for the rest of the century, and then gradually increased again between 1600 and 1675 to a point where the return from the stalls was three times what it had been at the end of Elizabeth's reign. Much of this was due to the increasing number of country butchers who chose to hire stalls in the city. In 1565 men from outside the city were hiring 37 stalls for a rent of just under £28. A century later the number of stalls had virtually doubled and the rents from the country butchers alone had reached £109, or virtually four times the earlier figure.[12]

The only remaining source of revenue of any significance was that derived from the profits of tolls and customs. Worth no more than £2 1s. 8d. in 1531, they had risen to £20 13s. 4d. four years later. Like the rents from the various stalls, they then remained virtually static for the rest of the century, but rose sharply to £69 7s. 10d. in 1615 and reached almost £78 by 1620. Subsequently profits declined, becoming stabilised at £56 3s. 4d. in the immediate post-Restoration period.[13]

Despite increasing difficulty in collecting rents during the 17th century, the overall picture which emerges is one of steadily rising income matched by ever-increasing expenditure. After an initial leap from just under £80 to almost £200 between 1531 and 1535, mainly due to increased rents, receipts rose steadily throughout the 16th and 17th centuries. The chamberlains were receiving more than twice as much money in 1600 as they were 70 years earlier and by 1620 the receipts had doubled again. The £1,000 mark was passed in 1645 and, apart from a temporary recession in 1660, continued at that level thereafter.

**Table 8.2 Receipts and expenditure of the Norwich chamberlains at five yearly intervals**

| Date | Receipts £ s. d. | | | Expenditure £ s. d. | | |
|------|-----|-----|-----|-----|-----|-----|
| 1531 | 79 | 16 | 1 | 70 | 8 | 6 |
| 1535 | 197 | 14 | 5 | 196 | 2 | 5 |
| 1540 | 253 | 8 | 0 | 232 | 6 | 1 |
| 1545 | 467 | 14 | 7 | 473 | 15 | 6 |
| 1552 | 213 | 5 | 4 | 210 | 7 | 7 |
| 1555 | 255 | 15 | 11 | 246 | 15 | 2 |
| 1560 | 213 | 19 | 4 | 195 | 14 | 10 |
| 1565 | 268 | 6 | 4 | 300 | 2 | 7 |
| 1580 | 351 | 6 | 0 | 475 | 16 | 10 |
| 1585 | 343 | 6 | 2 | 528 | 3 | 6 |
| 1590 | 620 | 14 | 8 | 740 | 19 | 2 |
| 1595 | 488 | 3 | 9 | 474 | 11 | 10 |
| 1600 | 401 | 1 | 9 | 489 | 6 | 10 |
| 1605 | 419 | 11 | 9 | 528 | 7 | 3 |
| 1610 | 558 | 17 | 11 | 658 | 7 | 10 |
| 1614 | 566 | 9 | 5 | 606 | 11 | 6 |
| 1620 | 926 | 5 | 4 | 769 | 19 | 5 |
| 1625 | 867 | 1 | 0 | 607 | 17 | 9 |
| 1630 | 819 | 3 | 2 | 675 | 6 | 5 |
| 1635 | 869 | 8 | 1 | 655 | 16 | 8 |
| 1640 | 946 | 4 | 4 | 758 | 6 | 9 |
| 1645 | 1,007 | 16 | 10 | 791 | 18 | 5 |
| 1650 | 1,074 | 18 | 10 | 965 | 2 | 3 |
| 1655 | 1,001 | 10 | 8 | 919 | 11 | 8 |
| 1660 | 884 | 14 | 6 | 846 | 2 | 11 |
| 1665 | 1,547 | 4 | 6 | 1,604 | 3 | 11 |
| 1670 | 1,184 | 17 | 5 | 1,076 | 1 | 11 |
| 1675 | 1,364 | 5 | 6 | 1,183 | 15 | 3 |

The accounts for the years 1530, 1550-1, 1570 and 1575 are missing. Collective accounts for the period 29 September 1614 to 15 August 1616 inclusive were presented for an unspecified reason. The receipts were £904 11s. 1d., the expenditure £812 2s. 1d.

The events outlined can probably be paralleled in most English towns of any size, differing only in the amounts of money actually received. Bristol, Exeter, Leicester and

Winchester, for example, all received the bulk of their income from property rented or leased within, or just outside, the town confines, the actual proportions varying from just over half in Leicester to between seventy-five and eighty-five per cent at different times in Bristol.[14] The major difference between those towns and Norwich is that the chamberlains there were concerned with virtually all financial matters whereas in the East Anglian town some responsibility was delegated to subordinates. Thus in all four towns the chamberlains were concerned with the receipt of sums of money due for admission to the freedom, a task which was the special responsibility of the foreign receiver in Norwich. In Leicester and Winchester respectively the chamberlains received fines for refusal to accept office and for the payment of aulnage, money which in Norwich would have been paid direct to the clavors.[15]

It is not a particularly profitable task to attempt a comparison of the relative receipts and expenditure of the various towns. The accounts of Exeter and Leicester have been printed for at least part of the period covered here, but those printed for Bristol and Winchester cover only single years while those of other cities are even less satisfactory.[16] It would, in any case, be mainly concerned with stressing the relative poverty of the smaller towns and the comparative wealth of the larger, a point which will emerge at least briefly in a discussion of expenditure.

The details of the city's expenditure between 1525 and 1675 are marginally more complex than those of the receipts. Two items stand out: the sums paid out on fees and wages and the relatively large amounts spent each year on repairs. With these exceptions, the money disposed of by the chamberlains tends to reflect the importance of particular issues at a given period of time. Thus the earlier accounts record the sums spent on monastic property following the Dissolution of the Monasteries. Elizabethan accounts are increasingly concerned with details of presents and rewards and, on occasion, with the payments necessary for mustering soldiers and sending them to their particular destination. As the 17th century progresses, there is increasing reference to the cost of sermons, and from 1645 onwards relatively large sums are recorded as having been paid to parliament.[17]

32. Augustine Steward, mayor 1534, 1546 and 1556.

The wages bill rose steadily from the £45 10s. recorded in 1531 to a peak of £398 13s. 6d. It fell to £385 4s. 8d. in 1646 and thereafter fluctuated between £340 and £350 a year.[18] In part this reflects the steady rise in prices, in part the equally steady increase in the number of officials employed. The mayor's salary, for example, rose from the £20 a year paid to the Henrician officers to the £100 a year received by their Elizabethan counterparts.[19] Fees to some other officials rose even more radically, albeit spread over a longer period. The five waits, for example, had their nominal salary of 13s. 4d. in 1531 increased to £15 by 1600 and £30 75 years later. The swordbearer, who initially earnt 10s., was paid £3 6s. 8d. in 1600 and as much as £20 in 1675.[20] The number of officials concerned is, perhaps, of greater significance than the salaries. In 1531 the chamberlain recorded his own fee and those of the mayor, the sheriffs, the recorder, the common clerk, the swordbearer, the waits, the clerk of the market, two mayor's servants and three men 'learned in the law'. By 1600 the number of entries had increased to 30 and by 1657 to thirty-five.[21] Apart from the major officials, fees were being paid to individuals as diverse as the water bailiff and the bellman, the sweeper of the assembly chamber and the trumpeter. One man was paid 8s. for keeping the mayor's place in church, another 6s. for sweeping the ground outside the New Hall. In the 1670s sums were being paid to the under-chamberlains, to men responsible for keeping the city's arms and for recording the christenings and burials in the city; even to the churchwardens of St Andrew's and St Peter Mancroft for arranging the Tuesday and Thusday lectures.[22] By 1675 the combination of increasing salaries and additional officials had produced a wages bill which bore comparison with the total city expenditure of a century earlier.

This again was a phenomenon common to most towns and cities of any size. Between 1556 and 1627 the number of officials employed by the Bristol corporation increased by almost fifty per cent while at the same time the wages bill virtually doubled.[23] In the latter year both Norwich and Bristol had to find some £300 for official salaries. The fortunes of the two towns varied. In Mary's reign the mayor of Bristol was receiving twice the salary of his Norwich counterpart but, whereas by 1627 his fee of £40 had risen to £52, the senior citizen of Norwich was allowed £100 and had been since the later years of the 16th century.[24] In contrast, the town clerk of Bristol was paid three times as much as the Norwich official and the swordbearer there was receiving £20 a year some time before the Norwich man achieved equality. The mayor of Exeter fared better than both his rivals, his Edwardian salary of £26 13s. 4d. being increased to £120 a year by the end of Elizabeth's reign.[25] Elsewhere the mayoral fees reflect the relative poverty of the towns concerned. In Leicester the mayor was receiving no more than £10 a year until 1572 when his salary was increased to £13 6s. 8d. 'for and towards the better maintenance of his housekeeping'.[26] Even this small amount, added to the fees of the recorder and the mayor's clerk, came to nearly half the town's expenses in 1558.[27] Nottingham and Winchester were both able to afford £20 a year for their senior officials during Elizabeth's reign, fees comparable to that paid in Norwich at the same time, and in the case of Nottingham this had been doubled by the early 17th century.[28] In every case, fees and wages made up between one-third and one-half of the total expenditure of the towns concerned.

While salaries and fees were obviously a major item in a town's expenditure, the repairs bill was often of even greater significance. The sums spent naturally varied from year to year but not infrequently they made up half, and occasionally more than half, of the total outgoings. The cost of repairs to the New Mills in Norwich has already been referred to. While less expensive than this, every major city building had to be attended to at least once during the second half of the 16th century. The common hall, for example, the former property of the Blackfriars which had been bought by the city after the Dissolution of the Monasteries at a cost of £54, had more than £70 spent on it in 1562, a further £44 three years later, and various smaller sums, often between £20 and £30, throughout the entire period.[29] As the rent increased from £6 7s. 8d. in 1558 to £36 11s. 0d. by 1601 and to £57 by 1660, however, it was still a profitable purchase.[30] The guildhall, the lazar houses, the common staithe, the butchery, to select examples at random, all had sums spent on them from time to time, and all were a source of profit to the city.[31]

Repairs of this nature were naturally intermittent. Much more frequent were the sums expended on the city's walls and gates. Every year the Elizabethan chamberlains made some reference to a section of the walls being repaired and the sums spent on them were often large. In 1558 and 1580, for example, the cost of repairs was £43. In 1585 the gates alone cost the city more than £74. In 1590 and 1595 sums in the region of £50 and £67

33. St Stephen's Gate.

34. Ber Street Gate.

respectively were disbursed in this direction.[32] When particularly large sums were required the chamberlains were provided with money under the heading of 'Foreign Receipts'. Certain sums of money could be called on which were specially set aside for this purpose, every alderman, for example, being obliged to contribute £2 towards the repair of the walls when he was sworn into office.[33] In addition, some legacies were specifically intended for work of this kind.[34] It was the responsibility of the mayor to check the walls and to decide when such money should be used. Thus in 1567 it was noted that the walls were greatly decayed and the mayor ordered that £20 a year should be spent on them for the next seven years.[35] Further action was taken in February 1576 when a workman was appointed to be specially responsible for such repairs. It was ordered that he should be paid 20s. a year for this task on top of his normal wages.[36]

Occasionally the repairs bill was increased by a natural disaster in the city. In 1590, for example, a fire destroyed the majority of the butchers' and fishmongers' stalls and shops, together with houses in the butchery, and over £156 had to be spent on their replacement.[37] The greater part of this sum was provided by the clavors, and as in the same year a new bridge was built at St Martin's at a cost of £177 5s. both the chamberlains' receipts and expenditure for that year were the highest recorded in Elizabeth's reign.[38]

Even allowing for the fact that the cost of repairs varied from year to year, there was a perceptible increase in the amounts spent in this direction as the years progressed. Much of this can be attributed to the rise in workers' wages and, less certainly, to the increasing cost of building materials. The wages of craftsmen and labourers approximately doubled

35.  The back of the fish market, showing the south porch of the Guildhall.

between 1540 and 1590, and rose by a further 50 per cent over the next 60 years. Thus carpenters, masons, reeders and tilers were being paid between 6d. and 7d. a day in 1540, 10d. a day by 1565 and as much as 1s. 2d. between 1590 and the turn of the century. Fifty years later the daily rate had risen to 1s. 6d. Labourers' wages rose in the same period from between 4½d. and 5d. to 9d. by 1590 and 1s. a day by the mid-17th century.[39] By the latter period wages were officially set by the justices of the peace. The Norwich assessment for 1657 was brief and to the point. 'Wages for men servants by the year £3, women servants 40s. and meat and drink, master workmen of carpenters, tilers, masons, reeders and the like to have 18d. a day and their labourers 12d. a day.'[40] Consciously or otherwise, these rates were in operation in the mid-1650s.[41]

It is impossible to be as precise about the cost of building materials, but the relatively high bills being submitted to the corporation during the 17th century bear some witness to its increase. In 1665, for example, Isaac Cooper and Thomas Austen, roughmasons, had bills paid to the value of £90 13s. 3d. and £154 3s. 7d. respectively; those of William Burgess and Robert Colman, carpenters, totalled £100 and £113 2s. 1d. Five years later Colman was paid £77 in part-payment of a bill totalling £120 19s. 7d.[42] The corporation was evidently satisfied with their work. Austen and Colman were submitting bills from 1650 and it was evidently official policy to maintain contact with the same people.[43] Some of these men were common councillors, but there were not enough of them to suggest that work was being deliberately farmed out to members of the council.

Among the minor items regularly recorded by the Elizabethan chamberlains were sums listed as presents. An average disbursement in this direction would be in the region of £20 but £50 was spent on presents in 1566 and almost £100 in 1584.[44] It is very probable that still higher sums were spent on the occasion of the Queen's visit in 1578, the clavors providing more than £700 towards its total cost, but the absence of the chamberlains' accounts for the relevant decade makes it impossible to be precise on the point.[45]

The only other item of major importance is the appearance of the monthly assessments in 1643. They are variously described as 'payments to the parliament' (1651-2), 'parliament rates' (1654-5), 'monthly taxes' (1655-6) and 'monthly rates' (1656-7), after their initial description as being 'for the advance of horse and for the British Army' (1644). The amounts were derived from a tax on city property and levied in accordance with the value of the buildings or lands concerned. At their highest in 1645 they brought in a total £109 2s. 8d. Usually the amounts fluctuated between £40 and £75, although on occasion they fell to as low as £4 or £5. Although originally intended to bolster the fortunes of parliament and the Commonwealth, the taxes continued to be levied after the Restoration and were still being collected in 1675. From their inception to that date they brought in just over £1,500, a sum which does not remotely correspond to the full amount demanded by the parliamentary assessors.[46] Between 1643 and 1659 Norwich should have contributed £23,866 7s. 7d., quite apart from its share of taxation levied on the county as a whole.[47] At best, the sums recorded were a contribution to this larger whole.

Other items of varying interest and importance appear intermittently in the expenses accounts. They range from the £54 paid in 1540 for the monastic property later known as Blackfriars' Hall, used to this day for civic and other purposes, and the £153 10s. 11d. paid a year later for lead from the churches and due to the king, to such mundane, but locally important, issues as paying the overseers of the poor and reimbursing a locksmith for providing a lock to the ducking stool.[48] In 1615 payments by warrant included: the wages of the marshals; expenses due to the clerk of the market; the re-imbursement of city officials for money spent while on business in London; and payment to a craftsman for repairing the city plate. The examples are selected arbitrarily. Although varied in content, these and similar items made up a substantial portion of the city's expenses, particularly during the 17th century.

For the greater part of the 16th century the chamberlains' accounts showed a deficit, even allowing for the sums paid to them by the city treasurers. It was one of the less pleasing aspects of the office that the chamberlains were expected to make good such loss to the city. Despite this, the post was not an unpopular one and, in contrast to such cities as Exeter and Nottingham, where the officials concerned with the town's finances were prepared to pay large sums to avoid the office, several chamberlains served for long periods of time.[49] A possible reason for this is that no undue pressure was placed on the people concerned, provided the debt was ultimately met. Ordinarily there is no record of this. The single exception occurred in 1549 when Robert Raynbald completed his tenure of office with debts of £157. Raynbald faithfully recorded the methods adopted to offset the debt. He was able to raise some £60 in cash and a similar sum from the sale of plate, all set down in great detail, and the residue from the sale of two tenements and a close in the parish of St Vedast. He received £60 from the latter transaction and was able to note, with some satisfaction, that the city was then in debt to him. The account is concluded with a record of the £23 then owed being duly paid to him.[50]

The 17th century saw the situation reversed, with the chamberlains in credit for virtually the entire period. One is left with a general impression of financial competence, with all the officials, whether clavors, chamberlains or auditors, normally well in command of the situation.[51]

*Chapter Nine*

# The Mayor's Court

Throughout the period 1525-1675 responsibility for law and order in Norwich was in the hands of three distinct, but interrelated, bodies. The least important of these was the old leet court, functioning under the sheriffs and operating at ward level. It dealt essentially with petty offences, malefactors being tried by a jury specially empanelled for the purpose from the inhabitants of the ward concerned. Those found guilty were fined sums ranging from a few pence to three or four shillings. The more serious offences, ranging from petty larceny to murder, were the prerogative of the Quarter Sessions, presided over by the mayor and such other justices as had passed the mayoral chair. The mayor's court effectively bridged the gap between the two. As the period progressed it gradually took over from the leet court jurisdiction which extended over nuisances, defective weights and measures, market offences, fraudulent manufacture and a variety of other breaches of the law. In common with Quarter Sessions, it had responsibility for the suppression of vagrancy, apprenticeship problems, tippling and gaming. Occasionally offenders in these areas would be sentenced at Quarter Sessions while the sentence itself would be executed in the mayor's court. Ordinarily, the majority of these offences would be dealt with at the twice weekly sessions of the mayor's court as a matter of course.[1]

The court met regularly on Wednesdays and Saturdays, with occasional additional meetings to deal with urgent business. Such aldermen as attended were expected to undertake specific duties, in addition to their judicial functions. Among others, these included the inspection of the work of the poor in the Bridewell, the auditing of accounts, making provision for the watch at the gates in time of plague, and acting as arbitrators between conflicting parties.

The court relied on the aldermen both for counsel and for the administration of its orders; legal advice was provided, when required, either by the recorder or, more rarely, the steward as chief justice of the sheriffs' court. The orders emanating from the court were enforced by a variety of officials, including the sergeants at mace, the ward constables, beadles, watchmen and marshals. The sergeant at mace, or mayor's sergeant, was a special attendant, particularly concerned with the oversight of markets and the making of summonses. The arrest of wrongdoers devolved on the regular and special constables. Twenty-four men were elected constable each year with responsibility to maintain law and order, supervise the keeping of the watch, and to execute all the mayoral orders. They were assisted from time to time by the appointment of auxiliary constables at large, appointed by the mayor and sworn in the court. The marshals and beadles were appointed as occasion demanded, usually for a few weeks at a time, and they were paid weekly.

The cases brought before the mayor's court naturally varied in number and importance from year to year. Some, such as theft and the necessity to arbitrate between conflicting parties, were ever present. Others, such as the provision of grain in time of dearth and the implementation of plague regulations were issues which concerned the court intermittently, but were dealt with at least once in every decade. As the late 16th and 17th centuries progressed, an increasing amount of time had to be devoted to the steadily rising numbers of vagrants and other poor people attracted to the city as a potential provider of relief or employment.[2]

36.  A street scene near St Laurence's church.

Until their hand was forced by external events, the Norwich ruling body was little concerned with the problem of the vagrant, who often avoided work, or with those itinerant craftsmen and others who travelled from place to place actively seeking employment.[3] From time to time the authorities fulminated against the admission and settlement of unacceptable newcomers, even threatening to impose really large fines on transgressors, but they undermined their case by tacitly ignoring their own regulations whenever it suited them to do so. In 1570, for example, a census of the local poor revealed the fact that the alderman and councillor class was the landlord of almost forty per cent of such people, despite the fact that local authorities specifically forbade such action. Prospective settlers were able to flout the entrance regulations with such impunity that at least sixty families from Norfolk and Suffolk alone were able to make their home in Norwich between 1560 and 1570, and travellers from much further afield found it equally easy to settle there. In the same period itinerants from London, Cambridgeshire, Essex, Northamptonshire, Yorkshire, Lancashire, Westmorland and Hertfordshire established themselves in the East

Anglian city, as well as some from Ireland and unspecified northern territories. Not surprisingly, the city's generosity – or laxity – in this respect became widely known and if the trickle of vagrants did not become a flood it at least developed into a fast flowing stream.

Initially, the reaction of the authorities was one of apparent indifference. Four people were ordered to leave the city in 1550, one in 1555, but it was not until 1560 that a vagrant was punished as such; in that year two of the three people ejected were whipped and given passports ordering them to return to their place of origin.[4] Thereafter the attitude of the justices was more rigorous.[5] By 1570 the mayor's court had dealt with 62 cases of vagrancy or unauthorised entry to the city in the years sampled, the majority involving men and women travelling on their own.[6] The figure had doubled by the end of the century, and increased enormously in the succeeding two decades when the local authorities had to deal with eight times as many cases as their early Elizabethan predecessors. Thereafter the numbers declined again and in the Commonwealth and Restoration eras the numbers arrested for this offence were minimal.[7] The evidence for the Commonwealth period, in particular, may reflect under-recording rather than actuality, and those that were listed were almost exclusively described as vagrants. For the bulk of the 17th century, however, wanderers of all sorts were listed, with vagrants being clearly differentiated from the rest. On the evidence of the court books, far more people were on the move from the late 16th century onwards but many of them were recognisably above the level of the vagrant.

Unless they could provide sureties that they would not be a charge on the town the newcomers were ordered to leave as a matter of course with the threat of punishment if they returned, but they were not punished indiscriminately as their forefathers had been. The constables were unwilling to whip every poor man or woman who was genuinely travelling in the hope of obtaining employment but, like many of their neighbours, they felt uneasy at the prospect of too many strangers flooding the labour market. Under such circumstances they were more than willing to escort the newcomer to the town boundary. If he chose to return they would have fewer scruples about using the whip as a deterrent.

**Table 9.1 Cases of vagrancy and other unauthorised travel brought before the mayor's court, 1550-1675**

M = Men     C = Children
W = Women     F = Families

| Periods | Vagrants | | | | Others | | | | Totals | | | | Vagrants (%) | | | |
|---|---|---|---|---|---|---|---|---|---|---|---|---|---|---|---|---|
| | M | W | C | F | M | W | C | F | M | W | C | F | M | W | C | F |
| 1550-70 | 29 | 11 | - | 5 | 7 | 5 | 1 | 4 | 36 | 16 | 1 | 9 | 81 | 69 | - | 56 |
| 1575-95 | 50 | 8 | - | 1 | 21 | 13 | - | 20 | 71 | 21 | - | 21 | 70 | 38 | - | 5 |
| 1600-20 | 105 | 43 | 18 | 9 | 127 | 88 | 2 | 45 | 232 | 131 | 20 | 54 | 45 | 33 | 90 | 17 |
| 1625-45 | 87 | 23 | 11 | 10 | 97 | 32 | 4 | 27 | 184 | 55 | 15 | 37 | 47 | 42 | 73 | 27 |
| 1655-75 | 11 | 8 | 4 | 6 | 1 | 1 | - | 2 | 12 | 9 | 4 | 8 | 92 | 89 | 100 | 75 |

The men, women and children referred to above were all travelling on their own. The families were arrested as such and no distinction was made between younger and older children when their cases were recorded in the court books.

If the number of wandering families and individuals increased, so did the areas from which they were drawn. If Norfolk is included, immigrants entering Norwich in the first of the periods considered above came from nine different counties. In the last quarter of Elizabeth's reign the figure had risen to 14, while during the reigns of James I and his successor the city saw travellers from no fewer than 29 different areas including vagrant families from as far afield as Scotland, Wales and Ireland. The summary below provides details of the 12 areas from which most of them came.

**Table 9.2 Twelve most common areas of origin of vagrants etc. entering Norwich between 1550 and 1675**

|  | 1550-70 | 1575-95 | 1600-20 | 1625-45 | 1655-75 | Totals |
|---|---|---|---|---|---|---|
| Norfolk | 12 | 22 | 167 | 135 | 5 | 341 |
| London | 17 | 1 | 24 | 24 | 4 | 70 |
| Suffolk | 3 | 6 | 25 | 15 | - | 49 |
| Yorkshire | 1 | 1 | 19 | 13 | 8 | 42 |
| Essex | 1 | 3 | 11 | 7 | 2 | 24 |
| Cambridgeshire | - | 2 | 9 | 7 | 4 | 22 |
| Lincolnshire | 1 | 2 | 11 | 8 | - | 22 |
| Kent | - | 1 | 3 | 8 | 1 | 13 |
| Nottinghamshire | - | - | 4 | 7 | 2 | 13 |
| Northamptonshire | - | 2 | 6 | 1 | - | 9 |
| Leicestershire | - | - | 5 | 3 | - | 8 |
| Wales | - | - | 6 | 1 | - | 7 |
| Totals | 35 | 40 | 290 | 229 | 26 | 620 |
| Totals for whom place of origin is given | 39 | 45 | 321 | 254 | 34 | 693 |
| Total number of vagrants etc. apprehended | 76 | 153 | 535 | 355 | 47 | 1,166 |
| Percentage for whom place of origin is given | 51 | 29 | 60 | 71 | 62 | 49 |

With the possible exception of Wales, the places of origin provide few surprises. The same counties had been sending apprentices to Norwich for a considerable time.[8] While it was hardly this which provided the impetus for the vagrant classes they were at least treading well-worn paths. During the first half of the 17th century, the period for which we have most information, just over half of the immigrants came from Norfolk itself, 13 per cent from the Midlands and North (Yorkshire, Lincolnshire, Nottinghamshire, North-amptonshire and Leicestershire), 12 per cent from London and the South-east and 10 per cent from Suffolk and Cambridgeshire.[9]

The possibility of work in a city which catered for much more than the textile worker, the knowledge that the Norwich merchant classes were at least relatively generous to the itinerant poor, a realisation that a city so often decimated by plague would need a transfusion of labouring people – any or all of these factors may have encouraged the wanderer in the earlier of the periods under review. At the end of the 16th century, and for much of the 17th, one needs to look no further than harvest failure and severe economic depression to account for the general influx of people. Desperate men sought sustenance wherever they thought it was to be found. Those seeking work in an often overcrowded labour market were usually turned away, but they were seldom required to depart immediately. Most were given a few days grace, with the threat of punishment if they delayed their departure too long. The professional vagrant neither received nor expected such latitude. Most of them sought quick gains, either in money or in kind, before continuing their travels. If they were whipped in the process it was accepted as an occupational hazard. Some may have returned to their place of origin. Others may have eventually settled down if they could escape the vigilance of the local constables. Either way, their numbers remain problematical.

In 1577 a contemporary estimated the number of vagrants in England at ten thousand.[10] Just over one hundred years later the statistician, Gregory King, considered that there were as many as sixty thousand vagrant families on the road.[11] Alarming reports of their numbers appear at intervals throughout the 16th and 17th centuries. John Aldrich, the mayor of Norwich, spoke with some exaggeration of the influx of beggars to the city before the reorganisation of its poor law scheme in 1570.[12] The oft-quoted letter of the Somerset J.P., Edward Hext, complains of virtual anarchy in his county at the end of the 1590s.[13] In 1649 Liverpool was apparently thronged with beggars,[14] and as late as 1678 Gloucestershire complained of the 'dayly concourse and great increase off Rogues, Vagabonds and Sturdy Beggars'.[15] All of the reports share a common vagueness, an imprecision of detail, and most of them were written in times of dire economic distress. It is extremely rare to have precise statistics, even of vagrants actually apprehended. A welcome exception is provided by Salisbury which kept a register of over six hundred vagrants whipped out of the town between 1598 and 1638.[16] The details provided can be compared with those of Norwich for a similar period although, as the Norwich figures have been collected at five-yearly intervals, only the percentages are directly comparable.

**Table 9.3 Numbers and categories of vagrants punished at Salisbury and Norwich between 1598 and 1645**

|  | Husbands and wives | Single men | Single women | Children | Totals |
|---|---|---|---|---|---|
| Salisbury 1598-1638 | 86 | 343 | 171 | 51 | 651 |
| *Percentages* | *13.2* | *52.7* | *26.3* | *7.8* | |
| Norwich 1600-45 | 36 | 192 | 66 | 29 | 323 |
| *Percentages* | *11.1* | *59.4* | *20.4* | *9.0* | |

Both the figures and the percentages relate strictly to people actually punished for vagrancy and give no indication of the relatively large number of people being ordered to depart without being actually punished.[17] As such, the proportion of vagrants in the different categories is broadly similar in the two cities and the number arrested per year suggests that under normal circumstances vagrancy was fairly easily contained. This was the case in some places even during the economic depression of the 1630s. At Guildford in Surrey, for example, the mayor informed the central authorities in 1631 that 'verie few or none are found to wander nor any come to this Towne'. In Shropshire it was apparently 'rare to see any wandering person', while the Derbyshire justices were to write that 'our country is cleerly delivered of them', and similar reports were received from counties as far apart as Somerset and Yorkshire.[18] In contrast, Norwich, which was in the throes of a trade depression, received a fresh influx of wanderers in the 1630s, and many of the examples collected by Dr. Slack date from the same period. In every case these examples reflect the efficiency of the local authorities and, even more so, the prevailing state of the economy.[19]

As defined by the Act of 1597, virtually every poor person leaving his home town or village could be designated vagrant. Officially they comprised 'all wandering persons and common labourers being persons able in bodye using loytering and refusing to worke for such reasonable wages as is taxed or commonly gyven in such partes where such persons do or shall happe to dwell or abide, not having lyving otherwise to maynteyne themselves'.[20] Sixty years later the parliament of 1657 took a similar attitude, enacting that 'any and every idle, dissolute person who was discovered wandering away from his place of abode and was unable to give adequate reason for his wandering should be judged a rogue and punished as such, although he was not taken begging'.[21] It was left to the magistrate to decide what was meant by 'able in bodye'. The very old and completely indigent, in theory at least, would be unable or unlikely to wander far from their homes. Those that did were subject to the full rigour of the law. As fear dictated the actions of many J.P.s, they tended to use the lash rather than the threat of it. From 1565, when vagrancy was first recognised as a problem in Norwich, until the end of the century, the usual sentence of the mayor's court was that a vagrant, whether man, woman or child, should be whipped and returned to his or her place of origin. Only rarely was he given the chance to leave with the threat of punishment hanging over his head.

Examples of all types of vagrant can be found in the pages of the mayor's court books. Among those whipped and passed on were: a bagpipe player from Ipswich; 'an old man of lowe stature' and his wife; a blind man and his son; a one-armed man from Monmouthshire taken 'roginge and beginge'; and a number of runaway servants and apprentices, including the very young.[22] One such was William Margaret, an eight-year-old apprentice, 'having a paire of pothookes about his necke'.[23] The little boy had apparently fled from his master on more than one occasion for both runaway servants and apprentices were marked in this way, a sentence apparently having its origins in the savage vagrancy laws of the mid-16th century.[24] Adults were differentiated from children by having iron collars fixed around their necks instead of the pair of pot hooks common to the apprentice, but both man and boy were clearly identifiable.[25] The sentence was in use over an extended period. In Norwich, isolated examples have been discovered ranging in date from 1565 to 1625, and the practice may have continued until well into the 17th century.[26]

Local children were usually treated kindly. Reference is made elsewhere to civic concern for the orphaned and homeless, culminating in the foundation of the Boys' and Girls' Hospitals, and those brought before the court almost invariably received some assistance.[27] In most cases, the justices insisted that the parishes concerned accepted their responsibility although occasionally they went further and provided help themselves. Thus John Games, 'a vagrant under the age of seaven yeres', was placed in the care of the parish of St Peter Permountergate, while the mayor himself clothed two older boys who were found begging before returning them to their native parish.[28]

Where outsiders were concerned, however, the city fathers adopted a rigid attitude, their sole concern being the cost to the community. If anything, their attitude to wandering children was even more severe than it was to adults. Thirty-three of the 40 youngsters from other places who were described as vagrants were whipped and sent on their way, six were threatened with punishment if they were found in Norwich in the future.[29] For a short period in the 17th century entries in the court books concerning punishment to children occur with almost monotonous regularity. Children from the age of eight upwards were entering the city having travelled, in many cases, more than one hundred miles. An eight-year-old girl, almost incredibly, had come from as far away as Staffordshire, and an 11-year-old boy had tramped the hundred miles and more from London.[30] In both cases they were summarily whipped and ordered to be returned to their birthplaces. No thought was given to the possible dangers of travel. It was presumed, as a matter of course, that vagrants travelled in bands, even if taken singly, and certainly children of that age must have received some assistance.[31] On one occasion a tailor offered to escort a little girl of 10 back to her birthplace in East Tuddenham, some nine miles from Norwich, but this was a rarity.[32] Not surprisingly, children and adults occasionally resisted such pressures and they were quick to discover that sanctuary was still available in the cathedral precincts. An entry in the court books for January 1600 noted that 'the Bedells of the cittie doe this day complayne that rogishes boys and beggers escape from them and runn into the liberties of Christes Churche wher they are harbored and not punished and in the eveninges they goe abroade in the cittie begging'.[33]

If some escaped the attentions of the beadles many did not. In 1600 alone more than one hundred and sixty people were brought before the mayor's court for illegal entry to the city, and the numbers dealt with for this offence remained high for the next half century.[34] The disastrous harvests of the late 1590s were, no doubt, partially responsible for the large number of itinerants at the turn of the century, and a combination of harvest failure, plague and trade depression guaranteed the continued presence of such people throughout the 17th century and beyond.

Many of the individuals and families entering the city were recognisably not of the beggar class. There was all the difference in the world between Thomas Draper, deemed a dangerous rogue and branded on the shoulder for his offence when he arrived in Norwich in 1620, and the travelling shoemakers and blacksmiths who arrived there five and ten years later.[35] Nevertheless, any newcomer was a prospective charge on the city and viewed with the utmost suspicion. If he was well-behaved but poor he was ordered to depart, with the threat of punishment as a vagrant if he remained. It was accepted that immediate departure might cause undue hardship and a time-limit was usually imposed, varying from a few days to as much as three weeks.[36] The majority of those affected left without trouble. Some returned at a later date, either to be actually punished or to be given a further warning to depart. Most sought the shelter of their own homes again or looked, optimistically, for a warmer welcome elsewhere.

The magistrates never used the whip indiscriminately. As early as 1550 two undesirable women were simply ordered to 'departe out of the cittie and go whether they woll', as was one Margaret Thacker, ordered to leave in 1555 'for her vycyous and incontynent lyving'.[37] Despite being regarded unfavourably, wandering players and musicians were usually treated with the same latitude. John Gyrlynge of King's Lynn, 'callyng himselfe a musitian and beyng founde in this cytie exercysyn the ydle trade of mynstralsy' was called before the mayor in 1580 and warned to cease his activities or be punished as a rogue. Twenty years later Richard Rogers, described by the mayor as 'a ballett synger' and 'no better than a rogishe vagrante' received similar treatment. Even out-and-out vagrants could be released with a warning of future punishment, as could those that harboured them. On at least one occasion a man was returned to his home town with half-a-crown, rather than a whipping, to speed him on his way.[38]

The dividing line between the decision to mete out punishment or otherwise must have been a fine one. There is no obvious reason – other than local knowledge – why one vagrant should be whipped while another escaped with a warning, any more than there is for one family to be ordered to leave almost immediately while another was given several weeks grace. Even stranger was the attitude of the justices in the 1630s when they ordered men who had lived in the city for between four and seven years to depart or be punished as vagrants.[39] This exceptional severity can be paralleled elsewhere, however, a Yorkshire woman and her children being compelled to leave their homes after a stay of seven years.[40]

If the city was inconsistent in this respect, it was also transgressing against its own laws and against general judicial sentiment in the country at large. As early as 1547, an otherwise exceptionally severe statute had granted immunity from expulsion after a residence of three years, and this had been recognised in a local ordinance in 1557 and in the 'Orders for the Poor' in 1571.[41] Matters were taken a stage further in 1629 when Sir Francis Harvey, presiding over the summer assizes in Cambridge, decreed that J.P.s 'were not to meddle either with the removing or settling of any poor, but only of rogues', a declaration which received the full support of the Judges of Assize in 1633 who condemned the 'illegal unsetling, which the law forbiddeth, for none must be forced to turn vagrant'.[42] Two years later the same sentiments appeared in Michael Dalton's 'Country Justice' where it was asserted that 'no man is to be put from the town where he dwelleth, nor to be sent back to their place of birth, or last habitation, but a vagrant rogue'.[43] The Norwich authorities could hardly claim to be ill-informed in this respect for, apart from their own ordinances, they specifically ordered a copy of Dalton's book for use in the mayor's court soon after it was published.[44]

The reasons for inconsistent punishments can only be surmised. The men on the spot had to judge the relative poverty or aggressiveness of the individuals brought before them. In times of dearth, too, they had to protect their own citizens, whether from an increase in the poor-rate or from undue competition from outsiders. It was possibly these considerations which led the magistrates to authorise the settlement of a joiner who had rented a house and shop, and who could afford to pay 12d. a week towards the relief of the poor, and to order the displacement of a cordwainer as a prospective vagrant, despite the fact that he had succeeded in finding employment.[45] In general, any person who appeared likely to be a future charge on the community was ordered to depart. The economic climate was too uncertain to risk the indiscriminate settling of all and sundry, and excessive unemployment could always lead to a prospectively dangerous situation. As late as 1666, when plague increased unemployment, fears were expressed about the demeanour of the poor. Many of the wealthy fled, leaving their workmen unemployed, and those that remained were in constant fear of mob rule. The Norwich town clerk, Thomas Corie, who remained at his post, expressed the views of many when he wrote that 'wee are in greater feare of the poore then the plague' and at least one correspondent was convinced that the poor intended to take over the houses of those that had gone and plunder them at their convenience.[46]

37. A range of 16th and 17th-century houses in Bedford Street.

Plague, of course, was an intermittent problem and is considered in more detail below.[47] Harvest failure and economic crisis occurred all too frequently. In 1614, for example, James I was persuaded to forbid the export of unfinished cloth to the Continent. A company headed by William Cockayne, a London alderman, was given the sole right to bleach and dye such cloths and to export them to the European markets. The quality of the English finishing was poor, however, and it proved extremely difficult to sell the products abroad. Within two years cloth exports had fallen by more than one-half, leading to a crisis of over-production and widespread unemployment in the clothing industry.[48] The Cockayne fiasco was followed by further crises in 1621-2 and 1630-1, the latter linked with harvest failure, while the years 1646-50 saw one of the worst periods of successive harvest failure in the century. As ever, different parts of the country were affected at different times. In Warwickshire, cases involving resettlement of vagrants jumped from 29 in 1630-41 to 100 for the period 1649-60.[49]

Where Norwich is concerned, the evidence is conflicting. Rice Bush in his book, *The poor man's friend*, published in 1649, was able to assert that there were no beggars in such towns as Norwich, Ipswich and Dorchester, and judged by the number of cases brought before the mayor's court the problem in Norwich was certainly easing by the 1650s.[50] In contrast, a Norwich petition to parliament in 1649 declared that the trade of the city's merchants was utterly ruined, and that prices were inordinately high, wheat being 40s. a comb, rye 22s. and other provisions at proportionately high rates.[51] As the petition was one to reduce taxation, one is inclined to be very suspicious, but it is a picture which conforms with that painted for the rest of the country. Throughout much of the 1640s parliament was inundated with petitions complaining of the general state of trade, a situation which led Miss James to assert that 'there is little doubt that the Civil Wars increased the numbers both of genuine rogues and of those workless men who were too often confused with them'.[52] The story is much the same in 1659. A letter from the gentry of Norwich and Norfolk spoke of 'the loud outcryes of multitudes undone and almost famished people, occasioned by the generall decay of trade, which hath spread itself throughout the whole Nation, and these Counties in particular'.[53]

Inevitably, many people sought work in areas outside their immediate locality and just as inevitably they were turned away. The uncertainty of the Civil War and Commonwealth periods prevented any serious discussion of the problem, but within two years of the Restoration the government had produced the Act of Settlement, an act which, according to the Webbs, theoretically immobilised nine-tenths of the nation.[54] Any person not belonging to the propertied classes was prevented from settling in a new area unless he could provide absolute surety that he would never be a charge to the parish. It was not sufficient to prove employment. The justices had to be satisfied that a man had reserves to draw on in times of economic depression, otherwise he and his family were liable to summary removal to his last dwelling place.

The central authorities were doing no more than regularising an existing situation. Resistance to any impecunious newcomer had become almost commonplace in mid-17th century England, and at least one modern authority has seen the Act of Settlement as the final inevitable link in an evolutionary chain.[54] The act was by no means universally popular, however. Roger North, writing about the year 1670, was particularly scathing in his criticism: 'The poor are imprisoned in their towns[hips], and chained down to their wants, so that they are deprived of means to mend their condition, if their own wits or their friends should suggest any, by removing to places more proper for them either for sort of work or of friends to employ them. But if any chance to remove for experiment, they are sent back, and tossed from pillar to post in carts, till they return to their old settled misery again'. He concluded, 'surely it is a great imprisonment, if not slavery, to a poor family to be under such restraint by law that they must always live in one place whether they have friends, kindred, employment or not, or however they might mend their condition by moving; and all because they had the ill-luck to be born or to have served or resided a certain time there'.[55]

The act may have caused the genuine workman to hesitate before seeking employment elsewhere, but it was no more successful than its predecessors in restraining the professional vagrant. The Gloucestershire magistrates complained in 1678 of rogues and vagabonds 'grown soe insolent and presumptuous that they have oft by threates and menaces extorted money and victualls from those who live in houses far remote from neighbours'. Forty years after the act became law Defoe, when entering Wellington in Somerset, found himself surrounded by so many beggars that he had difficulty in keeping them from under his horse's hoofs.[56]

It remains true, nevertheless, that Norwich in the Commonwealth and Restoration periods was singularly free of unauthorised entrants if the numbers apprehended can be taken at all as a guide. The court kept a wary eye on the situation, and as late as November 1675 ordered the churchwardens to keep a register of all newcomers to the city. The registers were drawn up 'for the preventing of poore people comeing out of the country to inhabit in thys city', and had to be presented to the aldermen of the wards of the first Monday of every month when requisite action would be taken.[57] For whatever reason, vagrancy and illegal entry had ceased to be a major concern of the Norwich authorities before the advent of the Act of Settlement, and the stipulation referred to above seems to have been no more than a tightening of the screw. Poverty within the walls, in contrast, continued to demand their attention, and the extent of that problem can be gauged by the fact that some sixty per cent of the population were exempted from the payment of Hearth Tax in 1671, but the city fathers ensured that the burden did not become an insupportable one because of the intrusion of poverty-stricken outsiders.

The problem of the vagrant, while always kept within reasonable bounds, was one which occupied the attention of the court for much of the period under review. Other cases brought before the mayor's court occurred less frequently and, as such, merit less detailed treatment. They were, nevertheless, numerous. In 1570, for example, the justices dealt with cases involving arbitration between contending parties, adultery, apprenticeship misdemeanours, assault, begging, craft inquisitions, counterfeit passports, disobedience of officials, debt, disturbance of the peace, food and drink offences, the appointment and discharge of various officials, people charged with using seditious words, scolds, theft, and unlawful games.[58] Sixty years later the authorities were more concerned with drunkenness and swearing, but these offences apart they were dealing, in all essentials, with the same problems as their Elizabethan forebears.[59]

Punishments for the various offences altered little throughout the entire period. Assault, one of the more serious offences, was invariably rewarded with the cage, the whip, or a period in the Bridewell. The scold was either ducked or spent a period in the cage. 'Michery', a local expression for petty theft, was a frequent charge. In most cases, the material stolen was the produce of orchards and gardens, sometimes it was fence-rails or wood. The offences were seldom sufficiently serious to be transferred to Quarter Sessions, and normally resulted in a whipping for a child or a period in the stocks for an adult.[60]

People accused of immorality were brought before the court as often as those charged with theft. In the Elizabethan period the usual sentence was one of the public disgrace, the offending parties being paraded around the market place with paper hats on their heads and followed by a crowd tinkling basins. Subsequently, the sentence was one of whipping, ducking or a period in the House of Correction. Thus one woman was placed in the Bridewell for entertaining three men in her house after midnight while another was paraded around the market place with a placard reading, 'For keeping a house of bawdry'.[61]

The city's policy regarding immorality was influenced in part by the fear of incurring unnecessary costs. An illegitimate child could become a charge on the rates and in consequence the court was scrupulous in seeking out the father of a bastard child. The men concerned were usually bound over to Quarter Sessions, but once security had been given that the community would not be held responsible the father was released and discharged from his recognisance.[62]

If the official attitude to immorality was influenced by increasing costs, the court's policy towards drunkards, swearing and games players was influenced by a growing leaning towards Puritanism. As early as 1572 17 Dutchmen had been expelled from Norwich for 'the disgraceful vice of drunkenness' and, according to Camden, their English neighbours learned this art even more quickly than they absorbed the new methods of spinning and weaving. Offenders were fined 5s. or sentenced to six hours in the stocks, while those drinking after hours were required to pay 3s. 4d. or spend a period in the pillory.[63]

A surer way of preventing drunkenness was to limit the number of alehouses in the city, and it was the mayor's court which set their number, specifying precisely how many were to be allowed in each ward and liberty. In 1621, for example, it reduced the number from 54 to thirty-seven.[64] Eleven years later the individual aldermen were called upon to take a census of 'all inkeepers, alehouse keepers, cooks and sellers of bragget', both licensed and unlicensed.[65] In theory, no-one was supposed to keep an alehouse unless licensed to do so in Quarter Sessions, a stipulation dating back to the last years of Edward VI's reign, but many people ignored the ruling. In 1630 the court imposed a penalty of 20s. or the whip for each offence and vigorously pursued offenders, sending them to the House of Correction if they transgressed on more than one occasion. Similarly, existing alehouse keepers were brought before the court if they allowed patrons to tipple

38. *The Church Stile Inn.*

after hours or if they sold less than a full ale-quart for a penny. Offenders were usually forbidden to keep an alehouse for three years, the penalty being imposed either by the mayor's court or by the same justices at Quarter Sessions.[66]

Alehouses were seen as prospective haunts of idlers and vagabonds and the magistrates were most reluctant to see the lower classes spending an undue period of time in them. Partly because of this, they also took a somewhat repressive attitude towards popular amusements. Warrants were issued, for example, to prevent 'poor, idle, unruly and disordered persons' from frequenting a bowling alley, and the names of all those committed to Bridewell for haunting such a place were posted in a prominent position to act as a deterrent to others.[67] Even greater concern was expressed when such games took place on a Sunday. In 1589 the authorities noted that games players were entering the city on that day and playing during time of preaching, resulting in 'quarrels and brawls whereby murder hath ensued'.[68] Freemen were fined 16d. for participation, a fine which was increased to 3s. 4d. in 1596 when the offending games were listed as table tennis, cards, dice and bowls.[69] The city fathers had little success in their endeavours, individuals still being punished for the same offence 40 years later.[70]

Sabbatarian laws, as such, appear in the city records for the first time in 1570. In that year it was ordered that the city gates were to remain locked from Saturday night to Monday morning to prevent carts entering or leaving on the Sabbath, and to prevent beer carts being in the city on that day. No shops were allowed to open for buying, selling, or retailing on pain of a 3s. 4d. fine.[71] Trade regulations contain similar provisions, the cobblers, for example, being fined 1s. if they worked on Sundays.[72] By 1580 the punishments had become much more severe, a fine of £3 6s. 8d. being levied on every cart travelling to or from London on the Sabbath and one of 20s. for every laden horse.[73] Tradesmen were also dealt with more harshly towards the end of Elizabeth's reign. In 1660 a man was imprisoned for working on Ascension Day and two years later butchers were forbidden to kill on Sundays on pain of a fine of between ten and twenty shillings. They were not allowed to go to markets or fairs to buy animals on that day unless they had first heard evening prayer.[74]

In a city so obviously inspired by the puritan ideal, one would have expected increasing evidence of sabbatarianism during the 17th century. In fact, the entries relating to this offence are relatively few. This may do no more than indicate that breakers of the Sabbath were few and far between for, according to Strype, 'it was preached in Norfolk that to make a feast or wedding-dinner on that day was as great a sin as for a father to take a knife and cut his child's throat'. Laws were, nevertheless, enacted to avoid 'prophanation of the Lord's day' in 1615, 1623 and 1631, and in the first instance a campaign was subsequently launched against offenders; it was not repeated with the same enthusiasm after the subsequent enactments, possibly because the need was less great.[75] On occasion, as in the Elizabethan period, fines were levied on people who saw fit to travel on the Sabbath, 10s. being taken for each offence. In February 1655, however, the penalty notwithstanding, Robert Cawston had offended on eight occasions, Lidea Cawston on four and her sister Anne twice. By this time the court's patience had worn thin and it threatened to levy distresses on the parties concerned unless their fines were paid promptly. Outsiders were subjected to more summary treatment. Five butchers from Wymondham who arrived in Norwich on a Sunday were promptly placed in the stocks as they had no money to pay their fines. Inevitably, there were always some who resisted such enactments. At frequent intervals attempts were made to prevent carriers and watermen from plying their trade on the Lord's day, but the very need for repetition implies a reluctance to comply with the orders and the readiness of a few to disobey them.[76]

The mayor's court was equally concerned with the formal attendance of its own members at church and memorial services. In addition to regular attendance on Sundays, the members of the court were expected to appear at commemorative ceremonies for deceased benefactors and, during the Civil War period, at relatively frequent thanksgiving services for the successes of the parliamentary armies. Other services were held on the king's birthday and accession day and on 5 November. Sermons were anything but brief. On Gild Day, 1638, the members of the court listened to a sermon which, when printed, filled 150 pages.[77]

Sabbatarianism apart, much of the legislation referred to above reflects the attitude of the city fathers to the problem of the idle poor, and the same attitude was prevalent where wandering actors and entertainers were concerned. Elizabethan statutes against vagrancy classified all such people as idle rogues, and until the Restoration any man claiming to be one was lucky to escape without a whipping.[78] Groups of players were not frowned on to the same extent and they were occasionally licensed to perform in the city, particularly if they were under the patronage of a great personage or had a licence from the Master of the Revels, but whenever possible the magistrates resisted their pleas. Large gatherings could lead to the spread of plague or possibly to riots and disorders, and the city frequently petitioned the privy council to prevent such people from coming to Norwich. In 1623 it complained that it had recently been 'disquited' by players, tumblers and other entertainers, whose presence was prejudicial to local manufacturers, a petition which led the council to forbid such entertainers to enter the city until further notice. Subsequent petitions complained that plays consumed a large portion of the earnings of poor workmen, drove their families to want and imposed a financial burden on the city. On more than one occasion the magistrates went so far as to pay players to depart.[79] After the Restoration attitudes changed to some extent. In 1675, for example, a fire-eater was authorised to perform on more than one occasion, as was a woman who wanted to show two mermaids and a 'devouring great eating quaker'.[80]

The city's attitude was conditioned to a large extent by fear of increasing the poor rate, and entries abound in the court books concerning the methods adopted to relieve the local poor. These will be more properly considered in the next chapter. Here it is sufficient to note that the magistrates concerned themselves with providing work for the unemployed, with the appointment of officials and the organisation of the various city hospitals, with the provision of money and a supply of corn in times of dearth, with the organisation of the poor rate, and with the administration of endowments and bequests of various kinds.

The provision of work for the unemployed was only part of the city's responsibility. It was also concerned with apprenticeship regulations and with the appointment of male and female servants. In the case of apprentices, the court authorised the premium payable and kept a fairly conscientious watch over their welfare. Cases where a master had refused to accept an apprentice or had abandoned him were settled, a new master was provided if the original one died before the end of the apprenticeship, and any masters guilty of ill-treatment were suitably dealt with. Almost invariably, however, the apprentice was at fault, usually for refusing to work or running away. In either case, he received short shrift from the magistrates. Refusal to work in his master's house led to compulsory toil in Bridewell. Flight meant a whipping and a prompt return, sometimes with a pair of pothooks round his neck.[81]

At intervals the court concerned itself with the hiring of servants and, less frequently, with disputes between employer and employee. Thus in May 1563, in conformity with the Statute of Artificers, the magistrates ordered a man to serve in husbandry for a year at an annual wage of 33s. 4d., the person concerned being paid a retainer of one penny.[82] Seventy years later the rates of pay were much the same.[83] Thomas Games, who hired himself to a twisterer in 1630, was promised 30s. and a pair of shoes; Henry Bussey was put to service in the same year for a similar sum plus meat and drink.[84] By 1657, however, servants' wages had doubled, a man receiving £3 a year and a woman £2 with the addition of meat and drink.[85] Similar details of the hiring of servants are recorded in the court books throughout the Tudor and Stuart periods, but disputes between master and servant were seldom sufficiently serious to be brought to the attention of the court. A few examples occur in the early part of Elizabeth's reign. In February 1559, for example, the court had to arbitrate between a baker, who had hired himself to two masters, and the employers concerned. He was ordered to serve one for a week and then to go to the other.[86] Two years later a man who had promised the authorities that he would let his servant go to another master attempted to override the authority of the magistrates and appealed to the Duke of Norfolk. He was fined 10s., both for his effrontery and the fact that he had tried to conceal his original promise.[87] Physical assault was treated more seriously. A servant accused of beating his master and dame was placed in the stocks. Another, who broke his master's head with a pair of tailor's shears, was imprisoned. In the latter case insult was added to the master's injury for he was also imprisoned for not reporting the offence.[88]

As well as maintaining law and order in the city, the mayor's court was responsible for the welfare of the citizens of Norwich in other spheres. Poor relief has already been mentioned. Price regulation, market offences and the provision of corn in the time of dearth are discussed below. All were items of almost daily importance, and never more so than in time of plague.[89] The citizens of Norwich were well acquainted with this phenomenon. From its positive re-emergence in the middle years of the 16th century until its final disappearance in 1666, men were always present who could remember the previous outbreak. Plague had been present in a virulent form in both 1544-5 and 1555-6, being followed in the latter years by an influenza epidemic which itself swept away half of the city's ruling body as well as large numbers of its lesser citizens. In every decade from the middle years of Elizabeth's reign onwards the court had to make provision for plague victims. Severe attacks of bubonic plague occurred in 1579-80, 1584-5, 1589-92, 1625-6, 1636-8 and 1665-6, with less severe attacks in the intervening periods. That of 1579 may well have been as serious as the original onslaught of the Black Death in 1349, being responsible for the deaths of some six thousand people, or approximately one-third of the city's population. At least three thousand, five hundred people perished in the subsequent Elizabethan outbreaks, and almost as many again in both 1603-4 and 1625-6. For more than a century scarcely a decade passed without the presence of plague, its final disappearance in 1666 being preceded by the deaths of more than two thousand, two hundred individuals in a single year.[90]

39.   Inner courtyard of a 16th-century house in Coslany.

In the 1579 outbreak the authorities seem to have been aware of the existence of plague as early as February. On the 25th of that month it was alleged that the common well of the city in St Andrew's had been poisoned by people throwing in carrion and other filth 'to the great peril and danger of infection', and the aldermen of the ward were ordered to assess the inhabitants for the cost of a new pump which was to be erected as quickly as possible. It was not until the last day of March that it was admitted officially that plague had broken out, and then only in the parishes of St Stephen's and All Saints. In June when it became obvious that the infection was spreading the city appointed one Thomas Usher to record the weekly numbers of deaths, and his figures enable the course of the plague to be followed. For the week ending 27 June 1579 there were 56 deaths; by August the number had reached 244 and twice during that month the figures exceeded three hundred, reaching an appalling 352 towards its end. The weekly figures remained above two hundred until the middle of October and then slowly decreased to below fifty by December, but six months were to elapse before this severest of outbreaks finally petered out.

The authorities could do little to counter the onslaught. In July they made an order forbidding the victims to leave their houses for six weeks and provided money to sustain them during this period. Aldermen were expected to contribute 20s. each, past and present sheriffs 13s. 4d. and the common councillors 10s., 5s. or 2s. 6d. according to their status. The following year attempts were made to stamp out the plague before the summer months. Nobody living in an infected house was allowed out unless he carried a two-foot white wand as an indentification mark. The parish sextons were ordered to fix papers to the doors of the afflicted inscribed with the words, 'The Lord have mercye upon us', and in a further effort to avoid the infection spreading it was ordered that no household stuff was to be sold before the end of May.[91]

Precautions proved to be of little avail during the 16th-century outbreaks, but the city fathers were at least prepared for subsequent attacks. At the first suggestion of plague the aldermen were required to acquaint themselves with the parishes and houses affected, a requirement which was largely accomplished by the searchers appointed by the court. The bearers, buriers and searchers were given wages for the duration of the outbreak, and were forbidden to mix with the public without a distinguishing mark on their clothing or a red wand in their hands. Special arrangements were made to feed them and provide them with other necessaries while they were carrying out their duties. As in the 16th century, the houses of those afflicted were nailed up, suitable marks were placed on them, and watchmen were posted outside. The period of quarantine varied. In 1637 the court agreed it should last six weeks, but this could be waived provided the released person was 'wary not to put himself unnecessarily into company'. Apart from individual dwellings, pest-houses were provided where the same regulations were applied. The clothing of infected people was usually burned and as a further precaution wandering animals of any sort were summarily despatched.

It was accepted that the poor would be more adversely affected than others and special rates were levied to provide for their maintenance. The sums collected were paid to the Treasurers of the Infected Poor, officials specially appointed for the purpose, and minor officials were called upon to distribute the money to those in greatest need.[92]

The presence of plague accentuated the ever-present problem of the poor. Its presence meant a temporary increase in the poor rate, a more careful regulation of the price of corn, and increased efforts to see that grain was fairly distributed.[93] Normally, only the absolutely destitute could expect to receive such assistance. To ensure that the number of people in this category was kept to an absolute minimum the court kept a careful watch on prices. The mayor, as clerk of the market, regulated the price of both corn and beer and, from time to time, saw to it that prices of other commodities were kept at a reasonable level.[94] Tradesmen accused of selling bad, or underweight, food were examined by a jury appointed for the purpose, and if found guilty were fined sums which ranged from 1s. at the beginning of Elizabeth's reign to between 10s. and £1 by the middle years of the 17th century.[95] Innkeepers were told the maximum price they could charge for meals, while anyone found guilty of forestalling was suitably punished.[96]

If the number of cases brought before the justices is any guide at all, the city was successful in its endeavours and succeeded in establishing a firm hold on the trading activities of the people concerned. Between 1630 and 1635 the mayor had to act in his capacity as clerk of the market on only eight occasions, fining butchers for various offences in each case. Regulation of corn prices was a more frequent occurrence, being governed in part by both plague and harvest failure, but the evidence available suggests that market offences were a relatively minor source of irritation to the local justices.[97]

The offences brought before the mayor's court remained much the same throughout the Tudor and Stuart periods. Vagrants increased in numbers during the first half of the 17th century but never, apparently, to the extent that they caused the city any serious problems. Whenever possible, they were treated leniently by the standards of the time and a careful distinction was usually made between the obviously professional vagrant and the man desperately seeking work, an attitude which had evolved from the city's experiments with poor relief in the early years of Elizabeth's reign. A determination to keep the populace at work, to suppress idlers wherever possible, to look after the interests of the poor, whether by the provision of work or the supply of corn, were the constant concerns of the city fathers. A blend of paternalism and occasional repression ensured that the city was usually well governed. In times of plague or severe economic depression the task was made more difficult and sometimes, in those circumstances, the burden proved almost too heavy. Normally, a combination of aldermanic vigilance and zealous work by the officials concerned was enough to make Norwich one of the best-governed provincial cities in the kingdom.

*Chapter Ten*

# The Wage-Earning Classes and the Treatment of Poverty

## I The wage-earning classes

Under normal circumstances, the lives of the poor are shrouded in obscurity. It is generally assumed that they comprised between one-quarter and one-third of the urban population, with the amount of absolute destitution being gauged from the numbers actually receiving poor-relief.[1] With more certainty, it is similarly assumed that the wage-earning classes immediately above them made up some 40 per cent of those assessed for taxation in 1524-5 or, to look at it in another way, a further one-third of the population.[2] It has been common practice to link these two groupings together, to suggest that the urban poor accounted for anything up to two-thirds of a town's inhabitants, and to apply emotive terms such as 'grinding poverty' to these statistics to portray a situation of all-pervading gloom.

This is no longer satisfactory. In recent years historians have become more and more aware that even the apparently desperately poor were sometimes better off than was previously thought possible. In his recent study of Coventry, for example, Charles Phythian-Adams has emphasised that some of those given nil assessments in the 1522 military survey had domestic servants resident in their households, as did a few of the Norwich poor in 1570. He considers that 20 per cent would be a realistic estimate of the true rate of poverty in the town, a figure broadly in line with that of the poor in Elizabethan Norwich. It is also apparent that some of the wage earners, or people assessed on £1 worth of goods, were land or property owners in their own right, the proportion varying from 15 per cent in Sudbury to as much as 29 per cent in Great Yarmouth, and there seems no good reason to assume that the figures were not similar in other large towns.[3]

Statistical details apart, the only positive materials concerning the poor are contained in the various censuses which were compiled from time to time and in those inventories which were drawn up for the goods of a minority of them. Very little of the census material survives. The most comprehensive, by far, is the Norwich survey which was made in 1570 as a prelude to the complete reorganisation of the city's poor law scheme.[4] It lists 525 men and 860 women over the age of sixteen as well as almost a thousand of their children. The information provided is far-ranging. Ages and occupations are given in almost every case, as are details of house-ownership and the provision of alms. Where it is relevant to the city's purpose, information is also given about a person's place of origin and his period of residence in the city. Similarly, it is clearly stated whether an individual was employed or not at the time of the census and, in the cases of the children, the numbers receiving some form of education. From the details provided it is possible to establish the areas of the city in which the poor were most abundant, to place them in specific age groups, to estimate the average size of their families and the extent to which their children were educated, to draw up a complete trade structure of the poor, both male and female, and in the process get an impression of the importance of female and child labour, to estimate the extent of unemployment among people of this class, to gauge the interest of the various classes in housing the poor and discover how far they had to be self-supporting, and, finally, to get some impression of the amount of mobility among the city's destitute.

Norwich, in 1570, had an English population of some eight thousand people, a population which was expanding rapidly as the steady trickle of Dutch and Walloon refugees grew into a flood. The aliens, many of whom were poor, tended to crown into the industrial areas of the city, particularly those situated beyond the river. It was a move which was necessary for the exercise of their crafts but it exacerbated an already difficult situation, for it was here that the native poor were most heavily concentrated. More than half of the English poor recorded in the census lived in a broad band of territory stretching from St Giles in the extreme west of the city, through the ward of West Wymer, and on to the three wards of Coslany, Colegate and Fyebridge situated beyond the river. The small ward of St Giles had the heaviest concentration of poor in the city, with more than half of its inhabitants finding their way into the town's poor books. Large numbers of native poor were also to be found in the southern parts of Norwich, something like forty per cent of the total population of Conesford falling into this category. The adjoining ward of St Stephen's had a quarter of its inhabitants recorded in the census. In complete contrast, these predominantly poor areas of the city were separated by the three large and wealthy wards of St Peter Mancroft, and Middle and East Wymer which, between them, housed fewer than one-eighth of the city's destitute. Middle and East Wymer, with poor populations of only nine and 11 per cent respectively, were particularly free of such people and had a correspondingly heavy burden to bear when the poor rate was radically increased later in the year.[5]

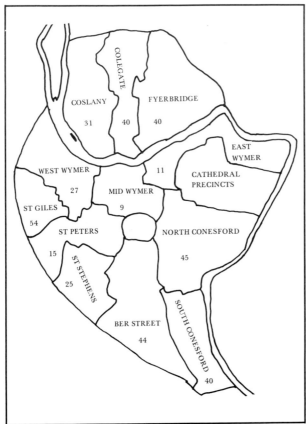

40. The distribution of poverty in Norwich in 1570. The figures represent the poor as a percentage of the estimated population of each ward.

Table 10.1 provides supporting evidence for the figures discussed above, as well as indicating the heavy demands placed on the rest of the population for the provision of poor relief. The over 60s comprised 13 per cent of the adult males named in the census of the poor, but I have followed the guidelines provided by the Ealing census of 1599 and have assumed seven per cent for the city as a whole, distributed among the wards in the same proportions as in the muster totals. The under 16s are assumed to comprise 40 per cent of the population and the women to number the same as the men.

While caution is obviously necessary where population estimates are concerned, the figures for the estimated population compare interestingly with those in the penultimate column and lend some credence to the suggestion given elsewhere that few people not named in the census escaped the necessity of contribution to poor relief. Virtually everybody not named in the census – as well as 20 families who were – was called upon to contribute, the thousand or so people listed in 1575-6 contrasting starkly with the 612 recorded in the subsidy roll for the same year.[6]

**Table 10.1 The extent and distribution of poverty in Norwich, c. 1575**

| Ward | Muster totals 1569 | Estimated: Over 60s | Estimated: Total males | Total adults | Total pop. | Number of poor | % of poor | Number in 1575-6* | Contributors: × 4.75 + poor | Contributors: × 4.75 + poor as % of est. pop. |
|---|---|---|---|---|---|---|---|---|---|---|
| South Conesford | 101 | 8 | 109 | 218 | 363 | 147 | 40 | 45 | 361 | 99 |
| North Conesford | 110 | 9 | 119 | 238 | 397 | 180 | 45 | 27 | 308 | 78 |
| Ber Street | 217 | 17 | 234 | 468 | 780 | 341 | 44 | 82 | 730 | 94 |
| St Stephen's | 186 | 14 | 200 | 400 | 667 | 170 | 25 | 78 | 540 | 81 |
| St Peter's | 207 | 15 | 222 | 444 | 740 | 109 | 15 | 114 | 650 | 88 |
| St Giles' | 35 | 3 | 38 | 76 | 127 | 69 | 54 | 24 | 183 | 144 |
| West Wymer | 305 | 22 | 327 | 654 | 1,090 | 298 | 27 | 134 | 934 | 86 |
| Middle Wymer | 208 | 15 | 223 | 446 | 743 | 69 | 9 | 109 | 587 | 79 |
| East Wymer | 258 | 19 | 277 | 554 | 923 | 106 | 11 | 105 | 605 | 66 |
| Coslany | 227 | 17 | 244 | 488 | 813 | 251 | 31 | 76 | 612 | 75 |
| Colegate | 172 | 14 | 186 | 372 | 620 | 246 | 40 | 79 | 621 | 100 |
| Fyebridge | 259 | 19 | 278 | 556 | 927 | 373 | 40 | 122 | 952 | 103 |
| Totals | 2,285 | 172 | 2,457 | 4,914 | 8,190 | 2,359 | 29 | 995 | 7,083 | 86 |

*Based on the maximum number of contributors in each of the two years

At the time of the census the vast majority of the Norwich poor were in some form of employment. They included master craftsmen who had fallen on hard times and journeymen who had completed an apprenticeship but had yet to attain their freedom, as well as a miscellany of individuals following a variety of trades. Thirteen of the families were actually contributing to the poor rate, despite being included in the census, a number which was to be increased to 20 when the city widened its net considerably after the results of the census were known.[6] It was the prospect of employment, rather than the lure of easy pickings, which had encouraged most of the non-local families to come to the city in the first place. In 1570 at least half of the city's poor were not local born, although many had lived in Norwich for so long that they were virtually natives by default. Seventy-five families, or just under 11 per cent of those for whom the requisite information is recorded, had lived there for more than twenty years. A further 261 families, or 38 per cent of the whole, had migrated there during the previous 20 years. The Norwich authorities were particularly concerned with the most recent arrivals, the thirty or so families which had been resident for three years or less. Wherever possible, they sought information not only about their actual period of residence but also about their place of origin. Significantly, as the following table indicates, the details become progressively less the longer a family had established itself. The city was concerned to rid itself of these recent arrivals, if it was at all justified. It was less worried about the long-established groups, provided they were not too great a strain on the local resources.

It becomes apparent, from such details as we have, that the majority of the immigrants were from Norfolk and Suffolk. Nevertheless, one-third of the known cases came from further afield. Eleven of the 27 families who had settled in Norwich in the previous 10 years, and who had origins outside East Anglia, came from the northern counties. Individual families came from as far afield as Wales and Ireland. Others came from the West Country, the Midlands, London and Cambridge. An apparently single man came from Scotland.

All found the city sufficiently congenial to cease their wanderings, and they had settled in without any undue pressure from the authorities.

**Table 10.2 Origins of Norwich immigrants with up to twenty years residence in the city**

| Years of residence | Places of origin | | | | Totals | Percentages | |
|---|---|---|---|---|---|---|---|
| | Norfolk | Suffolk | Elsewhere | Unknown | | Known | Unknown |
| 1 to 5 | 27 | 3 | 8 | 19 | 57 | *66.66* | *33.33* |
| 6 to 10 | 20 | 10 | 19 | 42 | 91 | *53.85* | *46.15* |
| 11 to 20 | 3 | - | 1 | 109 | 113 | *3.54* | *96.46* |
| Totals | 50 | 13 | 28 | 170 | 261 | *34.87* | *65.13* |

If the census is less than full about a person's origins, it is the reverse where details of age and marital status are concerned. Almost every adult over the age of 16 had his or her age clearly stated, little more than three per cent of the men and just under six per cent of the women having this information unrecorded. The same is true of marital status. Few of the men were unmarried, and the women are normally indicated as either married, widowed or deserted. Where this is not stated, even in the case of elderly women, it seems probable that they had never married. Sometimes this is clearly apparent. At others, particularly where the surnames of mothers and children are the same, the details are rather ambiguous. As precise information is given in 85 per cent of the cases, however, the problem is a small one.

A large proportion of both sexes were aged between thirty-one and forty, almost 29 per cent of the men and 26 per cent of the women falling into this category. Just under one-quarter were younger, their ages varying between sixteen and thirty. Of greater significance, however, is the relatively large number of people who had survived into old age. Just over one-fifth of the men and a quarter of the women were aged 60 and above, a significantly high total in an age when 50 was considered elderly and the poor might have been expected to succumb more quickly than their wealthier counterparts. Among the aged poor, seven men and 15 women were aged 80 and above, two of the women allegedly being centenarians.

Evidence of this sort does not square too easily with the official assertion that the city's poor were almost universally disease-ridden. Some were, and are described as such. Several were maimed in some way, others had lost limbs, but such people were in a distinct minority. For the older among them their environment may have at least partially contributed to their longevity. Norwich had always had a reputation for cleanliness, and until the advent of the Dutch and Walloons caused severe overcrowding in some areas there is little evidence that the poor were unduly congested. Fewer than one family in five lived in households containing more than four people, and although many of these lived in tenements, one house sometimes containing several families, congestion was rare. Three-quarters of the 459 dwellings of the poor contained six people or less; one-quarter of them housed no more than one or two.

With one or two exceptions which will be dealt with below, the houses or buildings containing relatively large numbers of poor were not in private hands. All belonged to the church or civic authorities. There were 12 church and two college houses in the city which between them provided shelter for 95 poor people. The two college houses were in the parish of St Michael's at Coslany. One was apparently a small dwelling and housed a single widow. The other was large and contained eight families comprising, between them, no fewer than 29 people. The church houses were scattered about the city. Four in St Benedict's housed 23 people; a single house in St John's, Maddermarket, provided shelter for 12; another in St Stephen's was the home of two childless married couples, a single person and a family of five. A number of people were also housed in the hospital precincts within the city. Twenty-four people lived in the 13 houses in the main city hospital known

41. A yard opposite St Benedict's church.

as the Normans, several of them being widows. St Giles' Hospital provided homes for 16 individuals. Another large hospital house in St Augustine's sheltered 19 people. The parish houses, too, were sometimes large if the numbers contained within them are any guide. Thus one house in the parish of St John at the Gates in Ber Street contained six families, totalling 19 people, another in St Stephen's housed fifteen. Between them the nine parish houses described as such provided shelter for 62 of the city's poor. Finally, 58 people lived in eight gatehouses and 12 of the towers around the city walls.

**Table 10.3 Number of poor housed in civic and church property**

| Description of property | Number of houses | Numbers within them | Percentage housed in such property |
|---|---|---|---|
| Church houses | 12 | 65 | 21.7 |
| Parish houses | 9 | 62 | 20.7 |
| Hospital houses | 4 | 35 | 11.7 |
| Gatehouses | 8 | 33 | 11.0 |
| College houses | 2 | 30 | 10.0 |
| City houses | 3 | 26 | 8.7 |
| Towers | 12 | 25 | 8.3 |
| Normans | 13 | 24 | 8.0 |
| Totals | 63 | 300 | |

The remaining 396 houses of the poor in the city were in private hands. By far the majority of these belonged to people who were either already serving the city as aldermen and councillors, or who were to do so in the immediate future. John Aldrich, the mayor, owned five such houses, two in North Conesford and one each in St Mary's Coslany, St Botolph's and St Clement's. Between them they provided shelter for 33 of the people he condemned so sweepingly in the preamble to the orders of the poor. John Sotherton and Robert Suckling also owned five houses apiece while Edward Pye had no fewer than seven. Others owned two or three, many had no more than one. A few of the city's ruling classes had turned over really large houses to the poorer classes to be used as tenements, presumably with the intention of extracting what profits they could from the transaction. Thus one of John Blennerhasset's houses in St Paul's contained eight families, or a total of 23 individuals. John Sotherton owned a house in St Mary's, Coslany, which housed even more, 11 families, comprising 34 people, being crowded into its confines. One of Thomas Parker's houses in Pockthorpe contained 20 people; Augustine Steward's two properties in North Conesford contained 17 and 14 people respectively; Edward Warden's house in St Gregory's housed 15; one of Aldrich's in St Mary's Coslany had 13 people living in it; while John Rede's property in St Saviour's housed two families, each containing six people. Several of the city fathers owned properties which were let to 10 people; many had tenements which contained six people or more. Despite their subsequent protestations, it is clear that the propertied classes in the city saw the poor as a source of income as well as a prospective nuisance. In the process, they may well have been guilty of severe overcrowding in a minority of cases, although in the absence of precise details about the size of houses one cannot be dogmatic on the point. It is most unlikely that either they, or the other freemen referred to below, sheltered the poor out of any feelings of pity. Indeed, more than twenty years previously they had passed laws specifically forbidding such 'charity' and they continued to pay lip service to this ideal.[7]

Apart from the owner-occupiers among the poor themselves, the rest of the privately owned property in the city was distributed among 55 freemen who were never to attain civic importance, 58 men who either for lack of money or lack of inclination never took up their freedom, and 22 women. Most of these people owned single houses, but there were exceptions. Thus among the freemen Nicholas Kent, baker, owned five properties in All Saints'; Christopher Austen, a cordwainer, had three houses, one large enough to contain 12 people; one of John Gose's two houses in St Benedict's sheltered 16 of the poor; while eight families, containing 22 individuals, were crowded into John Lynge's two properties in Pockthorpe. Among the non-freemen, Humphrey Rant, a man of some substance, had a house in All Saints' large enough to contain 17 people; Thomas Richman owned one of a similar size in St Swithin's; while John Hemming's five properties in St Andrew's and St Julian's, none apparently exceptionally large, provided accommodation for a further 19 individuals. Few of the women owners possessed more than one house or had large properties, the major exceptions being a Mrs. Felix who owned four houses in North Conesford and one in St Giles', Mrs. Norgate, whose single house in St Augustine's contained 15 of the poor, and Mrs. Croke, one of whose houses contained 25 people.

The final group of house-owners in the city come from within the ranks of the poor themselves. Sixty-one families, or between eight and nine per cent of the whole, owned their own property. Ten of the householders were widows, with labourers, textile, leather and building workers predominating among the men. In one or two cases the houses had been mortgaged, others were still 'in purchase'. Occasionally the sums owed are quoted. Thus a widow in the parish of St John at the Gates was said to owe £8 for her property, another had a further £5 to pay. In the majority of cases, however, the families concerned were in full possession of their properties. Not surprisingly, they took in lodgers whenever possible. A weaver in St Paul's had 16 people in his house, and this was hardly likely to have been a large dwelling. Two of the families were sufficiently prosperous to own more than one house. A currier in the parish of St John on the Hill had two, a haymaker in St Augustine's had three.

**Table 10.4 Owners of private property used to house the poor**

| Category | No. of owners | 1 | 2 | 3 | 4 | 5 | 6 | 7 | No. of houses | Total housed | Av. No. per house | % of houses owned |
|---|---|---|---|---|---|---|---|---|---|---|---|---|
| | | No. of houses owned | | | | | | | | | | |
| Aldermen and Councillors | 78 | 48 | 11 | 11 | 2 | 4 | 1 | 1 | 144 | 792 | 5.5 | *36.3* |
| Other freemen | 55 | 36 | 11 | 4 | 3 | 1 | - | - | 87 | 454 | 5.2 | *21.9* |
| Non-freemen | 58 | 46 | 7 | 3 | - | 1 | - | - | 75 | 375 | 5.0 | *18.9* |
| Owner-occupiers | 61 | 59 | 1 | 1 | - | - | - | - | 64 | 289 | 4.5 | *16.1* |
| Non-poor women | 22 | 20 | 1 | - | - | 1 | - | - | 26 | 149 | 5.7 | *6.8* |
| Totals | 274 | 210 | 31 | 19 | 5 | 7 | 1 | 1 | 396 | 2,059 | 5.2 | *100.0* |

Whether tenant or owner-occupier, paying rent, however nominal, or paying off a mortgage, some form of income in addition to that required for normal family needs was essential. In fact, the vast majority of both men and women were in some form of employment. Despite the steady decline of the textile industry in 16th-century Norwich, and the decreasing number of people being admitted to the freedom of the city in such occupations, a number of the poor were employed as worsted weavers. No more than eight of the 68 described as such in the census were unemployed, and in the textile industry as a whole 106 of the 120 workers had employment of some kind. The same story is true of the other occupational groupings. In those in which relatively large numbers were employed, 75 per cent of the leather workers and over 60 per cent of the labourers were in gainful employment. In the building trades, in contrast, some difficulties were obviously being experienced, rather more than half of such workers being described as unemployed. Four out of the five glaziers were in this category and seven out of the 11 masons. It was only among the men where no specific occupation was given that unemployment was really rife, however, and it may be guessed that these 39 included a proportion of genuine beggars. Some, of course, were simply too old to work any longer. The overall position is summarised below.

**Table 10.5 Occupational groupings of poor men**

| Occupational groupings | Numbers | | Percentages |
|---|---|---|---|
| Labourers | 120 | *75* | 23.4 |
| Textiles | 120 | *106* | 23.4 |
| Leatherwork | 64 | *47* | 12.5 |
| Building | 50 | *24* | 9.7 |
| Miscellaneous | 27 | *19* | 5.3 |
| Clothing | 26 | *16* | 5.1 |
| Food & Drink | 23 | *18* | 4.5 |
| Metalwork | 21 | *15* | 4.1 |
| Transport | 8 | *7* | 1.6 |
| Woodwork | 5 | *4* | 1.0 |
| Distributive | 4 | *3* | 0.8 |
| Professional | 4 | *4* | 0.8 |
| Unspecified | 41 | *2* | 8.0 |
| Totals | 513 | *340* | |

The figures in italics indicate the numbers in employment in the various occupational groupings. The residue were unemployed.

Important though the earnings of the head of the household were, they were seldom sufficient for the needs of the family as a whole, and the census reveals the very great reliance placed on both female and child labour. Like the men, almost all of the women were in some form of employment. Spinning bulked large in the female occupations, over three-quarters of the employed women being engaged in some form of this work. Those spinning white warp were the most numerous, the 348 women thus designated making up 42 per cent of the total female labour force. Important subsidiary occupations were sewing, knitting and weaving which between them employed a further 100 people, or some 12 per cent of the whole. These occupations apart, the women were engaged in a variety of jobs. Some sold *aqua vitae*, flesh, sauce and links (probably sausages). Others were pedlars, pipe fillers, servants, washerwomen and teachers of knitting. Many combined more than one occupation. Thus we have women who knit and sew, who sew and make buttons, and who sew and sell bread and other victuals. Others spin and make malt; some combine spinning with dressing meat and drink, with picking chalk and selling fish. One was employed in teaching children to spin, another travelled on her husband's behalf. Little more than 12 per cent of the women have no occupation to their names and, as in the case of the men, a number of these were beyond work of any description.

Most of the children were employed as well as their parents. The third definitely described as being aged between one and five years old can almost certainly be supplemented by many of those of unspecified age who are referred to as being very young, thus raising the total to somewhere between forty and forty-five per cent of the whole. A majority of these children were far too young to work, but a child living in St Peter's Southgate had begun to weave at the age of four, and others were in employment by the time they were five. In all, some three hundred and thirty children and young people between the ages of four and 20, or about three-quarters of those for whom we have positive ages, helped to supplement the earnings of their elders. Where the sex of a child is given, it seems that girls were more likely to be employed than boys, but as this information is provided in only 30 per cent of the recorded cases, such a suggestion must necessarily be tentative. As in the case of the women, many were concerned with spinning and weaving. Others had a miscellany of occupations. One boy kept a bowling alley; another, a tinker's son, carried his father's bag; a girl looked after an elderly couple and a boy acted as guide to a blind man. Few of the latter 'occupations' can have added much to the family income, but the earnings of the children as a whole were not unimportant. On two occasions, both relating to girls spinning great hose, the children were described as the families' chief source of income. Poor as many of them may have been, not all of the parents felt obliged to make their children work. A minority of the boys and girls (77 in all, or perhaps 16 per cent of those aged between five and 12) were sent to school, even when their fathers were unemployed. In some cases, the schools were almost certainly of an industrial nature where the children would be taught the rudiments of spinning or weaving but a few, at least, were concerned with teaching of a more academic nature and at worst combined this aspect with preparing the children for some sort of future occupation. The city authorities considered schooling to be sufficiently important to make special provision for it when they reorganised their poor law scheme. Twelve youngsters kept in St Giles' Hospital were ordered to be taught their letters by the resident bailiff and his wife 'as their capacities shall be hable to attayne', a provision which was still, apparently, in force some twenty years later.

**Table 10.6 Occupational groupings of poor women**

| Occupational groupings | Numbers | Percentages |
|---|---|---|
| Spinning | 563 | 67.2 |
| Textiles* | 41 | 4.9 |
| Clothing | 91 | 10.9 |
| Miscellaneous | 28 | 3.3 |
| Food & Drink | 12 | 1.4 |
| Unspecified | 103 | 12.3 |
| Total | 838 | |

* This refers to textiles other than spinning. Of those with occupations to their names, five spinners of white warp, a knitter, a kersey spinner, a mentle-warp spinner, a carder and spinner, a white-webbing spinner and a teacher of children were described as unemployed.

Almost all of the adult males listed in the census were married men. One-third of them had no children, several of these being young men in the 21-30 age-group. A further 40 per cent had families containing either one or two children, just over one-fifth had families with three or four, and fewer than one in twenty had large families with five or more children. As might be expected, men in the 31-40 age group had the largest number of resident children, although the few really large families belonged to still older men. Labourers tended to have smaller families than those in skilled occupations, no more than nine per cent of them having four or more children compared to the 15 to 17 per cent of the textile, building and leather workers.[8]

Apart from the married couples two men, probably widowers, and 112 women had children. Sixty-seven of the women were widows, 27 deserted wives and 18 were of no clear status.

**Table 10.7 Distribution of children among the poor**

| Category | No. of families with children | No. of children | | | | | | | | Total children | Average per family |
|---|---|---|---|---|---|---|---|---|---|---|---|
| | | 1 | 2 | 3 | 4 | 5 | 6 | 7 | 8 | | |
| Married couples | 331 | 115 | 85 | 67 | 38 | 16 | 5 | 2 | 3 | 786 | 2.37 |
| Widows | 67 | 40 | 15 | 6 | 4 | 2 | - | - | - | 114 | 1.70 |
| Deserted wives | 27 | 13 | 7 | 2 | 3 | - | 1 | 1 | - | 57 | 2.11 |
| Others | 20 | 9 | 9 | 2 | - | - | - | - | - | 33 | 1.65 |
| Totals | 445 | 177 | 116 | 77 | 45 | 18 | 6 | 3 | 3 | 990 | 2.22 |

The number of children had little or no bearing on the amount of support a family might expect from the city authorities. If the main bread-winner, whether man or woman, was designated 'able' the city was seldom prepared to subsidise his or her family. The fact that a man might be temporarily unemployed made no difference to the officials concerned. It was considered his responsibility entirely, and if in times of real distress he begged his bread from his more affluent neighbours he was vigorously denounced for his temerity. With this attitude prevailing, it is not surprising to find that on the eve of the census more than 75 per cent of those subsequently recorded were receiving no support at all. The rest received relatively small sums of money, little more than 10 per cent of the families getting sums in excess of twopence a week.

Life was especially burdensome for those women who had no husband to support them. There were 366 of these in the city; 46 had been deserted by their husbands, 183 were widows and 137 had no status attributed to them. Many of those deserted had not seen their husbands for some considerable time. In a few cases, the men had left to seek work elsewhere and maintained contact with their families. A boy of 13 was reported to have joined his father in London, possibly as a prelude to a general exodus for the details of the family were later crossed out in the census. In another case a woman knew that her husband was ill in one of the London hospitals. Almost invariably, however, such desertion was permanent. The widows were in a slightly better position for they always had the chance of another marriage even, apparently if they were quite elderly. The census records a number of examples of married women who were considerably older than their husbands, in exceptional cases twice their age. The fact remains that until such marriage, or re-marriage, took place, their position was that much more tenuous than their fellows. If they had children it must have been virtually untenable.

Poor though these people were some, at least, gathered sufficient possessions to make it worth an appraiser's while to draw up an inventory of their goods at the owner's death. While seldom dealing with the absolutely poverty-stricken, these inventories provide us with an alternative source from which to obtain details of the poor and one which gives another dimension to the evidence discussed above.

In this context people are deemed poor who owned property worth up to £10 before 1600 and up to £15 in the subsequent period. Their inventories follow a general pattern and lend themselves to analysis in five ways. About a quarter of them provide details of the various rooms in the house – or section of a house if the building was subdivided – which can be compared with the dwellings of the farm labourers discussed by Professor Everitt.[9] Both these and the remaining inventories can be analysed to ascertain the proportion of domestic goods in the households, the value of the bedding, the relative value of the clothing and, finally, details of those households containing books and animals.

The vast majority of the inventories give no indication of the number or type of rooms in the various houses. Fewer than one-quarter provide details of this sort in the Elizabethan period and, although subsequent inventories are more informative, this basic information is still lacking for some two-thirds of the houses in the late 17th century. This was not an unusual situation. Some seventy per cent of the inventories examined by Professors Barley and Everitt were equally uninformative. In many cases they were almost certainly one-roomed houses, possibly medieval survivals open to the roof. In others, the lack of detail may do no more than indicate the impreciseness of the appraisers, particularly where details of living and sleeping accommodation are followed by those of kitchenware, indicating progress from one room to another.

One is on safer ground when dealing with the documents which provide positive details of the various rooms. During the whole of the period 1584-1675 this information is given in 70 instances, or about twenty-five per cent of the whole. Approximately 26 per cent of these houses contained two rooms, 60 per cent had between three to five, distributed in roughly equal proportions, and a further 14 per cent contained six or more rooms.[10]

In contrast to the houses of the typical rural labourer, there was a tendency for the proportion of city dwellers with two-roomed houses to increase as the century progressed, twice as many being thus housed in the post-Jacobean period as in the Elizabethan. The same period saw a radical decline in the number of houses with six rooms or more, but this may do no more than reflect the chance survival of inventories recording this information. Nevertheless, in the middle and later years of the 17th century three-quarters of these people lived in houses which had at least three rooms, a proportion which corresponds closely with the situation in rural areas in general and may, indeed, reflect a general trend.

Within these general figures, one can observe some changes in the actual structure of the houses. The hall, which was named or obviously present in two-thirds of the Elizabethan and three-quarters of the Jacobean inventories, was mentioned in only one-quarter of those surviving for the later 17th century. In part, this is explained by the increasing use of what was the hall for a cooking area. In no more than a dozen cases, distributed equally between the three periods, were the hall and kitchen referred to together. In contrast, the kitchen is mentioned as a distinct unit on 17 occasions, 10 of these occurring the period after 1625. This is a phenomenon which Professor Barley has observed elsewhere and the Norwich inventories may again reflect a general trend.[11] The same is true of the less frequent use of the medieval term 'buttery'. More than 58 per cent of the late Elizabethan inventories record such a unit whereas the proportion had fallen to a little more than 17 per cent in the post-Jacobean period.

More surprising is the decline in the use of the parlour or, to be more precise, the less frequent references to it. In the years up to 1600 this room was mentioned in 74 per cent of the relevant inventories, in the first 25 years of the 17th century it was referred to in more than half the recorded cases, while in the post-Jacobean era the proportion had fallen to as low as 22 per cent. This is puzzling, particularly as almost all of these houses had upstairs chambers. It would suggest that such innovations in house structure as had taken place were restricted to the provision of an upstairs room, probably reached by a ladder rather than stairs, which was used for storage as well as for sleeping purposes. This particular point is discussed more fully below, but one would have expected a reversal of the trend with increasing sub-division of the lower rooms as the century progressed, rather than the reverse. It may be that this again reflects the chance survival of particular inventories rather than a positive trend, but it is impossible to be dogmatic on the point.

42.  Weavers Lane.

43.  Bear Yard, Gentleman's Walk, 1862.

There was greater consistency in the number of chambers recorded. From the age of Elizabeth to that of Charles II fewer than one house in five comprised a single storey, while almost 40 per cent of the inventories record the presence of a second upstairs room and one in 10 a third.

Apart from these more usual rooms, a number of others are referred to in the individual inventories. Shops are mentioned on 17 occasions, one man, Thomas Mace of the parish of All Saints, owning no fewer than three, a distinction which was still unable to raise the total value of his inventory to much above £15. Other rooms referred to include cellars, working houses, vaults, attics and, in a few individual cases, pastry cellars and brewhouses.[12]

On the evidence available, it would seem that the housing revolution had affected more poorer people in Norwich than in most rural areas. Virtually all of the labourers' inventories analysed by Professor Everitt make reference to a hall while no more than one-fifth refer to a kitchen, implying a slower rate of adaption.[13] The same is true where an upper chamber is concerned. Four out of five of the city dwellers had had their houses converted in this fashion compared to the three in five of their rural counterparts, and the contrast is greater still where additional chambers are concerned. Twice as many Norwich men had a second compartment upstairs and three times as many a third. In contrast, when it comes to older established rooms such as the buttery and the fire-house the situation is very similar in both rural and urban areas. The latter term, almost certainly a medieval survival, is met with in Norwich as late as 1640.[14]

Turning to the contents of the rooms, one is again aware of the sharp contrast between the living conditions of the townsman and the countryman. Professor Everitt has pointed out that very few labourers in rural areas could afford the luxury of domestic ware, by far the greater part of their possessions comprising their domestic animals and stock.[15] In contrast, over 60 per cent of the men and women whose goods were assessed in late Elizabethan Norwich owned little more than their furniture, and the proportion rose to as high as 70 per cent in the succeeding years.[16]

The value of individual goods over the period as a whole ranged from just under £1 to in excess of £13, with a notable increase in value as the century progressed. At the end of Elizabeth's reign no more than one-third of the people here designated as poor owned domestic goods worth more than £5 whereas in the Caroline and Commonwealth periods the proportion had increased to one-half.

Typical of the less wealthy was Robert Teale who died in 1595 possessed of property assessed at £1 7s. 3d.[17] His domestic ware, including his bedding worth 4s. 8d., made up £1 1s. 11d. of this sum, the remainder comprising his clothing worth 5s. and his bow and arrows which were priced at four pence. Similar in status was Thomas Gray, 'a pore lame man & almost blind which reseived wekely collection'.[18] At his death in 1618 Gray was worth £2 6s. 8d. Apart from his apparel which was worth 6s. 8d. and his bedding which, at £1, made up half the total value of his domestic wares, his sole possessions were three old kettles valued at 6s. 8d., an old frying pan, two earthen pots, six dishes and wooden platters, a 'cowl', two old coffers, a little box, an old tub, a little sieve, a spinning wheel, two or three old pieces of board, a pail, a little gridiron, a little pair of hakes, a 'towcome', two little pewter dishes, three saucers and six trenchers. He apparently possessed neither chairs nor table in his single-roomed house, indeed very little apart from his eating and drinking utensils and his bed, and must have eked out a precarious living supported by his wife's activities at the spinning wheel. Edmund Ransom, who died 20 years later, was poorer still if the value of his inventory is a true indication.[19] The appraisers summed up his worldly possessions in 24 words: 'An old bedstead, fetherbed nat & cord and an old cubbart and an old tables, a forme and thre old chayres prised at 25s.' Ransom must have had some clothes and, presumably, something from which to eat and drink but, like Gray and Teale, he was desperately poor.

Where a man was wealthier at this level it was only in a relative sense. Perhaps he had a little more pewter or brassware, some cushions or the occasional trappings of luxury such as a looking-glass or some pieces of joined furniture, even, on occasion, some animals. One such was Thomas Plowman who died in 1584 worth £5 19s. 3d. He owned feather, trundle and transome beds in addition to a couple of chests, a table and chairs, some pewter candlesticks, oddments of kitchenware and a cow worth 30 shillings. Each of his possessions was carefully itemised in his will and duly bequeathed to a relative or friend. His clothing was enumerated in some detail, and was in sufficiently good condition to be valued at 18s. 3d., or some 15 per cent of the total inventory. It included black and white doublets, blue, grey and velvet hose, three shirts, black, white and frieze coats, an old cloth gown and black drawers. Like most of his class, Plowman had little or no ready money in his possession and had to make arrangements for the sale of his cow to meet his few monetary bequests. The picture which emerges is one of a soberly-dressed man, probably just above the poverty line, extracting a meagre living from his activities as a husbandman or general labourer, and dying secure in the knowledge that his relatives were not left in absolute penury.[20]

Almost without exception, the most important item of a man's domestic ware was his bedding. Throughout the entire period three men in five owned bedding which made up between thirty and sixty per cent of their household goods, and in a few cases it was the only property an individual owned, apart from his clothing. As an item, the value of bedding increased markedly during the ninety or so years under discussion. Between 1584 and 1600 no more than 14 per cent of the inventories record bedding worth £3 and above. The proportion doubled in the Jacobean period and rose to as high as 45 per cent in the years up to 1675. In part, this increase is clearly attributable to the price revolution, but it rose at a far faster rate than other items of domestic furniture.

In contrast to Professor Barley's evidence for Lincolnshire up to the mid-17th century, the most usual place for the bed to be stored was in the chamber, although not infrequently it shared this room with such diverse objects as pitchforks, looms, yarn and other miscellaneous lumber.[21] Beds were also to be found in the parlours, in the hall, even, on occasion, in the kitchen. One man went so far as to have a separate bed chamber in the yard. Where there was more than one bed chamber, it sometimes housed a servant or perhaps an apprentice. Thus John Nobbes, who lived in a seven-roomed house in the parish of St Andrew's, and apparently carried on business as a pointmaker, had his own bedding worth £2 5s. 4d. in the main chamber while his servant was supplied with a trundle bed worth no more than 2s. in the servants' chamber. Nobbes must have been above the level of the very poor, but his property was worth no more than £4 8s. 4d., almost 90 per cent of it being made up of his domestic wares.[22]

The one other item which is contained in most of the inventories is the apparel of the deceased. This was rarely a major item and seldom exceeded 20 per cent of the value of the inventory, but even so it was worth twice as much, in general, as the clothing of an agricultural labourer. The average value of an individual's clothing rose little. At the end of Elizabeth's reign the median stood at 15s. and it rose to no higher than £1 in the succeeding years. The few occasions when clothing formed a major part of an inventory may imply absolute poverty, that a man literally owned little more than the clothes he stood up in or, in some cases, that the bulk of his property had been disposed of before his death. In contrast again to the inventories of the rural labourers, a number of the Norwich ones give precise details of a person's apparel.[23] Thomas Plowman's has been listed above. William Roberts, described as the guider of the poorhouse outside St Stephen's gates, possessed a doublet, a pair of breeches, an old hat, a gown, 2 pairs of old stockings, a pair of shoes, 2 shirts and 3 old shirt bands.[24] William Smyth, a fishmonger, owned 3 doublets, 2 cloaks, 2 pairs of 'Venetians', 3 pairs of stockings, a pair of shoes, 2 girdles, 2 shirts, 2 shirt bands and a hat.[35] John Partan, a draper, despite living in an eight-roomed house and having property valued at £8 10s. 8d., appeared worse off in this respect. His clothing, valued at 10s., consisted simply of an old gown, a threadbare cloak, a pair of hose and an old jerkin.[26] In contrast, the apparel of Robert Reade, a clerk, was assumed to be worth £2 13s., or almost 40 per cent of the value of the entire inventory, and included a gown of Norwich stuff worth £1 6s. 8d.[27] Jean de Grave, a widow of the parish of St Michael at Coslany, possessed little apart from her bedding, which at £3 3s. 6d. comprised over 90 per cent of the value of her furniture, but her clothing was valued at £1 9s. 6d. She evidently took great care of what she had for her neighbours noted, possibly with some satisfaction, that her apparel included an 'ould hatt of the ould fashion'.[28]

The close proximity of town and countryside and indeed the semi-rural nature of part of the area within the city walls is indicated by the minority of people actually owning farm animals. Some, without any occupation to their names, may well have farmed in a small way. In a few cases, animals were kept as a form of insurance, a useful addition to a man's main occupation and a saleable commodity either at his death, as in the case of Thomas Plowman or, feasibly, to offset the rigours of unemployment during a period of depression or dearth. Very few of the poor could afford such additional security. No more than a dozen people owned animals in the whole of the period 1584-1675, and where they were present they were usually one of the most valuable possessions of the person concerned. Eight people owned cows, ranging from the guider of the poorhouse to three tailors and two weavers. The value of the animals was normally much the same, ranging from 20s. to 30s., but in one case a milch cow was priced as highly as £2 13s. 4d. – half the total value of the man's possessions.[29] Two men, one a tailor, owned more than one animal. The tailor's additional stock – 2 hens and 4 pullets worth 2s. – added little to the value of his property. His fellow in this respect maintained what were described as an old lean gelding and two old diseased mares, the three being valued at 27s., or 14 per cent of the total value of the inventory.[30] Two other people owned horses. One, belonging to a widow, was valued at 15s. while the other, the property of a person of unspecified occupation, was worth four times as much.[31]

A much higher proportion of the poor had books recorded in their inventories, ranging from 20 per cent in the late Elizabethan period to 16 per cent in the years after 1625. The owners followed a variety of occupations, no one group being outstanding in any of the periods. Most numerous were the five tailors, followed closely by three weavers and, in the later 17th century, three women. There were two examples each of clerks, ministers and schoolteachers, all relatively poor but having a proportion of their inventories devoted to what were, in a very real sense, the tools of their trade. Individual examples include painters, masons, joiners, basketmakers, hatters, coopers and beerbrewers. While the possession of books is not in itself absolute proof of literacy it seems reasonable to assume that someone in the household was capable of reading them, and it is interesting to speculate on where these people obtained their education. It is at least possible that a few of them may have been products of the system of elementary education set up by the Norwich authorities in the 1570s and which seems to have been maintained for an extended period.[32]

As might be expected, the value of the books varies considerably. A musician who owned only two books – a copy of Fox's *Martyrs* and a Bible – had them valued at 20s. while another man, possibly a bookseller, had 70 books which were priced at no more than £1 6s. 3d. Thus, while the hosier whose 'library' was presumed to be worth £1 6s. 4d., and the minister and clerk, each with a collection worth £1 10s., undoubtedly owned several books, it would be unwise to speculate on the actual number.[33]

Without exception, those books specified were of a religious nature. Bibles, prayer books and psalm books abound. A weaver had a Bible, testament and psalm book worth 6s. 7½d., a brewer's seven sermon books were valued at 1s. 4d., a widow's service book at 1s. 6d., an alien, possibly bilingual, had both French and Dutch Bibles which, with a testament, were valued at 11s. 5d.[34] As books of this sort were apparently always clearly indicated, it seems reasonable to assume that the simple term 'books' refers, in at least some cases, to books of a different nature. A joiner owned 13 of these, valued at £1.[35] Other owners of books of a non-religious nature include tailors, a basketmaker and a painter as well as schoolmasters and ministers of religion.

One general point which emerges is the steady decline in the value of the books, the median falling from 7s. 4d. in the late Elizabethan period to 4s. in the post-Jacobean era. In the former period, six people owned books worth more than 10s., while in the Jacobean period the number had fallen to two and in the succeeding years only a tailor, who owned a Bible and 18 little books worth 11s. 4d., was in this category.[36] How far this reflects a general trend is open to question. As in other cases, it may do no more than relate to the chance survival of certain inventories, but one would have expected to see at least some indication of the price rise unless, in virtually every case, these were old books handed down from one generation to another.

Working tools were of far greater use to a man at this level than books, but very few of the inventories record these in any detail. Six weavers owned looms ranging in value from about 2s. 6d. to 10s. and in quantity from one to 10, while one alien, in addition to his loom which was worth 6s., owned wool combs, bay yarn and coarse nyles valued at £2 12s. 3d.[37] The inventories of two building workers provide greater detail. James Tomson, a mason who died in 1589, possessed a rough saw, three trowels, a brick axe, a hammer axe, a plumb rule, a level, a square, two 'whiten' brushes, a little hammer and a hand pickaxe, valued, between them, at the princely sum of 2s. 6d.[38] Six years later the appraisers began to list the property of William Morley, carpenter. When they came to his tools they noted wimbles, planes, saws, chisels, moulds, and then, possibly through lack of technical knowledge, gave up, concluding with '& other thinges belonging to carpenters craft by what name soever they be called'.[39] In all they were priced at 6s. Henry Cockly, a fletcher who died in the same year as Tomson, owned working tools priced at no more than 5s., but his stock, which included 3,000 feathers priced at 10s. and a sheaf of arrows valued at 7s., was assumed to be worth eight times as much.[40] Even better off in this respect was James Mountfort, fisherman, who owned boats worth £2 and working tools valued at £4 4s. at his death in 1602.[41] A lone labourer had a spade listed at 1s. 6d. and a hoe at 3d. in addition to unspecified tools valued at 1s. 8d., all worth considerably less than his clothes which were priced at £1 15s. His property was valued at £9 5s. 2d. at his death in 1635, which probably placed him above the level of absolute poverty.[42]

People who belonged to the wage-earning classes were, in a sense, walking a perpetual tightrope. Under normal circumstances they could survive without undue difficulty. In a few cases they may have lived in relative comfort. But with even the threat of industrial depression they could find themselves in severe difficulties. In such circumstances there was always the possibility that the more unruly among them would react violently, and in the uncertain economic climate of the times they were always a potential threat to the wellbeing of the community. It was essential that they should be well contained and it explains, at least in part, why cities such as Norwich took their poor law problems so seriously, and what prompted many of them to take action which anticipated all, or much, of governmental legislation in this respect.

## II The treatment of poverty

The treatment of poverty in Norwich in the 16th and 17th centuries falls into three well-defined, but unequal, phases. The first, which ends in 1570, sees the principle of a compulsory poor rate established, the foundation of a permanent grain stock and the beginnings of that flood of mercantile charity which was a welcome and necessary complement to the city's efforts; the second is concerned exclusively with the establishment of the Norwich scheme for the relief of the poor in the decade 1570-1580 and its immediate aftermath; and the third phase sees the city responding to national legislation while still following its own bent whenever the situation seems to demand it.

In 1525 about one-quarter of the Norwich population was considered sufficiently poor to be exempted from a subsidy which was purposely as all-embracing as it could possibly be. The proportion was not significantly high, bearing comparison with the situation prevailing in other provincial capitals and large towns, and the numbers of poor remained at this level throughout the 16th century and beyond. Probably the greatest single cause of poverty where Norwich was concerned was the instability of the labour market. The cloth industry, in particular, was at the mercy of the prevailing political climate, and many an urban craftsman became temporarily or permanently unemployed as the result of continental warfare which led to the closure of the main trade routes and less demand for the staple product.[43] Economic instability affected all the wage-earning classes from time to time, but the numbers of the poor were swelled at intervals by a host of other factors which varied in extent from area to area and in importance from decade to decade. Enclosure of common land affected few, if any, of the Norwich labouring classes and the same is probably true of the dissolution of the monasteries, although a few ex-monastic retainers may have sought a living in the locality. The city would have had its share of demobilised soldiers and sailors who may, or may not, have been re-absorbed into the local economy, and the pressures of the price-rise, as well as the adverse effects of plague and harvest failure, would have affected Norwich as elsewhere.[44]

Numerous though the poor may have been, there is no indication that they caused the city authorities any real problem until the onset of Kett's rebellion in 1549, and even then the insurgents almost certainly included many itinerant vagrants and other outsiders as well as a sprinkling of the local poor. When, in accordance with the statute of 1531, Norwich surveyed its beggars, the city authorities could find no more than 51 who were sufficiently destitute to be authorised to beg.[45] Monastic charity provided succour for many others of the local poor and in the case of Norwich Cathedral Priory they could rely on the beneficence of one of the most generous houses in the whole of England.[46] Hospital facilities, providing both shelter and medical care for those in need, were available both before and after the Reformation, and some local merchants were already instituting loan funds for the more needy members of their own occupations.

It seems, in fact, that a combination of authorised and unauthorised alms-giving, combined with the eleemosynary activities of the monastic houses, was more than sufficient to maintain the needy or, if not to maintain them, at least to keep them quiescent. Even so, the events of 1549 were sufficiently serious to hurry through a local plan for compulsory contributions to poor relief, and in that year Norwich became the first provincial city to institute regular collections for the relief of its deserving poor.[47] No rate-books survive for this period and it is impossible to tell whether the scheme was long-lasting or whether, as was so often the case, it was a temporary remedy for a temporary problem. Certainly begging was again authorised in 1556, which implies that many of the poor were uncared for, but equally certainly a well established rate was still in existence during the first decade of Elizabeth's reign.[48] In addition, a permanent corn stock had been established in 1554 under the terms of the will of William Castleton, the last Prior and the first Dean of Norwich. Castleton made provision for 100 quarters of wheat to be sold to the poor in small quantities whenever the market price was high, and the city fathers, in their turn, guaranteed to make good any deficiency which might accrue.[49]

The combination of an established rate, a permanent corn stock, hospital facilities for the indigent, and the steadily increasing charitable donations of all classes combined to give Norwich a poor law scheme which compared favourably with others in existence in the first decade of Elizabeth's reign. It is thus somewhat surprising to find the mayor, John Aldrich, complaining in 1570 that vagabonds were becoming an intolerable nuisance in the city and inaugurating comprehensive regulations for their treatment in the future, particularly as the numbers apprehended rarely exceeded twenty-five or so a year.

It is quite possible that the impetus, both for the original census discussed above and the reorganisation of the city's poor law scheme, was a political one. The rebellion of the Northern Earls had taken place in the previous year and had been followed by a plot by malcontents in the Norwich area. Ostensibly it was aimed at the increasing numbers of

Dutch and Walloons settling in the neighbourhood, but the participants were chiefly Catholics and there was some talk of a link-up with the northerners if it was successful. The mayor and the local J.P.s were aware of it from the first and arrested the conspirators at their convenience, but even the potential threat greatly concerned the central government. They investigated the incident closely and on or about 11 July 1570 William Cecil wrote to the Deputy Lieutenants of the county. As well as making arrangements for mustering, the provision of volunteer bands and the availability of warning beacons, he made special reference to the 'great multitude of people of mean and base sort' resident in Norwich whose very presence caused uncertainty among their wealthier counterparts. In an effort to offset this uncertainty he ordered the Lieutenants to reside at least intermittently in the city, together with gentry such as Edward Clare and Drew Drury, in order that 'the heads and governors of the City may be emboldened to retain the multitude in quietness and obedience'.

Whether outside events led to the taking of the census or not, the numbers contained within it must have shaken the local authorities. They responded initially by a blanket denunciation of all those it recorded. Although most of the poor claimed to follow a trade, it was alleged that this was merely a pretence, the majority of them continually begging from door to door to the irritation of the citizens and their own degradation. According to Aldrich, the local citizens were so beneficent in their almsgiving that many of those normally prepared to follow a trade were taking to permanent begging as a more profitable occupation. They were so well supplied with food that they threw the surplus into the streets. The vagabonds among them were not concerned with permanent dwelling-places but used church porches, cellars, barns and hay chambers as resting places and, as they rarely changed their clothes, most of them were disease-ridden and thus a source of physical as well as moral contagion. When not begging they spent their time in victualling houses which were filled with drunkards and abusive individuals throughout much of the day.

44. *The Old Barge*, King Street. Houses converted from a long 15th-century warehouse.

Although some of the poor may have been permanent beggars and others may have resorted to begging in times of extraordinary dearth, it was far too sweeping to lump them all together in this one general category. It seems, in fact, that although speaking in general terms, the authorities were concerned with two distinct groups of poor, the relatively passive natives and an increasing number of normally itinerant beggars drawn to the town by the generosity of its merchant class. The census itself to some extent substantiates this point of view. As well as giving the occupations of all those in actual employment at the time it was taken, it specifically states which people were unemployed, differentiating between the able and those who were too old or too infirm to work. A majority of both men and women were in work and it was rare to find a household where neither adult was employed. If they were all vagrants, it would have been a pointless task to distinguish so carefully between employed and unemployed and it must be assumed that the majority of the native poor were in at least temporary employment at the time of the census. This is not to suggest that any of this section of the community were comfortably off. Some of them may well have resorted to begging on occasion, a few may have found it more profitable to beg than to work, but the very fact that the more unruly elements were stated to be homeless makes it clear that they were professional vagrants. All of the poor referred to in the census had houses or accommodation of some kind, and many of them were owner-occupiers.

Whatever the impetus, it seems fairly clear that the action of the Norwich authorities was taken as much with a view to the future as with solving an immediate problem. It almost certainly reflects their anxiety about the results of the misplaced generosity of certain of the merchant class, a generosity which made it increasingly difficult to prevent beggars settling in the city, and which might ultimately corrupt the native poor and undermine what had been until then a fairly satisfactory poor law system.[50] The action taken was drastic. It incorporated all aspects present in other towns, but in four major respects it went much further. Begging of any kind was absolutely forbidden within the city precincts; an all-embracing organisation was provided which dealt adequately with every aspect of poor relief, including the provision of work for the able-bodied; regular funds were provided which were essential for the smooth running of the system; and finally, and perhaps most important of all, the city's system was consistently applied throughout the decade 1570-80 and at least intermittently thereafter. These aspects combined to give Norwich a poor law system far in advance of its contemporaries, for it was here that other towns failed most noticeably. Financial difficulties caused the collapse or virtual cessation of many of the municipal schemes and the fact that begging was tolerated, even if theoretically confined to the impotent, undermined much of their efforts.[51]

The financial aspect was of primary importance. A beginning was made by trebling the existing sums donated for poor relief and, where necessary, by taxing people for the first time. Virtually everybody above the status of wage-earner was a contributor – including 20 families actually named in the census itself – the amounts varying from $\frac{1}{2}$d. to 1s. 4d. a week. As might be expected, most people paid small amounts, almost two-thirds contributing twopence or less. Those paying the higher amounts included the city aldermen and the Bishop of Norwich who was alone in being assessed at 1s. 4d.[52]

The wealthiest parishes naturally had the largest number of contributors and the smallest number of poor to deal with, for there was a tendency for the less wealthy to congregate in certain areas of the city. Thus a parish such as St Peter Mancroft, with 111 people contributing to the poor rate and with only 22 individuals considered worthy of support, was expected to provide for the poor of other parishes as well as its own and did, in fact, make contributions to six other areas. St Andrew's, with 54 contributors and no more than six of its own parishioners to care for, made donations to four other parishes. Altogether nine of the Norwich parishes provided support for their less fortunate fellows.[53]

Within a few years of the inception of the city's poor law scheme the numbers of contributors and recipients had become roughly stabilised. Throughout most of the 1570s some nine hundred and fifty people were providing support for about three hundred and eighty regular 'pensioners'. By 1574-75 the annual receipts for poor relief exceeded £530 and they continued to be above £500 for the rest of the decade. The Norwich chamberlains received less than this for normal city business, a fair indication of how seriously the problem of the poor was regarded. In normal circumstances the numbers contributing were sufficiently high for the deacons to collect more money than they actually paid out, and this surplus was used as a reserve stock to be drawn on in cases of special need. The usual beneficiaries were people who were sick or who were suffering from broken limbs. Such people would not be permanent 'pensioners', and their ability to draw what amounted to unemployment or sickness benefit removed any excuse they may have had to beg.

Adequate financial provision was an absolute pre-requisite if the city's system of poor relief was to be a success. Once this was established to their satisfaction, the authorities thoroughly reorganised the existing system. Vagabonds were placed in the Bridewell, a building which had been purchased for the purpose in 1565. Certain of the begging women and some of the younger children were put in the charge of 'select women' who were specially chosen for the task. Other young people were sent to St Giles' Hospital to be educated. The aged and impotent were sustained by increased alms and, where possible, work was provided for those willing and able to do it.

A number of new officials were appointed at the same time to see that the scheme worked smoothly. The mayor himself took over the position of Master of the Bridewell and four of the aldermen were made responsible for the four great wards of the city. They, in turn, appointed a host of minor officials. The deacons were the most important of these. Two were appointed for each petty ward (24 in all) and they were initially responsible for recording the names of all the poor, including those of children whose parents were unable to support them adequately; these children were put out to service. Those poor with less than three years' residence were sent away while all newcomers unable to support themselves were refused admittance. It was the deacons' responsibility to see that all capable of work did work, all vagabonds, loiterers, idlers or drunkards that remained being punished. In addition to these punitive duties, they were expected to know how many poor there were in the city with insufficient alms, so that they could be provided for, and to see that any money, wood, or other gifts to the poor were duly distributed.

The Bridewell, which was an essential part of the city's poor law system, was also provided with new officials. The most important was a resident bailiff who was appointed at a salary of £30 a year. From this he was expected to provide for his wife, children, servants and a surveyor who was made responsible for the arrest of idle rogues. He was assisted by two wardens who were concerned with the provision of household utensils and the year's supply of food. Twelve vagabonds were to be housed in the Bridewell for a period of at least twenty-one days and obliged to work from 5 a.m. to 8 p.m. in the summer and from 7 a.m. to 6 p.m. in the winter. Half an hour was to be allowed for a meal break and a quarter of an hour for prayer, and it was expressly ordered that if they refused to work they were to receive no food.

The 'select women' were paid a salary of 20s. a year. Each woman was made responsible for between six and twelve people, and while primarily concerned with seeing that they worked she was also expected to teach the children the rudiments of reading and writing. If this task was done properly, and if the census of the poor is to be believed, it would suggest that something like one in ten of the poorer children received at least a basic education, and that the level of literacy among these people was higher than is generally believed. The women and children worked shorter hours than the men. In the winter months they began at 8 a.m. and continued until 4 p.m., while in the summer their hours of labour extended from 6 a.m. until 'paste vii of the clocke at nighte'. Throughout the year they had a two-hour dinner break from 11 a.m. to 1 p.m. Provided they supplied their own materials, they were allowed to keep the profits from their work, Otherwise they had to be content with the wages paid them by the 'select women'. Although their treatment seems to have been relatively mild for the times, some unruliness was expected for the women were empowered to give loiterers six stripes with a whip and if they retaliated they were to be handed over to the deacons for a double punishment or be sent to Bridewell.

These orders made provision for the most unruly inhabitants of Norwich, but the stipulations were by no means entirely coercive. The authorities went out of their way to provide instruction in reading and writing for the children sent to St Giles' Hospital, for example. Twelve children were to be kept there in the charge of the Bailiff and his wife who were responsible for teaching them letters and and other exercises 'as their capacities shall be hable to attayne'. They were also to provide them with clothes, meat and drink and see that they went to church on Sundays. Provision was also made for the impotent poor and those prepared to work, two hospitals being maintained for the former and stocks of materials being provided for the latter.

The Norwich authorities were not content to rest on their laurels. They not only maintained the existing scheme, but supplemented it at intervals throughout the decade 1570-80. Some of the action taken was specifically geared to avoid a return to wholesale vagrancy. A law passed in 1574, for example, stipulated that all unemployed men were to assemble at the Market Cross at 5 a.m. each day with the tools of their trade and wait there for an hour in the hope of employment. Further laws were passed to prevent the housing of vagrants, and the city authorities dealt promptly with complaints that artisans were losing money by appearing on juries by ordering that in future they should be paid at the rate of twopence per man. Rigorous settlement regulations were enforced, any newcomers that appeared at all likely to be a charge to the city being refused admittance. At the other extreme, all affluent newcomers were brought before the mayor after 1576 to be assessed for their contribution to the relief of the poor. The reserve fund was regularly drawn on to sustain people who were temporarily incapacitated and on occasion the city went beyond this, supplementing the alms given for poor relief by making grants in kind. Thus in 1580 a lame boy was supplied with a joint of mutton or veal twice a week, as well as being treated by a surgeon. The 'medical staff' was improved in 1573 by the appointment of one Richard Durrant, 'a man very skillful in bone setting and of good will to dwell in the cittie', as the municipal bonesetter. He was to be responsible 'for the releyfe of souch as shall fortune by misfortune to have ther legges, armes, or the bones of other partes of ther lymes to be broken and of souche as be poore and not able to pay for ther heling'. Durrant was obviously an able man. His initial salary of £4 a year was soon increased to £10 and he seems to have built up a clientele of private patients as well. At his death in 1602 he left bequests amounting to £282 10s.[54]

It would be misleading to suggest that the Norwich scheme was infallible. From time to time itinerant beggars proved themselves a nuisance, but references to them in the Court Books are even fewer than before 1570 and the authorities were clearly well in command of the situation. After the scheme had been made in operation for a year the officials concerned reported on its progress. They were able to state that during the year 950 children had earned 6d. a week, 64 men 1s. and 180 women between 1s. and 2s. 6d. a week, all of whom, it was alleged, had previously been beggars. It was calculated that if the yearly earnings of these people were added to the sums previously given in alms, both for healing and general maintenance, the city had profited by more than £3,000. Much of this transformation was attributed to the 'feare of the terrour of the house of Bridewell', with vagrants apparently preferring to seek normal employment rather than be compelled to work there. The figures for the children are almost certainly exaggerated, representing virtually the total number recorded in the census, but those given for the men and women are probably correct and may well represent the numbers of known beggars among the poorer classes.

Even allowing for possible over-exuberance where the figures are concerned, the scheme was clearly a success. The Norwich authorities had succeeded in just those respects that had caused, and were to cause, the collapse of so many apparently sound urban schemes.[55] They had forbidden begging entirely, thus preventing any abuse of the licensing system. Before parliamentary sanction had been given for compulsory taxation for poor relief,

Norwich had not only taxed its citizens for the purpose but had trebled the initial contributions and regularly collected and distributed such sums of money throughout the whole of the decade 1570 to 1580; and provision was made for all categories of poor, even to the extent of finding work for the able-bodied. Perhaps the most significant thing about the Norwich scheme, however, was the consistency with which it was applied, and it was this consistency above all else which made it superior to those undertaken by other towns and ultimately brought the city national acclaim. Matthew Parker, the Archbishop of Canterbury and himself a Norwich man, specifically asked for details of the Norwich methods and John Aldrich, its originator, sat on a parliamentary committee which discussed the whole question of poor relief in 1572. It is no coincidence that the Act passed in that year incorporated several aspects of the Norwich scheme.[56]

The official records of the Norwich scheme cease in 1580, a year in which plague was still at its height, and the decimation of the poorer classes, in particular, must have led to the disappearance of several of the city's pensioners. Nevertheless, the loss of the principal breadwinner in some cases, the disappearance of an employer in others, must have caused considerable hardship to individual families and some form of relief continued to be absolutely essential. Between 10 August 1590 and May 1592, for example, years in which plague was again present, the citizens were assessed on four separate occasions for the relief of the afflicted poor.[57] Although direct evidence is lacking for the remainder of the 16th century, it seems highly likely that the poor rate continued to be collected in individual parishes and distributed according to need. In 1584 one Robert Gyrdeler was disfranchised for refusing to contribute to the poor rate and to the charges of the church and parish.[58] Collections were made at intervals to provide the able-bodied with work and when it was thought necessary the Bridewell regulations were revised. One such revision took place in 1588 when, rather surprisingly, the services of the select women and the deacons were dispensed with, ostensibly so that the 'artycles tuching Bridewell bee not repugnant or contrary to the lawes and statutes of this realme'.[59]

It became impossible to maintain the laws against begging, however. A few years after the first attack of plague in 1579 complaints were again made that the taverns were filled with idlers who had little or no concern for their dependants. The city authorities feared, with reason, that this would be a direct encouragement to begging. A law passed against such people in 1586 referred to wives and families who 'suffer much penury, wanting competent sustenance and are likely dayly more and more to becom greatly burdenous and chardgeable to this worshippful citie'.[60] The following year specific reference was made to wives and children forced to go begging from door to door.

It remains an open question as to whether collections for the poor continued to be levied in every parish during the last two decades of Elizabeth's reign. Certainly the auditors for the poor continued to be appointed, which implies a regular income, as does the disfranchisement of Robert Gyrdeler referred to above. The only accounts for the overseers of the poor which survive for this period relate to the large and wealthy parish of St Peter Mancroft, and are concerned with the years 1598-1634.[61] Significantly the accounts begin in a period of acute famine and it is possible that they are a response to the parliamentary legislation of that year rather than a continuation of the existing Norwich scheme. The inhabitants collected over £100 for poor relief in 1598, donating almost half of this to three poorer parishes. It seems very probable that the other wealthy areas of the city responded in the same way. At the same time the Norwich aldermen provided 4,600 quarters of rye for the poorer inhabitants, selling it at 4s. a bushel, a considerably cheaper rate than that prevailing in most other towns.[62]

The combination of municipal and parochial benevolence shielded the citizens from the worst effects of the harvest failures of the 1590s but, almost inevitably, the generosity of the merchant classes led to a further influx of undesirables. In 1601 the mayor, Alexander Thurston, felt obliged to take drastic action. It was stipulated that a weekly search was to be made for all newcomers likely to be a charge to the city; that the numbers of unemployed single women, particularly those pregnant, were to be listed, together with the numbers of known idlers and those sick and infirm; the names of those hiring poor people and giving them lodging were to be recorded; and it was again insisted that all over the age of 14 were to be apprenticed. Reference was made to those refusing to contribute to the poor rate but surprisingly, although both national and local legislation had made this compulsory, the overseers were merely ordered to see 'what you can by good means bring them willingly to give'.[63]

The principles formulated during the reign of Elizabeth continued to be followed during the succeeding century. It seems fairly clear that a poor rate was levied regularly on those individuals who could afford to pay, the accounts surviving for 14 of the city's parishes for the 17th century and beyond.[64] From 1616 the Quarter Sessions books make reference to the necessity for the wealthier parishes to support their poorer neighbours and the principal inhabitants are accordingly required to provide sums in addition to those already paid by them.[65] In exceptional circumstances, such as severe economic distress, even this was considered insufficient and rates were collected in 1634 and in the 1670s which appear to be additional to those already gathered.[66] In the latter period between 750 and 850 people were regularly maintained from the rates or, to put it another way, about one quarter of those considered too poor to contribute to the Hearth Tax.

Norwich was unusual in consistently levying a poor rate over an extended period. Most towns adopted compulsion only in times of dire necessity. In part, this apparent indifference was dictated by sheer economic necessity, in part by a realistic response to an existing situation. In normal times, much of the responsibility for the relief of the poor fell on the shoulders of the merchant classes in particular and, to a lesser degree, on those of anybody willing and able to bear the burden. In the post-Reformation period members of every class from the humblest artisan upwards contributed to the relief of the poor. In urban areas especially, the wealthier merchants became almost obsessed with the problem and, far from being concerned exclusively with immediate relief, in many cases they made positive efforts in their lifetimes and through bequests to prevent their poorer neighbours from sliding into this particular abyss.[67]

Sometimes the provisions of a will were general such as that of William Castylton in 1550 which allocated £40 for the purchase of gowns, shirts or smocks for poor boys and 100 quarters of wheat to be sold under the market price in times of dearth; and those of Thomas Gray and Thomas Harleston who, at their deaths in 1559, provided, respectively, £6 13s. 4d. for the town granary and £10 for the relief of the poor.[68] Increasingly, however, the merchant classes looked to the future. The provision of loan funds, usually intended to aid the poorer members of the donor's own trade, was a particularly popular device. Examples of charities of this sort can be found from the middle of the 16th century onwards.

In 1553 William Rogers left not only £7 16s. as outright doles for the poor but also £300 to be employed for interest-free loans to needy merchants and other inhabitants of the city, stipulating that no more than £20 was to be lent to any one person.[69] Richard Head, a haberdasher who died in 1568, in addition to £22 5s. left exclusively for poor relief and £4 2s. for the support of almshouses, donated £100 to be lent to poor men in sums not exceeding £10, the amounts to be lent without interest but on security.[70] Thomas Pettus, a tailor and mayor in 1590, made bequests of £20 to be used as a stock to set the poor to work in the Bridewell, £86 for general charitable purposes and £100 for a loan fund. The latter sum was to be loaned in sums of £5 and £10 on proper security, half among poor worsted weavers and half among needy dornix weavers, none of whom were to retain the money for longer than two years.[71]

The most notable among benefactors of this sort was Henry Fawcett, a Norwich woollen merchant and alderman who died in 1619. In all, Fawcett donated £1,394 13s. 4d. to charitable purposes in the city and county including £94 6s. 8d. outright to the poor of Norwich as well as £40 as a stock for the poor among the Dutch and French communities in the city. A sum of £45 6s. 8d. was provided to enable the churchwardens of six parishes to buy coal for the poor in winter; £40 was left to be advanced each winter to any local entrepreneur who provided work for poor masons in the local 'stone mines' during those months; and £360 was made available for loan funds, £300 of this for as many as 30 poor worsted weavers, £30 to be distributed among six dornix weavers, £20 to shoemakers and £10 to poor smiths.[72] The fact that security was demanded for loans of this sort in virtually every case meant, inevitably, that they would have been of little use to the very poor. They were meant to prevent destitution and to take some of the weight from the shoulders of the city fathers. As such, they played a valuable role in the city's system of poor relief.

The same object was undoubtedly behind the founding of the Boys' and Girls' Hospitals in 1621 and 1650 respectively.[73] Many citizens were concerned that so many children were wholly or partially uncared for, and sought means to look after them while young as well as arranging for them to be apprenticed when they were older. The attitude of the philanthropists in the city was made clear in the will of Thomas Anguish, mercer and sometime mayor of Norwich, who died in 1618.[74] Anguish was the founder of the Boys' Hospital, and he suggested that such an institution had been 'for many years wished and desired'. He spoke of 'compassion and great pitye' for the young and poor children 'borne and brought up in this city . . . and specially suche as for wante, lye in the streetes . . . whereby many of them fall into great and grievous diseases and lamenesses, as that they are fitt for no profession, ever after'. He intended that as many as 40 boys and girls should be maintained in his hospital, under the tuition of a master and mistress as well as other teachers. They were to be admitted at between five and seven years and kept until they were about fifteen. Anguish himself provided the house for this purpose, 'being large, spacious and new built, and many rooms therein', as well as an endowment comprising urban real estate for the support of the property. The hospital, which was opened on 1 January 1621 when 14 boys were admitted, proved a popular institution. Numerous bequests were received in the following decade, the largest being the £525 from the estates of Nicholas Reeve, a London scrivener, and Mirabell Bennett, widow of a prosperous London merchant. In all, some £2,150 was donated between 1619 and 1630, providing an income in excess of £100 a year, and by 1660 the endowments for the Hospital stood at £4,260, an amount sufficient to provide complete maintenance and training for about fifty-three children.

Despite Anguish's original intention, it seems probable that no girls were ever admitted to the original hospital and a separate institution was founded for them in 1650. The founder was Robert Baron, parliamentarian mayor of the city, who left £250 for the purpose at his death in 1649. He directed that the sum should be used 'for the training up of women children, from the age of seaven, untill the age of fifteen years, in spinning, knitting, and dressing of wooll' under the guidance of a discreet and religious woman to be appointed by the magistrates. Although less popular than the Boys' Hospital, some £790 was bequeathed in support of the venture during the next 10 years, and the institution became as firmly founded as its male counterpart.

The role of the merchant classes, both in relieving the poor and, where possible, preventing poverty was as significant in Norwich as elsewhere in the country. Even so, the East Anglian city was never wholly dependent on philanthropy. Apart from a well-established and long-standing poor rate and a normally well-stocked granary, a number of individual parishes devised methods of their own to assist the poor in their immediate locality. Many of them instituted loan funds in the 17th century, the sums lent varying from £2 to £10.[75] Security was demanded in every case. Usually, items of household furniture were provided; not infrequently, silver spoons were 'pawned'. Quite often loans were taken up again for a further period. No interest was payable on such loans but, as with the bequests discussed above, the demand for security must have placed them beyond the reach of the very poor. The aged and impotent continued to be supported by the parish concerned, with some parishes supplementing their normal almsgiving at specific times of the year. In the parish of St Benedict's, for example, it was usual to provide alms for the poor in general on the first Monday of each year and again at Easter. The funds for this were provided in part from the rents of parish houses.[76]

In times of dearth or general economic instability the impetus came from the ruling body. Extraordinary rates have been referred to already. In addition to the provision of corn which was, and always had been, a feature in times of dearth, there were frequent attempts to restrict the use of corn by members of various trades. Brewers, maltsters and starch makers were especially vulnerable in this respect, and in the 1630s they were frequently hauled before the mayor's court to be dealt with.[77] Attempts were made to forbid, or restrict, the numbers of country workers employed in the city while at the same time ensuring, as far as possible, that additional hands were taken on in time of distress. Thus, both in 1625 and 1630 work was provided at the local stone mines for poor masons, the produce being used to pave the streets.[78] Entrepreneurs, who in some cases employed hundreds of people in country districts, were asked to take on additional employees in the city, and usually responded with apparent ease.[79] Knitting schools were established in those parishes where they did not already exist, and the poor were allowed to keep some of the profits of their activities.[80] Bread baked against the court's order was usually given to the poor.[81] There were also further attempts to prevent the settlement of undesirable newcomers, the authorities levying a tax not only on the newcomer himself but also on his landlord and employer.[82] A person who was allowed to stay for an indefinite period had to provide sureties that he would not become a charge on the city, and he had to be prepared to contribute to the existing poor rate. From time to time the justices exercised their power of removal. Despite the legal ruling that a person who had settled in an area for a month without complaint could be deemed to be settled there, on occasion the court banished individuals who had been resident in the community for years. Nor was it a respecter of domestic ties. Husbands were separated from wives, elderly parents from their children, if it seemed at all likely that the city would have to pay for their upkeep.[83]

Under normal circumstances, the Norwich ruling body had little difficulty in supporting its poor, the combination of a regular rate, a permanent corn stock, the philanthropy of its merchant classes and the extraordinary contributions of the parishes being more than sufficient to maintain its 'pensioners'. Hospitals for the aged and the young and a Bridewell for the idle and unruly ensured that other sections of the poor were not neglected. The city was by no means entirely successful, as is evinced by the numbers of poor children lying unattended in its streets as late as 1618, and it would be foolish to assume that every unwanted child was subsequently cared for in either the Boys' or the Girls' Hospital. Nevertheless, the Norwich authorities accepted their responsibilities and dealt with them to the best of their abilities. Their beneficence was restricted to those born within their boundaries, but within these confines they maintained a poor law system which had few rivals elsewhere and which from the point of view of continuity may have had no rivals at all.

*Chapter Eleven*

# Tudor and Stuart Norwich

Between 1525 and 1675 the population of Norwich more than doubled, the eight thousand or so resident in the Tudor city swelling to more than twenty thousand by the second decade of Charles II's reign. In addition to natural increase and immigration from the outlying districts, the city had to absorb an ever-increasing number of Dutch and Walloon refugees, the aliens ultimately comprising about one-third of the total population.[1] Almost incredibly, it seems that the bulk of the increased population was absorbed not only within the walls but mostly within the same houses, many of which underwent conversion into tenements to house the larger numbers.

In consequence, the traveller to Restoration Norwich would have seen a city which looked in all essentials very similar to its early Tudor counterpart. It was surrounded by the same walls and dominated by the same castle and cathedral. The vast majority of the churches were still standing and the open areas remained effectively what they had been 150 years earlier. The only major buildings to have disappeared were those of the monastic houses, with the notable exception of the chancel and nave of the Blackfriars which had been bought specifically for civic use. The huge mansion of the Dukes of Norfolk was soon to be in sad decline, however.

As late as the 1690s the city still presented an antique appearance to that intrepid traveller, Celia Fiennes, but change had obviously taken place, not least in those areas seldom, if ever, frequented by the wealthy. Many of the existing houses had been renovated internally, even where the outside structure remained essentially the same. In addition, a number of small dwellings of the cottage type had been built in the existing yards to house the ever-increasing numbers of poor, while elsewhere many houses had been converted into tenements for the same purpose. In a city which had far more people exempted from the Hearth Tax than other towns of comparable, or even smaller, size, poverty was ever-present and the destitute were more than ready to take possession of the houses vacated by their betters.[2] Change of this type is most in evidence in the ward of South Conesford, where there was hardly a household with more than a single hearth, but overcrowding was equally rife in the industrial quarters to the north of the city, parts of Norwich which absorbed thousands of Dutch and Walloon immigrants without noticeably expanding their built-up areas. The examples noted earlier, particularly in St Martin at Palace where 70 people were crowded into a single tenement, were almost certainly no more than the tip of a decidedly larger iceberg.

Broadly speaking, the occupations practised in those areas, and in the wealthier wards towards the centre of Norwich, remained very similar throughout the Tudor and Stuart periods. The wards of Wymer and Ultra Aquam continued to be peopled primarily by textile workers, while the central districts of the city housed the merchant and professional classes. The distributive trades which were of some importance in Conesford in 1525, however, were ousted in favour of the clothing trades by 1671, and there are other examples of individual change. The food and drink trades, for example, which were of general importance in the Henrician period, employed relatively few people in the wards of Mancroft and Wymer in 1671. The metal trades, which were of some significance in Wymer alone in 1525, had changed their major venue to Mancroft by Charles II's reign, to be replaced by building and clothing workers. Tailors and the like were also of some importance in Ultra

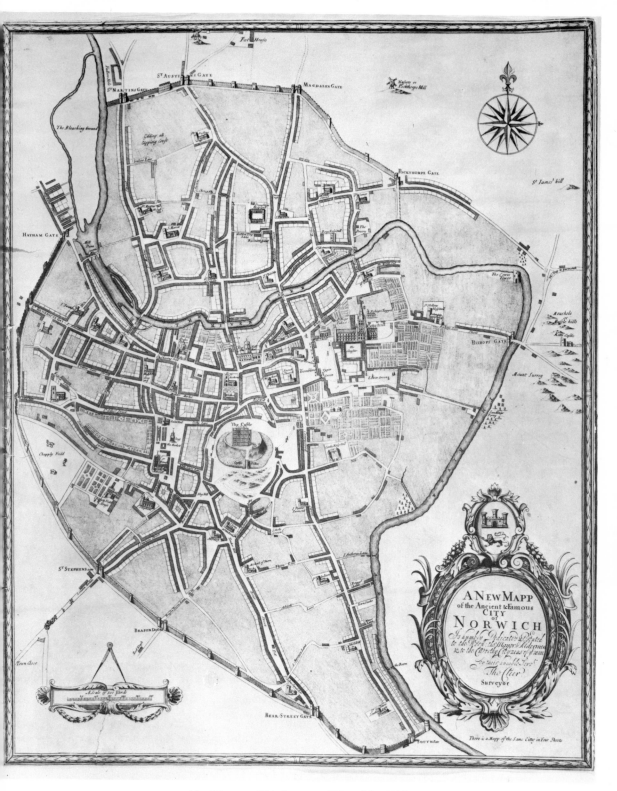

45.  Thomas Cleer's map of Norwich, 1696.

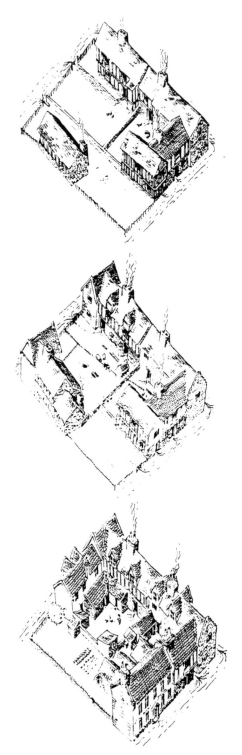

Aquam by 1671, whereas those concerned with the distributive trades were, at best, of secondary importance.

Throughout the whole of the 16th and 17th centuries the textile industry was of prime importance in Norwich, and outstandingly so in the 17th century. At its lowest point it employed at least twenty per cent of the working population of the city, quite apart from the unknown, but substantial, number of people dependent on it in the surrounding districts; at its highest it provided work for twice as many.[3]

Nevertheless, the story of the Norwich textile industry is by no means one of unqualified success. The 16th century saw its steady decline, the nadir being reached in the last years of Elizabeth's reign when fewer than fifteen per cent of those admitted to the freedom of the city were textile workers. Significantly, almost one-quarter of the Norwich poor either were, or had been, textile workers when the census was taken in 1570. With the advent of the Dutch and Walloons a slow but steady resurgence took place. During the reign of James I just over one-quarter of those admitted to the freedom of the city were textile workers. By 1675 the proportion had reached more than forty per cent.

The waxing and waning of the textile industry is reflected in the changing aspirations of the apprentices' fathers. When the industry was in decline only the conservative husbandmen continued in any numbers to send their sons to be apprenticed to it. The gentry were never attracted to it in the 16th century, the clergy hardy at all, while the yeomen and tradesmen looked to more prosperous avenues for their sons' advancement. All classes were quick to notice a changing situation, however, and the upper classes were as willing as the tradesmen and farmers to set their progeny on what appeared to be a potentially rewarding path. During the 17th century at least half of the sons of the gentry and clergy were apprenticed to the textile trades. A similar proportion of yeomen's sons were appren-

46.  A reconstruction of the buildings on Alms Lane about 1520, 1650 and 1720. Not only were more houses built on the site during the period, but the existing ones were subdivided. Pottery evidence suggested that the inhabitants were immigrants from the Low Countries. St George's Street ran along the bottom right-hand frontage, Alms Lane along the top right and Muspole Lane on the top left.

ticed to the industry during the same period but the husbandmen, while being initially attracted, subsequently apprenticed an equal proportion of their sons to the clothing and leather trades. Many of the apprentices came from Norwich itself and the surrounding county, but a substantial proportion came from further afield, especially from the Midlands and North.[4]

Despite its pre-eminence in the 17th century, in particular, it would be misleading to discuss the industrial development of Norwich solely in terms of the city's textile industry. Even when that industry was at its height, six out of every 10 freemen were employed in other spheres, while during the reign of Elizabeth other occupations were of far greater significance.[5] With Norwich becoming increasingly important as a regional capital, more and more people turned their attention to providing for the needs of the city's neighbours, whether visiting countrymen or gentry in residence for the season. Individual trades prospered exceedingly, the number of freemen grocers increasing sevenfold between 1525 and 1569, with other trades catering for the visitors also growing in importance.

Many of these – grocers, mercers, drapers – were prestigious occupations and provided ample opportunities for social mobility. Whenever possible, city and county tradesmen and the wealthier yeomen apprenticed their sons to the distributive trades. During the 16th century the gentry and clergy looked virtually nowhere else. Even in the textile industry's boom years, greater fortunes were still to be made by grocers and merchants, despite the fact that their share of the city's freemen had fallen.[6]

Some broad trends can be discerned by an analysis of probate inventories but the distribution of wealth in Norwich can only be measured with reasonable accuracy at the beginning and end of the period under consideration. The full subsidy return survives for 1525, a return which included the majority of men, and some women, of the status of wage-earner and above, and the Hearth Tax assessment of 1671 survives sufficiently fully to enable a reasonably accurate picture to be derived from it. In 1525 the numbers of poor have to be estimated. In 1671 those excluded from payment on the grounds of poverty are clearly listed.[7]

The two tax assessments were obviously made on an entirely different basis, the earlier of them being based on broadly accurate assessments of the wealth of the people concerned, while the latter was concerned solely with the number of taxable hearths in a particular household. Nevertheless, comparison is possible. In a society very much concerned with the status of the individual a man tended to live up to, and occasionally beyond, his means and, with the notable exception of innkeepers, the size of his house is normally a fair indication of his wealth. Assuming this to be true of Henrician and Caroline Norwich, comparison of the two returns suggests that the distribution of wealth in the city had altered litte, proportionately speaking, during the 150 years concerned. In 1525 six per cent of the taxable population owned 60 per cent of the city's wealth. In 1671 seven per cent of the citizens were living in houses containing six or more hearths and, as the wealthiest section of the community, may be presumed to have been at least as rich as their Henrician forebears. Poverty was acute in both periods. In 1525 more than forty per cent of the taxpayers were wage-earners, with perhaps one-quarter of the population too poor to contribute at all. In Restoration Norwich some sixty per cent of the city's householders were exempted from paying hearth tax on the grounds of poverty, and while this undoubtedly comprised groups corresponding to both the very poor and the wage-earners of the Tudor period it is clear that the situation had not improved.

A minority of people thus continued to be in possession of most of the wealth in the city while the majority were either poor or relatively poor. It should be stressed, however, that whereas in 1525 the proportion of wage-earners in Norwich – and possibly the proportion of those below that status – was very similar to that to be found in other provincial towns, in 1671 the percentage of people exempted from paying hearth tax was distinctly higher than that found elsewhere. This suggests that Norwich was either a poorer town than its rivals elsewhere by the late 17th century or that wealth had come to be distributed on a more equal basis in other provincial centres.

47.   Samson and Hercules House, Tombland.

As one would expect, the bulk of the wealth in both Henrician and Caroline Norwich was to be found in the hands of the governing classes of the city and those of equivalent status, whether resident or potential aldermen and councillors. These people were merchants almost to a man, whether they were described as such or given a more specific designation such as grocer, mercer or draper. Occasionally men from other occupations were to be found among them, including goldsmiths, scriveners and, especially during the 17th century, the wealthier members of the textile trades, but the lion's share of the city's wealth remained in the hands of the merchant classes throughout the Tudor and Stuart periods. This is not to say that other classes were necessarily poor. Certain of the clothing and food and drink trades prospered during the reign of Elizabeth, for example, and the introduction of the New Draperies saw a steady rise in the living standards of those textile workers for whom we have the requisite information. Individual members of the building and metal trades also accumulated personal fortunes. None of these, however, bore comparison with the wealthier members of the merchant classes.

Nevertheless, whatever their occupation, the evidence of surviving inventories suggests that the wealth of the more affluent citizens rose steadily throughout the 16th and 17th centuries. When all due account has been taken of inflation, it seems reasonably certain that the top third of the city's population not only saw their incomes rise as the cost of living rose but in many cases their incomes rose faster than prices. By no means all of those with their possessions recorded were wealthy, as the previous chapter indicates, but the broad picture of a rise in the living standards of the upper strata seems undeniable. Certainly a proportion of these people had sufficient cash in hand to lend it to other individuals, and the number of people with debts due to them increased radically between the end of Elizabeth's reign and the beginning of that of Charles II.[8]

While a minority of the city's population may have lived in comfort, the vast majority lived in conditions of extreme poverty. Norwich was by no means unique in this respect. Poverty was a feature common to any English town of reasonable size. Something like one in five of the inhabitants of the larger towns were desperately poor and up to sixty per cent were dependent on wages for their livelihood. Poverty is necessarily an all-embracing term and people's standards of living varied and fluctuated despite being subsumed under the blanket term, 'the poor'. Provided they were employed at reasonably regular intervals they could normally expect to have sufficient to feed and clothe themselves and their families and, on occasion, have a little to spare. Their situation was necessarily an uncertain one. Even if they chose to work regularly – and few did – work was seldom available to them on a regular basis. When they were in employment there was always the danger of a sudden recession which could reduce them to the level of a beggar at a stroke.[9]

Nevertheless, a proportion of the Norwich poor – we cannot be sure of what proportion in the absence of figures for the poor, as such, for much of the period – were sufficiently well-off, in a relative sense, to leave enough property to be recorded in an inventory; and analysis of this material allows us to paint a very broad picture of those living above the level of absolute poverty. Sixty per cent of these people lived in houses containing between three and five rooms, and a few lived in still larger dwellings. No more than a quarter of them inhabited houses with two rooms or less. A small minority owned animals – cows, pigs, horses and chickens – which provided a cushion against unemployment, but most of them possessed little more than their personal property. Of this, bedding was by far the most valuable item, followed by personal clothing and books. Every fifth person owned a few books, some among them owning several, which suggests a reasonable level of literacy among people of this class. A number of the poor lived in property which had been renovated, either by themselves or their landlords, and one is conscious when examining the inventories of the slow change taking place in the domestic architecture of Norwich, even at this level.

The very poor were less fortunate. A substantial number lived in church property, in civic property made available for the purpose, even, in a minority of cases, in the towers along the walls. Others were housed in property belonging to aldermen, common councillors and other rate-payers of Norwich while a few were owner-occupiers.[10] As no more than a quarter of them were in receipt of alms when the census of the poor was taken in 1570, both sexes were obliged to work until it was no longer physically possible to do so; very few were unemployed. A majority of the men were textile workers or labourers. Most of the women were concerned with spinning or similar work. The rest were employed in a miscellany of occupations.[11] Poor though they were, a minority of them sent their children to school, either to learn their letters or to learn a trade, and they were encouraged to do so by the city fathers who themselves provided teachers for a proportion of the children. That they were at least relatively successful is indicated by the number of books recorded in the inventories of those a rung or two higher up the ladder.[12]

As early as 1549 the Norwich authorities had organised support for the resident poor, the first provincial city to insist on compulsion in this respect, and 20 years later external events caused the city fathers to take the problem even more seriously. The threat of insurrection in 1570 led to the inauguration of a system of poor relief which had no parallel in England at the time, and one which was regarded as sufficiently important to serve as a model for the first major Elizabethan Act of Parliament concerning the matter, two years later. Exacerbated at intervals by plague, harvest failure and industrial depression, the problem of poverty was never completely eradicated either in Norwich or elsewhere, and if anything the lot of the poor was probably worse in 1670 than it had been a century earlier. The census of the poor suggests that overcrowding was limited in Elizabethan Norwich, but by the second decade of the 17th century the problem was becoming progressively more acute. The Hearth Tax returns suggest that many of the poor in Restoration Norwich were crowded tightly together in tenements, a natural result of an expanding population being crammed together in a restricted built-up area.

Despite this unsatisfactory situation, there is evidence that the city looked after its worst cases. The authorities did all they could to avoid illegal settlement and were ruthess where professional vagrants were concerned, whether they were adults or children. The native poor, however, were provided for, at least at parochial level, throughout the Elizabethan and Stuart periods and some, almost certainly, received assistance from the reign of Edward VI onwards. By the middle years of the 17th century the worst cases of orphaned children were cared for in the newly-established Boys' and Girls' Hospitals, and there was adequate provision for the aged and incapacitated. Within limits, the city fathers did well by their own poor, although neither they nor their counterparts elsewhere were ever entirely successful.

It is against this background that the city's government and governing classes can be considered. The framework of government remained the same throughout the 16th and 17th centuries. An upper house of 24 men, divided equally among the 12 petty wards, had executive power. From their ranks were chosen the mayor, one of the sheriffs (until it was decreed that all potential aldermen should have served in that capacity), the justices of the peace and most of the important office-holders. Similarly, 60 common councillors were chosen throughout the period. The most affluent among them replenished the ranks of the aldermen whenever a vacancy occurred. They supplied the second of the sheriffs until the 17th century, a common speaker to represent their views to their superiors, and they filled a host of minor offices. Aldermen and councillors apart, the most important officials were the recorder, steward and chamberlain, the last of these being responsible for the financial affairs of the city.

All of these men were comfortably off or wealthy. Most of them, whether aldermen or common councillors, were drawn from little more than a dozen or so trades, the same occupations being represented throughout the entire period. Inevitably, the success or failure of a particular occupation was reflected in the ranks of the ruling body. Thus of all men entering civic service in the period 1576-1600 no more than 11 per cent were textile workers, whereas 100 years later the proportion had risen to 39 per cent. Similarly, for much of the Tudor and Stuart periods four out of every 10 men serving the city in an official capacity were members of the merchant classes, the proportion falling to 22 per cent between 1651 and 1675 when the textile trades were at their height. Representatives of other trade groupings – butchers, bakers, cordwainers and ironmongers, for example – also varied in number depending on the success or failure of the textile industry.

While many of the merchants regarded it as their duty to serve the community, if chosen to do so, few of them were prepared to serve for long periods in the pre-Elizabethan era. Just over twenty per cent of those elected between 1526 and 1550, for example, served for a single year, and less than one-third of them were prepared to devote more than five years as a common councillor. Their successors tended to be wealthier men, many of them coming from gentry backgrounds, who were willing and able to devote more time to civic service. By the end of the reign of James I the situation had been reversed, the majority of those elected serving for periods in excess of five years.

Broadly speaking, the majority of the common councillors were the sons or apprentices of men who had themselves represented the city in that capacity. Many of those who came from a different background were wealthy merchants who had purchased their freedom on coming to Norwich, although this element was radically reduced in the 17th century at the instigation of the aldermen themselves. Most of the potential councillors could expect to be elected within ten years or so of becoming freemen, although a minority took considerably longer than this to achieve office.

The same pattern is discernible among the aldermanic ranks, the major difference being that potential aldermen were elected to the council ranks twice as quickly, on average, as those persons who never aspired to, or never attained, this office.

The Civil War and Restoration led to both a change of personnel and a change of outlook among the city's ruling body. Despite its apparent parliamentary affiliations, Norwich contained a solid core of royalist sympathisers and, as might be expected, many of them were to be found among the ranks of the aldermen and common councillors. They were not especially vociferous or aggressive, however, and the more fervent Puritans found little

48. Bacon's House, with St George's church, Colegate, in the background. Bacon was mayor *c.* 1556.

49. The courtyard of Bacon's House.

difficulty in ousting them from their positions of authority. The lower house was purged so drastically that few of the surviving members had had more than a year or two's experience of local government. The new men were drawn from among the lesser lights of the freemen, men who under normal circumstances would never have been elected to such a position. In many cases they had been trading in the city for more than twenty-five years, a situation which produced a lower house comprised of men who were either elderly or in advanced middle age.

The purge of the upper house was, if anything, even more ruthless. Those who resisted were liable to be imprisoned, as in the case of William Gostling, mayor in 1642, or falsely accused of behaviour unbecoming an alderman, as in the case of Alexander Anguish. Attempted neutrality was of little avail. Unless a man was an avowed parliamentarian, he was thrust from office, either immediately or at the first reasonable opportunity.

The stability which emerged from the events outlined above was of short duration. The inevitable Royalist reaction in 1660 brought another series of purges, events which were to be repeated yet again, for different reasons, under James II.[13]

Such drastic upheavals caused a radical change in the city's outlook. From the reign of Henry VIII to that of James I the city fathers had been concerned with internal affairs above all else. Fiercely proud of their independence, they had brooked no interference from outsiders whatsoever. Change was, perhaps, inevitable, as more and more of them emerged from gentry backgrounds or married into the gentry. Horizons were widened with interests extending to the county if not beyond. The Civil War forced them to look further still until by the Restoration, if not before, the upper house had a stake in national politics as well as those nearer home. Significantly, admissions to the freedom of the city in 1678 were closely linked to the aspirations of rival Whig and Tory groups. More than 300 worsted weavers alone were admitted in January of that year, all of whom, it was hoped, would vote for the party concerned.[14]

If the type of man governing Restoration Norwich was different, in some ways at least, from his Henrician forebears, the problems confronting him were very much the same. The most important of these concerned finance, law and order, and the treatment of the poor.

In apparent contrast to other cities of comparable size, Norwich had two major financial bodies, those organised by the chamberlain and the clavors respectively. The chamberlain was responsible for normal day-to-day financial affairs, recording both receipts and expenditure and paying workmen weekly from the accrued funds. The clavors, four of whom were appointed each year, took charge of surplus funds and recorded any extraordinary receipts and expenditure. Whereas the chamberlains were almost invariably in arrears during the 16th century, if solvent thereafter, the clavors rarely recorded a loss and were normally in a position to bolster the funds of the chamberlains and, if necessary, the other financial bodies operating in the city.

In broad terms, the financial history of the city, from the chamberlains' point of view, can be summed up as one of impecuniousness in the 16th century and of relative prosperity in the 17th. Deficits were seldom large and could normally be met by the clavors who, in return, received such surplus funds as became available. While the actual sums of money involved inevitably increased during a period of raging inflation, the source of revenue and the areas of expenditure remained much the same throughout the entire period under consideration.

Rents from city property provided much of the city's income, salaries and repairs to city property the bulk of the expenditure. From time to time additional items appeared, mainly reflecting the temporary importance of a particular issue, but the additions were never sufficiently onerous to make the chamberlains' task a severe one. In consequence, in contrast to such towns as Exeter and Nottingham, the post was a relatively popular one, and its occupants invariably held office for a number of years.

The success of the city fathers in this respect is matched by their similar success in the role of justices of the peace. Serving mayors and all those who had aready passed the chair were entitled to sit in the mayor's court and to participate at Quarter Sessions. Throughout the period some petty offences were still dealt with at parish level, the sheriffs' court fining people for such misdemeanours. By Elizabeth's reign at the latest, however, the majority of such offences, together with those of a more serious nature, had become the responsibility of the mayor's court.

Some offences, as might be expected, were ever-present, varying only in the number of people actually indicted. These included: pilfering; breaking the peace, whether through swearing, scolding, drunkenness or assault; market offences of various kinds; and immorality. Offenders were usually sentenced to be fined or whipped, ducked or put in the cage for scolding, or paraded around the market place for immorality. Vagrancy was a much more serious problem, particularly during the 17th century, but is discussed more appropriately in the section below dealing with poor relief.

50.   Norwich Guildhall.

The court was by no means concerned with crime and punishment alone. The mayor, as clerk of the market, was responsible for the pricing of victuals and for ensuring that any commodities sold were fresh and wholesome. Closely linked to this function was the provision of grain, especially in time of dearth, the members of the court ensuring that it was sold at a reasonable price to prevent starvation among the poor.

Dearth was often linked with plague, a scourge that appeared all too often in Tudor and Stuart Norwich. Epidemic influenza was rampant in the city during the middle years of the

16th century, striking suddenly at both rich and poor, and had been preceded by a relatively serious outbreak of plague in the mid-1540s. The outbreak of bubonic plague which followed the queen's visit in 1578 was much more serious than either of these, however, and before it had run its course in 1580 it was responsible for the deaths of at least one-third of the city's population. For the next quarter of a century plague recurred about once every five years, culminating in a severe outbreak at the beginning of James I's reign. Subsequently it appeared intermittently, notably in 1625 and the 1630s, until its final disappearance after a further catastrophic onslaught in 1665.

Although initially caught off guard, the corporation responded to the best of its abilities, providing money and corn for the afflicted as well as keeping a strict watch on their houses and, ultimately, on the pesthouses provided for them.

A combination of plague and shortage of food made the problem of dealing with the city's poor infinitely more difficult. Fortunately for the town, its poor law system was firmly established by 1579. After the extent of the problem had been made clear by taking a census of the poor in 1570, the authorities trebled the poor rate and took responsibility for some four hundred people who, temporarily or permanently, were incapable of looking after themselves. Special provision was made for the old and incapacitated, and subsequently for children; recalcitrant vagrants were dealt with ruthlessly in the House of Correction. Continuity was essential if the scheme was to be at all successful, and although there may have been a temporary breakdown of the system during the initial outbreak of plague there is evidence that this continuity was maintained well into the 17th century and beyond.

The very success of the scheme encouraged a certain class of vagrant who was prepared to risk the Bridewell in return for potential gain, and initially this class was treated in the most ruthless fashion. Subsequently, severity was tempered with mercy. The city authorities were never prepared to support wanderers from other towns or villages, but they would distinguish between the professional vagrant and those, travelling either singly or as a family, who sought nothing more than a place to work. No work was provided for the non-native poor and they were expelled, but a feature of the 17th century was that such expulsion was not necessarily immediate. Both individuals and families were given as long as three weeks to depart and, on occasion, they were provided with money to speed them on their way. If they returned the authorities were less inclined to leniency.

The constables clearly knew their men and anybody remotely resembling a professional vagrant was treated with the utmost severity. Small children were as subject to a whipping and order to depart as their elders, and there are several examples in the mayor's court books of children under 10 years of age being set adrift outside the city gates with nobody to care for them.

Generally speaking, a combination of severity tempered with mercy to outsiders and a general concern for the welfare of the native poor helped to keep the city authorities in control of the poor law problem. Certainly in the 16th century, possibly in the 17th, Norwich led the rest of England in both its attitude to, and its treatment of, the poor. If it was never entirely successful in this respect it was because the problem was beyond the resources of any community until well into the 20th century. Ironically, too, the problem of poverty was accentuated at intervals by the continuing success of the textile industry. Any temporary depression in this area tended to upset the whole urban economy with consequent pressures on poor relief which the city could ill afford to meet.

But despite occasional vicissitudes of this kind, all commentators were agreed in their praise of the city's size and importance by the reign of Charles II. By then Norwich was far more cosmopolitan than its early-Tudor counterpart. A winter season was well established, with theatres, shows and assemblies which attracted the surrounding gentry even if few of them continued to maintain a town house there. The summer Assizes provided the occasion for similar activities, while for the less wealthy there was the mayor's inauguration, popular entertainments of various kinds and even the county elections which brought in droves of people from outside the city with money to spend. Professional services were increasingly available as was a money market for those who chose to take advantage of its facilities.

Norwich ended the 17th century as it began the 16th, as the largest and wealthiest provincial town in England, well-governed, well-organised and with every reason to look forward to continuing prosperity in the immediate future.[15]

# Abbreviations

| | |
|---|---|
| Ec.H.R. | *Economic History Review* |
| E.H.R. | *English Historical Review* |
| N.R.O. | Norfolk Record Office |
| N.R.S. | Norfolk Record Society |
| *Norf. Arch.* | *Norfolk Archaeology* |
| P.R.O. | Public Record Office |
| V.C.H. | *Victoria County History* |

# Notes

References to documents in the N.R.O. are given below in a slightly abbreviated form. For the full references, *see* the Bibliography.

## Chapter One: Wealth and Occupation in Tudor and Stuart Norfolk

1. W. White, *Norfolk*, 1845 (Reed and Charles reprint, 1969), p. 13; A. H. Smith, *County and Court: Government and Politics in Norfolk, 1558-1603*, 1974, p. 4. Some of these men had flocks of well in excess of 13-14,000 sheep, with many others numbering their animals in thousands rather than in hundreds.
2. A. M. Everitt, 'The Market Towns', in P. Clark, ed., *The Early Modern Town*, 1976, p. 176.
3. N. Williams, 'The Maritime Trade of the East Anglian Ports, 1550-1590', Univ. of Oxford D.Phil. thesis, 1952, p. 63.
4. Ibid., pp. 175 and 186.
5. Ibid., p. 72.
6. Ibid., pp. 256-8.
7. Ibid., p. 258, n. 11, and p. 290.
8. J. Patten, 'The Urban Structure of East Anglia in the Sixteenth and Seventeenth Centuries', Univ. of Cambridge Ph.D. thesis, 1972. I have extracted the Norfolk material from Dr. Patten's tables on pp. 154, 188 and 218 of his thesis and reworked them to conform to the occupational categories used elsewhere in this book.
9. A. M. Everitt, 'The marketing of agricultural produce' in J. Thirsk, ed., *The Agrarian History of England and Wales, IV, 1500-1640*, 1967, pp. 589-92.
10. J. Patten, 'Changing occupational structures in the East Anglian countryside, 1500-1700', in H. S. A. Fox and R. A. Butlin, eds., *Change in the Countryside: Essays on Rural England, 1500-1900*, Institute of British Geographers Special Publication No. 10, 1979, pp. 103-121. I have used the tables on pp. 109, 111 and 113 of this article, again extracting the Norfolk material and modifying it as in note 8.
11. The details given here are based on figure 60, p. 280, in H. C. Darby, ed., *A New Historical Geography of England before 1600*, 1976.
12. P.R.O., E36/22 for the hundreds of Walsham, Brothercross and Gallow; E36/25 for Great Yarmouth and the hundreds of East and West Flegg, Tunstead and Happing; E101/61/16 for South Erpingham; E315/466 for Holt; SP1/234 for Blofield; and N.R.S., i, 1931, for North Greenhoe.
13. N.R.O., Bradfer-Lawrence Papers, XIb, *passim*.
14. *Norfolk Antiquarian Miscellany*, ii, 1883, pp. 399-410.

15. R. M. Dunn, ed., *Norfolk Lieutenancy Journal, 1660-1676*, N.R.S., xlv, 1977, pp. 38-69; M. S. Frankel and P. J. Seaman, eds., *The Norfolk Hearth Tax Assessment, Michaelmas 1664*, Norfolk Genealogical Society, xv, 1983, *passim*.

16. For a fuller discussion, *see* my article, 'Clerical Poverty in Early Sixteenth Century England: some East Anglian Evidence', *The Journal of Ecclesiastical History*, 37, no. 3, July 1986, pp. 389-96.

17. P.R.O., E36/25, f. 91.

18. J. F. Pound, 'The Social and Trade Structure of Norwich, 1525-1575', reprinted in P. Clark, ed., *The Early Modern Town*, 1976, p. 131.

19. R. H. Tawney, *The Agrarian Problem in the Sixteenth Century*, 1967 edn., p. 26.

20. *Norfolk Antiquarian Miscellany*, ii, 1883, pp. 400, 401, 404.

21. Ibid., p. 401.

22. J. F. Pound, ed., *The Military Survey of 1522 for Babergh Hundred*, The Suffolk Records Society, xxviii, 1986, *passim*; and for Norwich pp. 32, 35, above.

23. Dunn, *op. cit.*, p. 17.

24. Tilney cum Islington was rated at £32 1s. 6d., Walpole at £32 6s. 2d. Ibid., p. 49.

25. Frankel and Seaman, *op. cit.*, *passim*.

26. Smith, *op. cit.*, pp. 351-5, for a full list of Norfolk J.P.s.

27. Dunn, *op. cit.*, p. 155, for a full list of Norfolk lieutenants in the period 1660-76, and ibid., p. 151 for a brief biography of Astley.

## Chapter Two: The Physical Appearance of the City

1. B. Green and R. Young, eds., *Norwich – the Growth of a City*, 1963, p. 13.

2. R. Taylor, *Index Monasticus*, 1821, p. 75.

3. L. Toulmin Smith, ed., *The Itinerary of John Leland in or about the years 1535 to 1543*, 1909, IV, p. 33; W. Camden, *Britannia: or a Chorographical Description of Great Britain and Ireland together with the adjacent lands*, 1722, I, p. 461.

4. Between 1521 and 1591 four of the city's five bridges were repaired and put on firmer foundations, the single, and notable, exception being the old Bishops' Bridge, originally built in 1275 and restored in its present form in the 14th century. Anon., *A Topographical and Historical Account of the City and County of Norwich*, 1819, pp. 105-7.

5. W. G. Hoskins, *Provincial England*, 1963, pp. 131-48. For a contrary view, suggesting a later date, *see* R. Machin, 'The Great Re-Building: A Re-assessment', *Past and Present*, 77, 1977, pp. 33-56.

6. I owe this information, and that in the subsequent paragraph, to Mr. Alan Carter, Director of the Norwich Survey, Univ. of East Anglia.

7. M. W. Atkin, H. Sutermeister *et al.*, 'Excavations in Norwich, 1977/8: The Norwich Survey – Seventh Interim Report', *Norf. Arch.*, xxxvii, Part I, 1978, pp. 32-3; J. F. Pound, ed., *The Norwich Census of the Poor, 1570*, N.R.S., xl, 1971, p. 13.

8. M. W. Atkin, A. Carter *et al.*, 'Excavations in Norwich, 1975/6: The Norwich Survey – Fifth Interim Report', *Norfolk Archaeology*, xxxvi, Part III, 1976, p. 197. *See also* R. Smith and A. Carter, 'Function and site: Aspects of Norwich Buildings before 1700', *Vernacular Architecture*, 14, 1983, p. 16.

9. For a fuller discussion *see* pp. 42-3.

10. E. A. Kent, 'The Houses of the Dukes of Norfolk in Norwich', *Norf. Arch.*, xxiv, 1932, pp. 74, 83; B. Cozens-Hardy, 'The Norwich Chapelfield House Estate since 1545 and some of its Owners and Occupiers', *Norf. Arch.*, xxvii, 1941, pp. 352, 357; N.R.O., Norwich City Assessment Books, 1671, no foliation.

11. C. Morris, ed., *The Journeys of Celia Fiennes*, 1947, p. 148

12. J. Nichols, ed., Thos. Fuller, *The History of the Worthies of England*, 1811, p. 154.

13. E. S. de Beer, ed., *The Diary of John Evelyn*, 1959, pp. 562-9.

14. Morris, *op. cit.*, pp. 148-9.

15. N.R.O., Chamberlains' Accounts, 1674, ff. 2-3.

16. Morris, *op. cit.*, pp. 148-9.

## Chapter Three: Population

1. J. F. Pound, 'The social and trade structure of Norwich, 1525-1575', *Past and Present*, 34, 1966, p. 49, reprinted in P. Clark, ed., *The Early Modern Town*, 1976, pp. 129-47.

2. The multiplier used here is the average of the 4.75 suggested by T. P. R. Laslett, 'Size and Structure of the Household in England over Three Centuries', *Population Studies*, xxiii, no. 2, 1969, pp. 207, 211, and the 4.2 suggested by D. V. Glass, 'Two Papers on Gregory King', in D. V. Glass and D. E. C. Eversley, eds., *Population in History*, 1965, p. 177. This may be unnecessarily cautious but recent research has suggested that 4.25 is a safer multiplier for the second half of the 17th century when the population was static or declining and 4.75 may be too high for the early 16th century when many towns, including Norwich, were experiencing at least partial decline. A multiplier of 4.75 would give Norwich a population of approximately 8,950. For the suggested 4.25 *see* Anne Whiteman, ed., *The Compton Census of 1676*, Records of Social and Economic History, New Series, x, 1986, p. lxvii. For the figures on which the population estimates for the other towns are based, *see* Table 4.1, p. 33.

3. E. A. Wrigley and R. S. Schofield, *The Population History of England, 1541-1871: A Reconstruction*, 1981, pp. 207-13, for a discussion of population trends in this period, and especially Table 7.8 on pp. 208-9.

4. P. Clark and P. Slack, *English Towns in Transition, 1500-1700*, 1976, pp. 82-96, for a general discussion of the population history of towns in the 16th and 17th centuries. The figures for the larger provincial towns provided on p. 83 seem high to me. I would doubt if any of them had yet reached 10,000, a modification of my earlier view expressed in the article referred to in n. 1., above.

5. N.R.O., Muster Rolls, Henry VIII to Charles II, no foliation; J. F. Pound, ed., *The Norwich Census of the Poor, 1570*, N.R.S., xl, 1971, p. 95; *idem*, 'Social and Trade Structure', 1966, p. 53. The supporting documentary material is provided on p. 126 above.

6. J. F. Pound, 'The Elizabethan Corporation of Norwich, 1558-1603', Univ. of Birmingham M.A. thesis, 1962, pp. 253, 260.

7. The method is suggested in W. G. Hoskins, *Local History in England*, 1972 edn., p. 169. The figures are derived from Pound, 'Elizabethan Corporation', p. 265, and K. J. Allison, 'The Wool Supply and the Worsted Cloth Industry in Norfolk in the Sixteenth and Seventeenth Centuries', Univ. of Leeds Ph.D. thesis, 1955, p. 607. *See also* Wrigley & Schofield, *op. cit.*, p. 174.

8. P. Corfield, 'A Provincial Capital in the Late Seventeenth Century', in P. Clark and P. Slack, eds., *Crisis and Order in English Towns, 1500-1700*, 1972, p. 268.

9. J. F. Pound, 'The Social Structure and Governing Classes of Norwich, 1525-1670', unpublished paper presented to the meeting of the Urban History Group at Norwich, April 1968; F. Blomefield, *An Essay towards a Topographical History of the County of Norfolk*, 1806, iii, pp. 410-11; Corfield, *loc. cit.*, p. 267. Weavers' and dyers' furnaces were exempt provided their chimneys had already been paid for. For the most recent discussion of the Compton Census for Norwich, *see* Whiteman, *op. cit.*, pp. 193-4. The returns for 17 parishes in 1696 suggest a mean household size of 4.26, *idem*, pp. 198-9.

10. Corfield, *loc. cit.*, p. 267.

11. For Bristol in 1607, *see* D. M. Palliser, *The Age of Elizabeth*, 1983, p. 204, and for Bristol and Salisbury in the 1690s, Clark and Slack, *English Towns in Transition*, p. 83. The other figures are based on the Hearth Tax material referred to on p. 42.

## Chapter Four: The Pattern of Wealth

1. P.R.O., E179/150/218; N.R.O., Case 7, shelf i; P.R.O., E179/154/701; N.R.O., Case 13, shelf a, Norwich City Assessment Books, 1671; N.R.O., Inventories 1 to 65. Seventeenth-century rates are discussed in J. T. Evans, *Seventeenth Century Norwich*, 1980, pp. 14-16, 22-4, 34-9.

2. The percentages of those exempted vary from 18 and 21 per cent at Sudbury and Coventry to 31 per cent at Great Yarmouth and 40 and 41 per cent at Aylsham and Exeter respectively. *See*: J. F. Pound, ed., *The Military Survey of 1522 for Babergh Hundred*, Suffolk Records Society, xxviii, 1986, p. 131, for Sudbury; C. Phythian-Adams, *Desolation fof a City: Coventry and the Urban Crisis of the Later Middle Ages*, 1979, pp. 318-9, for Coventry; P.R.O., E36/25 and E101/61/16 for Great Yarmouth and Aylsham; and, for Exeter, M. M. Rowe, ed., *Tudor Exeter*, Devon and Cornwall Record Society, 22, 1977, pp. 7-33. In the latter town, a further 41 peoople, or seven per cent, were assessed on amounts of less than £1 in the Military Survey of 1522, from which all of these estimates are taken. It is of some significance that many of those given nil assessments at Exeter were servants or apprentices, and that everywhere a proportion of such people were taxed on goods or wages in either 1524 or 1525.

3. W. G. Hoskins, *Provincial England*, 1963, p. 84.

4. Phythian-Adams, *op. cit.*, p. 132. The Norwich census of the poor, in contrast, contains references to only two servants among almost 800 households, with two other girls possibly fulfilling this function. J. F. Pound, ed., *The Norwich Census of the Poor, 1570*, N.R.S., xl, 1971, pp. 29, 40, 61.

5. J. F. Pound, *Poverty and Vagrancy in Tudor England*, 2nd edn., 1986, p. viii.

6. P.R.O., E179/250/263 for Thetford, and *Suffolk in 1524: Subsidy Return*, Suffolk Green Books, x, 1910, pp. 348-58, for Bury St Edmunds.

7. Hoskins, *op. cit.*, p. 73; *Norfolk Antiquarian Miscellany*, ii, 1883, p. 406, for Guybon, and *Suffolk in 1524*, p. 30, for Smyth.

8. P.R.O., E179/150/208 and J. F. Pound, 'The social and trade structure of Norwich, 1525-1575', *Past and Present*, 34, 1966, reprinted in P. Clark, ed., *The Early Modern Town*, 1976.

9. This situation was not unusual and undoubtedly could be paralleled throughout the country. In Babergh hundred in Suffolk, for example, it is possible to compare the assessments of 1,309 men who appeared in both 1522 and 1524, 169 of whom were given nil assessments in the former year and were taxed for the first time in the latter. Of the remaining 1,140, 578, or just under 51 per cent, had their assessments reduced while 476, or 42 per cent, remained the same. While some of these cases reflect a genuine change in fortune – see, for example, the appeals against the 1524 assessments in Exeter in Rowe, *op. cit.*, pp. 79-80 – there are too many for this to apply universally, and they probably reflect the opposition of the upper classes, in particular, to an unpopular tax. The Babergh details are derived from Pound, ed., *Military Survey*, and *Suffolk in 1524, passim*.

10. F. J. Fisher, ed., Thomas Wilson, 'The State of England, A.D. 1600', in *Camden Miscellany*, xvi, 1936, p. 20.

11. J. F. Pound, 'The Elizabethan Corporation of Norwich, 1558-1603', Univ. of Birmingham M.A. thesis, 1962, pp. 82-94, for these and other aldermanic wills.

12. Ibid., pp. 92-3, 97-106.

13. E. H. Phelps-Brown and S. V. Hopkins, 'Seven Centuries of the Price of Consumables, compared with Builders' Wage-rates', in E. Carus-Wilson, ed., *Essays in Economic History*, II, 1962, p. 195. Wages began to move ahead of prices in the first half of the 17th century, but builders' wage-rates fluctuated, and after a rise of approximately forty per cent between 1625 and 1650 fell again in the succeeding period to a level little higher than at the end of Elizabeth's reign. P. Bowden, 'Agricultural Prices, Farm Profits and Rents', in Joan Thirsk, ed., *The Agrarian History of England and Wales, IV, 1500-1640*, 1967, p. 609.

14. A table analysing the types of rooms mentioned in the inventories is provided in Pound, 'Government and Society in Tudor and Stuart Norwich', Univ. of Leicester Ph.D. thesis, 1974, p. 43. The details given there have been substantiated over a wider period in a recent article by U. V. M. Priestley and P. J. Corfield, 'Rooms and Room Use in Norwich Housing, 1580-1730', *Post-Medieval Archaeology*, 16, 1982, pp. 93-123. A detailed analysis of all the Norwich inventories surviving locally, by value and occupation, is given in Pound, *op. cit.*, pp. 310-18. There are relatively few Norwich inventories surviving in the P.R.O., and all of them date from the Restoration period onwards. The median value of 21 of these, dated between 1661 and 1675, is £878, with a range from £222 to £7,851. Apart from the latter, nine of them varied between £1,049 and £4,592. N.R.O., MF 506.

15. N.R.O., Inv. 27, No. 161.

16. P.R.O., Prob.4/1687.

17. Pound, 'Government and Society', p. 40, for a table contrasting the last years of Elizabeth's reign with the period 1651-75.

18. Ibid., p. 41 and P.R.O. inventories on microfilm in the N.R.O., MF 506.

19. R. H. Tawney, ed., Thos. Wilson, *A discourse on usury*, 1925, introduction, *passim*, for the prevalence of moneylending in Elizabethan England.

20. N.R.O., Inv. 27, No. 131, for Edgeley and Inv. 22, Nos. 310 and 358, and Inv. 46, No. 137, for the others.

21. P.R.O., Prob. 4/1606, 10289, 4051 and 3602. The linen draper's inventory is numbered 1756. All can be found on MF 506 in the N.R.O.

22. Ibid., No. 1528.

23. N.R.O., Invs. 5, Nos. 119, 161; 15, Nos. 128, 14, 18; 9, No. 79; 17, Nos. 79 and 121.

24. N.R.O., Invs., 3, Nos. 42 and 30, No. 37.

25. N.R.O., Inv. 30, No. 65.

26. The inventories of the relatively poor can be made to yield interesting information, however. *See* Chapter 10, pp. 135-40.

### Chapter Five: The Trade Structure of Tudor and Stuart Norwich

1. P. Millican, *The Freemen of Norwich, 1548-1713*, 1934; P. Millican and W. Rising, *An Index of Indentures of Norwich Apprentices enrolled with the Norwich Assembly, Henry VII-George II*, N.R.S., xxix, 1959; J. F. Pound, ed., *The Norwich Census of the Poor, 1570*, N.R.S., xl, 1971; *idem*, 'The validity of the Freemen's lists: some Norwich evidence', Ec.H.R., 2nd ser., 34, 1981; W. J. C. Moens, *The Walloons and their Church in Norwich: their History and Registers*, 1887-8, pp. 152-6, 207-16.
2. P. Clark, 'The migrant in Kentish towns, 1580-1640', in P. Clark and P. Slack, eds., *Crisis and Order in English Towns, 1500-1700*, 1972, pp. 134-5.
3. This paragraph, and those following, is based on Table XXII in Pound, 'Government and Society in Tudor and Stuart Norwich', Univ. of Leicester Ph.D. thesis, 1974, pp. 59-60.
4. A detailed breakdown of the trades followed by the Norwich apprentices, indicating those who followed their fathers as well as those who were apprenticed in other spheres, is provided in Pound, 'Government and Society', pp. 62-6.
5. Pound, 'The Social and Trade Structure of Norwich, 1525-1575', in P. Clark, ed., *The Early Modern Town*, 1976, pp. 137-8.
6. Pound, 'Government and Society', p. 67.
7. *See* p. 48.
8. *See* p. 50, for some indication of the time taken to attain the freedom.
9. Richard Grime, for example, was apprenticed as a worsted weaver early in James I's reign until he was 27 years and 16 weeks old. Millican and Rising, *op. cit.*, p. 78.
10. W. Hudson and J. C. Tingey, eds., *The Records of the City of Norwich*, II, p. 382.
11. Ibid., I, p. 106.
12. Millican and Rising, *op. cit.*, p. ii.
13. For a discussion of the accuracy of the freemen's lists, *see* Pound, 'Validity of the Freemen's Lists', 1981, *passim*.
14. Millican, *op. cit.*, p. xx.
15. Pound, 'Government and Society', Appendix VIII. For a comparison with the occupational structure of other towns in the 16th century, including Coventry and Northampton in the 1520s, *see idem*, Table XXXI, p. 76, and for a fuller survey, Palliser, *The Age of Elizabeth*, p. 243.
16. *See* Appendix I for the value of the moveable goods owned by various tradesmen and others.
17. Many of these were poor only in a relative sense. Most historians would now regard those worth between £2 and £4 in moveables as being a buffer between the true poor and their more affluent fellows.
18. *See* Pound, 'Government and Society', p. 6, for a full tabulation.
19. Ibid., Appendix I, pp. 295-6.
20. K. J. Allison, 'The Norfolk Worsted Industry in the Sixteenth and Seventeenth Centuries', *Yorkshire Bulletin of Economic and Social Research*, xii, 1960; N. Williams, 'The Maritime Trade of the East Anglian Ports, 1550-90', Univ. of Oxford D.Phil. thesis, 1952, pp. 38 and 74.
21. K. J. Allison, 'The Norwich hatters', *East Anglian Magazine*, xvi, p. 138.
22. D. Knoop and G. P. Jones, *The Medieval Mason*, 1933, p. 209.
23. F. J. Fisher, 'Influenza and inflation in Tudor England', Ec.H.R., 2nd Ser., xviii, 1965.
24. F. Blomefield, *History of Norfolk*, iii, p. 276.
25. W. G. Hoskins, *Provincial England*, 1963, pp. 86-7; A. G. Dickens, 'Tudor York', in *The City of York*, V.C.H. Yorks., 1961, pp. 127-8.
26. N. Williams, *op. cit.*, p. 216.
27. Ibid., p. 73.
28. Norwich Consistory Court, 273 Flack and 150 Candler for Stingate and Durrant respectively.
29. Williams, *op. cit.*, pp. 77 and 205.
30. *See* Chapter Ten, pp. 131-3.
31. It may have been houses such as these which some of the aldermen and councillors were letting to the poor in 1570. *See* Chapter Ten, pp. 130-1.
32. W. Rye, 'The Dutch Refugees in Norwich', *Norfolk Antiquarian Miscellany*, ii, p. lxxix.
33. *Idem*, iii, p. 185; Moens, *op. cit.*, pp. 29, 152-6, 207-16.

34. Hudson and Tingey, II, p. lxxx.
35. K. J. Allison, 'The Norfolk Worsted Industry in the Sixteenth and Seventeenth Centuries: Part II. The New Draperies', *Yorkshire Bulletin of Economic and Social Research*, 13, No. 2, November 1961, pp. 63-4.
36. *See* Pound, 'Validity of the Freemen's Lists', for a fuller discussion of this important document.
37. *See* Table 5.5, p. 51.
38. It was an expensive privilege for some. Jacques Dehem, for example, paid £50 when admitted as a merchant in March 1601. Millican, *op. cit.*, p. 104.
39. P. J. Bowden, *The Wool Trade in Tudor and Stuart England*, 1962, p. 53.
40. Charles Wilson, *England's Apprenticeship, 1603-1763*, 1965, p. 76.
41. Joan Thirsk and J. P. Cooper, *Seventeenth Century Economic Documents*, 1972, p. 731.
42. Millican and Rising, *op. cit.*, *passim*.
43. The numbers of potential freemen in this sphere were far from exhausted. In January 1678, 194 of the 362 men enfranchised to vote in a parliamentary election were worsted weavers. Millican, *op. cit.*, pp. xvi and 182-5.
44. Moens, *op. cit.*, p. iii.
45. Pound, 'Government and Society', p.87; C. Webster, ed., *Health, Medicine and Mortality in the Sixteenth Century*, 1979, p. 225; Margaret Pelling, 'Occupational Diversity: Barber Surgeons and the Trades of Norwich, 1550-1640', *Bulletin of the History of Medicine*, 56, 1984, p. 484; John H. Raach, *A Directory of English Country Physicians, 1603-43*, 1962, pp. 15, 110.
46. Pound, 'Validity of the Freemen's Lists', p. 54.
47. Pound, 'Government and Society', p. 95.
48. Millican, *op. cit.*, *passim*.
49. N.R.O., Case 16, shelf a, Mayors' Court book, 1562-69, ff. 95-7; Millican, *op. cit.*, p. 65.
50. Millican, *op. cit.*, pp. 34, 131.
51. Pelling, 'Occupational Diversity', p. 504.
52. Millican, *op. cit.*, p. 86.
53. J. F. Pound, 'The Social Structure and Governing Classes of Norwich, 1525-1670', unpublished paper circulated and discussed at the meeting of the Urban History Group at Norwich, April 1968, pp. 9-10.
54. Ibid., p. 8.
55. Thirsk and Cooper, *op. cit.*, p. 27.
56. P. Corfield, 'A Provincial Capital in the Late Seventeenth Century: the Case of Norwich', in Clark and Slack, *op. cit.*, p. 280.
57. *See* p. 42.
58. T. B. Macaulay, *History of England from the Reign of James II*, 1906 edn., I, p.261.
59. Wilson, *op. cit.*, p. 77.

## Chapter Six: The Government and Governing classes of Norwich, 1525-1625

1. W. Hudson and J. C. Tingey, *Records of the City of Norwich*, I, Norwich, 1910, pp. xv-xxviii.
2. Ibid., p. lix.
3. Ibid., pp. cxxix-xxx, quoting Gough Mss Norfolk, 33, f. 46d in the Bodleian Library, Oxford.
4. D. M. Palliser, *Tudor York*, 1979, pp. 60-91; W. T. MacCaffrey, *Exeter, 1540-1640*, 2nd edn. 1975, pp. 26-53; A. D. Dyer, *The City of Worcester in the Sixteenth Century*, 1973, pp. 189-202; C. I. Hammer, 'Anatomy of an Oligarchy: the Oxford Town Council in the Fifteenth and Sixteenth Centuries', *Journal of British Studies*, xviii, 1978-9, pp. 1-27.
5. Palliser, *op. cit.*, p. 61.
6. Conesford and the Ward across the Water each had 12 representatives, Mancroft had 16 and the larger Wymer ward twenty.
7. Hammer, *loc. cit.*, p. 4.
8. Two aldermen were elected to represent each of the 12 petty wards of Norwich, the great wards of Conesford, Mancroft, Wymer and Ultra Aquam being each subdivided into three parts.
9. As with John Spencer in 1540, for example.
10. Hudson and Tingey, *op. cit.*, p. xc.
11. Ibid., p. 126.

12. This should not be seen as a 'flight from office' as such. Those seeking to avoid election completely were normally less wealthy men. In many cases office was deferred rather than avoided. The same situation was to be found in many large and middling towns. *See* the references cited in note 4 and, for medieval parallels,. Jennifer Kermode, 'Urban Decline? The Flight from Office in Late Medieval York', Ec.H.R., 2nd Ser., xxxv, 1982, pp. 179-98.

13. *See* J. F. Pound, 'Government and Society in Tudor and Stuart Norwich, 1525-1675', Univ. of Leicester Ph.D thesis, 1974, p. 105, for appropriate references.

14. J. F. Pound, 'The Social Structure and Governing Classes of Norwich, 1525-1670', unpublished paper circulated to the meeting of the Urban History Group at Norwich, April 1968.

15. Ordinances were passed in that year authorising cordwainers to become members of the common council. Before then they were deemed an unacceptable trade. Hudson and Tingey, *op. cit.*, II, p. 135.

16. *See* Pound, 'Government and Society', p. 111, for the table on which this discussion is based.

17. On average they were then between 28 and 30 years of age if the aldermanic evidence is a reliable guideline. *See* below, note 23, for details of the ages of aldermen in the centuries concerned.

18. Pound, *op. cit.*, pp. 113-14, for statistical evidence of this.

19. Pound, *op. cit.*, pp. 116-17.

20. J. F. Pound, 'The Elizabethan Corporation of Norwich, 1558-1603', Univ. of Birmingham M.A. thesis, 1962, p. 49.

21. Pound, 'Government and Society', p. 122.

22. V. Pearl, *London and the outbreak of the Puritan Revolution*, 1961, p. 60.

23. It has been possible to establish the ages of 37 of the Norwich aldermen at various times during the 16th and 17th centuries. If one takes the median, an alderman became free at the age of 28, was elected a common councillor seven years later, attained the shrievalty at the age of 46, became an alderman the following year and was elected mayor when he was fifty-nine. He could expect to serve as an alderman for 23 years. The extremes ranged from election as alderman at 35 to service of almost 50 years. This accords closely with the situation at York discussed in Palliser, *op. cit.*, p. 71, although in Oxford aldermen averaged 55 when elected. *See* Hammer, *loc. cit.*, p. 24.

24. Pound, 'Government and Society', p. 128.

25. Ibid., pp. 130-3 for supporting tables.

26. N.R.O., Assembly Book, 1585-1613, ff. 53 and 64.

27. J. T. Evans, 'The political elite of Norwich, 1620-1690', Univ. of Stanford Ph.D. thesis, 1971, pp. 61-6.

28. B. H. Allen, 'The administrative and social structure of the Norwich merchant class, 1485-1660', Univ. of Harvard Ph.D. thesis, 1951, pp. 281-2.

29. Allen, *op. cit.*, pp. 344, 350.

30. Norwich Consistory Court Wills, 134 Goldingham and 161 Skyppow.

31. Pound, 'Elizabethan Corporation', p. 15.

32. Pound, 'Government and Society', pp. 143-51 for these and several other examples.

**Chapter Seven: Civil War and Instability, 1620-1675**

This chapter draws heavily on the accounts of J. T. Evans (*Seventeenth Century Norwich*, 1979) and R. W. Ketton-Cremer (*Norfolk in the Civil War*, 1969 reprinted 1985). I have given specific references to these works where it seems appropriate up to the Norwich riot of 1649, and I have referred to whole sections of their books thereafter. My own contribution is confined to the analyses of the aldermanic and common councillor bodies at the time of the 'purges' of 1649-50 and 1661-2. They modify those put forward in Dr. Evans' account.

1. B. L. Beer, 'The Commoyson in Norfolk, 1549': a Narrative of Popular Rebellion in Sixteenth Century England', *Journal of Medieval and Renaissance Studies*, vi, 1976; J. Cornwall, *Revolt of the Peasantry*, 1577. *See also* A. Fletcher, *Tudor Rebellions*, 3rd edn., 1983, pp. 54-68.

2. *See* pp. 104-5.

3. *See* pp. 73, 78, 81.

4. Evans, *op. cit.*, p. 48.

5. *Calendar of State Papers Domestic*, 1619-23, p. 40.

6. Evans, *op. cit.*, pp. 56-7.

7. F. Blomefield, *An Essay towards a Topographical History of the County of Norfolk*, 1805-10, iii, p. 373.

8. Evans, *op. cit.*, p. 80.
9. A. D. Bayne, *A Comprehensive History of Norwich*, 1869, p. 243. Norwich was also the home of an early separatist movement, the Brownists.
10. K. Shipps, 'Lay Patronage of East Anglian Puritan Clerics in Pre-Revolutionary England', Univ. of Yale Ph.D. thesis, 1971, pp. 267-70.
11. Evans, *op. cit.*, pp. 85-8.
12. Ketton-Cremer, *op. cit.*, p. 62.
13. Ibid., pp. 67-8.
14. Evans, *op. cit.*, pp. 89-90.
15. Ketton-Cremer, *op. cit.*, p. 77.
16. Ibid., p. 79.
17. Evans, *op. cit.*, pp. 91-3.
18. Ketton-Cremer, *op. cit.*, p. 84
19. Evans, *op. cit.*, p. 96.
20. Ibid., pp. 121-2.
21. Ibid., pp. 122-3.
22. Ibid., pp. 126-7.
23. Ketton-Cremer, *op. cit.*, pp. 232-3.
24. Evans, *op. cit.*, p. 129.
25. Ibid., pp. 132-3.
26. For a thorough discussion of the events leading up to the riot of 1649, *see* Evans, *op. cit.*, pp. 151-74. The riot itself is described most graphically in Ketton-Cremer, *op. cit.*, pp. 334-49, and the events leading up to the Restoration and beyond in Evans, *op. cit.*, Chapter Six.
27. Evans, *op. cit.*, p. 228.
28. J. Miller, 'The Crown and the Borough Charters in the Reign of Charles II', E.H.R., 1985, pp. 53-84.

**Chapter Eight: Financial Affairs**
1. N.R.O., Clavors' Accounts, 1555-1646, *passim*.
2. Ibid., f. 53d.
3. Ibid., f. 43d.
4. Ibid.: ff. 50d, 52, 78, 127d, 144d, 152d; June 1649-May 1651, n.p.; 1665, n.p.
5. W. Hudson and J. C. Tingey, eds., *The Records of the City of Norwich*, 1910, I, p. 67.
6. N.R.O., Chamberlains' Accounts: 1532-49, f. 8d; 1531-37, f. 73; 1537-47, f. 56; 1551-67, f. 164; Assembly Book, 1551-68, f. 57; Chamberlains' Accounts: 1580-89, f. 222d; 1589-1602, f. 305d; 1603-25, n.p.; 1614-16; 1625, n.p.; 1655-6, f. 6d.
7. Assembly Book, 1551-68, f. 161.
8. Chamberlains' Accounts, 1551-67, f. 258d; 1580-9, f. 287d.
9. Ibid., 1558-1603, *passim*. The volume containing the accounts for the years 1550-79 inclusive is missing.
10. J. F. Pound, 'Government and Society in Tudor and Stuart Norwich, 1525-1675', Univ. of Leicester Ph.D thesis, 1974, p. 339.
11. Chamberlains' Accounts, 1625, n.p.
12. Pound, 'Government and Society', pp. 339-41.
13. Chamberlains' Accounts: 1531-37, ff. 8, 89-92; 1589-1602, ff. 176, 179; 1610-15, 1620, n.p.; 1665-6, ff. 4, 6, 6d.
14. W. G. Hoskins, *Provincial England*, 1963, p. 99; D. M. Livock, ed., *City Chamberlains' Accounts of the Sixteenth and Seventeenth Centuries*, Bristol Record Society, xxiv, 1966, p. xxii.
15. Hoskins, *op. cit.*, p. 98; T. Atkinson, *Elizabethan Winchester*, 1963, p. 127.
16. W. T. MacCaffrey, *Exeter, 1540-1640*, 1958, p. 56; Hoskins, *op. cit.*, p. 99.
17. Chamberlains' Accounts: 1541-9, ff. 152d-157; 1589-1602 and 17th century, *passim*.
18. Ibid.: 1531-37, ff. 9d-10; 1625-48, n.p.; 1648-75, *passim*.
19. Ibid.: 1531-37, f. 9d; 1589-1602, f. 290d.
20. Ibid. and 1673-83, f. 25.
21. Ibid.
22. Ibid., 1673-83, f.25.
23. Livock, *op. cit.*, p. xxii.

24. Ibid.
25. MacCaffrey, *op. cit.*, p. 50.
26. Hoskins, *op. cit.*, p. 98.
27 Ibid., p. 99.
28. Atkinson, *op. cit.*, p. 131; W. H. Stevenson, ed., *Records of the Borough of Nottingham, IV, 1547-1625*, pp. 117, 281.
29. Chamberlains' Accounts: 1540; 1551-67, ff. 142, 250d, 326; 1589-1602, f. 307d.
30. Ibid., 1558-1660, *passim*.
31. Ibid., 1580, 1585 and 1590.
32. Ibid.: 1551-67, f. 154d; 1580-9, f. 21; 1589-1602, ff. 26d, 194d.
33. N.R.O., Hanaper Accounts, *passim*.
34. Assembly Book, 1551-1568, f. 142.
35. Ibid.
36. Ibid., 1568-85, f. 244.
37. Chamberlains' Accounts, 1589-1602, ff. 65d, 81.
38. Ibid.
39. Ibid.: 1537-49, ff. 38, 38d, 39d, 46, 46d, 128d; 1551-67, ff. 49, 146d, 152d, 320, 320d, 321, 322d, 329; 1589-1602, f. 321d; 1648-63, ff. 16, 191, 268d.
40. W. E. Minchinton, ed., *Wage regulation in pre-industrial England*, 1971, p. 104.
41. Chamberlains' Accounts, 1648-63, f. 16.
42. Ibid., 1663-73, ff. 57-57d, 156-7.
43. Ibid., 1648-1663, f. 60.
44. Ibid.: 1551-67, f. 359d; 1580-89, f. 164.
45. Clavors' Accounts, 1555-1646, ff. 40d, 43, 44.
46. Chamberlains' Accounts: 1648-63, ff. 152, 114, 132d, 14d; 1645, n.p.
47. C. H. Firth and R. S. Rait, *Acts and Ordinances of the Interregnum*, 1911: I, pp. 224, 273, 292, 323, 615, 631, 742, 763, 810, 959, 1,074, 1,109; II, pp. 28, 53, 288, 459, 655, 904, 1,031, 1,060, 1,236, 1,358.
48. Chamberlains' Accounts: 1537-47, ff. 39, 173-173d; 1614-16, n.p.
49. MacCaffrey, *op. cit.*, p. 63; Stevenson, *op. cit.*, pp. 272, 286, 296, 320, 339, 342. In Norwich, Peter Peterson served for nine years, Richard Skottow for 10, and Robert Goldman for 14 years. M. Grace, 'The Chamberlains and Treasurers of the City of Norwich, 1293-1835', *Norf. Arch.*, xxv, 1935, pp. 199-200.
50. Chamberlains' Accounts, 1541-50, ff. 343-4.
51. *See* Table 5.2.

**Chapter Nine: The Mayor's Court**

 1. W. Hudson and J. C. Tingey, eds., *The Records of the City of Norwich*, I, 1910, pp. cxxvii-cxxxiv. For a discussion of Quarter Sessions in the reign of Elizabeth I, *see* J. F. Pound, 'The Elizabethan Corporation of Norwich, 1558-1603', Univ. of Birmingham M.A. thesis, 1962, pp. 285-93.
 2. The period 1525-1675 is covered by no fewer than 23 volumes, each of which contains more than 700 pages. They are thus far too detailed for minute analysis, but they have been examined for every fifth year throughout the 150 year period and the discussion is based on this survey.
 3. For a fuller discussion of the events referred to in this paragraph, *see* Chapter Ten, p. 141 *et seq.*
 4. Mayor's Court Book: 1549-55, f. 19; 1555-62, f. 37.
 5. This was almost certainly in response to a letter from Sir Nicholas Bacon, written in 1562, exhorting the justices to be more diligent in their duties. Vagrants were to be apprehended according to the statutes of 1531 and 1550.
 6. *See* the breakdown of cases in Table 9.1, p. 111.
 7. Considerable under-recording must have taken place in the middle years of the 17th century, but such evidence as we have does suggest that vagrancy was becoming less of a problem by the second decade of Charles II's reign. *See* pp. 117-8.
 8. *See* Chapter Five, pp. 46-7, for geographical origins of apprentices.
 9. The percentages are based on the totals for whom a place of origin is given, not on the total number apprehended in a given period.
10. J. F. Pound, *Poverty and Vagrancy in Tudor England*, 1971, p. 27.

11. Sidney and Beatrice Webb, *English Poor Law History, I: The Old Poor Law*, 1962 edn., p. 356.

12. Pound, *Poverty and Vagrancy*, p. 61.

13. Ibid., pp. 94-7. It should be stressed that Hext was writing of exceptional conditions at an exceptional time. They are in no way typical of the 16th century as a whole, nor, indeed, of the country at large.

14. Webbs, *op. cit.*, p. 359.

15. Ibid., pp. 361-2.

16. P. Slack, 'Vagrants and Vagrancy in England, 1598-1664', Ec.H.R., 2nd series, xxvii, 3, 1974, p. 366.

17. For much of the 17th century, vagrants made up fewer than half of those brought before the mayor's court in Norwich. The average number arrested per year in Salisbury was 16, in Norwich twice that number, but in neither case sufficient to cause any major problems.

18. E. Leonard, *The Early History of English Poor Relief*, 1900, pp. 250, 299, 358.

19. Slack, *loc. cit.* While males continued to predominate, especially in the North, one in five of the vagrants apprehended in Colchester and Hertfordshire in the 1630s were children travelling on their own, and the proportion was only slightly less (16 per cent) in Devon and Cornwall.

20. P. Styles, 'The evolution of the law of settlement', *Univ. of Birmingham Historical Journal*, ix, 1963-4, pp. 34-5.

21. Margaret James, *Social Problems and Policy during the Puritan Revolution*, 1966, p. 287.

22. Mayor's Court Book: 1624-36, f. 70d; 1615-24, f. 306; 1603-15, ff. 82 and 97.

23. Mayor's Court Book, 1624-36, f. 32.

24. Hudson and Tingey, *op. cit.*, II, p. xcix.

25. Mayor's Court Book, 1562-9, ff. 194, 196, 326.

26. Ibid., and 1615-24, f. 275; 1624-36, f. 32.

27. *See* Chapter Ten, p. 148.

28. Mayor's Court Book: 1615-24, f. 6; 1654-66, f. 112.

29. Ibid., 1603-75, *passim*.

30. Ibid.: 1654-66, f. 239; 1624-36, f. 37.

31. The numbers travelling together remain problematical. I inadvertently exaggerated the size of the groupings when I misquoted the well-known letter from the Somerset magistrate, Hext, and suggested that in times of stress gangs of soldiers could reach forty or fifty strong. (Pound, *Poverty and Vagrancy*, first edn., 1971, p. 29.) They met in barns in groups of this size, but actually travelled in twos or threes. Dr. Beier, in his anxiety to prove the contrary, is similarly misleading. he refers to '*one* instance when '40, sometimes 60 [sic]' gathered weekly in a remote hay-house'. (A. L. Beier, *Masterless Men: The Vagrancy Problem in England, 1560-1640*, 1985, p. 124.) *Weekly* gatherings of forty to sixty men hardly relate to a single instance, and reflect the unsettled conditions in Somerset, in particular, during the late 16th century.

32. Mayor's Court Book, 1603-15, f. 459. Examples could undoubtedly be paralleled throughout the country. Beier refers to a boy of 10, taken in Leicestershire in 1586, 'almost devoured with lice', and two others, aged five and six, who were taken at Stafford in 1614 and said to come from school at Shrewsbury, 30 miles distant. Beier, *op. cit.*, p. 55.

33. Mayor's Court Book, 1595-1603, f. 399.

34. *See* Table 9.1, p. 111.

35. Mayor's Court Book, 1615-24, f. 304d; 1625-36, ff. 28a, 58, 279, 279d.

36. Ibid., 1603-75, *passim*.

37. Ibid., 1549-55, f. 19; 1555-62, f. 37.

38. Ibid., 1576-82, f. 515; 1595-1603, f. 498 and 470.

39. W. L. Sachse, ed., *Minutes of the Norwich Court of Mayoralty, 1630-31*, N.R.S., xv, 1942, pp. 107, 151.

40. James, *op. cit.*, p. 291.

41. Hudson and Tingey, *op. cit.*, II, pp. 132, 353.

42. Webbs, *op. cit.*, p. 319; Styles, *loc. cit.*, p. 43.

43. Webbs, *op. cit.*, p. 329.

44. Mayor's Court Book, 1634-46, f. 62d.

45. Sachse, *op. cit.*, pp. 77, 99.

46. R. H. Hill, ed., *The correspondence of Thomas Corie*, N.R.S., xxvii, 1956, pp. 19-20.

47. *See* pp. 121-3.

48. D. L. Farmer, *Britain and the Stuarts*, 1965, p. 34.

49. A. L. Beier, 'Poor relief in Warwickshire, 1630-1660', *Past and Present*, 35, 1966, pp. 82, 86, 90.

50. Jordan, *op. cit.*, p. 207. Beier has recently suggested that the problem of vagrancy eased from the mid-17th century due, at least in part, to the widespread enforcement of statutory poor relief. Beier, *Masterless Men*, p. 18.

51. James, *op. cit.*, p. 50.

52. Ibid., p. 286.

53. Ibid., p. 76.

54. Styles, *loc. cit.*

55. Webbs, *op. cit.*, pp. 328, 330n.

56. Ibid., pp. 359, 361-2.

57. Mayor's Court Book, 1666-76, f. 333d.

58. Ibid., 1569-76, ff. 49-133, *passim*.

59. Sachse, *op. cit.*, pp. 24-7.

60. Ibid., p. 25.

61. Mayor's Court Books, 1555-1603, *passim*; Sachse, *op. cit.*, pp. 25-6.

62. *See*, for example, Mayor's Court Book, 1595-1603, f. 55.

63. Sachse, *op. cit.*, p. 27.

64. R. Fitch, 'Notices of Norwich Brewers' Marks and Trade Regulations', *Norf. Arch.*, v, 1859, pp. 326-7.

65. Mayor's Court Book, 1624-34, f. 416. The census does not survive. Innkeepers, tapsters and tipplers predominate among the occupations which are listed in full in the St Peter Mancroft parish registers for the period 1538-48 and again from 1598 to the mid-1630s. Twenty-two distinct inns are named in this rich and central parish which may, however, be atypical in this respect. N.R.O., PD 26/1 (S), 8 (S) and 16 (S).

66. Mayor's Court Book, 1624-34, ff. 421 and 435. For the increasing importance of tipplers in 17th-century Norwich *see* p. 62.

67. Mayor's Court Book, 1615-24, f. 218.

68. Ibid., 1585-1613, f. 54.

69. Ibid., 1595-1603, f. 55.

70. Sachse, *op. cit.*, p. 27.

71. Assembly Book, 1568-85, ff. 24d-25. For a general discussion of Sabbatarianism in this period *see* Christopher Hill, *Society and Puritanism in Pre-Revolutionary England*, 1966, pp. 145-218.

72. Assembly Book, 1568-85, f. 235.

73. Ibid., f. 188d.

74. Mayor's Court Book, 1595-1603, p. 438; Assembly Book, 1585-1613, ff. 272d-273.

75. Sachse, *op. cit.*, p. 51.

76. Mayor's Court Book, 1655-66, f. 2; 1634-46, f. 457d.

77. Sachse, *op. cit.*, p. 51.

78. For other examples, *see* p. 115.

79. L. G. Bolingbroke, 'Players in Norwich from the accession of Queen Elizabeth until their suppression in 1642', *Norf. Arch.*, xiii, 1898, p. 15.

80. Mayor's Court Book, 1666-76, ff. 331d, 333d, 334.

81. Sachse, *op. cit.*, p. 38.

82. Pound, 'Elizabethan Corporation of Norwich', p. 283.

83. Wage rates remained virtually static between 1580 and 1640. Christopher Hill, *Reformation to Industrial Revolution*, 1969, p. 57.

84. Sachse, *op. cit.*, pp. 87, 100.

85. R. K. Kelsall, 'Wage Regulation under the Statute of Artificers', in W. E. Minchinton, ed., *Wage Regulation in Pre-Industrial England*, 1972, p. 104.

86. Mayor's Court Book, 1555-62, f. 366.

87. Ibid., f. 472.

88. Ibid., ff. 507, 548.

89. For a general discussion of plague in early-modern Norwich, *see* P. Slack, *The Impact of Plague in Tudor and Stuart England*, 1985, pp. 61-2 and 126-43. The Elizabethan outbreaks are dealt with in Pound, 'The Elizabethan Corporation of Norwich', pp. 249-66, with a table of births and deaths for the decade 1582-92 on p. 265.

90. In the six months between the end of June and the end of December 1579 eight times as many people were buried as would normally have been interred in a twelve-month period. At a time when the average number of yearly burials was below five hundred, 1,827 people were buried in 1585 and a further 1,646 in 1592. Almost 3,000 of the 3,481 interred between August 1603 and July 1604 were plague victims – possibly one-quarter of all the inhabitants. Slack, *op. cit.*, pp. 129, 131.

91. Pound, 'Elizabethan Corporation of Norwich', pp. 249-51. Usher was originally appointed at a salary of 1s. 4d. a week when it was assumed that his position would be a temporary one. He was appointed permanently sometime between November 1581 and June 1582 when he was required to record both births and deaths, his salary having been fixed at £2 a year in September 1580. The post was maintained until 1646. Plague deaths were differentiated from others and Dutch and Walloons from English. The figures provided by Usher and his successors are the fullest population statistics available for any English city during the period concerned. They make it clear that the alien population suffered far more acutely than the English, not least because they were crowded together in the central and northern parishes in conditions that were far from salubrious.

92. Sachse, *op. cit.*, p. 45.

93. *See*, for example, Assembly Book, 1585-1613, ff. 66d-71d, and Sachse, *op. cit.*, pp. 82, 84, 87, 92 and 97.

94. Examples are given in: Mayor's Court Book, 1555-62, ff. 361, 498; Assembly Book, 1551-68, f. 91d; and Sachse, *op. cit.*, pp. 97, 102.

95. Mayor's Court Book, 1555-62, f. 623; Sachse, *op. cit.*, pp. 91, 240.

96. Sachse, *op. cit.*, p. 42.

97. Ibid., pp. 41-2.

## Chapter Ten: The Wage-Earning Classes and the Treatment of Poverty

1. W. G. Hoskins, *Provincial England*, 1963, p. 84; J. F. Pound, 'The Social and Trade Structure of Norwich, 1525-1575', *Past and Present*, 34, 1966, p. 50.

2. *See* pp. 31-2.

3. J. F. Pound, *Poverty and Vagrancy in Tudor England*, 2nd edn., 1986, p. viii; C. V. Phythian-Adams, *Desolation of a City: Coventry and the Urban Crisis of the Late Middle Ages*, 1979, p. 134.

4. The discussion of the Norwich census is largely based on the introduction to my edition of it in N.R.S., xl, 1971, pp. 9-21. A partial census of the Ipswich poor, taken in 1597, is printed in J. Webb, ed., *Poor Relief in Elizabethan Ipswich*, Suffolk Records Society, ix, 1966, and the Warwick census of 1587 is referred to in A. L. Beier, 'The Social Problems of an Elizabethan Country Town: Warwick, 1580-90', in P. Clark, ed., *Country Towns in Pre-Industrial England*, 1981, pp. 46-85.

5. It should be noted that the methods for calculating population given above differ from those provided by me in 1971, when I assumed that the proportion of over-sixties in the city as a whole was the same as that recorded in the census and that the numbers of women were larger than those of the men. The amended method has the inevitable effect of reducing the estimated population of the city and, if correct, implies that it had altered little from that suggested for the 1520s and may even have declined. I have preferred a multiplier of 4.75 here, rather than the 4.5 used in calculating the population for the 1520s. If the latter had been used contributors plus poor would have totalled 6,836, or 83 per cent of the whole – a minimal difference in this context.

6. The numbers of poor would, of course, have fluctuated according to the prevailing economic conditions and the problems of individuals. This is well brought out for 17th-century Norfolk in an article by Tim Wales, 'Poverty, poor relief and the life cycle: some evidence from seventeenth-century Norfolk', in R. M. Smith, ed., *Land, Kinship and Life-Cycle*, 1984, pp. 351-404.

7. The Elizabethan overcrowding palls into insignificance when compared with the situation in 17th-century Norwich. In August 1631 one Mary Newman was called before the leet court for allowing four families into her house, 'all wch ar lykly to be chargaball to the parish', the house in Mancroft 'not bein fit for more then toe dwelers and not having a howse of ofis'. (N.R.O., Sessions 29, No. 6, 8 August 1631.) Six years later Thomas Stalworthy of St Swithin's and his wife were similarly indicted 'for over chargeing & pestering theyr howses wth pore people . . . they takeing in severall persons from the lazar howse. There are severall famylys, 46 persons, under one rooff & some of them keep swyne in theyr dwelling howses'. At the same sessions, two other people were charged with having 14 and 15 householders respectively in their houses. (Sessions 37, No. 10, 17 July 1637.) A month later Edward Wyer was committed for letting a tenement to 12 tenants which had just one privy and one well for

all of them. The worst example concerned Thomas Harrald of Aylsham who owned a house in St Martin at Palace which he converted into 16 tenements, housing 18 families comprising over 70 persons. Several of the tenements had no toilet facilities. Harrald was twice indicted (Sessions, No. 3, September 1637, and Sessions No. 1, December 1637), but apparently did little to mend his ways. The evidence of the Hearth Tax returns suggests that an increasing number of houses were converted in this way. *See* pp. 42-5.

8. Pound, *Norwich Census*, pp. 17-18, provides tables giving full details of family size according to the age of the father, and of the number of children in families according to occupational grouping.

9. A. M. Everitt, 'Farm Labourers', in *The Agrarian History of England and Wales, IV, 1500-1640*, 1967, pp. 396-465.

10. J. F. Pound, 'Government and Society in Tudor and Stuart Norwich, 1525-1675', Univ. of Leicester Ph.D thesis, 1974, p. 237, for a detailed table showing the number of rooms listed in three distinct periods. The Norwich inventories begin in 1584. *See* also U. V. M. Priestley and P. J. Corfield, 'Rooms and Room Use in Norwich Housing, 1580-1730', *Post-Medieval Archaeology*, xvi, 1982.

11. M. W. Barley, *The English Farmhouse and Cottage*, 1967, pp. 44, 53, 138.

12. Pound, 'Government and Society', p. 239.

13. Everitt, *loc. cit.*, p. 444.

14. Barley, *op. cit.*, p. 76; N.R.O., Inventories 46, No. 160.

15. Everitt, *loc. cit.*, p. 453.

16. Pound, 'Government and Society', p. 241.

17. Inventories 12, No. 190.

18. Ibid., 29, No. 137.

19. Ibid., 44, No. 11.

20. Ibid., 2, No. 35; Norwich Consistory Court Wills, 393 Bate.

21. Barley, *op. cit.*, p. 152.

22. Inventories 6, No. 200.

23. Everitt, *loc. cit.*, pp. 449-50.

24. Inventories 17, No. 91.

25. Ibid., 6, No. 202.

26. Ibid., 19, No. 175.

27. Ibid., 10, No. 211.

28. Ibid., 41, No. 89.

29. Ibid., 25, No. 14.

30. Ibid., 29, No. 260.

31. Ibid., 41, No. 132.

32. *See* David Cressy, *Literature and the Social Order: Reading and Writing in Tudor and Stuart England*, 1980, for a general discussion of the standards of literacy during this period. Cressy emphasises that women were the least literate group in society. With this in mind, it is interesting to note that the teachers of the poor in Norwich were women and that some poor women, at least, were the owners of books.

33. Inventories 15, No. 146; 8, No. 114; 10, No. 372; 6, No. 97; and 10, No. 211.

34. Ibid., 46, No. 107; 36, No.18; 45, No. 192; 31, No. 104.

35. Ibid., 25, No. 40.

36. Ibid., 29, No. 229.

37. Ibid., 5, No. 200; 6, No. 218; 8, No. 138; 9, No. 53; 12, No. 120; 14, No. 71; 15, No. 147.

38. Ibid., 5, No. 127.

39. Ibid., 12, No. 22.

40. Ibid., 5, No. 152.

41. Ibid., 18, No. 248.

42. Ibid., 41, No. 121.

43. Seventy-one of the men recorded in the Norwich Census had attained their freedom at some time, while a further 41 had been apprenticed but had remained journeymen. Fifty-three of these were textile workers. Pound, *Poverty and Vagrancy in Tudor England*, 2nd edn., 1986, p. 27.

44. Ibid., pp. 1-22.

45. W. Hudson and J. C. Tingey, *Records of the City of Norwich*, II, 1910, p. xcviii.

46. G. W. O. Woodward, *The Dissolution of the Monasteries*, 1966, p. 22.

47. Hudson and Tingey, *op. cit.*, p. c.
48. Pound, *Norwich Census*, pp. 19-20.
49. Hudson and Tingey, *op. cit.*, p. ci.
50. The authorities themselves were hardly guiltless in this respect, many of them owning property which had been used to house poor families. *See* pp. 128, 130.
51. E. M. Leonard, *The Early History of English Poor Relief*, 1900, pp. 41-5.
52. *See* Pound, *Norwich Census*, pp. 19-20, for supporting tables.
53. The discussion of the Norwich scheme is based on pp. 62-66 of Pound, *Poverty and Vagrancy in Tudor England*, 2nd edn., 1986.
54. Inventories 18, No. 275; Norwich Consistory Court Wills, 150 Candler.
55. Leonard, *op. cit.*, pp. 41-5.
56. Pound, *Poverty and Vagrancy*, 2nd edn., p. 66. Where some towns were concerned, of course, the problem of poverty may have been an intermittent one.
57. Assembly Book, 1585-1613, ff. 80, 102d.
58. Ibid.: f. 316d; 1568-85.
59. Ibid., 1585-1613, f. 38d.
60. Ibid., ff. 40-40d.
61. N.R.O., PD 32/39.
62. Goddard Johnson, 'Chronological Memoranda touching the City of Norwich', *Norf. Arch.*, i, 1847, p. 150. The accounts for 1598-9 are printed in Pound, *Poverty and Vagrancy*, 2nd edn., pp.102-3.
63. Assembly Book, 1585-1613, ff. 244-5.
64. Pound, *Poverty and Vagrancy*, 2nd edn., p. 66.
65. N.R.O., Quarter Sessions Book, 1616, n.p.
66. W. Rye, *Norwich Rate Book, April 1633-April 1634*, 1903, *passim*. N.R.O., Documents relating to poor rates, 1677-89.
67. *See* W. K. Jordan, *Philanthropy in England*, 1961, *passim*, for a thorough discussion of the changing aspirations of the merchant classes. Jordan's failure to take inflation into account has come under fierce attack from other historians, notably W. G. Bittle and R. T. Lane, 'Inflation and Philanthropy in England: a re-assessment of W. K. Jordan's data', Ec.H.R., 2nd ser., xxix, 1976, and their response to criticisms of their own work in *idem*, 'A Re-Assessment Reiterated', xxxi, 1, 1978; and J. F. Hadwin, 'Deflating Philanthropy' in *idem*, xxxi, 1, 1978. Their criticisms, of which Hadwin's is the less severe, are summarised in Pound, *Poverty and Vagrancy*, 2nd edn., 1986, pp. xii, 75.
68. Norwich Consistory Court Wills, 75-78 Wellman, 102 Jerves, 219 Ingold.
69. Jordan, *op. cit.*, p. 102.
70. Ibid., p. 142.
71. Ibid.
72. Ibid., p. 108.
73. Hudson and Tingey, *op. cit.*, II, pp. cx-cxii.
74. Jordan, *op. cit.*, pp. 131-7, for this and the following paragraph.
75. N.R.O., Parish Register Lists, PRG/4-6.
76. A document published in 1720 provides details of the poor law receipts and expenditure of 14 of the city's parishes throughout the 17th century and beyond, details for all of the parishes in Norwich being provided from 1690 onwards. The author was probably B. Mackerell. (*An Exact Account of the Charge for supporting the Poor of the City of Norwich*, N.R.O., Local Studies Library, L. 102,774.) Examples provided above have been taken from parish registers in the N.R.O., PD 32/39. An individual account for the parish of St Michael at Thorn survives for 1656, MS 21,285, and the St Benedict's material can be found in PRG/4-6.
Leonard, *op. cit.*, pp. 318-26.
N.R.O., Mayor's Court Book, 1624-34, ff. 294d, 304d, 319, 320, 321d.
Ibid., duplicate book containing additional details, n.p., 2 November 1634.
Mayor's Court Book, 1624-34, f. 306.
Ibid., ff. 324d, 367d, 368d.
Ibid.: ff. 263, 311, 372d, 394, 432; 1634-46, f. 54d.
Ibid.: 1624-34, f.309; 1634-46, f. 89d.

**Chapter Eleven: Tudor and Stuart Norwich**
1. In this final chapter, which is effectively a synthesis of what has gone before, footnotes will be kept to a minimum.
2. Slack, *op. cit.*, p. 143.
3. These proportions refer to the freeman population. Many non-freemen were also textile workers, as were the bulk of the female working population.
4. J. F. Pound, 'Government and Society in Tudor and Stuart Norwich, 1525-1675', Univ. of Leicester Ph.D thesis, 1974, pp. 62-66.
5. As indicated in the previous chapter, many non-freemen and a majority of poor women were concerned with textiles at this time, quite apart from the unknown number of countrymen dependent on the trade.
6. Some of these men were themselves concerned with the textile trade, albeit as part of their wider activities.
7. The information from the Hearth Tax returns is derived from three sources, viz., three surviving books in the city's archives, a partial return in the P.R.O. and a box in the same repository containing lists of exemptions, the two latter being found in E179/254/701 and E179/336. These were first discussed in my paper presented to the meeting of the Urban History Group at the Univ. of East Anglia in April 1968 and have received subsequent treatment in Penelope Corfield's paper, 'A provincial capital in the late seventeenth century: the case of Norwich', reprinted in P. Clark, ed., *The Early Modern Town*, 1976, pp. 235-6.
8. This type of activity was discussed in some detail sixty years ago in R. H. Tawney's edition of Thomas Wilson's *A discourse upon usury*, 1926, pp. 17-42.
9. Modern estimates of the level of poverty are dealt with in J. F. Pound, *Poverty and Vagrancy in Tudor England*, 2nd edn., 1986, p. viii, and attitudes to work in D. C. Coleman, 'Labour in the English Economy of the Seventeenth Century', reprinted in E. Carus-Wilson, ed., *Essays in Economic History*, II, 1962.
10. J. F. Pound, ed., *The Norwich Census of the Poor, 1570*, N.R.S., xl, 1971, pp. 13-15.
11. Ibid., pp. 97-9.
12. Ibid., p. 17.
13. For a thorough discussion of the political issues in late-Stuart Norwich, *see* J. T. Evans, *op. cit.*, pp. 263-354.
14. P. Millican, ed., *The Freemen of Norwich, 1548-1713*, 1934, pp. xvi, 182-6.
15. Penelope Corfield provides a good account of Norwich in the late 17th century in *loc. cit.*, pp. 233-72.

# Appendix I

## Occupation and wealth in early 16th-century Norwich*

| | £ Under 2 | £ 2-4 | £ 5-9 | £ 10-19 | £ 20-39 | £ 40-99 | £ 100-299 | £ 300-500 | £ Over 500 | Totals |
|---|---|---|---|---|---|---|---|---|---|---|
| **Building** | | | | | | | | | | |
| Carpenters | 3 | 10 | 4 | 4 | 2 | - | - | - | - | 23 |
| Freemasons | - | - | - | - | - | - | 1 | - | - | 1 |
| Glasswrights | 1 | - | 1 | - | - | - | - | - | - | 2 |
| Glaziers | - | 7 | - | 2 | - | - | - | - | - | 9 |
| Joiners | - | 1 | - | - | - | - | - | - | - | 1 |
| Masons | 3 | 10 | 3 | 2 | - | - | - | - | - | 18 |
| Millwrights | 1 | - | 1 | - | - | - | - | - | - | 2 |
| Reeders | 1 | 6 | - | 1 | - | - | - | - | - | 8 |
| Sawyers | - | - | 1 | 1 | - | - | - | - | - | 2 |
| Tilers | - | - | 1 | - | - | - | - | - | - | 1 |
| *Totals* | *9* | *34* | *11* | *10* | *2* | *-* | *1* | *-* | *-* | *67* |
| **Clothing** | | | | | | | | | | |
| Cappers | 2 | 1 | 1 | - | - | - | - | - | - | 4 |
| Hosiers | - | - | - | 1 | - | 1 | - | - | - | 2 |
| Tailors | 9 | 20 | 7 | 8 | 3 | 1 | - | - | - | 48 |
| *Totals* | *11* | *21* | *8* | *9* | *3* | *2* | *-* | *-* | *-* | *54* |
| **Distributive** | | | | | | | | | | |
| Drapers | - | 1 | - | 4 | 2 | 3 | 1 | - | 1 | 12 |
| Grocers | - | 6 | 2 | 5 | 5 | 4 | 3 | - | 1 | 24 |
| Haberdashers | - | 3 | - | - | - | - | - | - | - | 3 |
| Mercers | - | 3 | 6 | 10 | 8 | 10 | 8 | 1 | 1 | 47 |
| Raffmen | 4 | 4 | 5 | 1 | 3 | - | - | - | - | 17 |
| Waxchandlers | 1 | 1 | 1 | - | - | - | - | - | - | 3 |
| *Totals* | *5* | *18* | *14* | *20* | *16* | *17* | *12* | *1* | *3* | *106* |
| **Food & Drink** | | | | | | | | | | |
| Bakers | 4 | 6 | 2 | 5 | 1 | 4 | - | - | - | 22 |
| Brewers | 3 | 4 | - | 1 | 1 | 1 | 1 | - | - | 11 |
| Butchers | 10 | 11 | 3 | 4 | 3 | 1 | 1 | - | - | 33 |
| Cooks | 3 | 3 | - | - | - | 1 | - | - | - | 7 |
| Fishermen | - | 2 | 1 | 1 | 1 | - | - | - | - | 5 |
| Fishmongers | 2 | 4 | 1 | 5 | - | - | - | - | - | 12 |
| Millers | 1 | - | 1 | - | - | - | - | - | - | 2 |
| Spicers | - | - | 1 | - | - | - | - | - | - | 1 |
| *Totals* | *23* | *30* | *9* | *16* | *6* | *7* | *2* | *-* | *-* | *93* |
| **Leatherwork** | | | | | | | | | | |
| Cobblers | - | 1 | - | - | - | - | - | - | - | 1 |
| Collarmakers | - | 1 | - | - | - | - | - | - | - | 1 |
| Cordwainers | 6 | 8 | 5 | 3 | 2 | - | - | - | - | 24 |
| Curriers | 1 | 4 | 1 | 1 | - | - | - | - | - | 7 |
| Glovers | - | - | 1 | - | 1 | - | - | - | - | 2 |
| Parchmeners | - | - | - | - | - | 1 | - | - | - | 1 |
| Pointmakers | - | - | 1 | - | - | - | - | - | - | 1 |
| Saddlers | 2 | 4 | - | 1 | - | - | - | - | - | 7 |
| Shoemakers | 10 | 6 | 1 | 2 | 1 | - | - | - | - | 20 |
| Skinners | - | 2 | - | 1 | - | - | - | - | - | 3 |
| Tanners | 6 | - | 1 | - | 3 | 1 | - | - | - | 11 |
| *Totals* | *25* | *26* | *10* | *8* | *7* | *2* | *-* | *-* | *-* | *78* |

|  | £ Under 2 | £ 2-4 | £ 5-9 | £ 10-19 | £ 20-39 | £ 40-99 | £ 100-299 | £ 300-500 | £ Over 500 | Totals |
|---|---|---|---|---|---|---|---|---|---|---|
| **Metalwork** | | | | | | | | | | |
| Blacksmiths | 1 | - | - | - | - | - | - | - | - | 1 |
| Bladesmiths | 1 | - | 1 | - | 1 | - | - | - | - | 3 |
| Braziers | 1 | - | - | 1 | - | - | - | - | - | 2 |
| Goldbeaters | - | 1 | - | - | - | - | - | - | - | 1 |
| Goldsmiths | - | - | 1 | 2 | 1 | 1 | - | - | - | 5 |
| Hardwaremen | - | - | 1 | - | - | - | - | - | - | 1 |
| Locksmiths | 1 | - | - | - | - | - | - | - | - | 1 |
| Pewterers | - | - | - | 2 | 1 | - | - | - | - | 3 |
| Pinners | 1 | 1 | 1 | 2 | 1 | - | - | - | - | 6 |
| Sheargrinders | - | 1 | - | - | - | - | - | - | - | 1 |
| Smiths | 2 | 2 | 1 | 2 | 2 | - | - | - | - | 9 |
| Spurriers | 1 | 1 | - | - | - | - | - | - | - | 2 |
| *Totals* | *8* | *6* | *5* | *9* | *6* | *1* | *-* | *-* | *-* | *35* |
| **Professional** | | | | | | | | | | |
| Barbers | 3 | 6 | 3 | 1 | 1 | - | 1 | - | - | 15 |
| Mayor's sergeants | - | - | 1 | - | - | - | - | - | - | 1 |
| Minstrels | - | - | - | 1 | - | - | - | - | - | 1 |
| Scriveners | - | 1 | 2 | - | 1 | - | - | - | - | 4 |
| *Totals* | *3* | *7* | *6* | *2* | *2* | *-* | *1* | *-* | *-* | *21* |
| **Textiles** | | | | | | | | | | |
| Calendrers | 1 | 5 | 1 | 1 | 1 | 1 | - | - | - | 10 |
| Coverlet weavers | 3 | 6 | 3 | - | 3 | - | 1 | - | - | 16 |
| Dyers | 6 | 1 | 4 | 3 | - | 1 | 1 | - | - | 16 |
| Fullers | 3 | - | 2 | 1 | 1 | - | - | - | - | 7 |
| Shearmen | 8 | 11 | 1 | 1 | 1 | 1 | - | - | - | 23 |
| Staymakers | - | 1 | - | - | - | - | - | - | - | 1 |
| Thickwoollen weavers | 1 | 1 | - | - | - | - | - | - | - | 2 |
| Weavers | 1 | - | - | - | - | - | - | - | - | 1 |
| Wool chapmen | - | - | - | 1 | - | - | - | - | - | 1 |
| Woolmen | - | 2 | - | 1 | - | - | - | - | - | 3 |
| Worsted shearmen | - | 1 | - | - | - | - | - | - | - | 1 |
| Worsted weavers | 31 | 52 | 16 | 10 | 11 | 6 | 1 | - | - | 127 |
| *Totals* | *54* | *80* | *27* | *18* | *17* | *9* | *3* | *-* | *-* | *208* |
| **Transport** | | | | | | | | | | |
| Carriers | 1 | 1 | 1 | - | - | - | - | - | - | 3 |
| Carters | 1 | - | 1 | - | - | - | - | - | - | 2 |
| Keelmen | - | 1 | - | - | - | - | - | - | - | 1 |
| Loaders | 1 | - | - | - | - | - | - | - | - | 1 |
| Watermen | 3 | 1 | 1 | 1 | - | - | - | - | - | 6 |
| *Totals* | *6* | *3* | *3* | *1* | *-* | *-* | *-* | *-* | *-* | *13* |
| **Woodwork** | | | | | | | | | | |
| Bowyers | - | 1 | - | - | - | - | - | - | - | 1 |
| Coopers | 2 | 2 | 1 | - | 1 | - | - | - | - | 6 |
| Fletchers | 2 | 1 | 2 | - | - | - | - | - | - | 5 |
| Gravers | - | - | - | 2 | - | - | - | - | - | 2 |
| Pattenmakers | 1 | 1 | 1 | - | - | - | - | - | - | 3 |
| Ploughwrights | - | - | - | 1 | - | - | - | - | - | 1 |
| *Totals* | *5* | *5* | *4* | *3* | *1* | *-* | *-* | *-* | *-* | *18* |
| Grand Totals | 149 | 230 | 97 | 96 | 60 | 38 | 19 | 1 | 3 | 693 |

The table excludes a serving man assessed at £1.

* A table showing the distribution of these occupations throughout the city is provided in Pound, 'Government and Society in Tudor and Stuart Norwich, 1525-1675', Univ. of Leicester Ph.D. thesis, 1974, pp. 295-6. The actual value of the goods owned by these people is listed in *idem*, pp. 305-9.

# Appendix II

Admissions to the freedom in Norwich, 1501-1675

| | 1501 to 1525 | 1526 to 1550 | 1551 to 1575 | 1576 to 1600 | 1601 to 1625 | 1626 to 1650 | 1651 to 1675 |
|---|---|---|---|---|---|---|---|
| **Building** | | | | | | | |
| Bricklayers | - | - | 4 | - | 2 | - | 1 |
| Brickmakers | - | - | - | - | - | 1 | - |
| Carpenters | 27 | 17 | 14 | 32 | 24 | 29 | 46 |
| Freemasons | - | 2 | 2 | - | - | - | - |
| Glasswrights | 2 | - | - | - | - | - | - |
| Glaziers | 6 | 4 | 9 | 11 | 9 | 10 | 17 |
| Joiners | - | 3 | 19 | 22 | 21 | 14 | 14 |
| Limeburners | 1 | 2 | 4 | 2 | 2 | 1 | - |
| Masons | 21 | 18 | 24 | 29 | 19 | 26 | 5 |
| Millwrights | 2 | - | - | - | - | - | - |
| Painters | 1 | - | 4 | 4 | 6 | - | 5 |
| Reeders | 9 | 5 | 14 | 7 | 4 | 9 | 13 |
| Reed merchants | - | - | - | - | - | 1 | 1 |
| Roughmasons | - | - | 7 | 8 | 10 | 9 | 31 |
| Sawyers | 2 | - | 1 | - | - | - | - |
| Stainers | - | - | 2 | - | - | - | - |
| Stainers & glaziers | - | 1 | - | - | - | - | - |
| Tilers | 1 | 1 | 5 | 6 | 4 | 3 | 2 |
| *Totals* | *72* | *53* | *109* | *122* | *101* | *103* | *135* |
| | | | | | | | |
| **Clothing** | | | | | | | |
| Bodymakers | - | - | - | - | 4 | 6 | 2 |
| Cappers | 2 | 12 | - | - | - | - | - |
| Feltmakers | - | - | - | 8 | 9 | 8 | 19 |
| Hatband-makers | - | - | - | - | 1 | - | - |
| Hatters | - | 10 | 29 | 22 | 2 | 2 | 1 |
| Hosiers | - | 1 | 2 | 6 | 42 | 33 | 38 |
| Merchant Tailors | - | - | - | 1 | - | - | - |
| Milliners | - | - | - | - | - | 5 | 3 |
| Tailors | 67 | 74 | 142 | 170 | 165 | 160 | 192 |
| Upperbodymakers | - | - | - | - | 1 | 2 | 11 |
| *Totals* | *69* | *97* | *173* | *207* | *224* | *216* | *266* |
| | | | | | | | |
| **Distributive** | | | | | | | |
| Chandlers | - | - | - | - | 1 | 4 | 2 |
| Chapmen | - | - | - | - | 1 | 1 | - |
| Drapers | 12 | 13 | 17 | 27 | 29 | 23 | 2 |
| Grocers | 31 | 53 | 121 | 96 | 75 | 88 | 70 |
| Haberdashers | 1 | 6 | 20 | 18 | 17 | 20 | 7 |
| Haberdashers of small wares | - | - | - | - | - | 3 | 11 |
| Kyddyer | - | - | - | - | 1 | - | - |
| Linen drapers | - | - | 2 | - | 2 | 3 | 10 |
| Mercers | 70 | 69 | 49 | 22 | 36 | 27 | 19 |
| Merchants | - | - | 1 | 9 | 57 | 30 | 22 |
| Raffmen | 21 | 10 | 2 | - | 1 | - | - |
| Soap-boilers | - | - | - | - | - | - | 1 |
| Tobacco-pipe makers | - | - | - | - | - | - | 3 |
| Wax chandlers | 7 | - | - | - | - | - | 3 |
| Woollen drapers | - | - | - | 3 | - | 4 | 11 |
| *Totals* | *142* | *151* | *212* | *175* | *220* | *203* | *159* |

| | 1501 to 1525 | 1526 to 1550 | 1551 to 1575 | 1576 to 1600 | 1601 to 1625 | 1626 to 1650 | 1651 to 1675 |
|---|---|---|---|---|---|---|---|
| **Food & Drink** | | | | | | | |
| Bakers | 11 | 19 | 23 | 32 | 41 | 59 | 58 |
| Brewers | 8 | 7 | 12 | 1 | 22 | 11 | 2 |
| Brewers of Ale | - | - | 1 | 1 | - | - | - |
| Brewers of Beer | 2 | 9 | 16 | 24 | 12 | 8 | 21 |
| Butchers | 20 | 26 | 29 | 30 | 29 | 28 | 27 |
| Comfit-makers | - | - | - | - | 1 | - | - |
| Cooks | 3 | 2 | 6 | 5 | 13 | 6 | 2 |
| Fingerbread makers | - | - | 1 | - | - | - | - |
| Fishermen | 1 | 2 | 2 | 2 | 1 | - | - |
| Fishmongers | 12 | 6 | 18 | 13 | 15 | 7 | 5 |
| Freshwatermen | 4 | 4 | 3 | - | - | - | - |
| Gingerbread makers | - | - | - | - | - | - | 3 |
| Innholders | - | 1 | 7 | 13 | 17 | 11 | - |
| Innkeepers | - | 5 | 4 | 3 | - | 1 | - |
| Maltsters | - | 1 | - | 2 | 1 | 1 | 1 |
| Mealsellers | - | - | - | - | - | - | 1 |
| Millers | 1 | 1 | 3 | 1 | - | 1 | 2 |
| Oatmealmakers | - | - | 1 | - | - | - | - |
| Poulterers | - | 1 | - | - | - | 1 | - |
| Stillers of hot water | - | - | - | - | - | 1 | - |
| Sugar bakers | - | - | 1 | - | - | 2 | 1 |
| Victuallers | - | 1 | 4 | 1 | 1 | - | - |
| Vintners | 1 | 2 | - | 5 | 4 | 12 | 1 |
| *Totals* | *63* | *87* | *131* | *133* | *157* | *149* | *124* |
| **Leatherwork** | | | | | | | |
| Bagmakers | 1 | 2 | - | - | - | - | - |
| Bookbinders | - | - | 1 | - | 1 | 2 | - |
| Bridlemakers | - | - | - | - | - | 1 | - |
| Buttonmakers | - | - | - | - | - | 1 | - |
| Cobblers | - | - | 9 | 8 | 20 | 7 | 2 |
| Collarmakers | - | - | 1 | - | - | 1 | - |
| Cordwainers | 18 | 29 | 53 | 78 | 81 | 107 | 115 |
| Curriers | 3 | 2 | 6 | 6 | 4 | 3 | - |
| Fellmongers | - | - | - | - | - | - | 1 |
| Foisterers | 2 | 3 | - | 1 | - | - | - |
| Glovers | - | 11 | 16 | 32 | 21 | 24 | 16 |
| Heelmakers | - | - | - | - | - | 1 | - |
| Jackmakers | - | - | - | - | - | 1 | - |
| Jerkinmakers | - | - | 1 | - | - | - | - |
| Knackers | - | - | - | 1 | 1 | - | 1 |
| Leathercarvers | - | 2 | - | - | - | - | - |
| Leatherdressers | - | - | - | 3 | 3 | 8 | 3 |
| Parchmeners | 4 | 2 | 4 | 3 | 3 | 3 | 1 |
| Pointmakers | 4 | - | 2 | 2 | 1 | - | 1 |
| Saddlers | 9 | 8 | 10 | 9 | 8 | 8 | 11 |
| Shoemakers | 16 | 14 | 2 | - | - | - | - |
| Skinners | 4 | 2 | 8 | 5 | 3 | 2 | - |
| Stationers | - | - | - | 3 | 5 | 3 | 6 |
| Tanners | 14 | 25 | 22 | 15 | 27 | 24 | 11 |
| Translators | - | - | - | - | - | - | 5 |
| Trunkmakers | - | - | - | - | - | 1 | 1 |
| *Totals* | *75* | *100* | *135* | *166* | *178* | *197* | *174* |

| | 1501 to 1525 | 1526 to 1550 | 1551 to 1575 | 1576 to 1600 | 1601 to 1625 | 1626 to 1650 | 1651 to 1675 |
|---|---|---|---|---|---|---|---|
| **Metalwork** | | | | | | | |
| Armourers | - | - | 1 | - | 2 | 3 | 2 |
| Bellfounders | - | 2 | 1 | - | - | - | - |
| Blacksmiths | - | - | 10 | 19 | 27 | 27 | 26 |
| Bladesmiths | 5 | 5 | 7 | 5 | 4 | 4 | 2 |
| Braziers | 3 | - | 2 | 1 | - | 1 | 5 |
| Claspmakers | - | - | - | - | 1 | - | - |
| Clockmakers | - | - | - | - | 1 | 3 | - |
| Cutlers | - | 2 | 7 | 6 | 9 | 14 | 10 |
| Farriers | - | - | 1 | - | - | - | - |
| Furbishers | - | - | 1 | - | - | - | - |
| Goldbeaters | 2 | - | - | - | - | - | - |
| Goldsmiths | 4 | 7 | 9 | 8 | 9 | 7 | 7 |
| Gunsmiths | - | - | - | - | - | 3 | 2 |
| Hardwaremen | 2 | 2 | - | - | - | - | - |
| Hookmakers | - | 1 | - | - | - | - | - |
| Instrument-makers | - | - | - | - | - | - | 1 |
| Ironmongers | - | - | - | 1 | 6 | 7 | 9 |
| Latten-founders | - | - | - | - | 1 | - | - |
| Locksmiths | 2 | 2 | 5 | 8 | 18 | 18 | 14 |
| Pewterers | 2 | 3 | 4 | 5 | 5 | 5 | 6 |
| Pinners | 7 | 2 | 5 | 3 | 8 | 11 | 7 |
| Plumbers | - | - | 1 | 2 | 3 | 3 | 4 |
| Sievemakers | - | - | 1 | 1 | - | 1 | 1 |
| Smiths | 10 | 32 | 10 | 4 | - | - | - |
| Spurriers | 2 | - | 1 | 1 | 3 | 2 | - |
| Tinkers | - | 1 | - | - | - | - | - |
| Watchmakers | - | - | - | - | - | 2 | 1 |
| Wiredrawers | 1 | - | 1 | - | - | - | - |
| *Totals* | *40* | *59* | *67* | *64* | *97* | *111* | *97* |
| | | | | | | | |
| **Miscellaneous** | | | | | | | |
| Ashburners | - | - | 1 | 1 | - | - | - |
| Courtholders | - | - | 1 | - | - | - | - |
| Gardeners | - | - | - | - | - | - | 2 |
| Horseleeches | - | - | 1 | - | - | - | - |
| Labourers | - | - | 1 | - | - | - | - |
| Latheryvers | - | - | 1 | - | - | - | - |
| Plateworkers | - | - | - | - | - | - | 1 |
| Ploughwrights | 1 | 2 | 1 | - | - | - | - |
| Potters | - | - | - | - | - | - | 2 |
| Printers | - | - | 1 | - | - | - | - |
| Ropemakers | - | - | 1 | 1 | - | 1 | - |
| Stringers | - | 1 | - | - | - | - | - |
| Swordbearers | 1 | - | 1 | - | 1 | - | - |
| Upholsterers | - | - | 1 | 2 | 2 | 6 | 4 |
| Whiteplate makers | - | - | - | - | - | - | 1 |
| Whiteplate workers | - | - | - | - | - | 1 | - |
| *Totals* | *2* | *3* | *10* | *4* | *3* | *8* | *10* |

| | 1501 to 1525 | 1526 to 1550 | 1551 to 1575 | 1576 to 1600 | 1601 to 1625 | 1626 to 1650 | 1651 to 1675 |
|---|---|---|---|---|---|---|---|
| **Professional** | | | | | | | |
| Apothecaries | 1 | 1 | 1 | 7 | 12 | 11 | 11 |
| Barbers | 15 | 15 | 8 | 15 | 19 | 30 | 34 |
| Barber-surgeons | - | - | 1 | 1 | - | - | - |
| Chemists | - | - | - | - | - | - | 2 |
| *Juris periti* | - | 3 | - | - | - | - | - |
| *Legis periti* | - | 3 | - | - | - | - | - |
| Minstrels | 2 | 1 | - | - | - | - | - |
| Musicians | - | - | 2 | 5 | 3 | - | 2 |
| Notaries | - | 2 | - | - | - | - | - |
| Schoolmasters | - | - | - | - | 1 | - | - |
| Scriveners | 15 | 8 | 12 | 15 | 21 | 17 | 20 |
| Sergeants | 2 | - | - | - | - | - | - |
| Surgeons | 1 | 1 | 3 | 1 | 3 | 1 | 2 |
| *Totals* | *36* | *34* | *27* | *44* | *59* | *59* | *71* |
| | | | | | | | |
| **Textiles** | | | | | | | |
| Bayweavers | - | - | - | 4 | 1 | - | - |
| Bleachers | 1 | - | - | - | - | - | - |
| Calendrers | 10 | 10 | 3 | 2 | 2 | 9 | - |
| Cardmakers | - | - | - | - | - | 1 | - |
| Clothiers | - | - | - | 6 | 3 | - | - |
| Clothmakers | - | 1 | - | - | - | - | - |
| Clothmen | - | 1 | - | - | - | - | - |
| Cloth-shearmen | - | - | - | 1 | 2 | 1 | 8 |
| Clothworkers | - | 1 | - | 3 | - | - | - |
| Colourmakers | - | 1 | - | - | - | - | - |
| Combers | - | - | - | 1 | 4 | 12 | 2 |
| Coverletweavers | 12 | 8 | 2 | - | - | - | - |
| Dornixweavers | - | 2 | 27 | 38 | 45 | 27 | 14 |
| Dyers | 7 | 11 | 10 | 3 | 18 | 14 | 7 |
| Embroiderers | 1 | - | - | 3 | - | - | - |
| Fringemakers | - | - | - | - | 3 | 2 | - |
| Fullers | 4 | 4 | - | - | - | - | - |
| Hairmakers | - | - | 2 | - | - | - | - |
| Hairmen | - | 1 | - | - | - | - | - |
| Hairweavers | - | - | - | - | - | - | 1 |
| Hotpressers | - | - | - | - | - | - | 1 |
| Laceweavers | - | - | - | 1 | - | 1 | 1 |
| Linenweavers | - | - | 5 | 3 | 2 | 4 | - |
| Linen and woollenweavers | - | - | 4 | 2 | - | - | - |
| Natmakers | - | - | - | - | 1 | - | - |
| Ribbonweavers | - | - | - | - | - | - | 2 |
| Russellweavers | - | - | 2 | 1 | - | - | - |
| Sayweavers | - | - | - | - | 1 | 1 | - |
| Shearmen | 26 | 29 | 11 | 10 | 11 | 7 | 2 |
| Silkrasers | - | - | - | 1 | 3 | 4 | - |
| Silkweavers | - | - | - | - | 3 | - | 1 |
| Slaymakers | 3 | - | - | 2 | 2 | 1 | - |
| Slaywrights | - | 1 | - | - | 1 | 1 | - |
| Tachemakers | - | 1 | - | - | - | - | - |
| Thickwoollenweavers | 5 | 3 | - | - | - | - | - |
| Tuft-mockado makers | - | - | - | 1 | - | - | - |
| Twisterers | - | - | - | 1 | - | 3 | 2 |
| Waterers of stuffs | - | - | - | - | - | 1 | - |
| Weavers | 1 | - | - | 3 | 16 | 3 | - |
| Woolchapmen | 1 | - | - | 2 | - | - | - |
| Woolcombers | - | - | - | 1 | 7 | 6 | 4 |
| Woolmen | 1 | - | - | - | - | - | - |
| Worsted calendrers | - | 1 | - | - | - | - | - |
| Worsted shearmen | 3 | 1 | 2 | 1 | 1 | 2 | 1 |
| Worsted weavers | 134 | 114 | 103 | 74 | 261 | 392 | 680 |
| *Totals* | *209* | *189* | *171* | *164* | *387* | *492* | *748* |

| | 1501 to 1525 | 1526 to 1550 | 1551 to 1575 | 1576 to 1600 | 1601 to 1625 | 1626 to 1650 | 1651 to 1675 |
|---|---|---|---|---|---|---|---|
| **Transport** | | | | | | | |
| Carriers | 2 | 8 | 8 | 5 | - | 1 | - |
| Carters | 1 | 1 | - | - | - | - | - |
| Coachmakers | - | - | - | - | - | - | 2 |
| Keelmen | - | 5 | 7 | 2 | 8 | 2 | 1 |
| Loaders | 1 | - | - | - | - | - | - |
| Ships' carpenters | - | - | - | - | - | - | 1 |
| Watermen | 2 | 1 | 2 | - | 1 | - | 2 |
| Wheelwrights | - | - | 3 | 4 | - | - | - |
| *Totals* | *6* | *15* | *20* | *11* | *9* | *3* | *6* |
| **Woodwork** | | | | | | | |
| Basketmakers | - | - | 3 | 3 | 4 | 3 | 6 |
| Bowyers | 2 | 1 | 1 | - | - | - | - |
| Chairmakers | - | - | - | - | - | 1 | 1 |
| Coopers | 3 | 11 | 11 | 14 | 12 | 13 | 22 |
| Fletchers | 4 | 4 | 2 | 1 | - | - | - |
| Gravers | 5 | 4 | - | - | - | - | - |
| Organ makers | 1 | - | - | - | - | - | - |
| Patten-makers | 3 | - | - | - | - | - | 1 |
| Pedmakers | - | - | 1 | 1 | - | - | - |
| Skepmakers | 2 | 1 | - | - | - | - | - |
| Turners | - | 2 | 2 | 1 | 1 | 1 | 11 |
| *Totals* | *20* | *23* | *20* | *20* | *17* | *18* | *41* |

# Appendix III

Occupations and wealth in late seventeenth-century Norwich

| | Number of hearths per household: | | | | |
|---|---|---|---|---|---|
| | 1 | 2 | 3-5 | 6-9 | 10 and over | Total |

| **Building** | | | | | | |
|---|---|---|---|---|---|---|
| Brickmakers | 1 | - | - | - | - | *1* |
| Carpenters | 10 | 10 | 9 | - | 1 | *30* |
| Glaziers | 4 | 6 | 3 | - | - | *13* |
| Joiners | 8 | 3 | 5 | - | - | *16* |
| Masons | 10 | 2 | 1 | - | - | *13* |
| Painters | - | 3 | 1 | - | - | *4* |
| Reeders | 3 | 1 | - | - | - | *4* |
| Roughmasons | 19 | 9 | 2 | - | - | *30* |
| Ship's carpenter | - | - | 1 | - | - | *1* |
| Tilers | 6 | 1 | - | - | - | *7* |
| *Totals* | *61* | *35* | *22* | *-* | *1* | *119* |

| **Clothing** | | | | | | |
|---|---|---|---|---|---|---|
| Bodymakers | - | - | 1 | - | - | *1* |
| Feltmakers | 4 | 5 | - | - | - | *9* |
| Hosiers | 2 | 7 | 2 | 7 | 5 | *23* |
| Milleners | - | - | 2 | - | - | *2* |
| Tailors | 46 | 41 | 33 | 4 | 1 | *125* |
| Upperbodymakers | - | 3 | 1 | 1 | - | *5* |
| *Totals* | *52* | *56* | *39* | *12* | *6* | *165* |

| **Distributive** | | | | | | |
|---|---|---|---|---|---|---|
| Drapers | - | 4 | 3 | 2 | 1 | *10* |
| Grocers | 1 | 8 | 24 | 16 | 5 | *54* |
| Haberdashers | 3 | 1 | 7 | 6 | - | *17* |
| Linen-drapers | 1 | 1 | 2 | 2 | - | *6* |
| Mercers | - | 3 | 9 | 4 | - | *16* |
| Merchants | 1 | - | 1 | 9 | 3 | *14* |
| Starchmakers | - | 1 | 1 | - | - | *2* |
| Tallowchandlers | - | - | 1 | 1 | - | *2* |
| Woollendrapers | - | - | 3 | - | 1 | *4* |
| *Totals* | *6* | *18* | *51* | *40* | *10* | *125* |

| **Food & Drink** | | | | | | |
|---|---|---|---|---|---|---|
| Bakers | 7 | 9 | 17 | 7 | 1 | *41* |
| Brewers | 2 | 2 | 9 | 3 | 2 | *18* |
| Butchers | 15 | 19 | 9 | - | - | *43* |
| Cooks | - | 1 | - | - | - | *1* |
| Fishermen | 1 | - | - | - | - | *1* |
| Fishmongers | - | - | 1 | 1 | 1 | *3* |
| Innholders | - | - | - | 1 | - | *1* |
| Maltsters | - | - | 1 | - | - | *1* |
| Millers | 1 | 1 | 1 | - | - | *3* |
| Sugarbakers | - | - | 1 | 1 | - | *2* |
| Vintners | - | - | - | 2 | 1 | *3* |
| *Totals* | *26* | *32* | *39* | *15* | *5* | *117* |

| | 1 | 2 | 3-5 | 6-9 | 10 and over | Total |
|---|---|---|---|---|---|---|
| **Leatherwork** | | | | | | |
| Bookbinders | 1 | - | 1 | - | - | 2 |
| Cobblers | - | 2 | - | - | - | 2 |
| Cordwainers | 36 | 28 | 23 | 2 | 1 | 90 |
| Curriers | 1 | - | - | - | - | 1 |
| Glovers | 1 | 4 | 3 | - | - | 8 |
| Knackers | 1 | - | - | - | - | 1 |
| Leatherdressers | - | 2 | 1 | - | - | 3 |
| Parchmeners | 1 | - | - | - | - | 1 |
| Pointmakers | 1 | 1 | - | - | - | 2 |
| Saddlers | 1 | 3 | 2 | 1 | - | 7 |
| Stationers | 3 | - | 1 | - | - | 4 |
| Tanners | 6 | 6 | 7 | 1 | 1 | 21 |
| Translators | 1 | - | - | - | - | 1 |
| Trunkmakers | - | - | 1 | - | - | 1 |
| *Totals* | *53* | *46* | *39* | *4* | *2* | *144* |
| **Metalwork** | | | | | | |
| Armourers | 1 | 1 | - | - | - | 2 |
| Blacksmiths | 15 | 5 | 3 | - | - | 23 |
| Bladesmiths | - | 1 | - | 1 | - | 2 |
| Braziers | 1 | - | - | 1 | - | 2 |
| Clockmakers | - | 1 | - | - | - | 1 |
| Cutlers | 4 | 8 | 2 | - | - | 14 |
| Goldsmiths | - | 1 | 1 | 1 | - | 3 |
| Gunsmiths | - | 1 | 2 | - | - | 3 |
| Instrument-makers | - | 1 | - | - | - | 1 |
| Ironmongers | 2 | 1 | 1 | 3 | 1 | 8 |
| Locksmiths | 1 | 5 | 3 | - | - | 9 |
| Pewterers | - | 1 | 4 | 1 | - | 6 |
| Pinners | 2 | 2 | 4 | 1 | - | 9 |
| Plumbers | 1 | - | - | - | - | 1 |
| Spurriers | 1 | - | - | - | - | 1 |
| Watchmakers | 1 | - | - | - | - | 1 |
| *Totals* | *29* | *28* | *20* | *8* | *1* | *86* |
| **Miscellaneous** | | | | | | |
| Gardeners | - | - | 1 | - | - | 1 |
| Ropemakers | - | 1 | - | - | - | 1 |
| Tobacco-pipe makers | 1 | - | - | - | - | 1 |
| Whiteplatemakers | - | - | - | 1 | - | 1 |
| *Totals* | *1* | *1* | *1* | *1* | *-* | *4* |
| **Professional** | | | | | | |
| Apothecaries | - | - | 2 | - | - | 2 |
| Barbers | 4 | 10 | 6 | 1 | - | 21 |
| Barber-surgeons | 1 | - | - | - | - | 1 |
| Bonesetters | 1 | - | - | - | - | 1 |
| Chemists | - | - | 1 | - | - | 1 |
| Clerks | - | 2 | 5 | - | 1 | 8 |
| Doctors | - | - | 1 | 3 | 5 | 9 |
| Judges | - | - | - | 1 | - | 1 |
| Musicians | - | 1 | 1 | - | - | 2 |
| Prebendaries | - | - | - | 2 | - | 2 |
| Scriveners | 1 | - | 9 | 7 | 2 | 19 |
| Surgeons | - | - | 1 | - | - | 1 |
| *Totals* | *7* | *13* | *26* | *14* | *8* | *68* |

|  | 1 | 2 | 3-5 | 6-9 | 10 and over | Total |
|---|---|---|---|---|---|---|
| **Textiles** | | | | | | |
| Bay weavers | 1 | - | - | - | - | *1* |
| Chapmen | - | - | 1 | - | - | *1* |
| Clothworkers | - | 1 | - | - | - | *1* |
| Combers | 2 | 1 | - | - | 1 | *4* |
| Dornix weavers | 8 | 5 | 5 | 1 | - | *19* |
| Dyers | 2 | 2 | 6 | 1 | - | *11* |
| Fringemakers | - | - | 1 | - | - | *1* |
| Linen weavers | 1 | 1 | 1 | - | 1 | *4* |
| Natmakers | - | 1 | - | - | - | *1* |
| Sayweavers | - | 1 | - | - | - | *1* |
| Shearmen | 1 | - | 1 | - | - | *2* |
| Silkweavers | - | - | 1 | - | - | *1* |
| Slaywrights | - | 1 | - | - | - | *1* |
| Twisterers | 1 | - | 1 | - | - | *2* |
| Upholsterers | - | 1 | 1 | 2 | - | *4* |
| Weavers | 1 | 2 | - | - | - | *3* |
| Woolcombers | 4 | 5 | 8 | 1 | - | *18* |
| Worsted weavers | 182 | 141 | 140 | 44 | 14 | *521* |
| *Totals* | *203* | *162* | *166* | *49* | *16* | *596* |
| | | | | | | |
| **Transport** | | | | | | |
| Keelmen | - | 1 | - | - | - | *1* |
| Watermen | 2 | - | 1 | - | - | *3* |
| *Totals* | *2* | *1* | *1* | *-* | *-* | *4* |
| | | | | | | |
| **Woodwork** | | | | | | |
| Chairmakers | - | - | 1 | - | - | *1* |
| Coopers | 5 | 2 | 1 | 1 | - | *9* |
| Turners | 1 | 2 | 1 | - | - | *4* |
| Wine-coopers | - | 1 | - | - | - | *1* |
| *Totals* | *6* | *5* | *3* | *1* | *-* | *15* |

# Bibliography

## I. Principal Documentary Sources

### Public Record Office
Taxation records (all prefixed by E179): 113/192; 116/541; 124/188; 136/315; 136/323; 150/210; 150/218; 173/175; 197/154; 217/92; 218/180; 254/701; 336.
Prerogative Court of Canterbury Wills.

### Norfolk Record Office
*General Administration*
Assembly Minute Books, 1510-1683 (9 volumes), Case 16, shelf c.
Folio Books of Proceedings of the Municipal Assembly, 1491-1668 (3 volumes), Case 16, shelf d.
City Revenue and Letters, Case 17, shelf b.

*Finance and Taxation*
Chamberlains' Accounts, 1531-1684 (10 volumes, that for 1567-80 being missing), Case 18, shelves a and b.
Clavors' Accounts, 1550-1601, 1555-1646, 1647-1733, Case 18, shelf d.
Assessment of the City, 1576, Case 7, shelf i.
Hearth Tax returns, Case 13, shelf a.
Foreign Receivers' Rolls and Books of Accounts, 1548-89, 1589-1727, Case 17, shelf c.
River and Street Accounts, 1556-1618. Book of Accounts (Sewers Book), 1615-1715, Case 19, shelf b.

*Proceedings of the Mayor's Court*
Books of Proceedings, 1510-1677 (22 volumes), Case 16, shelves a and b.

*Poverty and the Treatment of the Poor*
'The Mayor's Booke of the Poore', 1571-79, Case 20, shelf c.
Volume of Poor Law Accounts, 1571-80, Case 20, shelf c.
Parcel of Books, 1571-2 (contains the census of the poor, taken in 1570), Case 20, shelf c.
Parcel of Poor Law Accounts, 1659-68, Case 15, shelf c.
Documents relating to Poor Rates, 1677-89, Case 15, shelf b.
Parish registers in the keeping of the Norfolk Record Office.

*Documents relating to the Trade Structure of Norwich*
The Old Free Book, 1317-1549, Case 17, shelf c.
Aylsham Papers, 156.
Boxes of inventories, 1589 to 1675 inclusive.

## II. Primary Sources in Print

E. S. de Beer, ed., *The Diary of John Evelyn*, 1959.
A. Campling, ed., *East Anglian Pedigrees*, N.R.S., xiii, 1940.
*Calendars of State Papers Domestic*, Edward VI to Charles II inclusive.
W. Camden, *Britannia: or a Chorographical Description of Great Britain and Ireland together with adjacent lands*, 1722.
B. Cozens-Hardy and E. A. Kent, *The Mayors of Norwich, 1403-1835*, 1938.

M. A. Farrow, ed., *Index to Norwich Consistory Court Wills*, 1550-1603, N.R.S., xxi, 1950.

M. A. Farrow and T. F. Barton, eds., *Index to Wills Proved at Norwich, 1604-1686*, N.R.S., xxviii, 1958.

C. H. Firth and R. S. Rait, *Acts and Ordinances of the Interregnum*, 1911.

F. J. Fisher, ed., 'Thomas Wilson, *The State of England*, A.D. 1600', *Camden Miscellany*, xvi, 1936.

S. H. A. Hervey, ed., *Suffolk in 1524*, Suffolk Green Books, x, 1910.

*Idem., Suffolk in 1674*, Suffolk Green Books, xi, 1905.

R. H. Hill, ed., *The Corie Letters, 1664-1687*, N.R.S., xxvii, 1956.

W. Hudson and J. C. Tingey, eds., *The Records of the City of Norwich*, 2 vols., 1910.

A. W. Hughes Clarke and A. H. Campling, eds., *The Visitation of Norfolk, 1664*, 1934.

M. F. Keeler, *The Long Parliament*, 1954.

H. Le Strange, *Norfolk Official Lists*, 1890.

D. M. Livock, ed., *City Chamberlains' Accounts of the Sixteenth and Seventeenth Centuries*, Bristol Record Society, xxiv, 1966.

B. Mackerell, *An Exact Account of the Charge for supporting the Poor of the City of Norwich*, Local Studies Library, Norwich, L. 102774.

P. Millican, ed., *The Freemen of Norwich*, 1548-1713, 1934.

P. Millican and W. Rising, eds., *An Index of Indentures of Norwich Apprentices Enrolled with the Norwich Assembly, Henry VII-George II*, N.R.S., xxix, 1959.

C. Morris, ed., *The Journeys of Celia Fiennes*, 1947.

J. Nichols, ed., Thomas Fuller, *The History of the Worthies of England*, 1811.

J. F. Pound, ed., *The Norwich Census of the Poor, 1570*, Norfolk Record Society, xl, 1971.

J. F. Pound, ed., *The Military Survey of 1522 for Babergh Hundred*, Suffolk Records Society, xxviii, 1986.

M. M. Rowe, ed., *Tudor Exeter*, Devon and Cornwall Records Society, xxii, 1977.

W. Rye, ed., *Norfolk Families*, 1913.

W. Rye, ed., *Norwich Rate Book, April 1633-April 1634*, 1903.

W. L. Sachse, ed., *Minutes of the Norwich Court of Mayoralty, 1630-31*, N.R.S., xv, 1942, and *idem* for 1632-35, N.R.S., xxxvi, 1967.

B. Schofield, ed., *The Knyvett Letters*, N.R.S., xx, 1949.

W. H. Stevenson, ed., *Records of the Borough of Nottingham*, published between 1882 and 1914.

R. H. Tawney, ed., Thomas Wilson, *A Discourse on Usury*, 1925.

R. H. Tawney and E. Power, eds., *Tudor Economic Documents*, 1924.

R. Taylor, *Index Monasticus*, 1821.

J. Thirsk and J. P. Cooper, eds., *Seventeenth Century Economic Documents*, 1972.

L. Toulin Smith, ed., *The Itinerary of John Leland in or about the years 1535 to 1543*, 1909.

Various eds., *Indexes of Wills Proved in the Prerogative Court of Canterbury, 1383-1675*, British Record Society, Index Library, 1893 to 1942.

J. Webb, ed., *Poor Relief in Elizabethan Ipswich*, Suffolk Records Society, ix, 1966.

A. Whiteman, ed., *The Compton Census of 1676*, Records of Social and Economic History, New Ser., x, 1986.

### III. Secondary Sources

**Books and theses**

B. H. Allen, 'The Administrative and Social Structure of the Norwich Merchant Class, 1485-1660', Univ. of Harvard Ph.D. thesis, 1951.

K. J. Allison, 'The Wool Supply and the Worsted Cloth Industry in Norfolk in the Sixteenth and Seventeenth Centuries', Univ. of Leeds Ph.D. thesis, 1955.

Anon., *A Topographical and Historical Account of the City and County of Norwich*, 1819.

T. Atkinson, *Elizabeth Winchester*, 1963.

M. W. Barley, *The English Farmhouse and Cottage*, 2nd edn., 1967.

A. L. Beier, *Masterless Men: The Vagrant Problem in England, 1560-1640*, 1985.

F. Blomefield, *A History of the City and County of Norwich*, 1741.

F. Blomefield, *An Essay towards a Topographical History of the County of Norfolk*, 1806.

P. J. Bowden, *The Wool Trade in Tudor and Stuart England*, 1962.

P. Clark, ed., *The Early Modern Town*, 1976.

P. Clark, ed., *Country Towns in Pre-Industrial England*, 1981.

P. Clark and P. Slack, eds., *Crisis and Order in English Towns, 1500-1700*, 1972.
P. Clark and P. Slack, *English Towns in Transition, 1500-1700*, 1976.
L. A. Clarkson, *The Pre-Industrial Economy in England, 1500-1750*, 1971.
J. Cornwall, *Revolt of the Peasantry*, 1977.
D. Cressy, *Literature and the Social Order: Reading and Writing in Tudor and Stuart England*, 1980.
A. Dyer, *The City of Worcester in the Sixteenth Century*, 1973.
J. T. Evans, *Seventeenth Century Norwich*, 1979.
A. M. Everitt, *Change in the Provinces: The Seventeenth Century*, 1969.
D. L. Farmer, *Britain and the Stuarts*, 1965.
A. Fletcher, *Tudor Rebellions*, 3rd edn., 1983.
D. V. Glass and D. E. C. Eversley, eds., *Population in History*, 1965.
B. Green and R. Young, eds., *Norwich – the Growth of a City*, 1976.
J. E. C. Hill, *Society and Puritanism in Pre-Industrial England*, 1966.
J. E. C. Hill, *Reformation to Industrial Revolution*, 1969.
J. W. F. Hill, *Tudor and Stuart Lincoln*, 1956.
W. G. Hoskins, *Industry, Trade and People in Exeter, 1688-1800*, 1935.
W. G. Hoskins, *Local History in England*, 2nd edn., 1972.
W. G. Hoskins, *Provincial England*, 1963.
R. Howell, *Newcastle-upon-Tyne and the Puritan Revolution*, 1967.
L. Howes, *Elm Hill*, 1961.
W. Hudson, *How the City of Norwich grew into Shape*, 1896.
M. James, *Social Problems and Policy during the Puritan Revolution*, 1966 edn.
W. K. Jordan, *Philanthropy in England*, 1959.
W. K. Jordan, *The Charities of Rural England*, 1961.
R. W. Ketton-Cremer, *Norfolk in the Civil War*, 1969.
D. Knoop and G. P. Jones, *The Medieval Mason*, 1933.
E. M. Leonard, *The Early History of English Poor Relief*, 1900.
T. B. Macaulay, *History of England from the reign of James II*, 1906 edn.
W. T. MacCaffrey, *Exeter, 1540-1640*, 1958.
W. J. C. Moens, *The Walloons and their Church in Norwich: their History and Registers*, 1887-88.
J. E. Neale, *The Elizabethan House of Commons*, 1949.
G. Owens, 'Norfolk, 1620-1641: Local Government and Central Authority in an East Anglian County', Univ. of Wisconsin Ph.D. thesis, 1970.
D. M. Palliser, *Tudor York*, 1979.
D. M. Palliser, *The Age of Elizabeth*, 1983.
J. Patten, *English Towns, 1500-1700*, 1978.
L. R. Paul, 'A Survey of the Ecclesiastical History of the Town of Norwich, 1500-1575', Univ. of Chicago M.A. thesis, 1958.
V. Pearl, *London and the Outbreak of the Puritan Revolution*, 1961.
N. Pevsner, *North-East Norfolk and Norwich*, 1962.
C. V. Phythian-Adams, *Desolation of a City: Coventry and the Urban Crisis of the Later Middle Ages*, 1979.
J. F. Pound, 'The Elizabethan Corporation of Norwich, 1558-1603', Univ. of Birmingham M.A. thesis, 1962.
J. F. Pound, 'Government and Society in Tudor and Stuart Norwich, 1525-1675', Univ. of Leicester Ph.D. thesis, 1974.
J. F. Pound, *Poverty and Vagrancy in Tudor England*, 2nd edn., 1986.
J. H. Raach, *A Directory of English Country Physicians, 1603-1643*, 1962.
A. Rogers, ed., *The Making of Stamford*, 1965.
W. Rye, *Norwich Houses before 1600*, 1916.
H. W. Saunders, *A History of the Norwich Grammar School*, 1932.
K. Shipps, 'Lay Patronage of East Anglian Puritan Clerics in Pre-Revolutionary England', Univ. of Yale Ph.D. thesis, 1971.
P. Slack, *Poverty in Early Stuart Salisbury*, Wiltshire Record Society, xxxi, 1975.
P. Slack, *The Impact of Plague in Tudor and Stuart England*, 1985.
J. Thirsk, ed., *Agricultural History of England and Wales, IV, 1500-1649*, 1967.

S. and B. Webb, *English Poor Law History. Part I: The Old Poor Law*, 1962 edn.

C. Webster, ed., *Health, Medicine and Mortality in the Sixteenth Century*, 1979.

T. S. Willan, *The Muscovy Merchants of 1555*, 1953.

N. Williams, 'The Maritime Trade of the East Anglian Ports, 1550-1590', Univ. of Oxford D.Phil. thesis, 1952.

B. M. Wilson, 'The Corporation of York, 1580-1660', University of York M.Phil. thesis, 1967.

C. Wilson, *England's Apprenticeship, 1603-1763*, 1965.

G. W. O. Woodward, *The Dissolution of the Monasteries*, 1966.

J. Youings, *Sixteenth Century England*, 1984.

## Articles

K. J. Allison, 'The Norwich Hatters', *East Anglian Magazine*, xvi, 3, 1957.

K. J. Allison, 'The Norfolk Worsted Industry in the Sixteenth and Seventeenth Centuries: Part I. The Traditional Industry', *Yorkshire Bulletin of Economic and Social Research*, xii, 1960; idem, 'Part II. The New Draperies', xiii, 2, 1961.

K. J. Allison, 'An Elizabethan Village Census', *Bulletin of the Institute of Historical Research*, xxxv, 1962.

K. J. Allison, 'Economic and Social History to 1545', V.C.H., *Warwickshire*, viii, 1969.

M. W. Atkin, A. Carter *et al.*, 'Excavations in Norwich, 1975/6: The Norwich Survey – Fifth Interim Report', *Norf. Arch.*, xxxvi, Part III, 1976.

M. W. Atkin, H. Sutermeister *et al.*, 'Excavations in Norwich, 1977/8: The Norwich Survey – Seventh Interim Report', *Norf. Arch.*, xxxvii, Part I, 1978.

B. L. Beer, 'The Commoyson in Norfolk, 1549: A Narrative of Popular Rebellion in Sixteenth Century England', *Journal of Medieval and Renaissance Studies*, vi, 1976.

A. L. Beier, 'Poor Relief in Warwickshire, 1630-1660', *Past and Present*, 35, 1966.

A. L. Beier, 'Vagrants and the Social Order in Elizabethan England', *Past and Present*, 64, 1974. See also the debate under the same title between Beier and J. F. Pound, *Past and Present*, 71, 1976.

W. G. Bittle and R. T. Lane, 'Inflation and Philanthropy in England: a re-assessment of W. K. Jordan's data', Ec.H.R., 2nd Ser., xxix, 1976.

L. G. Bolingbroke, 'Players in Norwich from the Accession of Queen Elizabeth until their suppression in 1642', *Norf. Arch.*, xiii, 1898.

D. Charman, 'Wealth and Trade in Leicester in the Early Sixteenth Century', *Transactions of the Leicestershire Archaeological Society*, xxv, 1949.

P. Clark, 'The Migrant in Kentish Towns, 1580-1640', in Clark and Slack, eds., *Crisis and Order*.

P. Clark, 'The Ramoth-Gilead of the good: urban change and political radicalism at Gloucester, 1540-1640', in Clark *et al.*, eds., *The English Commonwealth*, 1979.

D. C. Coleman, 'Labour in the English Economy of the Seventeenth Century', in E. Carus-Wilson, ed., *Essays in Economic History*, II, 1962.

P. Corfield, 'A Provincial Capital in the late Seventeenth Century: the case of Norwich' in Clark and Slack, eds., *Crisis and Order*, and reprinted in Clark, ed., *Early Modern Town*.

J. Cornwall, 'English Country Towns of the Fifteen Twenties', Ec.H.R., 2nd Ser., xv, No. 1, 1962.

B. Cozens-Hardy, 'The Norwich Chapelfield House Estate since 1545 and some of its Owners and Occupiers', *Norf. Arch.*, xxvii, 1941.

A. G. Dickens, 'Tudor York', V.C.H. *Yorkshire, The City of York*, 1961.

A. Dyer, 'The Economy of Tudor Worcester', *Univ. of Birmingham Historical Journal*, x, 1966.

A. M. Everitt, 'Farm Labourers' in J. Thirsk, ed., *The Agrarian History of England and Wales, IV, 1500-1640*, 1967.

F. J. Fisher, 'Inflation and Influenza in Tudor England', Ec.H.R., 2nd Ser., xviii, 1965.

R. Fitch, 'Notices of Norwich Brewers' Marks and Trade Regulations', *Norf. Arch.*, v, 1859.

G. C. F. Forster, 'York in the Seventeenth Century', V.C.H., *Yorkshire, The City of York*, 1961.

M. Grace, 'The Chamberlains and Treasurers of the City of Norwich, 1293-1835', *Norf. Arch.*, xxv, 1935.

C. Gross, 'A Plea for Reform in the Study of English Municipal History', *American Historical Review*, v, 1891.

J. F. Hadwin, 'Deflating Philanthropy', Ec.H.R., 2nd Ser., xxxi, 1, 1978, together with Bittle and Lane's 'A Re-assessment Reiterated' in the same number of the journal.

C. T. Hammer, 'Anatomy of an Oligarchy: the Oxford Town Council in the Fifteenth and Sixteenth Centuries', *Journal of British Studies*, xviii, 1978-9.

W. G. Hoskins, 'English Provincial Towns in the Early Sixteenth Century', reprinted in *Provincial England*, 1963, together with another article of his, 'An English Provincial Town: Leicester'.

W. G. Hoskins, 'The Elizabeth Merchants of Exeter', in S. T. Bindoff *et al.*, eds., *Elizabethan Government and Society*, 1961.

W. A. Jenkins and C. T. Smith, 'Social and Administrative History, 1660-1835', V.C.H., *Leicestershire*, iv, 1958.

G. Johnson, 'Chronological Memoranda touching the City of Norwich', *Norf. Arch.*, i, 1847.

R. K. Kelsall, 'Wage Regulation under the Statute of Artificers', reprinted in W. E. Minchinton, ed., *Wage Regulation in Pre-Industrial England*, 1972.

E. A. Kent, 'The Houses of the Dukes of Norfolk in Norwich', *Norf. Arch.*, xxiv, 1932.

J. Kermode, 'Urban Decline? The Flight from Office in Late Medieval York', Ec.H.R., 2nd Ser., xxxv, 1982.

E. Kerridge, 'Social and Economic History, 1509-1660', V.C.H., *Leicestershire*, iv, 1958.

T. P. R. Laslett, 'Size and Structure of the Household in England over Three Centuries', *Population Studies*, xxiii, 2, 1969.

C. A. F. Meekings, 'Cambridge Univ. and Borough Hearth Tax Assessments, 1662-1674', V.C.H., *Cambridgeshire*, iii, 1959.

J. Miller, 'The Crown and the Borough Charters in the Reign of Charles II', E.H.R., 1985.

D. M. Palliser, 'York under the Tudors: the Trading Life of the Northern Capital', in A. M. Everitt, ed., *Perspectives in English Urban History*, 1973.

J. Patten, 'Changing occupational structures in the East Anglian countryside', in H. S. A. Fox and R. A. Butlin, eds., *Change in the Countryside: Essays on Rural England, 1500-1900*, Institute of British Geographers Special Publication No. 10, 1979.

M. Pelling, 'Occupational Diversity: Barber-Surgeons and the Trades of Norwich, 1550-1640', *Bulletin of the History of Medicine*, 56, 1984.

E. H. Phelps-Brown and Sheila V. Hopkins, 'Seven Centuries of the Price of Consumables, compared with Builders' Wage-Rates', reprinted in E. Carus-Wilson, ed., *Essays in Economic History*, II, 1962.

J. F. Pound, 'An Elizabethan Census of the Poor', *Univ. of Birmingham Historical Journal*, viii, 1962.

J. F. Pound, 'The Social and Trade Structure of Norwich, 1525-1575', reprinted in Clark, ed., *Early Modern Town*.

J. F. Pound, 'The Validity of the Freemen's Lists: some Norwich evidence', Ec.H.R., 2nd Ser., xxxiv, 1981.

U. V. M. Priestley and P. J. Corfield, 'Rooms and Room Use in Norwich Housing, 1580-1730', *Post-Medieval Archaeology*, xvi, 1982.

W. Rye, 'The Dutch Refugees in Norwich', *Norfolk Antiquarian Miscellany*, iii, 1887.

P. Slack, 'Poverty and Politics in Salisbury, 1597-1666', in Clark and Slack, eds., *Crisis and Order*.

P. Slack, 'Vagrants and Vagrancy in England, 1598-1664', Ec.H.R., 2nd Ser., xxvii, No. 3, 1974.

R. Smith and A. Carter, 'Function and Site: Aspects of Norwich Buildings before 1700', *Vernacular Architecture*, xiv, 1983.

P. Styles, 'The Evolution of the Law of Settlement', *Univ. of Birmingham Historical Journal*, ix, 1963-4.

J. Thirsk, 'Stamford in the Sixteenth and Seventeenth Centuries' in Rogers, *op.cit.*

J. C. Tingey, 'Deeds Enrolled within the County of Norfolk', *Norf. Arch.*, xiii, 1898.

T. Wales, 'Poverty, Poor-Relief and the Life-Cycle: some evidence from Seventeenth Century Norfolk', in R. M. Smith, ed., *Land, Kinship and Life-Cycle*, 1984.

N. Williams, 'The Risings in Norfolk, 1569-1570', *Norf. Arch.*, xxxii, 1961.

# Index

Actors, 120
Acts of Parliament: Militia Act, 1662, 15; Act of Settlement, 1662, 118
Adkin, John, 62
Aldermen, 54, 57, 59-60, 68-9, 70-3, 76-87, 94-8, 109, 119, 123, 146, 156-7; ages of, 168 note 3
Aldermen of London, 7
Aldred, Robert, 40
Aldrich, John, 113, 130, 141, 146
Aldrich, Thomas, 32, 35
Aldrich family, 80
Alehouses, 119
Allen, Robert, 97
Allen, Samuel, 97
Alva, Duke of, 57
Andrewes, John, 97
Anguish, Alexander, 91, 158
Anguish, Thomas, 60, 148
Anguish family, 80
Anticipation, 6
Apprenticeship, 46-50, 60-1
Ashwell, Thomas, 94, 97
Assault, 121
Assembly-sweeper, 104
Astley, Sir Jacob, 17
Atkin, Thomas, 80
Attleborough, 2
Auditors, 74
Aulnage, 99
Austen, Charles, 131
Austen, Thomas, 107
Austin Friars, 82

Babergh hundred, Suffolk, 12, 15, 165 note 9
Bacon family, 82
Bailiffs, 68
Baker, Nicholas, 57
Baret, Thomas, 95, 97
Baret (Barett), family, 80
Barley, Prof. M., 91, 135
Baron, Robert, 148
Baskerville, Thomas, 20, 26, 27
Beadle, 109
Bedford, 41
Bedingfield, Thomas, 16
Bedingfield family, 17
Beecroft, Robert, 41
Beer, Barrett, 85
Bellman, 104
Bennett, Mirabell, 148
Berwick, 1
Bishop family, 10

Black Death, 122
Blennerhasset, John, 130
Blickling Hall, Norfolk, 16
Blofield hundred, 6-7, 12-15, 17-18
Boleyn, William, 7
Boys' Hospital, 114, 148-9
Brereton, Cuthbert, 78
Bridge, Wiliam, 88-9
Bristol, 1, 28, 30, 32-3, 43, 55, 60, 102-4
Brothercross hundred, 6, 12-14, 17-18
Browne, Sir Thomas, 67
Building activity, 57
Burgess, William, 107
Burman, Edmund, 97
Bury St Edmunds, 32-3
Bush, Rice, 117
Bussey, Henry, 121
Buttery (in houses), 40

Cambridge, 41, 115, 127
Cambridgeshire, 41, 46, 110, 112
Camden, William, 19, 118
Canterbury, 32-3
Castleton, William, 141, 147
Cawston, Anne, Lidea and Robert, 120
Cecil, William, 142
Chamberlains, 74, 85, 143, 158
Church, Bernard, 95-6
Churchwardens, 74, 85, 143, 158
Clackclose hundred, 13-14, 17-18
Clare, Edward, 142
Clarke, Richard, 41
Clavering hundred, 13, 15, 17-18
Clavors, 74, 99-100, 158
Clerk of the Market, 104
Cock, Col. C. G., 95-6
Cock family, 74
Cockayne, William, 116
Cockford, 7
Cockly, Henry, 140
Codd, Thomas, 85
Common Councillors, 54, 57, 69, 70-5, 78, 95-8, 123, 156-7
Common Speaker, 24
Composition of 1415, 68
Compton Census, 1676, 29-30
Constables, 68, 109, 112, 160
Cony, Thomas, 74
Corbet, Bishop, 88
Corie, Thomas, 116
Cornwall, Julian, 85
Coroners, 68, 74

193